Innovations in Digital Instruction Through Virtual Environments

Jason D. DeHart
University of Tennessee, Knoxville, USA

A volume in the Advances in Educational
Technologies and Instructional Design (AETID)
Book Series

Published in the United States of America by
IGI Global
Information Science Reference (an imprint of IGI Global)
701 E. Chocolate Avenue
Hershey PA, USA 17033
Tel: 717-533-8845
Fax: 717-533-8661
E-mail: cust@igi-global.com
Web site: http://www.igi-global.com

Library of Congress Cataloging-in-Publication Data

Names: DeHart, Jason D., 1982- editor.
Title: Innovations in digital instruction through virtual environments /
  edited by Jason D. DeHart.
Description: Hershey, PA : Information Science Reference, [2023] | Includes
  bibliographical references and index. | Summary: "Innovations in Digital
  Instruction Through Virtual Environments advances knowledge about the
  pedagogical decisions and lived experiences of researchers and educators
  both before and after the COVID-19 pandemic. It features research from
  those who have worked to sustain and develop digital/media pedagogical
  practices. Covering topics such as active learning environments,
  emotional labor, and textual engagements, this premier reference source
  is an excellent resource for educators and administrators of both K-12
  and higher education, pre-service teachers, teacher educators,
  librarians, researchers, and academicians"-- Provided by publisher.
Identifiers: LCCN 2022058432 (print) | LCCN 2022058433 (ebook) | ISBN
  9781668470152 (h/c) | ISBN 9781668470190 (s/c) | ISBN 9781668470169
  (eISBN)
Subjects: LCSH: Web-based instruction. | Internet in education. | Virtual
  reality in education.
Classification: LCC LB1044.87 .I534 2023 (print) | LCC LB1044.87 (ebook)
  | DDC 371.33/44678--dc23/eng/20230113
LC record available at https://lccn.loc.gov/2022058432
LC ebook record available at https://lccn.loc.gov/2022058433

This book is published in the IGI Global book series Advances in Educational Technologies and Instructional Design (AE-TID) (ISSN: 2326-8905; eISSN: 2326-8913)

British Cataloguing in Publication Data
A Cataloguing in Publication record for this book is available from the British Library.

For electronic access to this publication, please contact: eresources@igi-global.com.

Advances in Educational Technologies and Instructional Design (AETID) Book Series

Lawrence A. Tomei
Robert Morris University, USA

ISSN:2326-8905
EISSN:2326-8913

MISSION

Education has undergone, and continues to undergo, immense changes in the way it is enacted and distributed to both child and adult learners. In modern education, the traditional classroom learning experience has evolved to include technological resources and to provide online classroom opportunities to students of all ages regardless of their geographical locations. From distance education, Massive-Open-Online-Courses (MOOCs), and electronic tablets in the classroom, technology is now an integral part of learning and is also affecting the way educators communicate information to students.

The **Advances in Educational Technologies & Instructional Design (AETID) Book Series** explores new research and theories for facilitating learning and improving educational performance utilizing technological processes and resources. The series examines technologies that can be integrated into K-12 classrooms to improve skills and learning abilities in all subjects including STEM education and language learning. Additionally, it studies the emergence of fully online classrooms for young and adult learners alike, and the communication and accountability challenges that can arise. Trending topics that are covered include adaptive learning, game-based learning, virtual school environments, and social media effects. School administrators, educators, academicians, researchers, and students will find this series to be an excellent resource for the effective design and implementation of learning technologies in their classes.

COVERAGE

- Online Media in Classrooms
- Collaboration Tools
- Curriculum Development
- Instructional Design
- Web 2.0 and Education
- Hybrid Learning
- Bring-Your-Own-Device
- K-12 Educational Technologies
- Higher Education Technologies
- Social Media Effects on Education

IGI Global is currently accepting manuscripts for publication within this series. To submit a proposal for a volume in this series, please contact our Acquisition Editors at Acquisitions@igi-global.com or visit: http://www.igi-global.com/publish/.

Titles in this Series

For a list of additional titles in this series, please visit: http://www.igi-global.com/book-series/advances-educational-technologies-instructional-design/73678

Exploring Social Emotional Learning in Diverse Academic Settings
Regina Rahimi (Georgia Southern University, USA) and Delores Liston (Georgia Southern University, USA)
Information Science Reference • © 2023 • 412pp • H/C (ISBN: 9781668472279) • US $215.00

Strategies for Promoting Independence and Literacy for Deaf Learners With Disabilities
Nena Raschelle Neild (Ball State University, USA) and Patrick Joseph Graham (Rochester Institute of Technology, USA)
Information Science Reference • © 2023 • 320pp • H/C (ISBN: 9781668458396) • US $215.00

Implementing Rapid E-Learning Through Interactive Materials Development
Mohammad Issack Santally (University of Mauritius, Mauritius) Yousra Rajabalee (Mauritius Institute of Education, Mauritius) and Ravi Rajputh (University of Mauritius, Mauritius)
Information Science Reference • © 2023 • 300pp • H/C (ISBN: 9781668449400) • US $215.00

New Approaches to the Investigation of Language Teaching and Literature
Aitor Garcés-Manzanera (University of Murcia, Spain) and María Encarnacion Carrillo García (University of Murcia, Spain)
Information Science Reference • © 2023 • 325pp • H/C (ISBN: 9781668460207) • US $215.00

Agricultural Education for Development in the Arab Countries
Mohamed M. Samy (Independent Researcher, USA) and R. Kirby Barrick (University of Florida, USA (retired))
Information Science Reference • © 2023 • 364pp • H/C (ISBN: 9781668440506) • US $215.00

Digitalization, New Media, and Education for Sustainable Development
Lars Keller (University of Innsbruck, Austria) Gerd Michelsen (Leuphana University, Germany) Martin Dür (University of Innsbruck, Austria) Syamsul Bachri (Universitas Negeri Malang, Indonesia) and Michaela Zint (University of Michigan, USA)
Information Science Reference • © 2023 • 335pp • H/C (ISBN: 9781799850335) • US $225.00

Fostering Diversity and Inclusion Through Curriculum Transformation
Cily Elizabeth Mamatle Tabane (University of South Africa, South Africa) Boitumelo Molebogeng Diale (University of Johannesburg, South Africa) Ailwei Solomon Mawela (University of South Africa, South Africa) and Thulani Vincent Zengele (University of South Africa, South Africa)
Information Science Reference • © 2023 • 315pp • H/C (ISBN: 9781668469958) • US $215.00

IGI Global
PUBLISHER of TIMELY KNOWLEDGE

701 East Chocolate Avenue, Hershey, PA 17033, USA
Tel: 717-533-8845 x100 • Fax: 717-533-8661
E-Mail: cust@igi-global.com • www.igi-global.com

Table of Contents

Detailed Table of Contents

Chapter 1
What's Old Is New Again 1
    Kristen Hawley Turner, Drew University, USA
    Jill Stedronsky, William Anin Middle School, USA

Schools closed in March 2020, causing teachers to reinvent themselves. As classes were forced into remote learning, educators jumped into virtual instruction – to a variety of outcomes. This chapter documents one teacher's personal inquiry during the pandemic shutdown through a literacy lens. By asking the question, "How do teachers engage students during this difficult time?" she ultimately realized that what she had always known about good pedagogy in a face-to-face classroom transferred into virtual contexts: content needed to be relevant, assignments and assessments needed to be project-based and authentic, and students needed the opportunity to connect with others. The move to remote instruction may have made the pedagogical choices that surrounded her teaching beliefs even more important. For this teacher, the goal of developing her students' literacies in order to help them become critical thinkers was at the heart of her integration of technologies into her learning environment.

Chapter 2
Civic Deliberations in COVID-19 and Beyond 14
    Anita Chadha, University of Houston-Downtown, USA

With online pedagogy becoming mainstream during COVID, research on digital instruction grew dramatically, finding that online pedagogy was on par with face-to-face methods. Adding to this body of work this chapter assesses collaborations to provide meaningful student deliberations. Of particular importance was how students created dialogue and were academically reflective as they lived in geographically dispersed locations from Texas to California, New York, New Jersey, Maryland, and Wisconsin. Indeed, significant findings provided proof that over the course of sixteen plus years including during COVID students fostered a multiplicity of academic reflective deliberations. With the rapidly evolving educational landscape this chapter provides evidentiary proof that carefully designed online collaborations provide effective deliberative communities, an amenable design for any discipline.

    İlkay Ulutaş, Gazi Üniversitesi, Turkey
    Emine Bozkurt Polat, Gazi Üniversitesi, Turkey
    Feyza Aydin Bölükbaş, Aksaray Üniversitesi, Turkey
    Kadriye Selin Budak, Bilecik Üniversitesi, Turkey
    Kübra Engin, Gazi Üniversitesi, Turkey

With the rapidly developing technology, the use of AR applications in the educational process is becoming widespread as a new field of study. When the literature was examined, there were no studies investigating AR applications and evaluating them as a mathematics education tool in early childhood. In this context, this study aims to determine the AR applications that can be used in the early childhood mathematics education process and to examine the content, mathematical skills, and functionality of these applications.

    Tetiana Holovatenko, Borys Grinchenko Kyiv University, Ukraine & University of
       Minnesota, USA

Lockdown due to COVID-19 has rapidly increased the level of digitalization of higher education. The chapter dwells on the way how the TPACK framework enhanced by the development of digital skills and Bloom's taxonomy influence pre-service elementary school teacher's academic success rate, as well as their perceptions of preparedness to implement digital collaboration instructional strategies in teaching elementary school students. The study was set at Borys Grinchenko Kyiv University (Ukraine) in 2020-2022 academic years. Pre-service elementary school students (n=64), enrolled in two courses participated in the study. The study is mixed-method sequential explanatory design. The quantitative analysis of grades was followed by qualitative analysis of students' self-assessment and feedback. The data shows an increase in the student success rate and their interest towards implementing the digital technologies in their own practice. Further work needs to be done to disseminate an effective complex of activities for developing pre-service teachers' collaboration skills using specific digital tools.

    Matthew S. Macomber, Murray State University, USA
    Whitney N. Chandler, Murray State University, USA

Online technology tools eliminate the need for teachers to bend to the strictures of traditional essays during assessments. Inspired by a shift in teaching and assessment needs during the pandemic, the authors experimented with requiring students to submit oral responses to novel studies in their high school English classrooms. The benefits of the digital oral reading assessment persist even as pandemic learning restrictions loosen, and the authors have since incorporated oral reading assessments into their classrooms as a matter of routine. Recommendations are provided in structuring prompts, creating rubrics, and collecting filmed responses, and solutions are offered to the problems of teacher time constraints, student testing anxiety, and the relative ease of student plagiarism. The authors provide the reader with three oral reading assessment prompts for texts of literary merit, including Octavia Butler's Kindred, Ken Kesey's One Flew Over the Cuckoo's Nest, and James McBride's The Color of Water, along with rubrics that can be adapted for use with any novel.

Chapter 6

Lamia Büşra Yeşil, The Ministry of National Education, Turkey

The purpose of this action research is to transform the quality of teaching decisions and actions by adopting an active learning approach. The implementation was carried out as an eTwinning project for eight months in the 2021-2022 educational year with the first and second-grade 28 students in primary schools, aged six to nine, in Germany, Greece, and Turkey. Action research data collection techniques were used such as experiencing (by observing), enquiring (by asking), and examining (by using records of the poll questions answered by the pupils) and the results were reported with descriptive analysis. Learning was enriched with an emphasis on collaborative teaching and learning, active participation, and decision-making of learners. Learning methodologies such as inquiry-based, project-based, blended, and game-based learning increased learning motivation and engagement. Science, technology, engineering, and mathematics (STEM) helped foster the development of a range of competencies. Digital technologies contributed to capturing the multiple dimensions of learner progression.

Chapter 7

Jason D. DeHart, University of Tennessee, Knoxville, USA
Kate Cimo, North Coventry Elementary, USA

In this chapter, the co-authors explore the power of children's and youth literature as high-quality materials for building connections online during the pandemic. Both authors note their experiences, as well as texts that provided a range of connections. The chapter is a narrative case study of the first author's experiences, while the researcher/co-author includes experiences that line up both practically and theoretically. The difficulty of pandemic teaching, as mitigated by some steps in instruction, is a theme of the chapter.

Chapter 8

Niroj Dahal, Kathmandu University School of Education, Nepal

In this chapter, the author will discuss his experiences working collaboratively to teach and learn in order to create an engaged pedagogy by subscribing action research methodologies in various semesters that involves his (PGD, Master, and MPhil) students of 2019-2021 batches in techno-pedagogy and its trend in learning. This chapter presents the ongoing learning of research conducted within the context of the researcher's teaching practice. The author will provide examples of some of his PGD, Master, and MPhil students' technological learning collaborative activities (i.e., LMS, Google Apps, and other open sources), including forum discussions, choices, managing quizzes, lesson study, workshops, and Google Docs activities (Doc, PowerPoints, and Jamboard), which are created for on-campus, online, and distance teaching and learning in Nepali universities (namely, Kathmandu University and Nepal Open University).

Chapter 9

It can be called "digitalization" to first convert all kinds of data such as voice, text, document, image into computer bits consisting of 0 and 1 and then send it to another place with the help of telecommunication technology. The lifestyles of individuals and societies have started to become digital thanks to the whole of the data produced in the digital environment or later transferred to the digital environment. Technological developments in the information age we live in have changed the lifestyles of individuals along with the opportunities they provide. One of these technological developments, especially the internet, has rapidly increased its place in the lives of individuals since the 1990s, and has become effective in many areas such as education, communication, health, politics, industry, and media. Individuals share their feelings and thoughts in online environments, exchange information, and quickly become aware of events taking place in various parts of the world.

Chapter 10

In this chapter, the author relates an analytic description of the composing practices of a digital comics maker, linking print processes and digital processes. This narrative case study includes a focus on the titles that have been salient for the comics maker, as well as the linking that this composer includes in their work across video games, toys, music, podcasts, and other types of texts. The chapter includes a focus on what teachers can learn about the interconnected and intertextual, digital world in which students live, act, and practice.

Chapter 11

Digital environments offer opportunities and spaces for students to engage in critical literacy practices. This necessitates a teacher's critical understanding of the social structures at work in online environments while instructing students. In this chapter, findings are presented from a mixed-methods study of four practicing teachers who characterized themselves as having strong personal and pedagogical knowledge of critical digital literacies (CDL) and claimed to recruit that knowledge to their classroom practices. Data analysis of teacher surveys, lesson plans, classroom observations and interviews pointed to several obstacles the teachers faced with incorporating critical dimensions into their students' technology use. The obstacles include: school/district technology restrictions; a lack of in depth understanding of CDL, and limited modeling and opportunities during teacher education and teacher development programs to build and recruit CDL to their practices. Implications for teacher education and development and suggestions for future research are presented.

    Fatima A. Al Husseiny, Lebanese International University, Lebanon
    Jana M. Saab, Lebanese University, Lebanon
    Maya H. Abdallah, Lebanese International University, Lebanon
    Noura H. Wehbe, Al Ain University, UAE

The rapid development of technology and communication had given birth to a new world order that impacted all aspects of citizens' lives. This new world order was often known as a world driven by digital tools and innovations. In digital mobility, citizens' lives become faster so that the interaction among individuals has no boundaries. This resulted in the development of digital citizenship. The emergence of social media certainly disrupted citizens' behavior. Therefore, digital literacy was necessary for this era of disrupted society, so becoming a smart and good citizen would be someone's necessity, not a luxury.

    Fatima A. Al Husseiny, Lebanese International University, Lebanon
    Maya H. Abdallah, Lebanese International University, Lebanon

This chapter explores the educational changes and new trends that emerged after the COVID-19 pandemic with a brief review of how education looked like before it. The pandemic forced schools and educational institutions to adapt to new modes of teaching and learning, including online and remote learning. This chapter examines how these changes affected education, including curriculum, assessment, and pedagogy. It also explores the role of technology in education and the importance of digital literacy skills. Finally, it highlights the future trends that we need to watch for.

    Renee R. M. Moran, East Tennessee State University, USA
    Natalia A. Ward, East Tennessee State University, USA
    Monica T. Billen, California State University, Fresno, USA
    Lashay Wood, East Tennessee State University, USA
    Shuling Yang, East Tennessee State University, USA

This chapter reaffirms books clubs as a sound pedagogical strategy and considers how digital and virtual book clubs may allow us to meet this globalized moment in which technology has become a staple of our everyday lives. The authors provide two examples of how to integrate digital and virtual book clubs in both elementary classrooms and teacher education. The first demonstrates the promise of cross-country virtual books clubs as a way to help pre-service teachers access children's literature and consider diverse perspectives. The second case illustrates how one rural elementary school successfully made the shift from face-to-face to digital books in order to build motivation to read and increase authentic discussion between students. The authors argue that digital and virtual book clubs can expand access to text, empower and motivate students of all ages, and mirror real world literacy practices. The authors advocate for book clubs as a necessary literacy practice, which should be part of the science of reading movement.

Preface

An exploration of the digital comes at a point in which many literacy and communication practices are centered in virtual and hybridized settings. With the advent of the COVID-19 pandemic, educators are arguably in a new age. This age has, however, been in development for some time. Teachers and researchers know this trend first-hand through classrooms and instructional reporting, and through the active literacy lives that youth lead – often, outside of the domains of what is considered "literate" behavior by those in charge. Some innovations in practices and theoretical approaches chronicled in this volume are the result of the pandemic; others exist outside of this context, with author speaking to the wider view of innovation and transformation in instructional routines that maybe considered less routine through a research lens.

A generous portion of the editor's professional life for a period of almost three years was almost entirely housed in such a digital setting, interacting with colleagues and students across regional and chronological spaces via video conferencing. These interactions required screen time management and did not end when conference sessions were complete. Work extended into online design and further interactions across blog spaces and via email. Literacy scholars have noted the important intertextual work of exploring digital practices (Spires et al., 2019), and the continuing exploration of these practices is a bedrock of linking interdisciplinary instruction in meaningful and relevant ways for students.

Simply put, the digital is not only a representation of where we are in educational practice. It is where we have been for some time; or, more adequately, where we have been moving toward. Moreover, the changes and demands of society incorporate digital movements and trends in ever-changing ways, from social media to the interlinked network of resources that are now not only available but instrumental as part of every day living. The shift to online learning is one that is sometimes encouraged to increase enrollment or to provide a wider reach for access to courses. Often quoted, Cazden et al. (1996) envisioned a world in which the information superhighway would transform the manner in which communication occurs. This transformation has been in progress for decades now, and was rolling forward even prior to this 1996 piece.

Both teachers and researchers can benefit from the work contained in this volume. Authors speak to the work that is evolving in online instruction, and the ways that connections were established through virtual engagements during the pandemic and beyond. Some chapters conceptualize innovation through the lens of digital citizenship, while others focus on the necessary ground-level work of teachers through shared narratives in creating and sustaining welcoming learning environments during a stressful and unprecedented time, punctuated with uncertainty and even grief.

This text makes a contribution to the education field as a marker of time spent in pandemic teaching, as a testament to the movement forward in instructional practices and processes that once were the material of speculative fiction, and as a reminder that the most successful and long-lasting instructional engagements center voice, community, and collaboration in authentic ways. Each author speaks from a particular position geographically and in relation to the work of digital learning. In the next section, the editor traces the pathway of the book before returning to central themes to close this preface.

A ROADMAP FOR THE READER

Following this preface, I include an introduction that chronicles my work in comics and digital media prior to, during, and since the pandemic. It is important to note that while the pandemic provided a driving force for innovations in digital and virtual environments, these spaces were part of conversation in research and practice well before this time period. The introduction is a framing up of my thinking about digital literacy and instruction, as well as a snapshot of practice in uniting visual, verbal, and digital forms of communication in instructional processes.

In Chapter 1, "What's Old Is New Again," authors Kristen Hawley Turner and Jill Stedronsky revisit the closure of schools in March 2020, making the case that teachers went into an immediate and required reinvention. The chapter incorporates a literacies lens in examining one teacher's experiences, centering around the question of how teachers engage students during times of great difficulty. The chapter is a testament the powerful work of teachers, the innovation that educators employed and continue to employ, and the powerful skills that teachers use to create and sustain engagement.

In Chapter 2, Anita Chadha details "Civic Deliberations in COVID-19 and Beyond." Chadha explores the idea that research on instruction during COVID has helped us see online education in ways that link with face-to-face methods, and that quality instruction can indeed occur in online and digital spaces. The author emphasizes collaboration, dialogue, and academic reflection, and notes the ways virtual instruction lowered regional and geographic barriers to foster online community. This chapter speaks, in particular, to pathways in regards to critical dialogue.

In "Mathematics Education With Augmented Reality in Early Childhood Education," the author team of İlkay Ulutas, Emine Bozkurt Polat, Feyza Aydin Bölükbas, Kadriye Selin Budak, Kübra Engin craft a fifth chapter that focuses on the use of technology with Augmented Reality (AR) applications. The authors evaluate AR as tool for mathematics education in early childhood, with particular skills on the possibilities for thinking about skills and functionality in teaching processes. As is frequently the case with educational studies, the focus of the chapter is not only the tool, but on the experiences of students. It is a pleasure as a literacy scholar to present a chapter focused on mathematics education in this edited volume.

In Chapter 4, Tetiana Holovatenko offers ideas on "Developing Digital Collaboration Skills of Elementary School Pre-Service Teachers of English Using Bloom's Taxonomy," focusing the conversation from the lockdown perspective and speaking to the increased digitalization of higher education. Through a mixed-methods approach, Holovatenko uses the TPACK framework to explore approaches to digital skills that increase levels of learning, and traces the ways these concepts influence pre-service elementary school teachers. The author affords space to the teachers to share about their perceptions of preparedness through this chapter, and draws upon a framework that has been a fixture and worthy focus in innovative digital technology for the past few years.

Matthew Macomber reports on "Checking Students' ORAs: Oral Assessments with Butler, Kesey, and McBride" in Chapter 5. Macomber explores online technology tools and their role when considering traditional essay assessments. Students in the author's courses submitted oral responses, rather than traditionally-framed work, and Macomber shares the benefits of this approach, as well as some specific recommendations for ensuring the process works well. The chapter presents a unique blend of digital text production and typographic or traditional prose engagements, with attention to classic works through a unique digital lens.

Chapter 6 is authored by Lamia Büşra Yesil, and is titled "Improving the Key Competences in K12 by Collaborating in an Active Learning Environment Online." In this chapter, the author employs an action research approach to consider the ways that teacher decision making and action steps take place throughout an eTwinning project. Yesil implemented observations, questioning, and poll questions to consider responses and results in the study in an effort to capture the realities of classroom instruction across a range of data collection methods. The approach emphasized collaboration, inquiry, project-based learning, and game-based approaches, among other ideas that are reported in the chapter.

In the following chapter, the editor acts as co-author with Kate Cimo to share about "Empathy Through Textual and Dialogic Engagements: A Classroom Narrative Study." Cimo is the primary voice in this chapter and presents work that is focused on the ways that read alouds with middle grades students through online class gathering times. Cimo reported on the engagement that surrounded these textual invitations, as well as the opportunity for empathy that was discovered through these read alouds and strategic class meetings. This sense of community was reported by the teacher and observed through the reactions of students, logging in and building literacy connections in a challenging time.

Niroj Dahal reports on "Integrating Collaborative ICT Tools in Higher Education for Teaching and Learning: A Modest Proposal for Innovation in Digital Instructions" in Chapter 8. Dahal emphasizes a collaborative approach within an action research frame, and recounts his teaching experiences with students at a range of levels. (Dahal & Pangeni, 2019; McNiff, 2013) in various semesters that involves his (PGD, Master, and MPhil) students of 2019-2021 batches in techno-pedagogy and its trend in learning. Dahal shares collaborative strategies and includes approaches that can be implemented in a variety of face-to-face and digital settings.

In "A Systematic Review of the Literature on Digital Citizenship," Pelin Yolcu explores research that has been done in regard to digital citizenship through a meta-analysis of existing literature, noting the distinctions between digital natives and digital immigrants, as well as the overall importance of a theoretical application of the digital world. Yolcu notes the growing prominence of digital interactions in societies, and comments on the information age, along with insights into technological developments. This chapter works as a theoretical and research-based addition to the conversation, ripe for use as a foundational text for studies to come, and bringing together global thinking about digital innovations.

In "Transmedial and Transformational Practices in Comics Work," the editor shares once more. This time, the focus is on an adult comics maker whose interactions with digital creations, gaming, and film inform his work. For this comics creator, the traditional page and artistic tools were part of the approach, linking to additional sources of inspiration and including multiple and multimodal methods for print and digital canvas creations. What is more, the creator reports on the ways that digital and virtual environments have also fostered his continued involvement in fandom communities and in ongoing processes of making.

In Chapter 11, Dr. Vicki Hosek and Dr. Lara Handsfield share an invited contribution, "The Struggle Is Real: A Study of Teachers' Experiences With Recruiting Critical Digital Literacy to Their Practices," in which the authors consider the opportunities that digital environments offer for critical literacy practices. The authors discuss the implications of this criticality for teachers through a mixed-methods study of four in-service educators. The chapter draws upon personal and pedagogical knowledge of critical digital literacies (CDL), and speaks to teacher education and development, as well as avenues of future research.

In Chapter 12, authors Fatima Al Husseiny, Dr. Jana Saab, and Maya Abdallah comment on the rapid development of technology and communication, including wider social implications. The authors include a focus on tools and innovations, as well as lived experiences in this new digital context, with applications to digital citizenship, including ways to enact practices in social media environments.

Then, in Chapter 13, Fatima Al Husseiny and Maya Abdallah collaborate once more to explore educational transitions and trends since the COVID-19 pandemic, noting the nature of pre-pandemic instruction briefly before considering the adaptations that were necessitated during this time. The authors consider implications for the wider world of education, including curriculum and more, with a vision of what might be next in the world of instruction. The authors conclude this volume with a clear recording and positioning on what teaching life has been like during this era.

Finally, Natalia Ward, Renee Rice Moran, Jody Jennings, and Shuling Yang collaborate on the fourteenth chapter. These scholars bring the conversation back around to literacy, examining the ways that book clubs have taken place in virtual contexts. In particular, the authors take note of how readership and engagement connects with students, expanding existing concepts of literacy; what is more, the authors speak across contexts, examining this work in two distinct regions in the United States.

Dr. Damiana Gibbons Pyles presents a conclusion that centers the human in the midst of the digital as a way of thinking about the themes that run through many of the chapters in this volume. In many ways, Dr. Pyles provides a way of approaching these chapters and this volume, maintaining a focus on the essential personhood in the midst of discussions of tools, technology, and trends.

IMPLICATIONS AND IMPACT

Digital work is not some far-off dream, so lesser-than way of approaching instruction, nor is it regionally bound. As a long-time resident of Appalachia, I know the connections that were fostered for me across televised and digital communications. I never imagined that I would become a teacher, and I continue to grow in my practice through both reflection and research. This notion of innovation that forms a part of the title of this volume is constantly reflected in the work I engage with in in-person and online settings.

I recently had a dream in which I was teaching. At the end of the lesson, I was sure that I had bombed. I could point to a hundred ways the lesson could have gone better. In the dream, my first principal, who had just recently passed away, said to me, "Son, it looks like you still have a lot to learn," and handed my evaluation over. The marks were high and the words he wrote were kind. Sometimes the leaps we take in education are supported by a community of practice; at other times, they are misunderstood. The linking between technology and humanity in education is sometimes fraught with a focus on tools. A list of no's and not yet's often populate the ways in which we humans engage with media consumption and digital materials. Rightly so to some degree, as these are powerful tools. Yet, there is more to digital literacy and virtual innovation than fences.

As I reflect on my experiences, I recognize the ways in which digital instruction has shaped and re-shaped my thinking. I recently read an early copy of a text called *The He-Man Effect* by Box Brown. In this graphic novel, Brown takes on the role that media and materials play in shaping thinking. As a child of the 1980s, I recognized myself immediately in this book, reflecting on the experiences I had in linking television to movies to action figures. It was quite the web of creating/reading/visualizing material.

Students today live in a world of materiality. To suggest anything otherwise is anachronistic. I think about students who would not readily engage with a print text, but who spend hours perusing social media. These young people I am thinking of know how to edit, engage, and filter through a vast array of media in concise moments.

I think about students who linked mainframe to mainframe, material to material, and did so with varying degrees of family support during the pandemic. Again, I want to include the caveat that this is not a pandemic book – even so, much of educational experience in the years leading up to this publication have been shaped by the pandemic. I see these implications reflected in teaching training in which I have been involved, noting how instruction has been re-envisioned with opportunities for synchronous and asynchronous engagements. The move to digital instruction has resulted in a number of different avenues for considering how instruction is delivered (Miller et al., 2021).

In many ways, educators are still rising from the COVID pandemic and continuing to explore links with one another. There is ground to cover for students and teachers emotionally, and critical thinking to be done about framing work with students from an assets-based perspective. The chapters in this book present themes that have been resonant in this author's work, but which he was not fully aware were also part of others' experiences in additional studies, including the linking of digital texts to community involvement and the central necessity of authentic and meaningful collaborations.

The digital movement is hardly done as technology increases, and it is the aim of this volume to present stories of virtual and digital innovation that can inspire, inform, and empower educators for transformative work to come. What comes next is hard to specifically imagine, but the prowess and constantly evolving practices of educators will no doubt be essential for engaging students in whatever shape the next digital turn takes.

Of final note before embarking on the chapters in this book, I offer the reader a brief epistemology of a digital instructional architecture. This is not the epistemology, but rather an epistemology. It is my hope that this a topic to return to in time to come both for my research agenda, as well as for readers. Notably, this epistemology includes (1) a notion of pivot. At one point in time, universities and other educational institutions were faced with the immediate need to pivot to a new location – the digital space. This pivot, however, is perhaps captured less dramatically in moments when institutions reconsider the ways that barriers can be broken down, and new avenues can be explored digitally.

From this pivot, there is a phase of exploring tools and possibilities, which I would term (2) leveraging digital functionality. This is a process of matching tools to instructional purposes; endemic to this phase is the process of (3) exploring commonalities in digital space. We often begin with what we know. This is the stage at which an educator explores the possibilities inherent in digital spaces and either rejects or accepts them. If acceptance occurs, there is an operation within existing limitations or an extension of possibilities.

The personalities present in the digital infrastructure ideally occur in the next phase as educators infuse the notion of community into digital spaces. I term this (4) linking identity/ies, which occurs in close tandem with (5) textual/content links. The move to crafting environment or crafting content first, or at all, is likely determined by the educator's philosophy. This results in what should be a (6) networking space, complete with pratfalls and moments when instruction bombs and must be reconsidered. It is important to note that this space must be designed, redesigned, and refreshed to reflect contemporary needs. A static online space quickly becomes the instructional equivalent of a busted weblink.

While much is yet to be explored in digital innovation, these facets and steps will likely be involved in healthy and growing, consistently innovative spaces.

Jason D. DeHart
University of Tennessee, Knoxville, USA

REFERENCES

Cazden, C., Cope, B., Fairclough, N., Gee, J., Kalantzis, M., & Kress, G.,The New London Group. (1996). A pedagogy of multiliteracies: Designing social futures. *Harvard Educational Review*, *66*(1), 60–92. doi:10.17763/haer.66.1.17370n67v22j160u

Miller, A. N., Sellnow, D. D., & Strawser, M. G. (2021). Pandemic pedagogy challenges and opportunities: Instruction communication in remote, HyFlex, and BlendFlex courses. *Communication Education*, *70*(2), 202–204. doi:10.1080/03634523.2020.1857418

Spires, H. A., Paul, C. M., & Kerkhoff, S. N. (2019). Digital literacy for the 21st century. In M. Khosrow-Pour (Ed.), *Advanced Methodologies and Technologies in Library Science, Information Management, and Scholarly Inquiry* (pp. 12–21). IGI Global. doi:10.4018/978-1-5225-7659-4.ch002

Acknowledgment

I gratefully acknowledge Dr. Damiana Pyles for sharing a conclusion to this volume. I also wish to acknowledge the work of the authors in providing their insights and expertise through chapter contributions and peer reviews. Additionally, I send gratitude to Dr. Nicole Mirra, Dr. Damiana Pyles, and Antonio Santos for providing additional chapter reviews.

Chapter 1
What's Old Is New Again

Kristen Hawley Turner
Drew University, USA

Jill Stedronsky
William Anin Middle School, USA

ABSTRACT

Schools closed in March 2020, causing teachers to reinvent themselves. As classes were forced into remote learning, educators jumped into virtual instruction – to a variety of outcomes. This chapter documents one teacher's personal inquiry during the pandemic shutdown through a literacy lens. By asking the question, "How do teachers engage students during this difficult time?" she ultimately realized that what she had always known about good pedagogy in a face to face classroom transferred into virtual contexts: content needed to be relevant, assignments and assessments needed to be project-based and authentic, and students needed the opportunity to connect with others. The move to remote instruction may have made the pedagogical choices that surrounded her teaching beliefs even more important. For this teacher, the goal of developing her students' literacies in order to help them become critical thinkers was at the heart of her integration of technologies into her learning environment.

INTRODUCTION

And don't throw the past away
You might need it some other rainy day
Dreams can come true again
When everything old is new again
  "*Everything Old Is New Again,*" Allen & Sager

Education did a topsy-turvy in March 2020 when schools closed overnight, forcing teachers and students into remote learning contexts. As an eighth-grade language arts teacher, Jill had positioned herself as lead learner in a classroom of readers and writers who conducted their own inquiries throughout the year. By the time the pandemic hit, her students were regularly using technologies to consume texts that

DOI: 10.4018/978-1-6684-7015-2.ch001

interested them, create digital compositions that documented their personal inquiries, and connect with other readers and writers outside their classroom.

But that March, Jill was forced to step back from what she knew to be good pedagogy. Her school required all language arts teachers to work collaboratively to develop curriculum that would carry them through the early weeks of the shutdown. All students were to have the same experience, and Jill knew that her colleagues, not having experienced through their past practice the power of digital tools to engage students in authentic work, would revert to more traditional methods. In fact, the lessons that the team developed did not engage Jill or her students, and she made the decision to go rogue, to collaborate with a colleague outside of her school, and to use technologies to help students (1) learn and (2) process the moment in which they were living while it was happening.

By asking the question, "How do teachers engage students during this difficult time?" Jill embarked on her own teacher-inquiry. Ultimately, she realized that what she had always known about good pedagogy in a face-to-face classroom transferred into virtual contexts: content needed to be relevant, assignments and assessments needed to be project-based and authentic, and students needed the opportunity to connect with others. The move to remote instruction may have made the pedagogical choices that surrounded her teaching beliefs even more important. For Jill, the goal of developing her students' literacies in order to help them become critical thinkers was at the heart of her integration of technologies into her learning environment. This chapter documents Jill's personal inquiry during the pandemic shutdown through a literacy lens.

BACKGROUND

Foundation and Development of the Concept of Literacies

In the last decade of the twentieth century, the New London Group brought together inquiries on new literacies that changed the way that researchers and teachers both defined literacy and approached instruction. Prior to the global transformation that occurred in 2020 in response to a pandemic, educators had been integrating digital technologies into teaching and learning, and researchers had been studying the impact of these technologies on literacy practices both in and out of school.

In the 1990s The New London group began research on what they eventually called New Literacies theory and the new literacies that enabled participation in a digital world, resulting in an understanding that technology had been and continues to influence both literacy and learning. The internet itself required new literacies in order for users to fully realize its potential. Literacies included skills of both consumption and creation that made reading and writing in digital contexts different than in print-based contexts. Leu, et. al (2004) defined literacies as "multiple, multimodal, and multifaceted" and asserted that "new forms of strategic knowledge are required with new literacies" (p. 1589). As part of this argument the understanding that social practices influenced literacies was important.

Work in the field of literacy instruction continued through the 2000s with Hicks and Grabill (2005) making a call early in the new century to make digital writing a part of teacher education. Shortly thereafter, the National Writing Project published *Because Digital Writing Matters* (DeVoss, et. al, 2010), articulating that "Digital writing is about the dramatic changes in the ecology of writing and communication and, indeed, what it means to write—to create and compose and share" (p. 4). Building on these understandings of the importance of *digital* in literacy instruction through the early part of the 21st century, researchers such as Hicks and Turner (2013) made the call to English teachers that they "must advocate for digital literacy, not just technology, in a way that reconceptualizes [the] discipline" (p. 61). These researchers also investigated authentic literacy practices in digital spaces, identifying that digital reading was different from the print-based reading instruction that was prevalent in schools (Turner and Hicks, 2015).

Turner (2020) succinctly defined digital literacy as "the knowledge and skills that allows for critical consumption, creation, interaction and communication using digital technologies" (p. 1), and over the last decade research in the field of digital literacies has continued with efforts made in areas such as multimodal literacies (e.g., McGrail, et. al, 2021), gaming literacies (e.g., Garcia, et. al, 2020), and sub-screenic literacies (e.g., Lynch 2017), to name a few. In short, new literacies continue to evolve and English teachers who center an understanding of literacies in their practice support students to develop skills that will serve them in real-world contexts.

Views of Technology Integration

Alongside the research in the field of literacy instruction that focused on the impacts of technology on literacy practices emerged research in the field of education on the integration of technologies into instruction. Mishra and Koehler's (2006) TPACK framework became a standard for considering the knowledge that teachers needed in order to use technology effectively. Models for tech integration in practice, such as SAMR (Puentedura, 2010) and the Technology Integration Matrix (Harmes, Welsh & Winkelman, 2016), helped educators to consider the instructional purpose behind selecting tools and launched new lines of inquiry into the effective uses of technology in education.

After the invention of the iPhone and the subsequent development of social media as spaces where everyone gathered, literacy practices changed at a faster rate than schools could adapt. The question of the thousand-dollar pencil became commonplace as leaders in the education technology world advocated for thoughtful integration of technology into instruction and selective purchases that truly supported student learning. In fact, many teachers resisted incorporating digital tools altogether.

Despite the seemingly parallel and often overlapping trajectories of the fields of educational technology and digital literacy, seeing technology as interconnected with literacy, however, was not widespread in schools. In 2013 Hicks and Turner made the argument that "digital literacy can't wait" (p. 58), urging teachers to transform their practice and to re-define literacy through the lens of the digital tools used in authentic spaces found outside the classroom where students were "hanging out, messing around, and geeking out" (Ito, et. al, 2008). Individual teachers answered the call; however, as the shift to remote teaching and learning during the pandemic revealed, the system had not yet transformed.

In fact, when schools shut down, technology integration became a must-do overnight for *all* educators. Many teachers had to learn how to use the tools that would allow them to connect to their students; it was a big learning curve. Shifting their pedagogy was not the priority of learning when simply getting online was a huge challenge, and as the results bore out, even after teachers became more comfortable with the tools, simply knowing the technologies was not enough to provide effective instruction.

Pandemic Teaching

Faced with the need to teach remotely or virtually, many teachers reverted to teacher-centered instruction, call and response pedagogy, and traditional modes. As a result, they struggled with screens full of blank boxes when students refused to turn cameras on, rampant cheating, and an overall dearth of participation. Teachers were not prepared to use digital tools to engage students in consuming and creating content and in connecting them with others. Educators that did employ tools in this way were more successful in the abrupt shift to remote and virtual instruction.

Pandemic teaching could have been an opportunity to transform education; unfortunately, a line from the song "Everything Old Is New Again" appears to be all too relevant: "Let's go backwards when forward fails." Despite the long history and advocacy of research in the fields of literacy and technology integration, education as an institution had not adopted authentic technology practices and instruction at a mass scale that would have prepared it for the shift into virtual teaching and learning. In many cases, teachers had to learn how to use the technologies and did not have the capacity to learn pedagogies that would be most effective in virtual spaces. With overwhelming effort on simply adopting technologies, pedagogy reverted to more traditional instructional practices that seemed easier to manage than constructivist pedagogies like cooperative learning or small group discussion activities that had become the norm in many classrooms. For example, Initiate-Respond-Evaluate patterns punctuated Zoom rooms as teachers tried to engage their students in ways that seemed to have worked in face-to-face settings (Turner & Hicks, 2022). For many, the idea of asking students to participate in small group conversations and personal inquiries seemed daunting, when, in fact, these kinds of pedagogies would have aligned with best practices before, during, and after the pandemic.

Jill, an eighth-grade teacher, had created a classroom where conversations occurred constantly, inquiry grew, and students thrived. When she was forced into remote teaching, she clung to her beliefs of sound pedagogy, which included her dedication to resituating literacy, which is inherently digital in contemporary society, at the heart of teaching. Through reflecting on her pandemic experience, Jill concluded that "it's all about great pedagogy." This chapter turns now to Jill's personal inquiry during the pandemic shutdown.

ENGAGING STUDENTS IN REMOTE LEARNING (JILL'S STORY)

Pre-Pandemic

Until the pandemic, Jill's school did not have 1:1 access to devices for the students. In order for Jill to use digital tools, she had to reserve a computer cart, which she did regularly. In fact, because she wanted it so often, the school purchased additional carts, making it easier for her to have access most days. Her colleagues were not using the computers as frequently. Regardless, pre-pandemic Jill had to be intentional about when and why she planned for device use simply because of the logistics of getting the computers in her students' hands, powering them up, and making sure they were reconnected to the charging station at the end of each period.

Jill's students needed devices frequently because they were conducting inquiries into questions that they had devised themselves through a process of self-reflection and use of the tool Ikigai (Kudo, 2018) to uncover their purpose in life. Jill understood that literacies must be authentic and that any instruction in literacy in her classroom needed to draw on authentic audiences and purposes. To this end she had already transformed her classroom into a space where students could focus on personal inquiries, personal development, and personal reflection on their learning and growth (Stedronsky & Turner, 2020). She began the year with an exploration of asking students to evaluate their purpose which was supported by reflective writing that led to an inquiry. Whenever possible students used digital tools to help them with their inquiries. Students presented their journeys in the form of TED Talks at the end of the school year. Consuming digital texts to spark their curiosities and further their learning - and creating digital, multimodal compositions - were standard practice in Jill's classroom even before the pandemic started.

In March 2020 students were poised to make a turn from research to creation of their TED Talks, which would have taken the entirety of the final quarter of the year. As was the case for educators and students all over the world, Jill and her eighth graders entered a school shutdown that turned teaching and learning upside down. Not only did Jill have to contend with mandates from her district about what and how to teach in the early days of the pandemic, she also had to grapple with how to maintain pedagogies that engaged learners in truly student-centered ways.

Jill's first-person reflection of the days immediately following the shutdown captures her commitment to maintaining a pedagogy that drew on constructivist approaches - keeping her practice firmly grounded in what educational research had shown time and again to be effective.

Going Remote

In March of 2020, when schools initially prepared for two weeks of virtual instruction, the language arts teachers in my district were given two days to collaboratively write a curriculum to account for students being remote. I knew how my district worked. I would have to dump my student-driven, inquiry-based classroom that I had been developing over years, jump on board with writing teacher-centered, formulaic lessons, and fake enthusiasm and support for the plan. In two days, my colleagues and I created vocabulary quizzes using technology for the sake of it and composed lists of questions for each and every chapter of *The Miracle Worker.*

Even as we created these rote tasks for students, I didn't know how I would implement them. I believed completely in engaging students with the text by cultivating their critical thinking skills and asking them to read with a questioning mind and to disrupt their thinking (Beers & Probst, 2017), but these lessons we were creating did not allow for any voice or choice. We were not considering how students would do more than answer questions about the text. We would not be helping them to cultivate their own thinking.

Though I did my best to try to influence the process, offering ideas and activities that would allow students to create, consume and connect in authentic ways while they were at home, I knew that ultimately the planned lessons were going to be brutal for the kids. They would be working completely independently, completing mundane tasks that did not truly engage their thinking. However, I wanted to be a team player and honestly had no clue what Covid would bring. To be fair to all of us, the district had charged us to make sure our entire curriculum was scripted and every child had the same experience. They wanted to ensure that if one teacher became sick, a colleague could take over seamlessly. I understood that and knew how stressed many teachers were with the overnight shift to going digital.

I was sick to my stomach by the time we left school that last Friday, knowing that what my students were about to encounter was completely antithetical to how we had been working as a classroom community all year. I explained to them the district's rationale and told them I would post the common lessons, but I also admitted that I did not know if I could stick with the plan. They understood. They knew me, my years of research in uncovering effective teaching practices, and the successes they had already experienced as students in my classroom. We all jumped into remote learning with trepidation at how the prescribed curriculum would impact us.

A Time to Experiment

After two days of trying to be a team player and using the lessons my colleagues had created, I knew I could not continue. The moment we were experiencing was confusing and scary for both me and my students, and I knew we needed to process what was happening in the world around us. It was not the time for me to adopt traditional pedagogies; instead, it was a time for me to enact what I knew to be good teaching and to experiment in a new context.

By the second remote day, I ditched the prescribed lessons and my students wrote from their hearts about this new experience. We created personal reactions during the first week of the shutdown and compiled them into a book. Using a digital tool that allowed us to collaborate and connect together in real time brought us instantly back to the community we had built in our classroom. Students wanted to share with each other, to hear other's experiences, and to grapple with the unknown together. They wrote with honesty and emotion about their experiences as learners, providing detailed suggestions about how to improve the overall school schedule if we were to stay remote, and as each day passed, it looked more and more like that would be the case.

By the end of the week, we had a digital book of recommendations that I shared with the assistant superintendent. She read the book with the sixty pages of students' thoughts and responded to me quickly. I shared her email on my Google Classroom, so the students could see that she had read it and appreciated their feedback on how the school was adapting to Covid. My students had choice in the pieces they created that week and knew their ideas would be heard by an authentic audience. They received feedback from someone other than me. We did this all in the context of being shut in our own homes. This was good writing; it was good instruction. It had purpose and audience and impact. After this experience, I knew I could not use the plans my colleagues and I created the week before, abandoning everything I knew to be effective. Students' learning must have purpose, impact and be driven by their own curiosities, and I needed to remember that as I charged forward in remote learning.

Building Collaborations

With the success of that first shared book, I began to look for other ways my students could collaborate and connect beyond the walls of their homes. We knew that we were going to be remote for the long haul. I reached out to my friend and colleague, John Brum, who taught environmental science at the high school. Previously, we did some small collaborations where his seniors gave my students feedback on their TED Talks. Always interested in making school more real and relevant, John was intrigued by this unique opportunity that Covid presented. John and I decided we would join our expertise and move forward. Our district mandate that no student would fail meant that grades were not the driver in either of our classes. We needed to keep the students engaged, and to do so we needed to enact great instructional practice.

Knowing we could not ignore the historical event we were living through, we decided the students would co-create a book about their lives in the moment. Wasn't this the definition of relevance? We would teach the skills of our unique content areas through the project. Even though he was teaching environmental science to seniors, and I was charged with teaching English to eighth graders, we both saw content as a vehicle, not a transference of knowledge. Covid presented the content. We would use the joint book our students created to be the vehicle for them to gain all the reading, writing, and thinking skills that actually mattered.

We didn't view our two distinct content areas or age groups as obstacles but rather as an opportunity for our students to learn and grow from each other. We decided each person would contribute three pieces to our joint book: (1) an information article on any topic a student chose about COVID, (2) an artistic expression of COVID -- whether that be a poem, a creative story, a piece of art, a collage or anything else the student perceived as art, and (3) an interview with a person of their choice about their experience with COVID.

John and I began planning immediately, spending a full weekend constructing a rough outline of possible lessons and then creating our own personal pieces for our book to be the models for the students. It was important for our students to see us creating, consuming and connecting in the same ways we were asking of them. And, to be honest, it felt good to do it! Throughout the project, we decided we would draw on each other's skills to teach the students about research, credible evidence, voice, organization and a host of other literacy skills that we knew were in our curriculums and state standards but that we also knew were life skills - digital literacies they needed to be successful citizens. From dabbling in project-based learning previously, I knew the students would be motivated to learn the skills because they would have choice in what they would be researching, reading and writing, and that it would have a future impact. Their work would become a history book of Covid for future generations!

We set it up like the year-long, inquiry-based TED Talk project I had been working on pre-Covid. I told John that it was important that the students read with a wondering and curious mind, and I could show his environmental classes how my eighth graders were doing that. I introduced a bookmark my students used while reading informational text with three simple questions: What surprised me? What challenged, changed or confirmed what I knew? What did the author think I already knew? (Beers and Probst, 2015). Although reading like this was new to John and his students, it made sense to him that we spend the time teaching them to read so that the text sparked their own thoughts. He had followed a more prescribed curriculum because some of his classes were AP and he felt his students would need to know the content for the test, but he was convinced by my argument.

I shared a story from Jim Gray's *Teachers as Writers: A Memoir of the Early Years of the National Writing Project* (2000) about Bob Tierney, a science teacher, who had felt most of his career was helping students memorize and not think. After attending the Summer Institute at the Bay Area Writing Project, Tierney experimented with his class by using "writing project writing-to-learn ideas" (p. 106). He used a colleague's class as the control group, and when they assessed the students sixteen weeks later, Tierney's "students recalled 19 percent more than [his colleague's]" (p. 106). John understood. He wanted his students to be critical consumers of information, thinkers who would process content knowledge. If we approached the reading and content his kids needed to do with more of an inquisitive mindset, they would retain more. Though his students would look at Covid through an environmental lens, he planned to allow them to write about anything that resonated with them. Together we embarked on good teaching in the face of a pandemic.

The Tech of It All

Book Creator (https://bookcreator.com/) was a tool that allowed John's and my students to collaborate. Students could create professional looking work that incorporated audio and video, as well as image and text. It was intuitive to use, and I was able to demonstrate it for students in a short mini-lesson. All 120 students added their writing to a single book, and they were able to see the process of each other's pieces as they developed. This connection through drafting and development inspired and challenged students to create articles, interviews and art that would accurately communicate their thoughts and feelings about Covid.

Students reached out to grandmothers and professors, uncles who worked for the mayor in NYC, healthcare workers in hospitals, police officers, and cousins who worked for the government. The students had choice in how they captured the stories, using technology that felt right and comfortable to them, including the recording options within Book Creator. As students added their interviews, the book showcased many voices - young, old and expert - and the experience of the Covid shutdown. The authentic audience of their peers and the idea that they would be sharing this book to the world impacted their writing. Students cared how their pieces communicated their message because there was an audience and their thoughts would have an effect on people.

With Book Creator serving as the main tool that connected the 120 students, we also used Zoom to bring the classes together. We planned joint sessions during the afternoons, when the district had scheduled open time for extra help, where one of my classes would connect with one of John's. We hoped to expand the students' world beyond their bedrooms and original classmates. From the first synchronous meeting, students expressed enthusiasm for the project and for the opportunity to work together across the grades and content areas. My eighth graders were excited that they would be collaborating with seniors - that, yes, they were intelligent enough to work with someone four years older and provide feedback and insight - and the seniors were excited that they could help my eighth graders. As the students continued to collaborate, however, the age gap seemed to disappear. Very quickly the project became a group of students who saw each other as equals and humans experiencing something kind of extraordinary. The technologies allowed this shift to happen.

Zoom also allowed students to connect with experts outside of the classroom, and we took advantage. We invited a journalist who was writing about Covid and vaccines to teach students how to be critical consumers and credible creators of information. Students engaged with him, asking questions and developing an understanding of the importance of writing using facts from primary sources. Though the Zoom sessions were not required, as they were held during the district time allotted for extra help, the majority (including the seniors) showed up. They were engaged by both the project and the opportunities to connect through technologies.

Authentic Learning

The pandemic shut down brought us a gift that ultimately ignited and fueled me and John and our students. Learning developed from authentic activities that created a rich environment for teaching literacy, and students were engaged. They didn't ask questions about a rubric and what they needed to get a grade; they wanted to know about reporting and writing; they wanted to share their stories. When students could have just checked out (and many students across the nation did), our students checked in. At a time when school offered them a free pass, they engaged even more.

As we saw the pieces developing, we had sessions where students were grouped to spark ideas for articles based on what they were reading. The conversations were natural and authentic, not schoolish. "Where did you read that?" "Oh, I didn't know that, can you explain more in your article?" "I loved your interview--how powerful--was that someone you knew?" The natural questions they asked of each other fed the drive to revise and edit so pieces communicated the message students wanted to tell. We didn't need rubrics; the students provided more feedback to each other than any teacher ever could. This was authentic, relevant, rigorous, student-driven, project-based learning. It avoided all the pitfalls some of my colleagues were having with cheating. This reinforced for me again, and for John that this approach is how we must *ALWAYS* teach.

In the end, our students wrote a 579-page book filled with their thoughts and feelings. Five hundred and seventy-nine pages of different, personal topics about Covid, sparked by our students' concerns and interests. Five hundred and seventy-nine pages of personal interviews and voices about a historical moment we were all living through. Five hundred and seventy-nine pages of art that was created by kids and their parents. Five hundred and seventy-nine pages of interviews with people that lived across the country, conversations that so many students would not have had with these people if not for this project.

As an educator, suffering through the most challenging moment of my teaching career, the work of giving my students a voice became cathartic. The book exuded emotion. I cannot even describe how beautiful the process was. I could consult theory books and categorize why this met effective educational practices, but it was even more powerful and beautiful than that. I have no English words. I have to borrow a Latin phrase used by lawyers: Res Ipsa Loquitur - the thing speaks for itself.

Moving Forward

John and I both forged ahead the next year, cemented in what was good practice. What we both had learned years ago in graduate school was still true. Relevance, rigor and agency always matter. Somehow, maybe through the lack of professional development and how overwhelming first years of teaching can be with the excessive need our country has to numerically measure student progress, so many teachers fall to bad practices. In the moment of Covid lockdowns, many teachers reverted to traditional pedagogies that did not engage students, and in the desire to "catch up" with return to school, these practices often continued in face-to-face settings. However, John and I both moved our classrooms to be fully grounded in project-based and student-centered learning. Digital tools like Zoom, Book Creator, Kami and Parlay offered authentic ways to connect, create and consume information, and we were committed to rethinking what we had always done and to incorporating even more digital tools to help break down the walls of our classrooms.

That summer, John and I sat on his porch and re-worked his whole year's curriculum to model and incorporate what he saw happening with his students during the shutdown. We mapped a year-long project where his students would use the content of his class to feed their own environmental quests. It was thrilling. Students are humans. They are curious individuals that think deeply about life. That is what rigor means, allowing students to think by using content as starting and sparking points, not as a thing that needs to be transferred and soon forgotten. Helping students develop skills to be critical consumers and responsible creators of information became the heart of John's science classroom, and it became even more important in my eighth grade language arts setting.

In the fall of 2020 while I was teaching virtually and then in concurrent virtual/in-person contexts, I looked for more ways to collaborate with other schools and countries and explored opportunities to make sure my students' learning had an impact. Book Creator continued to be an important digital tool for this work because of the affordances it offered. Peers around the world could write about issues that mattered to them, discuss topics, and provide feedback. Through these authentic projects, students learned the necessary literacy skills of reading, writing, listening, speaking, thinking, creating, consuming, collaborating - all the skills needed for contemporary humans. This is work I continued even after my school returned to a normal schedule.

At the same time that I was thinking about how I could be even more project-based and student-centered during a time of virtual learning, realizing that tools like Book Creator and Zoom could allow for so many different types of collaborations and connections, my colleagues and district were planning ways to deal with rampant cheating that occurred during Covid. To me, it was simple. I had to offer choice and voice in every assignment, and the task must be relevant and allow students to have an impact on their world. If students worked just for the grade, and technology was used just to transmit knowledge, then students would cheat.

My district did not listen to my thoughts. They were intrigued by my pedagogies, but they believed my students were motivated and inspired by my attitude, not the structure of my class, the environment we created together, and the authentic, relevant tasks I offered. They spent their energy and time brainstorming statements that students would have to sign and paste to every assignment, promising that it was their work. They created rules for students to take assessments with cameras on and their phones right by them so teachers could watch for cheating. Meetings occurred about how we should upgrade software technology like Turnitin.com so we could catch plagiarism and instill more fear into our students to prevent cheating.

And all I could think about was a book with five hundred and seventy-nine pages of different thoughts, art and interviews - and not a single piece like another.

After the experience during the spring of 2020, I knew I could never go back to reading a whole-class book and giving questions for my students to answer as they read. My role is to cultivate mindsets and develop thinking routines (Project Zero, 2022). Connections to other humans, including interviews, would forever become a part of my classroom. I want my students to leave my classroom with a set of literacy skills that are transferable, not content that will soon be forgotten if not used. I want to cultivate independent, curious humans that are critical consumers and responsible creators

The students stayed interested in my class despite the craziness of their schooling because they were reading, writing and learning about topics they cared about. They were connecting with humans and learning together, just like we do in the real world. Relevance is not about showing kids how a topic is relevant to their lives; it is about starting with topics that *are* relevant to their lives and then letting them follow their own inquiries about it. It's really that simple. That's great pedagogy.

CONCLUSION: THE HEART OF GREAT PEDAGOGY

Jill's story showcases some important lessons. First, centering literacies in teaching allows for authentic learning, and second, great pedagogy evolves from truly student-centered, inquiry-driven practices that use technologies with purpose. Neither of these lessons is new. In fact, they are pretty old. From Dewey's writings in the early 1900s that argued that learning is both social and interactive to Vygotsky's mid-century theory of the zone of proximal development and the importance of mentoring in sociocultural learning to the connection between constructivism and technology in the late 20th century (Duffy & Jonassen, 1992), constructivism has a long-standing history in the field of educational research.

At its core, Jill's pedagogy rests on constructivist principles. However, it also relies on the work of literacies scholars over the past few decades. For Jill, skill development, or more specifically, literacies development, is the most important aspect of teaching and learning. She wants her students to gain transferable skills that will help them to become critical consumers, careful creators, and critical thinkers who can contribute to society. When looking at Jill's pedagogy during remote learning - and the pedagogy she continues to enact - Dewey would probably say, yes, "everything old is new again."

However, lessons can be learned from the integration of technologies in Jill's practice - especially those that she adopted during the pandemic and has carried with her into her current teaching. Even before the shutdown when she could only connect with her students remotely, Jill had incorporated digital texts and tools into her classroom in an effort to help her students uncover, follow, and document personal inquiries. Covid-19 brought with it an unexpected gift: her school purchased Chromebooks for every student.

With 1:1 to devices, Jill was able to use tech every day - whether her students were at home or in her physical classroom space. As Jill and John attempted to connect their students with them, with each other, and with experts in the field, the use of technology naturally allowed for students to be (1) active, (2) collaborative, (3) constructive, (4) authentic, and (5) goal-directed (Hermes, et. al, 2016). Because the technology was in service of the learning - or more specifically, the process of inquiry - Jill did not get stuck in early phases of the Technology Integration Matrix that limited use of tech to deliver content or in traditional applications. Rather, tech was infused, and in some cases transformative, simply because of the constructive pedagogies that Jill and John adopted in a virtual setting.

The lessons learned from pandemic teaching require a look back to what we already knew about effective pedagogy. Content needs to be relevant, assignments and assessments need to be project-based and authentic, and students need the opportunity to connect with others who can provide mentorship and feedback. Within and across this rather simple frame, technology needs to be integrated purposefully to support the learning.

To that end, simply having access to tools of technology does not lead to increased learning. Understanding how to employ those tools pedagogically, selecting them to meet purposeful goals, is the key. Perhaps Allen and Sager offer the most promising view of post-pandemic teaching and learning:

And don't throw the past away
You might need it some other rainy day
Dreams can come true again
When everything old is new again

By remembering that technology integration can be in service of developing literacies and that authentic, student-centered instruction leads to learning, educators can transform their classrooms - whether virtual or in-person - to environments that foster student growth.

REFERENCES

Beers, K., & Probst, R. E. (2015). *Reading nonfiction: Notice & note stances, signposts, and Strategies.* Heinemann.

Beers, K., & Probst, R. E. (2017). *Disrupting thinking: Why how we read matters.* Scholastic.

DeVoss, D. N., Eidman-Aadahl, E., & Hicks, T. (2010). *Because digital writing matters: Improving student writing in online and multimedia environments.* Jossey-Bass.

Duffy, T. M., & Jonassen, D. H. (1992). *Constructivism and the technology of instruction: A conversation.* Lawrence Erlbaum.

Garcia, A., Witte, S., & Dail, J. (Eds.). (2020). *Studying gaming literacies.* Brill. doi:10.1163/9789004429840

Grabill, J. T., & Hicks, T. (2005). Multiliteracies Meet Methods: The Case for Digital Writing in English Education. *English Education, 37*(4), 301–311.

Gray, J. (2000). *Teachers at the center a memoir of the early years of the National Writing Project.* Distributed by ERIC Clearinghouse.

Hermes, J. C., Welsh, J., & Winkelman, R. J. (2016). A framework for defining and evaluating technology integration in the instruction of real-world skills. In Rosen, Y., Ferrara, S. & Mosharraf, M., eds. Handbook of research on technology tools for real-world skill development. IGI Global.

Hicks, T., & Turner, K. H. (2013). No longer a luxury: Digital literacy can't wait. *English Journal, 102*(6), 58–65.

Ito, M., Baumer, S., & Bittanti, M. boyd, d., Cody, R., Herr-Stephenson, B., Horst, H. A., Lange, P. G., Mahendran, D., Martínez, K. Z., Pascoe, C. J., Perkel, D., Robinson, L., Sims, C., & Tripp, L. (2010). Hanging out, messing around, and geeking out: Kids living and learning with new media. MIT Press.

Kudo, A. (2018). *My little Ikigai journal.* St. Martin's.

Leu, D. J., Kinzer, C. K., Coiro, J., & Cammack, D. W. (2004). Towards a theory of new literacies emerging from the Internet and other information and communication technologies. In R. B. Ruddell & N. Unrau (Eds.), *Theoretical models and processes of reading* (5th ed., pp. 1570–1613). International Reading Association.

Lynch, T. L. (2017). *The hidden role of software in educational research: Policy to practice.* Routledge.

McGrail, E., & Turner, K. H. (2021). A framework for the assessment of multimodal composition. *English Education, 53*(4), 277–302.

Mishra, P., & Koehler, M. J. (2006). Technological pedagogical content knowledge: A framework for teacher nnowledge. *Teachers College Record, 108*(6), 1017–1054. doi:10.1111/j.1467-9620.2006.00684.x

Project Zero. (2022). *Project Zero's thinking routines toolbox.* Harvard. https://pz.harvard.edu/thinking-routines.

Puentedura, R. R. (2010). SAMR and TPACK: Intro to advanced practice. *Hippasus*. http://hippasus. com/resources/sweden2010/SAMR_TPCK_IntroToAdvancedPractice.pdf

Stedronsky, J., & Turner, K. H. (2020). Inquiry ignites! Pushing back against traditional literacy instruction. In J. Dyches, B. Sams, & A. Boyd (Eds.), *Acts of resistances: Subversive teaching in the English language arts classroom* (pp. 51–64). Myers Education Press.

Turner, K. H. (Ed.). (2020). *The ethics of digital literacy: Teaching students across grade levels*. Rowman and Littlefield.

Turner, K. H., & Hicks, T. (2015). *Connected reading: Teaching adolescent readers in a digital age*. NCTE.

Turner, K. H., & Hicks, T. (2022). Digital literacy (still) can't wait: Renewing and reframing the conversation. *English Journal*, *112*(1), 86–93. doi:10.2307/814427

Chapter 2
Civic Deliberations in COVID–19 and Beyond

Anita Chadha
University of Houston-Downtown, USA

ABSTRACT

With online pedagogy becoming mainstream during COVID, research on digital instruction grew dramatically, finding that online pedagogy was on par with face-to-face methods. Adding to this body of work this chapter assesses collaborations to provide meaningful student deliberations. Of particular importance was how students created dialogue and were academically reflective as they lived in geographically dispersed locations from Texas to California, New York, New Jersey, Maryland, and Wisconsin. Indeed, significant findings provided proof that over the course of sixteen plus years including during COVID students fostered a multiplicity of academic reflective deliberations. With the rapidly evolving educational landscape this chapter provides evidentiary proof that carefully designed online collaborations provide effective deliberative communities, an amenable design for any discipline.

INTRODUCTION

Research consistently finds that critical reflection is more effective than other, more expository instructional approaches, irrespective of face-to-face, hybrid to online modes of instruction (Ananga & Biney, 2017; Misra, 2021; Rossini et al., 2021; Megahed & Hassan, 2021). Research also finds that constructing critical reflection processes in online spaces offer several benefits for this evolutionary process (Burke & Larmar, 2021; Miller et al., 2021; Peimani & Kamalipour, 2021; Zeivots et al., 2021). Among these benefits are that online spaces are asynchronous which provide time to reflect, review concepts, respond and deliberate with others as one can respond any time after work and home obligations. This makes for greater convenience, ease of use and flexibility in participation as the content is more digestible. With asynchrony, learning happens at the learner's own pace allowing each student to view lectures, finish assignments, and take exams at any point before their deadlines. Additionally, students can kickstart in-course conversations at any point revisiting the deliberations.

DOI: 10.4018/978-1-6684-7015-2.ch002

While another benefit for critical reflection online is that there is anonymity which empowers students to speak their minds freely expressing varied perspectives. In addition, they know that someone is always listening, engaging, and reacting based on what they wrote at any time of day so that they can 'test the water' with their knowledge before unreservedly sharing perspectives (Carroll & Ryan, 2005; East, 2019; Easton, 2003). Research also concludes that anonymity creates a 'level playing field' amongst students (Blake, 2000; Easton, 2003), widening participation from cohorts such as international students, students returning to education, first generation students and more join as they are eager to engage and practice their voice.

Engagement with peers develops social capital amongst them whom they turn to when first stuck on a problem, sympathizing with shared struggles and experiences rather than asking the instructor (Boud & Cohen, 2014). And while student peers do not always lead to obtaining accurate information, there are advantages to learning from people we know is that they are, or have been, in a similar position to ourselves. They have faced the same challenges as we have in the same context, they talk to us in our own language and we can ask them what may appear, in other situations, to be silly questions. Learning from each other is not only a feature of informal learning, but it also occurs in all courses at all levels. The support and the engagement processes coupled with the online spaces providing convenient, flexibility, anonymity and asynchrony provide the scaffolded support each need (Peeters, 2019), along with the motivation and interest to continuously engage in reflective discourse (Volkovskii, 2021).

With online learning environments proliferating our times and the abundance of research on online pedagogy this chapter explores online collaborations during COVID to evaluate how collaborations affect the ecology of and deliberative practices inherent in education, albeit online among students no matter their mode of instruction or geographic location.

BACKGROUND

John Dewey's approach to education in 1933 was revolutionary for his time as he espoused that student learned through a 'firsthand' approach which involved developing their problem solving and reflective skills. While the educator became a facilitator encouraging students to think about what they are doing involving them in reflective practice (Dewey, 1933).

While Dewey's concept was intended for face-to-face classes integrating critical reflection online was extended by Garrison's Community of Inquiry Model (COL). The model proposed a Venn diagram of three overlapping "presences" – cognitive presence, social presence, and teaching presence to adapt the critical inquiry process to online pedagogy.

The COL Framework

According to the COL framework the teaching presence element was the "design, facilitation, and direction of cognitive and social processes for the purpose of realizing personally meaningful and educationally worthwhile learning outcomes" (Garrison et al., 2000, p. 5). To build the online teaching presence element Garrison espoused that the course design took on greater prominence therefore the design of the web site would need to be familiar to students such as Facebook so the focus would be on the course requirements. In addition, the course design would need to include activities such as locating and building curricular materials, sequencing lessons, and writing assignment guidelines and evaluation criteria.

And that a regularly schedule of engagement be provided for continuous interaction (Garrison et al., 2000; Moore, 1989; Moore, 1990).

While the facilitation was the regularly monitoring and commenting on students' postings to maintain their interest, motivation, and engagement in the course (Northeastern, 2022). With these in place research concludes that students challenge each other, reflect upon, and defend ideas, thereby constructing meaning which build a sense of community (Arasaratnam-Smith & Northcote, 2017; David, 2014; McDonald et al., 2021; Rowntree, 1995; Ruth & Houghton, 2009; Smith, 2021; Wilson, 2001).

The second COL element was the social presence element which was the extent to which members of an online community perceived each other to be "real" and feel a connection to one another. Thus, designing online deliberations that encouraged students to deliberate, relate to and collaborate with peers built an online 'we' community as Dewey had espoused. Thus, when students identified with each other and the course content they are building inter-personal relationships with each other as they "projected their individual personalities" which further elicited students relating to each other and the course content. (Garrison, 2009, p. 352).

While the third COL element was the building of cognition to construct meaning through sustained reflection and discourse (Garrison et al., 2001). Here a wide variety of strategies from collaborations, group projects, or team-based learning would encourage deeper reflection and critical thought about the material. Additionally, incorporating different tools for discussion such as Flipgrid, Project-based learning or other open annotation tools to facilitate discussion, engage and guide them added value and built cognition. By focusing on integration of materials and exposing them to multiple approaches/ideas while providing feedback sustained that cognition while making online learning less isolating.

Incorporating the three elements of Garrison's work researchers found that students did indeed think over issues or concepts, considered peer arguments, questioned, and reconsidered their own viewpoints even when it placed their own views in doubt (Boud & Cohen, 2014). As they deliberated, explained perspectives, revisited, and communicated with each other they were exposed to and reconsidered multiple explanations. And that they asked insightful and respectful questions that sought our more information, clarified perspectives, or challenged each other on their viewpoints which often lead to furthering the deliberative process as was espoused by Dewey (Chadha, 2022a; Jones & Ryan, 2017). This engagement process, of giving and receiving feedback mimicked face-to-face deliberative contexts (Bandura, 2001; Croxton, 2014).

Moreover, still other researchers found that in online classes that addressed learning challenges or other needs when students were paired together for assignments resulted in sharing of knowledge and feedback (Peeters & Mynard, 2019; Sato & Ballinger, 2016). Similarly, a study found that when a beginner -level oral b skills peers collaborated with a peer with stronger English language skills they completed a reading task (Bigelow & King, 2016). While another study found that an online peer interaction space supplemented with made-to-measure instructions, prompts and tasks facilitated engagement with the foreign language, increased motivation, and enabled further interaction with fellow learners socially and collaboratively (Lamy & Zourou, 2013; Sato & Ballinger, 2016).

Furthermore, research in subjects such as political science where civic tolerance, politeness and neutrality are of utmost importance, found that online discussions on the second impeachment of Trump were rational and positive from the point of view of civility (Volkovskii, 2021). And that that online deliberation was more convenient and flexible as well as low cost compared to opinion polls (Fishkin, 2006). Moreover, those that participated in political deliberations had an increase in their participation in politics (Price, 2009). While in yet other studies on politics still others concurred that student engagement on contentious political issues as each considered alternative solutions and potential consequences, while developing critical reasoning skills about an issue furthered academic content (Chadha, 2022a, b).

Synchrony or Asynchrony

Relatedly, other research focused on whether synchrony or asynchrony was the preferred method to promote critical inquiry deliberations. While some researchers valued both synchronous and/or asynchronous methods others found value in specifically asynchronous or just asynchrony (Biesenbach-Lucas, 2003; Hollenbeck et al., 2011; Glassmeyer et al., 2011; Morris et al., 2005; Tello, 2007).

The volume of research that preferred just asynchronous methods found that students valued the method as the demands on their time from school, work, and family made asynchrony easier. Moreover, asynchronous discussions made them "felt more comfortable and "free" to discuss their ideas and opinions finding these forms of discussions more intriguing in an online context than in face-to-face environments (Hollenbeck et al., 2011).

While others disagreed arguing that synchronicity forced discussions making them unnatural commenting that, "The requirement to react to and expand on an existing topic may stifle students' motivation to initiate new topics or raise alternative issues" (Biesenbach-Lucas, 2003, p. 91). In contrast with synchrony smaller group would form that offered each the opportunity to hear ideas from classmates who do not speak up to the whole group as much (Glassmeyer et al., 2011).

Nonetheless, despite the debate researchers agreed that online education could be lonely and isolating (Bibeau, 2001; Howland & Moore, 2002; Mann, 2005; Wanstreet, 2006). Additionally agreeing that interaction online lessened isolation while promoting a sense of online community (Hodge et al., 2006; Swan, 2002) which also reduced the likelihood of them dropping the course (Liu et al., 2007; Morris et al., 2005; Tello, 2007).

MAIN FOCUS OF THE CHAPTER

Adding to the continuing debate on building effective online pedagogy an online collaboration was assessed as a means to engage students in critical thinking and to create best practices. With these two goals in mind this study examined one semester of an online collaboration that has been used for the past sixteen plus years that was created to complement a traditionally required Introduction to American Government course taught throughout the country using the three elements in the COL framework. The project called the American Politics Project, represented various pedagogical goals such as that of encouraging and increasing student interaction and participation, development of and an understanding of opposing views, improving critical thinking, developing a deeper sense of community, and providing peer presence so that learner isolation did not occur.

This collaborative project would change every semester based on the participants, one which ranged from two to six universities across the sixteen plus years as shown in Table 1. In addition, as shown in the same Table the institutions ranged from public and private universities: four-year-degree universities, PhD-granting institutions, and a community college and they were dispersed across four time zones.

Furthermore, in each semester of iteration the participating universities would readdress the project requirements which ranged from discussion forums, virtual town hall meetings, live chats, and student-to-student interviews. This would mean that the participants varied in their demographics, to the full and part time student status and the course itself. While students did not know the geographic location of the other participating students yet could potentially identify participants as some chose to create profile pictures and names that contained those identifiers.

Table 1. University participants

City/State	Redlands CA	Baltimore MD	Adirondack N. Y.	Queens, N. Y	Waukesha, WI	Houston, TX
Region	Suburban West	Suburban Mid-Atlantic	Rural Northeast	Urban northeast	Suburban Upper mid-west	Urban Southwest
Overall demographics	Mostly white	Diverse	White	Nonwhite immigrant	Mostly white	Diverse ethnically/ racially
Student status	Full time	Full time	Mostly part time	Full time	Full time	Full and part time
Course Name	American Politics	Introduction to American Government & Politics	American National Government	American Politics	Introduction to American Politics	US Government I

The E-Collaborative Site and Requirements

With the intent of the collaboration to be an interactive space for academic deliberation across universities a site was rented as university LMS systems did not allow those outside the university to participate. Relatedly, a new website was created each semester for each set of participating classes. The URL has been from a ning.com site, typically called, https://ampoliticsfall2022.ning.com/, and the web site itself was designed for familiarity for students set up similar to Facebook, so that they would focus on the content and not the design per the COL framework teaching presence element.

On the site as shown in Table 2 a student would respond to the question and another student such that they could interact seamlessly. And although the forum had hundreds of participants their mind's eye narrowed to whom they were dialoguing with just as it is with someone across a candlelit table or looking at someone across a campfire creating "Candlepower" a term akin to a candle lit conversation (Rudestam & Schoenholtz-Read, 2009) building the COL frameworks social element. Insomuch that the weekly participation requirement and the feeling the presence of peers as real individuals builds and further sustained the social interpersonal element developing that intimate conversation.

Table 2. Interactivity among students

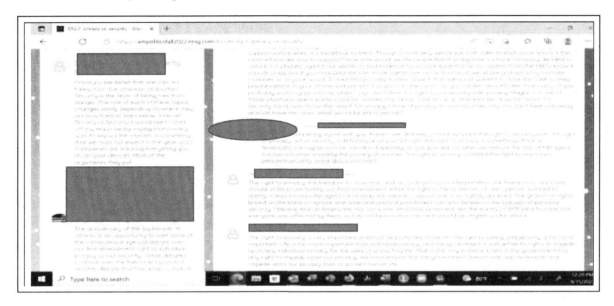

FERPA and Collaborative Requirements

Before semester start each participating instructor agreed to a common set of collaborative and syllabus requirements and applied for and gained human subject approvals as their campuses following FERPA protocols. Each instructor was also responsible for and performed any work in a timely manner, aside from obtaining human subject forms which had to be approved by each student. Relatedly, the site was accessible by invitation only after the instructor verified that each had signed human consent forms after which they had access to the site.

Before semester start the participating instructors additionally agreed to three identical collaborative requirements as shown in Table 3, which would allow for the COL frameworks cognition element to develop. The first requirement was 1) Students had to post eight (8) times and respond (8) eight times to the same minimum number of questions, for a total of sixteen times over the semester. A weekly question was posted by the professors on a rotation basis for all classes to post and respond which would build and maintain a discussion- oriented online community. 2) Second, students were required to post and respond using a minimum length of 75 words. Other than the minimum word guidance and the requirement to respond and reply to the same minimum number of discussion questions, no other guidance was provided to the students on how to make arguments, provide evidence and so forth. However, student conversations were monitored for signs that students were abiding by general rules of respect and civility. 3) Third, the professor assigned a course grade, to the collaborative activity as shown in the comparability table 3.

Table 3. Comparability of course e-collaboration

	Class X	**Class Y**
Course Name Course Level Collaboration requirement in Syllabus	American Government	
	First-year level	
	8 posts and 8 responses 75-word minimum length 10%	

Measuring the Dependent Variable: Academic Reflectivity

Alongside building each of the COL elements and the purpose of the collaboration to be a space for academic interactivity the dependent composite six variable measured for academic reflectivity as operationalized here.

- *Reflective/ deliberative:* This meant that students had reflected, deliberated, or reconsidered their own views when they responded to questions or when they commented on other students' posts. They pondered through their thoughts, questioned, and challenged others responding with reflective, deliberate comments.
- *Civic roles:* As this class was on American Government. Did students think about the questions posed and respond in ways that reflected a theoretical or practical application of American politics? Did they think about and discuss civic issues such as First Amendment or voting issues rather than just mention them? Did they engage each other, not just agreeing or disagreeing with each other, but did they challenge or push one another to think in a civil way?
- *Use of Classroom ideas or texts*: Did they post and respond referencing ideas that they had read about in class, mentioning their professor's material or in-class discussions?
- *Use of references or outside links*: Did they cite links to external websites when responding to questions, or did they refer to court cases that one might look up? Did they cite current events or media-related stories, and/or did they post real links to other related sources?
- *Posing honest questions*: Did they think about and ask one or more questions that enlarged the scopes of the discussions, not rhetorical question that assumed answers, but ones that expanded discussions.
- *Length:* This was a range of points as the total number of postings per student (example: student X posted six times a day, five days in a row) was not indicative of reflection but rather that reflectivity measured thoughtful understanding and contribution to a post or response. Therefore, a short response was usually 75 words or fewer, or up to 4 full lines of text; a medium response, between 5-9 lines of text; and a long response, longer than 10.

Measuring the Independent Variables

The study variables would depend upon which universities participated in the collaboration and their hypotheses. For instance, when two-year and four-year institutions participated the study variable might have been if students interacted with academic reflectivity across classes/institution types, identified with each other or personalized their posts and responses to each other. Similarly, if the collaboration was across different modes of instruction the study variables might have been if students interacted with academic reflectivity across online and face-to-face classes or online and hybrid classes.

Likewise, based on the pedagogical goals to further interaction and participation, develop their understanding of opposing views and developing a deeper sense of community, study variables would measure the differing forms of interaction. These forms of interaction could be students challenging each other, clarifying their perspectives, correcting other responses, agreeing, or disagreeing and or arguing their positions as these variables are the heart of the interaction story. Other variables could include if they identified with each other and built a community of learning. Therein these study variables were operationalized as follows.

- *Direct Address:* Did the student directly address someone when responding, or address comments to other participants on the site? "Hey guys;" "I agree with Patty..."
- *Knee-Jerk:* Did the student respond in a manner that was reactive and not reflective? Was it a response that was emotional, opinionated, and not well-reasoned?
- *Personal Experience/History*: Did they explicitly state or imply that they had some personal stake in the topic at hand? Did they have personal experience taking on the role in the discussions. For instance, "...I have experienced this before as a Muslim..." Or "...as a military man..."
- *Unsupported Generalizations* : Were the comments made by the student wrong or unsupported, "sweeping generalizations"?
- *Derogatory Comments:* Did students comment directly about an individual or group in a hostile and judgmental way? "You are stupid..."
- *Negative Tone:* This category measures a person's level of anger, rather than merely strong feelings about an issue. Such as irritated/abrasive tone; exclamation with some bolded letters capitalized to "shout" or "yell;" strong language or cuss words; direct accusations, hostile, uncivil.
- *The Prescriptive/Normative "Should":* Made at least one normative statement that includes a "should" as in, "...the US should get out of that war...," or "...the US should not send prisoners to war..."
- *Revisited:* Did the students revisit the questions they initiated, or did they revisit another student's question and respond?
- *Challenge:* Did students raise questions that challenged or contested a premise. In challenging a peer, they would support their challenged claims using counterclaims and academic materials accounting for these views.
- *Clarification:* Did students clarify their statement or position to each other as they explained or illustrated their points to be clear and unambiguous.
- *Correction:* Did students correct peers' discussions to remove errors while using academic materials to make accurate assessments to support these corrections.
- *Agreement/Disagreement*: Did students agree/disagree with discussion posts and offering a concurring/dissenting stance while using academic materials
- *Adding information*: Did students add knowledge to the discussion via class texts or outside media references such as court cases.
- *Identifying*: Did students identify with each other using personalized examples such as being a single mom or serving in the military online.

RESULTS OF PEER LEARNING

Indeed, over the sixteen plus years of the collaborative endeavor statistically significant results confirm that the across the two year, four-year and public/private institutions students were academically reflective. Similarly, across the differing mode of instruction from online, face-to-face and hybrid classes students were academically reflective. Furthermore, students directly addressed each other, personalized their experiences, identified with each other, and revisited the collaboration past syllabus requirements.

Furthermore, students interacted in various forms from challenging each other, arguing, clarifying their perspectives, correcting assumptions, agreeing, and disagreeing with each other. For instance, as shown in Table 4 on the discussion question (DQ2) having to do with the 2022 midterm elections and on DQ 5 balance between privacy versus security their interactions reveal that they were academically reflective. And that they challenged and pushed each to think over an issue more critically, more deeply as they developed an awareness of alternative points of view, a more reflective understanding of collective problems, and an appreciation of majority and minority rights (Guttman, 2000; Chadha, 2019; Chadha, 2022b).

Table 4. Reflexivity index by 'challenge' and 'clarify'

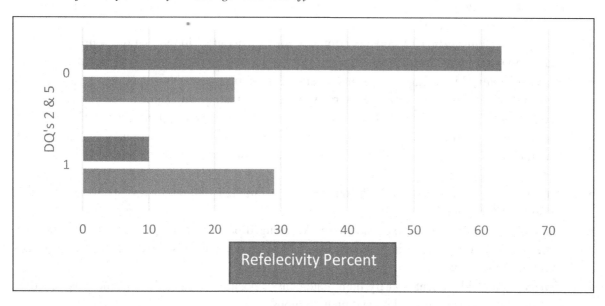

Furthermore, DQ 2 had asked them, "The 2022 midterm elections could be the most consequential in years, possibly defying political history and resetting modern political norms. Every seat in the House of Representatives is up for grabs, as are 35 U.S. Senate seats and 36 governorships. Considering the importance of this election what is really at stake this election season? While some argue that partisanship and who controls the presidency or congress matters for others such as Texans and three dozen states the governors' race would matter as they would be electing a new governor for the first time since the pandemic started. While for other issues such as how to handle violent crime, voting rights, racial discrimination, abortion access, global warming, health care among others matter. What is making this election season so tumultuous? And what is at issue in our democracy, make a case, defend your position, and deliberate.

In response a student wrote 238-word response which was academically reflective, while clarifying and explaining their perspectives commenting:

The November 2022 midterm election has more than 400 House of Representative seats being challenged and over one-third of the Senate, making this election extremely critical. Some Americans have little faith in the Presidential election because the popular vote does not guarantee it. However, it is the electoral college made of each state-elected House of Representatives & Senators, where the popular vote wins. This race could potentially shift House and Congress' majority from democratic to republican, ultimately determining what America would look like in the next few years. Regardless of party, change for better or worse is inevitable. The issues we see across the country, from human rights to the crime rate and increased inflation, have undoubtedly affected those interested in voting. While all these play a huge role in the high stakes the midterm election would mean for our country, I feel the most significant issue we have today are the false claims of widespread voter fraud and the validity of the 2020 election. Social media and new outlets constantly circulate misinformation, creating a world of skepticism, violence, and control. As important as the issues we face with the economy, healthcare, and human liberties, even more so are how we respond to those who bully their way through the election process. I believe the outcome we saw from the 2020 election is what makes the 2022 midterm one of the most chaotic yet crucial times to vote. (student response)

Similarly, on DQ 5 the question on 9/11 and the balance between privacy vs. security a student wrote 327 words which included citations, and references to the first amendment.

Another student wrote:

The 9/11 terrorist attack on the United States affected many spheres of people's lives, but the most prominent was heightened security measures globally. According to Koenig (2021), the terror attack on American airspace initiated stringent and tension-filled security measures worldwide. Unfortunately, the heightened security measures have brought about concerns about the equilibrium between people's right to privacy and their right to security. (Maniam (2016) aptly captures this dilemma, noting there are split decisions on whether the government should snoop on their citizens to ensure there is no repeat of the 9/11 terrorist attack on America. The aftermath of a major security scare or event usually leads to more people being supportive of the government infringing on their privacy to smoke out terrorists. Still, this support usually wanes over time, especially when the people have serious concerns about their government's intentions. Ultimately, both security and privacy are equally important to citizens, so it is vital that a balance between the two competing issues is achieved. Americans' privacy is enshrined in the First Amendment of the US constitution, especially in homes or places where an individual has a reasonable expectation of privacy. It is therefore expected that people should not have their personal spaces violated, which includes illegally accessing their emails, phone records, and general internet data. However, the same people expect their government to protect them from terror attacks, including using the intelligence service community to know the enemies' plans and acting in time to foil them. However, such a surveillance program would infringe on people's privacy rights, creating a conundrum that must be resolved. One way of resolving this dilemma is to involve the law courts to help draw the lines that must not be crossed. For instance, the intelligence community can seek permission from the courts to intercept email and phone communications of suspected terrorists or their sympathizers. This move will ensure that law enforcement agencies can only infringe on privacy rights with enough legal-based reasons. (student response)

In response to their post a student asked them an honest question:

The right to privacy is discussed in the 1st amendment when discussing the right of having assembly or the right of choosing the religion you want. When you think about it, how are you going to secure something when it is private? When discussing the effects of 9/11, there is not a decent balance between privacy and security because people want to protect themselves from people from the Middle East, while innocent people are trying to keep their religion, or place of origin a secret, or else they will be negatively judged. A way to ensure that both of these issues are protected is to stop discriminating against people by where they are from and their religion, by relying on those things, people are stripping those people their freedom of privacy. (student response)

Each of their interactions, whether they challenged, clarified, or argued they used and or added academic materials or cited evidence in support of an idea, action, or theory. As can be seen the aim of these interactions was not to persuade others to share their view, yet to be heard and provide their own justifications for their perspectives (Chadha, 2022b). These interactions, with the reciprocal process of asking questions answering it themselves, revisiting previous thought ideas if necessary, clarifying their perspectives they expanded their knowledge base together" (Angelino et., al, 2007, p. 10).

CONCLUSION

Indisputable evidence finds that the collaboration fostered multiple forms of interaction which fostered critical reflection and reassessment of views. And that peer learning cultivated lifelong learning in the student which becomes part of their repertoire of skills in their daily lives (Chadha, 2022a; Smith & Hatton, 1993). This is in contrast to studies were

students who learnt on their own without any participation with others lacked not only connections with their instructor but also a lacked connections with other students. The absence of connections lead to self-reports of isolation, a decrease in self-direction and self-management, a decrease in motivation and academic achievement (Abrami & Bures, 1996; Ludwig-Hardman & Dunlap, 2003; Rovai & Wighting, 2005).

Moreover, with the benefits of anonymity and asynchrony the online reciprocal peer engagement process also provided opportunities for deeper engagement in the learning process, as they reflected over knotty issues asking each other questions, seeking clarity of varied perspectives while being tolerant and respectful of differing viewpoints (Chadha, 2019; Sun et al., 2008; Wiecha et. al., 2003). With the reciprocal process of asking questions answering it themselves, revisiting previous thought ideas if necessary, clarifying their perspectives students "expand their knowledge base together" as students learn together through their relationships with peers, not just trying to 'beat the system' (Angelino et., al, 2007, p. 10).

Similarly, during the heightened state of online pedagogy during COVID research found that students bonded and engaged with their peers which motivated them to learn, their attitude toward learning, and created an online learning community akin to face-to-face learning despite being socially distanced (Chadha, 2022b; Hammer, 2019; Tang et al., 2022). A community of learning was formed online as learning becomes an interactive process with each sharing perspectives, their experiences, knowledge, and skills. This community of learning was sustained as they could deliberate at a time of their choosing day or night, they often revisited older posts asking more questions furthering the deliberation.

Undeniably, the central purpose of the collaborative website was effective which was to provide an educational space in which undergraduates could spend time understanding others, expressing themselves, applying knowledge, weighing, and refining positions while expanding their oral communication skills leading to effective civic engagement. This study concludes that using the three elements from the COL framework and creating a consistent schedule of interaction an online collaboration offers rich possibilities for learner interaction and effective deliberative communities during COVID and beyond without sacrificing substance.

This research received no specific grant from any funding agency in the public, commercial, or not-for-profit sectors.

REFERENCES

Abrami, P. C., & Bures, E. M. (1996). Computer-supported collaborative learning and distance education. *American Journal of Distance Education, 10*(2), 37–42. doi:10.1080/08923649609526920

Ananga, P., & Biney, I. K. (2017). Comparing face-to-face and online teaching and learning in higher education. *MIER Journal of Educational Studies Trends and Practices*, 165-179.

Angelino, L. M., Williams, F. K., & Natvig, D. (2007). Strategies to engage online students and reduce attrition rates. *The Journal of Educators Online, 4*(2), 114. https://eric.ed.gov/?id=EJ907749. doi:10.9743/JEO.2007.2.1

Arasaratnam-Smith, L. & Northcote, M. (2017). Community in online higher education: Challenges and opportunities. *The Electronic Journal of e-Learning, 15*(2), 188-198.

Bandura, A. (2001). Sociocognitive theory: An agentic perspective. *Annual Review of Psychology, 52*(1), 1–26. doi:10.1146/annurev.psych.52.1.1 PMID:11148297

Bibeau, S. (2001). Social presence, isolation, and connectedness in online teaching and learning: From the literature to real life. *Journal of Instruction Delivery Systems, 15*(3), 35–39.

Biesenbach-Lucas, S. (2003). Asynchronous discussion groups in teacher training classes: Perceptions of native and non-native students. *Journal of Asynchronous Learning Networks, 7*(3), 24–46.

Bigelow, M., & King, K. (2016). Peer interaction while learning to read in a new language. *Peer interaction and second language learning: Pedagogical Potential and Research Agenda*, 349-375.

Blake, N. (2000). Tutors and students without face or places. *Journal of Philosophy of Education, 34*(1), 183–196. doi:10.1111/1467-9752.00164

Boud, D., & Cohen, R. (2014). *Peer learning in higher education: Learning from and with each other*. Routledge. doi:10.4324/9781315042565

Burke, K., & Larmar, S. (2021). Acknowledging another face in the virtual crowd: Reimagining the online experience in higher education through an online pedagogy of care. *Journal of Further and Higher Education, 45*(5), 601–615. doi:10.1080/0309877X.2020.1804536

Carroll, J., & Ryan, J. (Eds.). (2005). *Teaching international students: Improving learning for all*. Routledge.

Chadha, A. (2019). Personalizing and extending deliberation in the online classroom: Future horizons. *Journal of Educators Online, 16*(2). https://eric.ed.gov/?id=EJ1223972. doi:10.9743/JEO.2019.16.2.4

Chadha. (2022a) Introspective interactions: Implications from an international collaboration. *Journal of Educators Online, 19*(1).

Chadha. (2022b) Pedagogical interrelationships: The transformed landscape of deliberations. *Journal of the Scholarship of Teaching and Learning, 22*(2).

Croxton, R. A. (2014). The role of interactivity in student satisfaction and persistence in online learning. *Journal of Online Learning and Teaching, 10*(2), 314–325.

David, B. (2014). Introduction: Making the move to peer learning. In D. Boud & Cohen, R. (Eds.), *Peer Learning in Higher Education* (pp. 1–17). Routledge.

Dewey, J. (1933). Philosophy and civilization. *Philosophy (London, England), 8*(31).

East, M. (2019). *Giving students a voice: The power of anonymity in a digital learning environment.* Talis. https://talis.com/2019/07/25/giving-students-a-voice-the-power-of-anonymity-in-a-digital-learning-environment/

Easton, S. (2003). Clarifying the instructor's role in online distance learning. *Communication Education, 52*(2), 87–105. doi:10.1080/03634520302470

Fishkin, J. S. (2006). The nation in a room: Turning public opinion into policy. *Boston Review*. https://deliberation.stanford.edu/mm/2006/bostonreview-nation.pdf

Garrison, D. R. (2009). Communities of inquiry in online learning. In *Encyclopedia of distance learning* (2nd ed., pp. 352–355). IGI Global. doi:10.4018/978-1-60566-198-8.ch052

Garrison, D. R., Anderson, T., & Archer, W. (2000). Critical inquiry in a text-based environment: Computer conferencing in higher education model. *The Internet and Higher Education, 2*(2-3), 87–105. doi:10.1016/S1096-7516(00)00016-6

Garrison, D. R., Anderson, T., & Archer, W. (2001). Critical thinking, cognitive presence, and computer conferencing in distance education. *American Journal of Distance Education, 15*(1), 7–23. doi:10.1080/08923640109527071

Glassmeyer, D. M., Dibbs, R. A., & Jensen, R. T. (2011). Determining utility of formative assessment through virtual community: Perspectives of online graduate students. *Quarterly Review of Distance Education, 12*(1), 23–35.

Hammer, E. (2019). Embracing a culture of lifelong learning–in universities & all spheres of life. *Proceedings of the International Astronomical Union. International Astronomical Union, 15*(S367), 316–322. doi:10.1017/S1743921321001010

Hodge, E., Bossé, M. J., Foulconer, J., & Fewell, M. (2006). Mimicking proximity: The role of distance education in forming communities of learning. *International Journal of Instructional Technology & Distance Learning, 3*(12). http://www.itdl.org/Journal/Dec_06/article01.htm

Hollenbeck, C. R., Mason, C. H., & Song, J. H. (2011). Enhancing student learning in marketing courses: An exploration of fundamental principles for website platforms. *Journal of Marketing Education, 33*(2), 171–182. doi:10.1177/0273475311410850

Hsiao, E. L. (2012). Synchronous and asynchronous communication in an online environment: Faculty experiences and perceptions. *Quarterly Review of Distance Education, 13*(1), 15.

Jones, M., & Ryan, J. (2017). The online space: Developing strong pedagogy for online reflective practice. In R. Brandenberg, (Eds.), *Reflective theory and practice in teacher education* (pp. 205–222). Springer. doi:10.1007/978-981-10-3431-2_11

Lamy, M., & Zourou, K. (2013). *Social networking for language education.* Palgrave Macmillan. doi:10.1057/9781137023384

Liu, X., Magjuka, R. J., Bonk, C. J., & Lee, S.-H. (2007). Does sense of community matter? An examination of participants' perceptions of building learning communities in online courses. *Quarterly Review of Distance Education, 8*(1), 9–24.

Ludwig-Hardman, S., & Dunlap, J. C. (2003). Learner support services for online students: Scaffolding for success. *International Review of Research in Open and Distributed Learning, 4*(1), 1–15. doi:10.19173/irrodl.v4i1.131

Mann, S. J. (2005). Alienation in the learning environment: A failure of community? *Studies in Higher Education, 30*(1), 43–55. doi:10.1080/0307507052000307786

McDonald, A., McGowan, H., Dollinger, M., Naylor, R., & Khosravi, H. (2021). Repositioning students as co-creators of curriculum for online learning resources. *Australasian Journal of Educational Technology, 37*(6), 102–118. doi:10.14742/ajet.6735

Megahed, N., & Hassan, A. (2021). A blended learning strategy: Reimagining the post-Covid-19 architectural education. *Archnet-IJAR: International Journal of Architectural Research.*

Miller, L. R., Nelson, F. P., & Phillips, E. L. (2021). Exploring critical reflection in a virtual learning community in teacher education. *Reflective Practice, 22*(3), 363–380. doi:10.1080/14623943.2021.1893165

Misra, P. K. (2021). Process of Teaching. In *Learning and Teaching for Teachers* (pp. 115–131). Springer. doi:10.1007/978-981-16-3077-4_7

Moore, G. (1989). Three types of interaction. *American Journal of Distance Education, 3*(2), 1–6. doi:10.1080/08923648909526659

Moore, G. (1990). Recent contributions to the theory of distance education. *Open Learning, 5*(3), 10–15. doi:10.1080/0268051900050303

Morris, L. V., Finnegan, C., & Wu, S.-S. (2005). Tracking student behavior, persistence, and achievement in online courses. *The Internet and Higher Education, 8*(3), 221–231. doi:10.1016/j.iheduc.2005.06.009

Northeastern Center for Advancing Teaching and Learning. (2022). *"Teaching presence" in the community of inquiry framework: What does it mean to "teach" online?* Northeastern University. https://learning.northeastern.edu/teaching-presence/

Peeters, W. (2019). The peer interaction process on Facebook: A social network analysis of learners' online conversations. *Education and Information Technologies, 24*(5), 1–28. doi:10.100710639-019-09914-2

Peeters, W., & Mynard, J. (2019). Peer collaboration and learner autonomy in online interaction spaces. *Relay Journal, 2*(2), 450–458. doi:10.37237/relay/020218

Peimani, N., & Kamalipour, H. (2021). Online education and the COVID-19 outbreak: A case study of online teaching during lockdown. *Education Sciences, 11*(2), 72. https://www.mdpi.com/2227-7102/11/2/72. doi:10.3390/educsci11020072

Price, V. (2009). Citizens deliberating online: Theory and some evidence. *Online deliberation: Design, Research, and Practice*, 37-58.

Rossini, T. S. S., do Amaral, M. M., & Santos, E. (2021). The viralization of online education: Learning beyond the time of the coronavirus. *Prospects, 51*(1), 285–297. doi:10.100711125-021-09559-5 PMID:33967347

Rovai, A. P., & Wighting, M. J. (2005). Feelings of alienation and community among higher education students in a virtual classroom. *The Internet and Higher Education, 8*(2), 97–110. doi:10.1016/j.iheduc.2005.03.001

Rowntree, D. (1995). Teaching with audio in open and distance learning. *British Journal of Educational Studies, 43*(2).

Rudestam, K. E., & Schoenholtz-Read, J. (2009). *Handbook of online learning*. Sage Publications.

Ruth, A., & Houghton, L. (2009). The wiki way of learning. *Australasian Journal of Educational Technology, 25*(2). https://ajet.org.au/index.php/AJET/article/view/1147. doi:10.14742/ajet.1147

Sato, M., & Ballinger, S. (2016). *Peer interaction and second language learning: Pedagogical potential and research agenda*. John Benjamins. doi:10.1075/lllt.45

Smith, M. D. (2021). CALL in a social context: Reflecting on digital equity, identity, and interaction in the post-COVID age. *Quality Assurance in Education, 29*(4), 537–549.

Sun, P. C., Tsai, R. J., Finger, G., Chen, Y. Y., & Yeh, D. (2008). What drives a successful e-learning? An empirical investigation of the critical factors influencing learner satisfaction. *Computers & Education, 50*(4), 1183–1202. doi:10.1016/j.compedu.2006.11.007

Swan, K. (2002). Building learning communities in online courses: The importance of interaction. *Education. Communication & Leadership, 2*(1), 23–49. doi:10.1080/1463631022000005016

Tang, Y. M., Lau, Y. Y., & Chau, K. Y. (2022). Towards a sustainable online peer learning model based on student's perspectives. *Education and Information Technologies*, *27*(9), 1–20. https://link.springer.com/article/10.1007/s10639-022-11136-y. doi:10.100710639-022-11136-y PMID:35668899

Tello, S. F. (2007). An analysis of student persistence in online education. *International Journal of Information and Communication Technology Education*, *3*(3), 47–62. doi:10.4018/jicte.2007070105

Volkovskii, D. (2021, June). Experience of Applied Research in Online Deliberation: An Analysis of Civility in American Online Discussions. In IMS (pp. 199-205).

Wanstreet, C. E. (2006). Interaction in online learning environments. *Quarterly Review of Distance Education*, *7*(4), 399–411.

Wiecha, J. M., Gramling, R., Joachim, P., & Vanderschmidt, H. (2003). Collaborative e-learning using streaming video and asynchronous discussion boards to teach the cognitive foundation of medical interviewing: A case study. *Journal of Medical Internet Research*, *5*(2), e13. doi:10.2196/jmir.5.2.e13 PMID:12857669

Wilson, M. S. (2001). Cultural considerations in online instruction and learning. *Distance Education*, *22*(1), 52–64. doi:10.1080/0158791010220104

Zeivots, S., Vallis, C., Raffaele, C., & Luca, E. J. (2021). Approaching design thinking online: Critical reflections in higher education. *Issues in Educational Research*, *31*(4), 1351–1366.

KEY WORDS AND DEFINITIONS

Asychrony: Engagements occurring across different times according to the individual schedule of the learner.

Community of Inquiry Framework: A model which proposed a Venn diagram of three overlapping "presences" – cognitive presence, social presence, and teaching presence to adapt the critical inquiry process to online pedagogy.

Deliberation: A word which indicates the online synchronous or asynchronous critical dialogue.

Distance education: Instruction that occurs in an online setting.

Learner autonomy: The notion of the learner as primarily responsible for their "stake" in the educational experience.

Social capital: Bandura's notion of the ways in which individuals gain an understanding of the network of communities around them through learning.

Synchrony: Simultaneous dialogic engagements.

Chapter 3
Mathematics Learning With Augmented Reality in Early Childhood Education

İlkay Ulutaş
Gazi Üniversitesi, Turkey

Emine Bozkurt Polat
Gazi Üniversitesi, Turkey

Feyza Aydin Bölükbaş
Aksaray Üniversitesi, Turkey

Kadriye Selin Budak
Bilecik Üniversitesi, Turkey

Kübra Engin
Gazi Üniversitesi, Turkey

ABSTRACT

With the rapidly developing technology, the use of AR applications in the educational process is becoming widespread as a new field of study. When the literature was examined, there were no studies investigating AR applications and evaluating them as a mathematics education tool in early childhood. In this context, this study aims to determine the AR applications that can be used in the early childhood mathematics education process and to examine the content, mathematical skills, and functionality of these applications.

DOI: 10.4018/978-1-6684-7015-2.ch003

INTRODUCTION

Early childhood is a critical period in which many skills, attitudes and competencies are acquired. For this reason, in order to support development at an optimal level, the content of the education to be given at this age should be planned in an appropriate way for their age, level of development and needs of children, contains rich stimuli, and ensures school-family-environment cooperation. Nowadays, the spread of technology often causes children to encounter technological tools in the environment they live in. In this context, it has become important to equip children with the competencies to handle these tools and integrate technology into their educational processes. Teachers will be provided with convenience in terms of time, effort, and economy as a result of materials and activities for mathematics to be developed with augmented reality (AR) technology, having been on the agenda quite a lot lately. Although there are some educational applications, these applications may not address the needs of every child, and constantly doing the same activity may limit the learning outcomes of children. This section provides explanations and application examples about mathematics education in early childhood and the use of technology in this process, AR technology, early childhood usability principles, and the use of AR technology in early mathematics education.

The Importance of Mathematics Education in Early Childhood

From the first moment they interact with objects and their environment, children are introduced to various mathematical contents, such as numbers, spatial perception, and patterns and acquire basic mathematical skills over time (Clements & Sarama, 2014). Children progress in mathematics in line with their individual interests and development; thus, different methods and techniques may be needed for them to form positive emotions toward mathematics, and to actively participate in the educational process (Cross et al., 2009; Fuson et al., 2015). Negative mathematics experiences and failure to provide qualified mathematics environments (Guss et al., 2022) may decelerate the tendency towards mathematics and this may cause differences between them and their peers (Copley, 2004; National Association for the Education of Young Children (NAEYC) & National Council of Teachers of Mathematics (NCTM) 2010; Rittle-Johnson, 2017). Instead of direct instruction in mathematics education, when educational environments and teaching processes are created to support children's thinking, questioning, and discovering mathematical procedures and discovering, children may have surprisingly flexible, complex, and critical mathematical thoughts and develop their own way of thinking (Clements, & Sarama, 2016).

Children become more effectively involved in the mathematics process in an educational environment prepared according to their own interests and needs. The NAEYC and NCTM (2010) emphasized that quality mathematics education provided before school is the basis for future mathematics teaching. They consider it necessary to present programs and teaching practices that are effective on children in this process, leading children to research and discovery. High-quality mathematics education in the early years also forms the infrastructure of children's academic skills in their future lives (NAEYC, 2010; Rittle-Johnson, 2017).

Technology is one of the important opportunities that can be used to support mathematical skills in early childhood, enrich the educational environment, and ensure the active participation of children in the educational process. Children need opportunities to think and learn mathematics in depth and comprehensively. It can be difficult to find quality technology-based early math experiences for children. For this reason, there is a need for studies about how the content of technology-based resources should be, usage areas, and how to integrate them into the education process for early mathematics teaching and learning (Guss et al., 2022).

The Use of Technology in the Process of Mathematics Education in Early Childhood

With the development of technology, the living standards of the 21st-century, and the competencies required, IT technologies have been used more frequently in education. Today, 21st-century skills are determined as 1) information, media, and technology skills, 2) learning and innovation skills, and 3) career and life skills (P21, 2009). According to the report of the European Committee (2013), it is essential that individuals have digital competence with 21st-century skills. In order for individuals with these skills and competencies to grow up, it is important to integrate technology into children's education starting from the preschool period (Martin et al., 2020). Technology integration in education can be seen as structured ways to improve and develop the performance of learners (Çiftçi & Topçu, 2021).

In the literature on technology integration in early childhood education, technology is one of the critical learning tools to improve the learning processes prepared for children (OECD, 2017), and the early childhood use of technology increases children's motivation and interest (Lavidas et al., 2022; Marsh, 2010; Muxiddinovna, 2022; Pitchford et al., 2016; Sundqvist, 2022); however, it was emphasized that technology usage periods and usage methods are essential. Having a direct effect on the processes of developing mathematics education programs for children in early childhood and teachers, and increasing quality in material selection and evaluation periods, the NCTM principles were determined as the principle of equality, the principle of education program, the principle of mathematics teaching, the principle of mathematics learning, the principle of evaluation, and the use of technology (NCTM, 2000). In the principle of technology use, it has been stated that the use of technology suitable for the development of children in mathematics education positively affects the mathematics learning process and that technology is one of the integral parts of mathematics education in early childhood (Clements & Sarama, 2008, NCTM, 2000).

Technology offers important contributions to ensure equality in children's learning processes. It can provide effective results quickly, especially in closing the learning gap caused by socioeconomic disadvantage (NCTM, 2010; Slavin & Lake, 2008). For example, Schacter and Jo (2016) showed in their study that socio-economically disadvantaged children increased their mathematical skills quickly with a math program that includes the use of tablets. In addition, it was stated that technology integration has effective results in distance mathematics education processes (Abdul-Majied et al., 2022; Nikolopoulou, 2022).

Preschool teachers can improve the quality of mathematics education with technology and provide children with rich learning processes (Ulutaş et al., 2022; Verbruggen et al., 2020).

Some studies have shown that teachers are turning to the sub-area of numbers and processes due to material insufficiency and that they devote very limited time to other sub-area (Björklund & Barendregt, 2016; Clements & Sarama, 2011). Digital mathematics applications or programs reduce the need for tangible materials in classroom applications and provide teachers with time and labor efficiency. Teachers can prepare digital materials for all kinds of concepts and content in a very short time in accordance with the needs of the children in the classroom. Digital materials can be used in teaching and reinforcing many mathematical concepts, such as space-time, orientation, classification, comparison, pairing, mathematical operations, patterns, volume, and dimension (Cheung & Slavin, 2013; Drigas & Kokkalia, 2014; Eleftheriadi et al., 2021).

By increasing the digital literacy skills of teachers for information technologies and informing them about different innovative applications, teachers can become producers and developers and users of information technologies. With the increase in the studies on the contributions of information technologies used in preschool education to mathematics (Cardenal & Lopez, 2015; Weiss et al., 2006), there is also an increase in the number of alternative approaches, such as robotic coding, digital games, digital stories, AR applications (Yuksel-Arslan et al., 2016). AR applications have a different effect among these methods in terms of providing the association of the learned with reality, being more practical and accessible.

Development of Augmented Reality Technology and Augmented Reality Environments

AR is expressed as the placement of digital objects such as sound, images, videos, animations, text, shapes, graphics on a real-world image through a screen (Zhou et al., 2008). AR applications can be easily developed and used with smart devices and applications on these devices without requiring a special device (Özel & Uluyol, 2016).

By combining real and virtual elements, AR increases learners' motivation with the three-dimensional images it reveals, which positively affect learning and decisiveness (Bamford, 2011; Dunleavy et al., 2009; Freitas & Campos, 2008; Liu et al., 2010). In education, AR allows accessibility of experiences that cannot be achieved in the real world for reasons such as security, cost, and time. In addition to the sense of vision and hearing, by activating vestibular and proprioceptive senses (Heffernan et al., 2021), it enables learners to experience learning processes that are interactive, concrete, and fun (Cai et al., 2014; Kerawalla et al., 2006; Özarslan, 2013; Yuen et al., 2011), constructivist, collaborative, creative, authentic, meaningful, and interesting, and support active participation and problem-solving (Dunleavy et al., 2009; Kerawalla et al., 2006; Liu et al., 2010; Shelton & Hedley, 2002). The interaction provided by AR increases the comprehension, comprehension, memory, and imagination skills of learners; it facilitates concept acquisition and prevents misconceptions (Chang et al., 2013; Shelton & Hedley, 2002).

AR is often confused with virtual reality. Virtual reality, unlike AR, takes the user out of reality and transports them to a virtual environment, in which the user cannot see the real world but experiences the virtual world completely (Azuma, 1997; Sin & Zaman, 2010; Zhou et al., 2008). In AR, it is necessary to combine real and virtual, to establish simultaneous interaction, and to make three-dimensional positioning. AR applications integrate real- and virtual-world contexts, increase interaction, and offer three-dimensional objects. It does not replace reality but enriches learning by providing complementary elements to reality (Azuma, 1977).

Figure 1. Virtuality continuity diagram
(Milgram & Kishino, 1994)

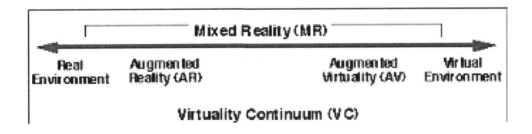

AR applications work with two different systems, image-based and location-based. Image-based applications use some markers and labels in order to correctly position the object to be added to the real environment through a technological tool. When applications recognize this marker through the camera, it creates a virtual image. The marker can be an image, graphic, or visual (such as a QR code) on a printed material (Cheng & Tsai, 2012).

Figure 2. Marker-based augmented reality application example
(Koong Lin et al., 2011)

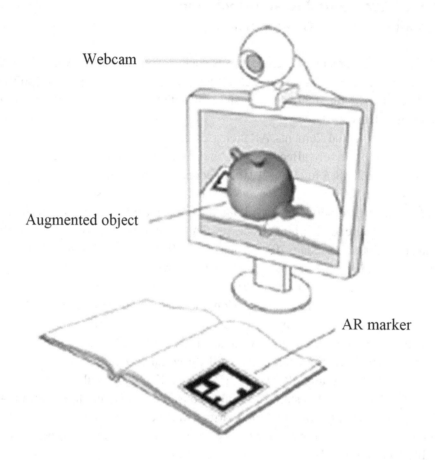

Location-based applications, on the other hand, offer data using the device's data, such as wireless network or GPS, instead of a marker. Depending on the perceived location, it provides information about the surrounding (pharmacy, school, etc.) (Cheng & Tsai, 2012). The famous game of an era, Pokemon Go, was developed using location-based AR technology.

Figure 3. An example of a location-based augmented reality application
(Cheng & Tsai, 2012)

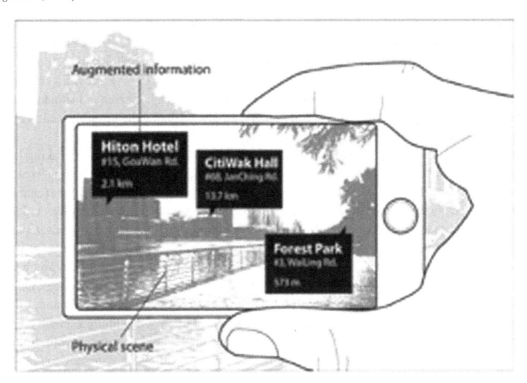

Preparing an AR environment requires hardware and software that can create virtual content that can reflect the real world, monitoring techniques so that the user can project the change in the position of the user to the object on the screen, calibration and recording tools for aligning real and virtual images when the user fixes the position, screen hardware that will combine virtual images with real-world view, computer processing hardware to run AR simulation code and support input-output devices, interaction techniques showing how the user will manipulate the AR content (Zhou et al., 2008). In this context, care can be taken to supply smartphones or devices to support the AR application.

When creating a simple marker-based AR environment, first decision is made for an application that will combine the marker and a three-dimensional digital object. Then, the material to be used as a marker and the three-dimensional digital object intended to be transferred to the real environment are prepared. Then, in the selected application, the marker and digital object are combined and visualized on the real image through hardware tools such as completed design, display, and glasses.

The Use of Augmented Reality Applications in Early Mathematics Education

In recent years, AR applications have been used quite frequently in educational environments (Bacca et al., 2014), and it is also known that AR is used at the preschool education level (Akçayır & Akçayır, 2017; Rambli et al., 2013; Yılmaz, 2016; Yılmaz, 2018). In early childhood, AR practices supported children's cognitive development and learning process, which increased the number of studies conducted on AR integration in the early years (Masmuzidin & Aziz, 2018; Oranç & Küntay, 2019; Yılmaz, 2016;

Yılmaz, 2018). These studies include language learning (Chen et al., 2017; Çevik et al., 2017; Redondo et al., 2020), Mathematics Education (Gecü-Parmaksiz, 2017; Zhu et al., 2017; Stotz, 2018; Agustika, 2021), Social Interaction (Albayrak & Yilmaz, 2021), Early Literacy (Cascales et al., 2013; Jeffri & Rambli, 2017; Özdamlı & Karagözlü, 2018; Pan et al., 2021; Rambli Et Al., 2013; Yılmaz & Goktas, 2018;), Alphabet Teaching (Jamiat et al., 2019; Safar et al., 2017), Concept Teaching (Yılmaz, 2016), Art Education (Huang et al., 2015), and Dramatic Games (Han et al., 2015). AR provides children with benefits of 1) learning content in 3D perspectives, 2) ubiquitous, collaborative, and situated learning, 3) learners' senses of presence, immediacy, and immersion, 4) visualizing the invisible, and 5) bridging formal and informal learning (Wu et al., 2013).

AR applications offer an alternative way to the classroom and individual learning, making learning experiences unique, interactive, motivational, and engaging (Estapa & Nadolny, 2015; Ihsan et al., 2017; Masmuzidin & Aziz, 2018; Wu et al. 2013). They increase children's experience of reality and enable them to benefit from the possibilities of the real world by providing contextual information (Wu et al., 2013).

Especially in the teaching process of abstract skills involving early mathematical thinking, technology integration is frequently preferred and provides benefits in terms of critical, creative, and innovative learning. However, in many studies, it is recommended to develop innovative math learning environments and integrate early mathematics education into children's daily activities with effective practices, innovative strategies, innovative strategies, as well as traditional teaching strategies (Guntur & Setyaningrum, 202; Rohibni et al., 2022). In the acquisition of early mathematical skills, young children should be offered experiences that expand their knowledge and development, and they should be provided with stimulating, high-quality content, and structured activities. In this process, providing studying environments with rich stimuli is seen as a necessary condition (Björklund et al., 2020).

AR applications that support the connection between the real world and the digital world appear as an arrangement that can replace 'tangible manipulatives' in early mathematical skills, support children's acquisition of mathematical skills, make learning processes fun, and support their abstract thinking through tangible materials. (Bujak et al., 2013; Gecu-Parmaksız & Delialioğlu, 2019; Stotz, 2018). These arrangements are expressed as virtual manipulatives that are expressed as "an interactive, technology-enabled visual representation of a dynamic mathematical object, including all of the programmable features that allow it to be manipulated, that presents opportunities for constructing mathematical knowledge" (Moyer-Packenham & Bolyard, 2016). In virtual manipulatives, the use of the 'visualization of the invisible' feature of AR applications for abstract content makes it easier for children in early childhood to understand and concretize concepts and situations (Bujak et al., 2013; Yilmaz, 2016).

There are studies such as 3D geometric objects and geometry, solid objects, coordinate plane, algebraic concepts, multiplication tables, probability, mathematical concepts, and problems in the further education stages where AR is integrated into mathematics education (Çetintav & Yilmaz, 2022; Stotz, 2018;). In addition, making two-dimensional books three-dimensional can be used in training technical works such as repair and maintenance, three-dimensional concept representation or experimentation in physics-chemistry and biology, visualizing concepts in geography, transferring knowledge in cultural institutions such as museums, concretizing concepts and spatial relations in mathematics/geometry, gaining experience and skills in the fields of health and military, gaining experience and knowledge about vehicles in engineering, and gaining classroom management experience in teacher education (Carmigniani & Furht, 2011; Johnson et al., 2012; Somyürek, 2014). In early childhood, number counting skills, geometry, spatial visualization, and spatial abilities that require mental rotation are taught by embodying them through virtual manipulators (Gecu-Parmaksız & Delialioğlu, 2019; Ihsan et al., 2018; Sontz, 2018; Zhou et al., 2020).

AR applications are decisively functional in terms of providing easy usability and accessibility to teachers. Aside from this, they should be prepared following the principles of consistency, fault management, graphic design, help, documentation, learnability, flexibility, interactivity, virtual-real-world interaction, low physical effort, user satisfaction, feedback, personalization, entertainment, multi-mode, attractiveness, controllability, convenience, effectiveness, durability, safety, simplicity, and predictability (Atkinson et al., 2007; Dünser et al., 2007; Gong & Tarasewich, 2004; Kim et al., 2008; Ko et al., 2013).

Tuli and Mantri (2021) stated that four usability principles, namely cognition, orientation, design, and support, should be paid attention to when preparing AR materials and environments for early childhood children (Figure, 4).

Figure 4. Principles of usability
(Tuli and Mantri, 2021)

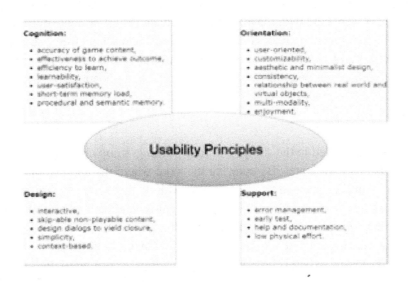

The arrangement of the application in such a way that it has these basic principles, allows children to go through the process more easily, efficiently, and interactively, without the need for support, to access and deconstruct information by establishing the relationship between the real and virtual world easily and quickly.

PURPOSE OF THE STUDY

With the rapidly developing technology, the use of AR applications in the educational process is becoming widespread as a new field of study. When the literature was examined, there were no studies investigating AR applications and evaluating them as a mathematics education tool in early childhood. In this context, this study aims to determine the AR applications that can be used in the early childhood mathematics education process and to examine the content, mathematical skills, and functionality of these applications. The research sought answers to the following questions;

- What features of AR applications can be used for mathematics education in early childhood?
- What are the teachers' views on AR applications with mathematical content?

METHOD

Aiming to provide basic information about AR applications in mathematics education in early childhood and examine the applications, this research was designed in a basic qualitative research pattern. The basic qualitative research pattern is used to investigate and categorize the concepts in the theoretical framework and explain them in detail (Caeli, Ray & Mill, 2003).

Within the scope of the research, online store searches regarding AR applications were made, and appropriate applications for early childhood mathematics education were selected and their features were listed. Then, interviews were held with the teachers to evaluate the reflections of the applications in the AR application list on the education process. In this direction, the teachers were asked to choose three of the determined practices and experience them with the children in their class. After these experiences, interviews were held with the teachers and the functionality of AR applications was tried to be determined.

Study Group

Two study groups were included in the study. The first working group consisted of AR applications in the store applications of smartphones. By entering the store where the applications are located on the mobile phone, the researchers scanned the applications with the keywords "augmented reality applications in mathematics" and "early childhood augmented reality applications" and downloaded them on the phone. The applications were first classified according to their "target age" by four field experts, and applications that were not suitable for the age of children in early childhood were removed from the phone. In the next stage, field experts classified the applications according to the "contents suitable for children" and applications that were not suitable for children's age were removed from the phone. Then, the experts made the classification of the applications regarding the "use in early childhood mathematics education" and the applications that were not suitable for use in mathematics education were deleted. At the last stage, "Preschoolers 2-4" and "Little Kids 5-" in the age filter of AR applications searched using the keyword "Augment Reality Apps" on the "Common Sense Media" website (https://www.commonsensemedia.org) Applications are listed by selecting 7" intervals. Attention was paid to the fact that the applications in the list included mathematics education and it was decided to include 14 applications in the scope of the research with the consensus of the field experts.

The second study created from preschool teachers who were working in a public kindergarten affiliated with the Ministry of National Education in Ankara and volunteered to participate in the "4005 TUBITAK Augmented Reality/AR and Multidimensional Mathematics in Preschool Education" project. The group consists of 8 teachers who voluntarily agree to support this study. All the teachers are women, and their ages range from 32 to 50. All teachers are graduated from pre-school education program and their years of service ranged from 9 to 21.

Table 1. Participants

	Gender	Age	Educational Level	Graduation	Years of Service
T1	Female	35	Bachelor d.	Preschool Teacher	14
T2	Female	35	Master d.	Preschool Teacher	13
T3	Female	34	Bachelor d.	Preschool Teacher	13
T4	Female	34	Bachelor d.	Preschool Teacher	12
T5	Female	41	Bachelor d.	Preschool Teacher	17
T6	Female	50	Bachelor d.	Preschool Teacher	21
T7	Female	32	Bachelor d.	Preschool Teacher	9
T8	Female	43	Master d.	Preschool Teacher	19
T9	Female	32	Bachelor d.	Preschool Teacher	10

Data Collection Tools

In this research, AR App Review Form and Teacher Interview Form were used as tools during data collection.

AR App Review Form

It has been prepared to examine and record the features of AR applications to be included in the study. This form includes the name of the application examined, the age group, the content of the application and the skills that it will support in the mathematics integration process. The researchers recorded each application with this form, had the opportunity to compare, and decided on the applications to be included in the research.

Teacher Interview Form

The Teacher Interview Form is a semi-structured interview form created by the researchers to evaluate the experiences, observations, and opinions of preschool teachers about AR applications with mathematics. The form consists of two parts. In the first part of the form, questions were asked to the teachers about the AR applications they used in the mathematics education process with the children in their classes, the effects of the applications on the process and the principles they paid attention to. Then, the teachers were presented with a list of 14 applications chosen by the researchers, and they were asked to choose three of these applications and experience them in their classrooms. The second part of the form was filled in one-on-one interviews with the teachers after these experiences. In this section, teachers are told which AR applications they choose and apply in their classrooms, how they find the purpose and functionality of this application, the difficulties, and conveniences they encounter, suggestions, etc. Open-ended questions were asked to teachers and their answers were recorded.

Data Collection

The data for the first study group were collected by scanning on the Google Play Store and Apple Store, and the determined features were recorded in the application review form.

After the data were collected from the teachers through the first part of the Teacher Interview Form, the preparation, implementation, and evaluation processes were followed in collecting data on AR experiences. In preparation, before using AR applications, teachers were informed about these applications by holding an online meeting. In these meetings, the features of the applications and how to use them were explained and an example application was made together. In the application phase, the teachers experienced the AR applications they chose with the children in the classroom and took audio or video recordings. In the evaluation phase, the teachers were met online and asked how they experienced the AR application they used. Interviews were recorded in audio and written form.

Data Analyses

When the screening process for AR applications was completed, the researchers evaluated the applications according to the criteria of age, the suitability of the content for the child, and their use in preschool mathematics education, and unanimously created a list containing 14 applications.

The interview data of the second study group were also analyzed by the researchers using the content analysis method.

FINDINGS

The findings will be reviewed under the headings of findings on application scanning and teachers' experiences of AR apps with math content.

Findings on AR Applications with Math Content

To create a qualified mathematics education environment, the content of AR applications, how they will be applied and teachers' views on this issue should be taken into consideration. In this direction, the findings obtained from the research are presented under two sub-headings the characteristics of AR applications that can be used for mathematics education in early childhood and the teachers' experiences of AR applications with mathematics content.

Early childhood mathematical skills used to support AR applications in marker-based and location-based applications are shown in Table 3.

Table 2. Marker-based and location-based applications in ar applications

Application Name	Age Group	Operating System	Application Content	Mathematical Skills	The AR system used
Block My World	+4 year age	IOS Android	It is a free-form AR game that allows the creation of structures in a real context.	Spatial Skills Counting Skills	Image-Based
Augmented Reality App	+4 year age	IOS	It is an application that allows you to create structures in a real context containing sections such as shapes, solar systems, measurement, surface detection, image detection, and AR physics.	Geometric Skills	Image-Based
Pokemon Go	+7 year age	IOS Android	It is a game that detects your location on the map with GPS in a real context.	Spatial Skills	Location-Based
MathNinjaAR	+6 year age	IOS	It is an AR game in which simple addition operations are performed in a real context.	Arithmetic Skills	Image-Based
Math Ninja BoxBattle	+4 year age	IOS	It is an AR-based multiple-player game in which simple addition operations are performed in a real context.	Arithmetic Skills	Image-Based
My Caterpillar	+3 year age	IOS	It is an AR application adapted from Eric Carle's book Very Hungry Caterpillar.	One-to-one matching Arithmetic Skills Pattern	Image-Based
ArLoon Geometry (Paid)	+4 year age	IOS	It is an application that has 3D models with AR for geometric shapes.	Geometric Skills	Image-Based
Substraction AR	+4 year age	IOS	It is an AR application in which simple subtraction operations are performed in a real context.	Arithmetic Skills	Image-Based
Addition AR	+4 year age	IOS	It is an AR application in which simple addition operations are performed in a real context.	Arithmetic Skills	Image-Based
Multiplication AR	+4 year age	IOS	It is an AR application in which simple multiplication operations are performed in a real context.	Arithmetic Skills	Image-Based

Continued on following page

Table 2. Continued

Mathematical Skills Substraction- F.ver (Paid)	+4 year age	IOS	It is an AR application in which arithmetic skills are performed in a real context	Arithmetic Skills	Image-Based
WizAR Kids	+4 year age	IOS Android	The application is structured so that there are many options, including mathematical skills.	Arithmetic Skills Geometric Skills	Image-Based
Arloopa	+4 year age	IOS Android	AR and virtual reality studies can be performed with the application. In the application, there are many AR materials such as education, art, dinosaurs, animals characters. 3D geometric shapes were also included in the training group.	One-to-one matching Arithmetic Skills Geometric Skills	Image-Based Location-Based

To create a high-quality mathematics education environment, the content of the AR applications, how to apply them, and the knowledge, competencies, and beliefs of teachers need to be taken into account. When the applications determined in the research were examined, it was seen that almost all of them (n = 13) were marker-based and that the applications were primarily designed to improve arithmetic skills as a mathematical skill (n = 8). In addition, at the stage of determining the applications, it was seen that the AR applications prepared for preschool children are often designed for science education and a limited number of applications for mathematics education. It is observed that there are sample applications related to the way applications are used in mathematics learning processes and that these sample applications mostly include three-dimensional geometric shapes. In addition, it was observed that the applications are mostly designed for the IOS operating system (n = 13), and some applications do not work on Android operating systems.

Although AR applications are a rapidly advancing technology, not many applications support mathematical skills in early childhood. The section below explains the usage of applications in mathematics education by the preparation of three examples of activities with Block My World, AR app, and Addition AR.

Table 3. Examples of augmented reality applications in early mathematics education

Targeted Mathematical Skills	Counting
The AR Application to be Used	Block My World
Application Process	The Block My World application allows building structures with blocks, dominoes, and balls. The created structures can be in the desired texture, structure, and colour. The application is available after downloading it for free. When it is turned on, the phone camera becomes active and the area where the images are wanted to be seen must be scanned with the camera. After the application has fully scanned the space, desired structures can be created with the buttons on the screen and the selection of the target area. The colour and size of the images can be changed and games can be played in the created structure. For example, after creating a block from squares, a sphere can be added by selecting the sphere shape, after clicking the hand button, the sphere can be moved by hand and the blocks can be knocked down. While creating the structure, the number of images can be increased or decreased with the + and − buttons on the screen. From the camera button, what you do in the application can be recorded. Even if the application is exited, it is possible to continue working on a previously worked structure when the application is reopened. The Block World application is introduced to children. A sample application is made with blocks together, they learn how to use them. Before using the application, they design the 3-dimensional shapes they want to create the structure are selected. Children create the structures they want and count how many blocks they use. (Before this application, children can be asked about the shapes of the wooden blocks in their classrooms. They can create structures by combining the blocks, and talk about how many blocks they use in the structures they create.)

Continued on following page

Table 3. Continued

Application Images	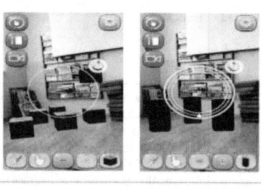
Other Mathematical Skills that can be Supported with Applications	**Geometric Shapes:** The views of different geometric shapes from different angles in the application are examined together with the children. Concepts of corner, edge, surface, and dimension can be studied. **Ranking:** Sorting studies can be included through concepts such as length and size. **Measuring:** The lengths of the materials in the classroom can be arranged on top of the shapes in the application, and measurement studies can be carried out with non-standard units. **Data Analysis/Graph:** Graphic creation and reading studies can be done with the shapes included in the application.

Continued on following page

Table 3. Continued

Targeted Mathematical Skills	Two- and Three-Dimensional Geometric Shapes
The AR Application to be Used	AR App
Application Process	After the AR App application is downloaded, when the application is opened, shapes, solar system, length measurement, horizontal and vertical surface detection, and image detection AR physics buttons appear. After selecting the button related to the content to be transferred to the real context, the button with AR on the screen is selected. For example, after 3D geometric shapes are selected, the AR button on the screen is clicked and the phone's camera becomes active. The images of 3D shapes are transferred to the real context in which they want to appear. The angle of the phone's camera can be moved according to the desired surface of the figures. The AR App application is opened, geometric shapes are shown and children are allowed to experience. Geometric shapes in the classroom environment and shapes in the AR app are brought side by side with AR and screenshots are taken. (Before this application, children can find shapes in their classrooms. They can match, group, etc. shapes.)
Application Images	

Continued on following page

Table 3. Continued

Other Mathematical Skills that can be Supported with Applications	**Counting:** Counting, addition, and subtraction studies can be performed with geometric shapes. **Classification:** Geometric shapes can be classified according to variables such as surface numbers and colours. **Pattern:** Pattern studies can be developed with the shapes included in the application. **Part-Whole Relationship:** The part-whole relationship can be studied using shapes forming the surfaces of geometric figures (such as squares from triangles, rectangles from squares, and rectangular prism from cubes). **Position in Space:** The concepts of above-under and above-below can be studied by showing visuals in the application in different areas in the classroom.

Targeted Mathematical Skills	Addition (Incrementing)
The AR Application to be Used	Addition AR
Application Process	The purpose of the application is to perform basic arithmetic skills through AR applications in a real context. The application is free to download and use, and in-app purchases are also available. In addition, the application objectives include the development of spatial perception and support of fine motor skills and coordination skills. The child must perform the operation given in the application and place it appropriately by pointing to the correct result. The app gives instant feedback on correct and incorrect answer. There are different levels within the applications. It can be supported by making a choice according to the level of the child's mathematical skills. When the application is entered, the camera access authorization is given to the device used and the game is started. When the game starts, a mathematical operation and images of different numbers appear on the screen. With the target area selection, the result of the operation should be selected by changing the angle of the camera and click the red button in the lower right corner. When the operation is done correctly, different operations appear on the screen. Children open the AR app and are shown how to use it and explained. The educator tells the children that other operations and numbers may be hidden in their classroom. Demonstrates an exemplary operation to children. After the kids experience the collection process in the AR app, chat about their app experience. (Before this application, the teacher can hang plus (+) and equals (=) symbols and numbers on the classroom board, children can do addition and subtraction with numbers or objects.)
Application Images	
Other Mathematical Skills that can be Supported with Applications	Problem solving: Problem solving skills of children can be supported by creating problem sentences related to the operations given in the application or by enabling children to create problem sentences according to the operation.

Teachers' Experiences of AR Apps With Math Content

The other question of the research is, "What are the teachers' views on AR applications with mathematical content?" To find an answer to the question, teachers' experiences with AR applications were examined. It was found that they also used "Block My World", "My Catterpillar", "Arloopa", "Augmented Reality AR", "Multiplication AR", "Math Ninja Bottle", "Augmented Reality App" applications. When the teachers' involvement with AR applications in the education process is examined, it is seen that it is generally between 20 and 40 minutes 2-3 times a week.

Teachers stated the reasons for preferring AR applications as attracting children's attention and providing permanent learning, being comprehensive in terms of subjects related to mathematics, being fun, being suitable for children's levels, and providing convenience in teaching mathematics subjects. T7's opinion on this was, *"I used Block my World as a mathematical skill about location in space. Because they were more interested, they asked more detailed questions and deeper learning took place."* While expressing that as T5 said, *"Arloopa included a lot of topics that I could use in the application, so I liked it very much, it was suitable for the level of children. It was easy to use, and the children enjoyed it very much."*

Figure 5. Opinions of teachers about AR application with mathematics content

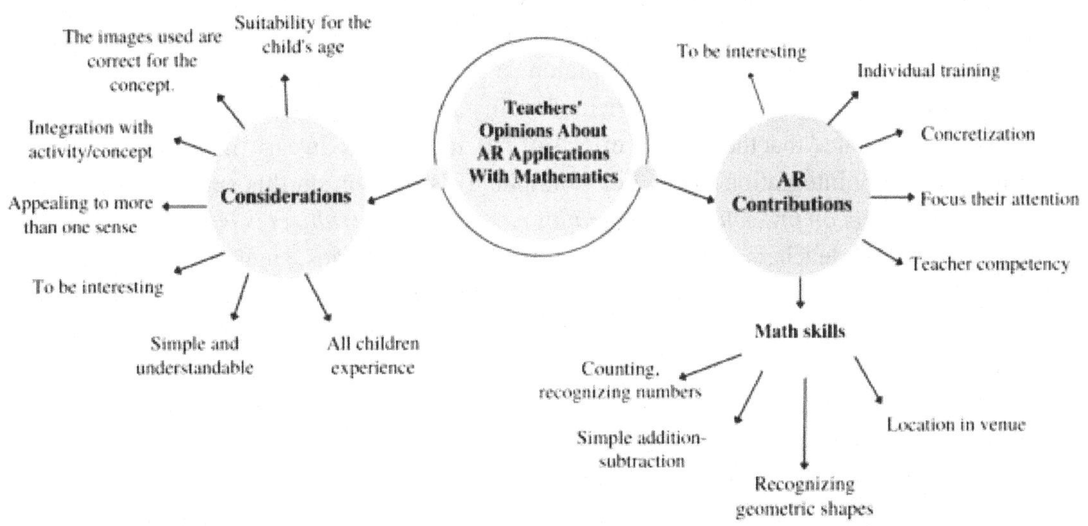

When teachers include AR in the education process, it should be appropriate for the age group of the children, each child can experience the process, the application is integrated with the activity and the concept, it is simple and understandable, the application is non-violent, interesting and appeals to more than one sense stated that they paid attention to the concept being correct and appropriate (Figure, 5). T2 *"I paid attention to the fact that it appeals to the concepts, focuses attention, and is interesting."* Then, T5's comment on the subject is as follows: *"It is suitable for age level, to include non-violent characters, to have a plain and understandable language."* T3: *"By dividing it into small groups, I allow each of my students to live with this experience. I measure the changes with individual observation and awareness*

in them." the words and T8: *"I take care to have all children apply it, under supervised control."* She emphasized individual experience with her explanation.

When the teachers used AR applications in mathematics education, they stated that the children were interested, had fun, and supported mathematical skills such as counting, recognizing numbers, simple addition and subtraction, and recognizing shapes and locations in the space, and the parents also gave positive feedback. For example, T1 said, *"I made a lesson by simply multiplying the additions with Multiplication and using Augmented Reality App with effective communication inappropriate lectures, it was effective, surprising and remarkable, I have attracted the attention of both children and parents."* While T3 expresses it as *"My Caterpillar provides the gain of counting as many objects as the object. Math Ninja creates a competitive environment in the game. It teaches number recognition and simple addition."* expressed as. At T7, *"I used Augmented reality AR for teaching shapes, My Caterpillar for simple addition and subtraction, and My block World for location in space."* stated as. In addition, teachers stated that AR applications embody visuals. T1 expressed his view as *"Sometimes with Arloopa, animals and objects are in their own hands".*

Some teachers, on the other hand, stated that children had difficulties in their experiences, they needed adult guidance, they also had difficulties in classroom management because children use the applications individually, technological inadequacies and lack of assistant teachers. T5 said that *"I chose the age level of the Multiplication AR application because it says 4 years old in the content, but even the advanced children in my class had a hard time doing it during the application. Therefore, I could not apply it to the whole class."* T6 stated that *"Adult guidance was needed more because My Block World is a somewhat difficult application".* T8 also said, *"It would be easier if there was a helper while using more screens and applications."* expressed an opinion.

All the teachers in the study stated that augmented reality applications should be used in mathematics teaching. Teachers also stated that the positive effects of AR applications in early mathematics education are related to technology integration skills. For example, T2's opinion on this subject is *"Augmented reality has a positive effect on pre-school mathematics education if the subject is learned."* expressed as.

The suggestions of the teachers were examined under three categories: suggestions for the features of AR applications, suggestions for teacher characteristics, and suggestions for the characteristics of the classroom (Figure, 6). Teachers stated that AR applications should be suitable for the age and development of the child, should be simple and understandable in terms of ease of use, should be designed to cover more than one subject, and adult guidance should not be required in the use of the application and should be free to ensure equality of opportunity among children. In addition, they stated that the teacher's technological competence and the presence of more than one teacher in the classroom would facilitate the use of the applications. In addition, the teachers stated that the classrooms where AR applications will be used should have technologies suitable for children appropriate class sizes with physical equipment, and individual teaching should be done. T4 expressed her opinion on this subject: *"During the education period, I used the application twice a week. It was a serious waste of time for all children to have the same application made with a single phone call. While one child was cultivating, the other children got impatient and pressed the practicing student by saying when it will be finished. I think that if every child has a phone or a device that can open the application, it will be very productive".* On the other hand, T6 expressed his opinion as *"I think that if there is a vehicle for each child, the practices will be very efficient."*

Figure 6. Teachers' suggestions for integrating AR applications into the education process

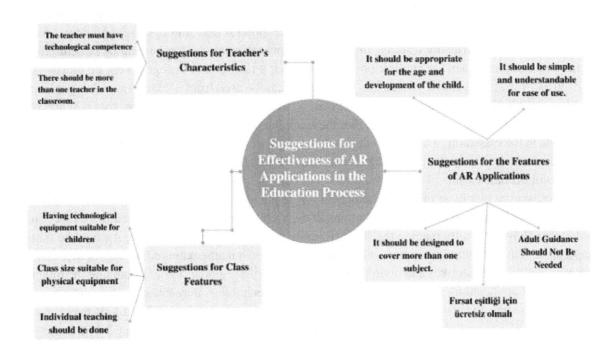

DISCUSSION AND RESULTS

When research and applications related to early childhood mathematics education are examined, it has been observed that digital materials or contents embody abstract mathematics content, stimulate curiosity with three-dimensional images and increase motivation for learning (Akçayır & Akçayır, 2017; Bamford, 2011; Gecu-parmaksız & Delialioğlu, 2019; Wu et al., 2013). AR applications can be seen as an interactive and individual teaching method alternative for children to learn mathematics content and skills such as numbers, measurement, geometry, algebra, operations, probability, problem, and spatial perception. The aim of this study is AR applications for children aged 3-6 easy to access and use are included. There are countless AR apps available in app stores, we aim to give an idea of how AR apps can be used rather than comparing all AR apps. In addition, in this direction, findings related to the AR applications of teachers and the results obtained by testing these applications were obtained.

When the AR applications in the application stores are examined, it is seen that the majority of them are spatial perception, geometry and operations. In the early years, mathematics content has a rich framework, and with ready-made AR applications, there will be limitations for many contents such as algebra, measurement, writing numbers. In this context, it can be recommended that educators increase their AR application development competencies as well as existing AR applications. In this way, richer and more targeted activities can be carried out.

While doing math activities with AR applications, children may lose the view, close the device's camera with a finger, cannot position the marker with one hand while holding the device with one hand, have difficulty in connecting the virtual world with the real world, and may need additional instructions during the application (Tuli & Mantri, 2021). These difficulties should also be seen as an important achievement of technology integration. Starting with more functional applications for children and changing the applications according to developmental gains will contribute to protecting children's motivation and increasing the impact of education. Another point is that although the applications have child-centered or child-friendly features, the interaction processes of children should be structured by parents and teachers. When the applications are examined, it is seen that the age levels are mostly determined as "4 years and above". Since it is stated that it can be used from a young age, adult guidance should be provided in the use of applications. Although AR technology has brought together the concrete and the abstract, it should not be forgotten that these applications support the process of working with real objects in the classroom. First, children should be allowed to gain experience with real objects and then reinforce and develop them with digital materials. Thus, the transition from concrete to abstract thinking will become easier.

It is noteworthy that most of the mathematical AR applications included in this study are marker-based. It is stated that marker-based applications in early childhood may cause difficulties in use, and children may have difficulty reading the signs (Rambli et al., 2013). In this context, it would be more beneficial to include digital applications with different features in mathematics education, both in terms of expanding their perspectives and improving their digital skills. Another issue is planning the time to be spent on AR applications. It is stated that long-term use of technology may cause negative effects such as physical ailments and obesity, social isolation, lack of motivation, decreased creativity, exposure to commercial exploitation and violence, and ethical problems in this age group (Bremer, 2005). It should not be forgotten that there is a time limit for children to become addicted to the digital environment, and most of the time is devoted to active practices in the classroom. AR applications can be realized with individual or small group work. Initial work can be done individually, and as children become familiar with AR applications, a transition can be made to small group work. In this way, social interaction between children is also ensured.

It is thought that the inclusion of sample applications regarding the use of AR applications in mathematics learning processes will facilitate the implementation of applications by teachers and parents. However, it is important that applications are designed for the IOS operating system, and that they can be run in both operating systems in order to increase their ease of use and accessibility in education.

AR environments are important in terms of providing the rich stimulus environment that children need in mathematics (Rasalingam et al., 2014; Tomi & Rambli, 2013; Yılmaz, 2016; Zarzuela et al., 2013; Zhu et al., 2017). AR technology meets the play and entertainment needs of children (Hsieh & Lee, 2008; Rambli et al., 2013; Tomi & Rambli, 2013; Yılmaz et al., 2016), and improves digital literacy skills, which are emphasized among 21st-century skills (Huang et al., 2015; Özdamlı & Karagözlü, 2018). With these applications, they can acquire many skills in the process of acquiring digital literacy skills, and they can structure their teaching processes in different ways.

Another limitation regarding AR applications is related to the access of schools and families to the technology through which they will use the relevant materials. The lack of access to technology by which schools and families will use the relevant materials should not hinder the implementation, even if it is limited. The teacher can work with the children alternately with their smart devices. The main thing here is the teacher's technological competencies, knowledge level, perception and beliefs about AR use (Huang et al., 2015; Yılmaz, 2016). As the willingness/attitude towards AR use in the education process increases, the efficiency of the process will also increase (Huang et al., 2015; Yılmaz, 2016). Teachers' openness to innovations while working with AR applications will enable them to comprehend AR applications and overcome the difficulties they will encounter. In this direction, it is thought that teachers' opinions will be important in this part of the research.

When the opinions of the teachers about the applications they use in the mathematics education process are examined, it is seen that the teachers often answered with general expressions such as "augmented reality cards" or "applications on the phone" instead of specific application names in the pre-interviews, and in the post-tests, they gave answers to the names of the applications used in mathematics. It has been seen that they use the "Block my Word" application. In this direction, it can be concluded that teachers' awareness of the applications increased after they experienced the applications in their classrooms, and they had more information about AR applications used in mathematics.

In addition, the teachers expressed their preference for using applications in the preliminary interviews as attracting the attention of the children, while in the final interviews, it was stated that it attracted the attention of the children and encouraged them to provide permanent learning. It can be said that teachers have gained experience in which they can have information about the effects of augmented reality applications on children's learning behaviours.

In the study, it was observed that teachers mostly used AR applications in teaching number concepts and spatial skills. The reason for this may be that teachers generally teach the concept of numbers as they are also basic skills in teaching mathematics. In addition, it can be said that teachers may think that reflecting three-dimensional visuals and mathematical concepts, which are frequently used in AR applications, to the learning space in three dimensions can increase children's spatial skills.

Each teacher preferred to use the augmented reality application at different times. It is thought that this may be because children's mathematics levels and attitudes towards technology are different from each other. In addition, the fact that the applications used by teachers are different from each other and that they have different usage patterns may also be effective.

Considering all the results, attention should be paid to the quality of the content, the quality of the children's age and developmental characteristics. In this direction, it is thought that this research, which was put forward to support the selection of applications in which both families and teachers can easily perform mathematics technology integration, will guide the preparation and application stages while performing integrations such as augmented reality applications in early mathematics education.

ACKNOWLEDGMENT

This study has emerged with the support of the 4005 TUBITAK Project "Augmented Reality/AR in Preschool Education". We thank TUBITAK 4005 Science and Society: Innovative Educational Practices and are supported by the Scientific and Technological Research Council of Turkey for their contributions.

REFERENCES

Abdul-Majied, S., Kinkead-Clark, Z., & Burns, S. C. (2022). Understanding Caribbean early childhood teachers' professional experiences during the COVID-19 school disruption. *Early Childhood Education Journal*, 1–11. doi:10.100710643-022-01320-7

Agustika, G. N. S. (2021). The influence of augmented reality-based learning media on the students' achievement of mathematics. In *2nd International Conference on Technology and Educational Science (ICTES 2020)* (pp. 47-56). Atlantis Press. 10.2991/assehr.k.210407.212

Akçayır, M., & Akçayır, G. (2017). Advantages and challenges associated with augmented reality for education: A systematic review of the literature. *Educational Research Review, 20,* 1–11. doi:10.1016/j.edurev.2016.11.002

Albayrak, S., & Yilmaz, R. M. (2021). An investigation of pre-school children's interactions with augmented reality applications. *International Journal of Human-Computer Interaction, 38*(2), 165–184. doi:10.1080/10447318.2021.1926761

Atkinson, B. F. W., Bennett, T. O., Bahr, G. S., & Nelson, M. M. W. (2007, July). Development of a multiple heuristics evaluation table (MHET) to support software development and usability analysis. *Proceedings of the 4th International conference on Universal Access in Human–Computer Interaction: Coping With Diversity,* Beijing, China. 10.1007/978-3-540-73279-2_63

Azuma, R. T. (1997). A survey of augmented reality. *Presence (Cambridge, Mass.), 6*(4), 355–385. doi:10.1162/pres.1997.6.4.355

Bacca, J., Baldiris, S., Fabregat, R., Graf, S., & Kinshuk. (2014). Augmented Reality Trends in Education: A Systematic Review of Research and Applications. *Educational Technology & Society, 17* (4), 133–149. https://www.jstor.org/stable/jeductechsoci.17.4.133

Bamford, A. (2011). *The 3D in education white paper.*

Björklund, C., & Barendregt, W. (2016). Teachers' pedagogical mathematical awareness in Swedish early childhood education. *Scandinavian Journal of Educational Research, 60*(3), 359–377. doi:10.1080/00313831.2015.1066426

Björklund, C., van den Heuvel-Panhuizen, M., & Kullberg, A. (2020). Research on early childhood mathematics teaching and learning. *ZDM, 52*(4), 607–619. doi:10.100711858-020-01177-3

Bremer, J. (2005). The internet and children: Advantages and disadvantages. *Child and Adolescent Psychiatric Clinics of North America, 14*(3), 405–428. doi:10.1016/j.chc.2005.02.003

Bujak, K. R., Radu, I., Catrambone, R., MacIntyre, B., Zheng, R., & Golubski, G. (2013). A psychological perspective on augmented reality in the mathematics classroom. *Computers & Education, 68,* 536–544. doi:10.1016/j.chc.2005.02.003

Caeli, K., Ray, L., & Mill, J. (2003). 'Clear as mud'. Toward greater clarity generic qualitative research. *International Journal of Qualitative Methods, 2*(2). Advance online publication. doi:10.1177/160940690300200

Cai, S., Wang, X., & Chiang, F. K. (2014). A case study of augmented reality simulation system application in a chemistry course. *Computers in Human Behavior, 37,* 31–40. doi:10.1016/j.chb.2014.04.018

Cardenal, F. J., & López, V. F. (2015) 'Education apps – one step beyond: it's time for something more in the education apps world'. *International Joint Conference, 369,* 571–581. https://doi.org/10.1007/978-3-319-19713-5_50

Carmigniani, J., Furht, B., Anisetti, M., Ceravolo, P., Damiani, E., & Ivkovic, M. (2011). Augmented reality technologies, systems and applications. *Multimedia Tools and Applications*, *51*(1), 341–377. doi:10.100711042-010-0660-6

Cascales, A., Pérez-López, D., & Contero, M. (2013). Study on parent's acceptance of the augmented reality use for preschool education. *Procedia Computer Science*, *25*, 420–427. doi:10.1016/j.procs.2013.11.053

Çetintav, G., & Yılmaz, R. (2022). A systematic analysis of published articles on augmented reality in the field of mathematics and geometry education. *Karaelmas Journal of Educational Sciences, 10* (1), 47-61. https://dergipark.org.tr/tr/pub/kebd/issue/70876/1077084

Çevik, G., Yılmaz, R. M., Goktas, Y., & Gülcü, A. (2017). Learning English word with augmented reality for preschool education. *Journal of Instructional Technologies and Teacher Education*, *6*(2), 50–57. https://dergipark.org.tr/tr/pub/jitte/issue/31327/303838

Chang, H. Y., Wu, H. K., & Hsu, Y. S. (2013). Integrating a mobile augmented reality activity to contextualize student learning of a socioscientic issue. *British Journal of Educational Technology*, *44*(3). Advance online publication. doi:10.1111/j.1467-8535.2012.01379.x

Chen, Y., Zhou, D., Wang, Y., & Yu, J. (2017, June). *Application of augmented reality for early childhood English teaching.* In 2017 International symposium on educational technology (ISET) (pp. 111-115). IEEE. 10.1109/ISET.2017.34

Cheng, K.-H., & Tsai, C. C. (2013). Affordances of augmented reality in science learning: Suggestions for future research. *Journal of Science Education and Technology*, *22*(4), 449–462. doi:10.100710956-012-9405-9

Cheung, A. C., & Slavin, R. E. (2013). The effectiveness of educational technology applications for enhancing mathematics achievement in K-12 classrooms: A meta-analysis. *Educational Research Review*, *9*, 88–113. doi:10.1016/j.edurev.2013.01.001

Çiftçi, A., & Topçu, M. S. (2021). Mental models and opinions of pre-service preschool teachers about stem education. *Milli Eğitim Dergisi*, *50*(231), 41–65. doi:10.37669/milliegitim.719596

Clements, D. H ve Sarama, J. (2008). Mathematics and technology: Supporting learning for student and teachers. In O.N. Saracho ve B. Spodek (Eds.), Contemporary perspectives on science and technology in early childhood education (pp.127-147). Information Age.

Clements, D. H., & Sarama, J. (2011). Early childhood teacher education: The case of geometry. *Journal of Mathematics Teacher Education*, *14*(2), 133–148. https://doi.org/110.1007/s10857-011-9173-0

Clements, D. H., & Sarama, J. (2014). *Learning and teaching early math: The learning trajectories approach*. Routledge.

Clements, D. H., & Sarama, J. (2016). Math, science, and technology in the early grades. *The Future of Children*, 75–94. doi:10.1353/foc.2016.0013

Copley, J. V. (2004) The Early Childhood Collaborative: A professional development model to communicate and implement. (Eds., Samara, D.H.) Enganging Young Children in Mathematics, Standards for Early Childhood Mathematics Education, 401-414. Lawrence Erlbaim Associates.

Cross, C. T., Woods, T. A., & Schweingruber, H. E. (2009). *Mathematics learning in early childhood: Paths toward excellence and equity.* National Academies Press.

Drigas, A. S., & Kokkalia, G. K. (2014). ICTs in kindergarten. *International Journal of Emerging Technologies in Learning, 9*(2), 52–58. doi:10.3991/ijet.v9i2.3278

Dunleavy, M., Dede, C., & Mitchell, R. (2009). Affordances and limitations of immersive participatory augmented reality simulations for teaching and learning. *Journal of Science Education and Technology, 18*(1), 7–22. doi:10.100710956-008-9119-1

Dünser, A., Grasset, R., Seichter, H., & Billinghurst, M. (2007, March). *Applying HCI principles to AR systems design.* 2nd International Workshop on Mixed Reality User Interfaces: Specification, Authoring, Adaptation (MRUI 2007) (pp. 37-42). Charlotte. http://hdl.handle.net/10092/2340

Eleftheriadi, A., Lavidas, K., & Komis, V. (2021). Teaching mathematics in early childhood education with ICT: The views of two contrasting teachers' groups. *Journal of Digital Educational Technology, 1*(1), 1–10. doi:10.21601/jdet/11117

Estapa, A., & Nadolny, L. (2015). The effect of an augmented reality enhanced mathematics lesson on student achievement and motivation. *Journal of STEM education, 16*(3). https://www.jstem.org/jstem/index.php/JSTEM/article/view/1981

European Committee. (2013). Monitor. *Education + Training, 2013,* http://educalab.es/documents/10180/14921/monitor13_en.pdf/23d54070-3136-4d22-8a95-9eb73123ad81

Freitas, R., & Campos, P. (2008). SMART: A system of augmented reality for teaching 2nd grade students. *22nd British HCI Group Annual Conference on People and Computers: Culture, Creativity,* Interaction Swinton, UK. 10.1145/1531826.1531834

Fuson, K. C., Clements, D. H., & Sarama, J. (2015). Making early math education work for all children. *Phi Delta Kappan, 97*(3), 63–68. doi:10.1177/0031721715614831

Gecü-Parmaksız, Z. (2017). *Augmented reality activities for children: A comparative analysis on understanding geometric shapes and improving spatial skills* (Publication No. 475084) [Doctoral dissertation, Middle East Technical University] Yükseköğretim Kurulu Başkanlığı Tez Merkezi. https://tez.yok.gov.tr/UlusalTezMerkezi/

Gecu-Parmaksiz, Z., & Delialioglu, O. (2019). Augmented reality-based virtual manipulatives versus physical manipulatives for teaching geometric shapes to preschool children. *British Journal of Educational Technology, 50*(6), 3376–3390. doi:10.1111/bjet.12740

Gong, J., & Tarasewich, P. (2004). Guidelines for handheld mobile device interface design. *Proceedings of DSI 2004 Annual Meeting,* 3751–3756. https://www.researchgate.net/publication/249916209_Guidelines_for_handheld_mobile_device_interface_design

Guntur, M. I. S., & Setyaningrum, W. (2021). The effectiveness of augmented reality in learning vector to improve students' spatial and problem-solving skills. *International Journal of Interactive Mobile Technologies, 15*(5), 159–173. doi:10.3991/ijim.v15i05.19037

Guss, S. S., Clements, D. H., & Sarama, J. H. (2022). High-Quality early math: Learning and teaching with trajectories and technologies. In A. Betts & K. Thai (Eds.), *Handbook of research on innovative approaches to early childhood development and school readiness* (pp. 349–373). IGI Global., doi:10.4018/978-1-7998-8649-5.ch015

Han, J., Jo, M., Hyun, E., & So, H. J. (2015). Examining young children's perception toward augmented reality-infused dramatic play. *Educational Technology Research and Development*, *63*(3), 455–474. doi:10.100711423-015-9374-9

Heffernan, A., Abdelmalek, M., & Nunez, D. A. (2021). Virtual and augmented reality in the vestibular rehabilitation of peripheral vestibular disorders: Systematic review and meta-analysis. *Scientific Reports*, *11*(1), 1–11. doi:10.103841598-021-97370-9

Hsieh, M., & Lee, J. (2008, March). *AR marker capacity increasing for kindergarten English learning*. International MultiConference of Engineers and Computer Scientists, Hong Kong, China. https://www. researchgate.net/publication/44261645_AR_Marker_Capacity_Increasing_for_Kindergarten_English_Learning

Huang, Y., Li, H., & Fong, R. (2015). Using augmented reality in early art education: A case study in Hong Kong kindergarten. *Early Child Development and Care*, *186*(6), 879–894. doi:10.1080/0300443 0.2015.1067888

Ihsan, A., Munawir, M., & Amir, F. (2017). Learning media of mathematical operations in early childhood based augmented reality. *In International Conference on Science, Technology and Modern Society*, *1*(1), 19-22. https://ejurnalunsam.id/index.php/icstms/article/view/498/346

Jamiat, N., & Othman, N. F. N. (2019, October). *Effects of augmented reality mobile apps on early childhood education students' achievement*. The 3rd International Conference on Digital Technology in Education (pp. 30-33). 10.1145/3369199.3369203

Jeffri, N. F. S., & Rambli, D. R. A. (2017). Design and development of an augmented reality book and mobile application to enhance the handwriting-instruction for pre-school children. *Open Journal of Social Sciences*, *5*(10), 361–371. doi:10.4236/jss.2017.510030

Johnson, L., Adams, S., & Cummins, M. (2012). *NMC Horizon Report: 2012 K–* (12th ed.). New Media Consortium., https://eric.ed.gov/?id=ED593595

Kerawalla, L., Luckin, R., Selijefot, S., & Woolard, A. (2006). Making it real: Exploring the potential of augmented reality for teaching primary school science. *Virtual Reality (Waltham Cross)*, *10*(3), 163–174. doi:10.100710055-006-0036-4

Kim, H. J., Kim, M. H., Chio, J. K., & Ji, Y. G. (2008, July). *A study of evaluation framework for tangible user interface*. 2nd International Conference on Applied Human Factors and Ergonomics AHFE2008, (pp. 14-17). Las Vegas, USA.

Ko, S. M., Chang, W. S., & Ji, Y. G. (2013). Usability principles for augmented reality applications in a smartphone environment. *International Journal of Human-Computer Interaction*, *29*(8), 501–515. doi:10.1080/10447318.2012.722466

Koong Lin, H. C. K., Hsieh, M. C., Wang, C. H., Sie, Z. Y., & Chang, S. H. (2011). Establishment and usability evaluation of an interactive AR learning system on conservation of fish. *Turkish Online Journal of Educational Technology-TOJET, 10*(4), 181-187. http://www.tojet.net/articles/v10i4/10418.pdf

Lavidas, K., Apostolou, Z., & Papadakis, S. (2022). Challenges and opportunities of mathematics in digital times: Preschool teachers' views. *Education in Science, 12*(7), 459. doi:10.3390/educsci12070459

Liu, T.-Y., Tan, T.-H., & Chu, Y.-L. (2010). QR code and augmented reality-supported mobile english learning system. In X. Jiang, M. Y. Ma, & C. W. Chen (Eds.), *Mobile Multimedia Processing* (pp. 37–52). Springer Berlin Heidelberg., https://link.springer.com/chapter/10.1007/978-3-642-12349-8_3

Marsh, J. (2010). Young children's play in online virtual worlds. *Journal of Early Childhood Research, 8*(1), 23–39. doi:10.1177/1476718X09345406

Martín, S. C., González, M. C., & Peñalvo, J. P. G. (2020). Digital competence of early childhood education teachers: Attitude, knowledge and use of ICT. *European Journal of Teacher Education, 43*(2), 210–223. doi:10.1080/02619768.2019.1681393

Masmuzidin, M. Z., & Aziz, N. A. A. (2018). The current trends of augmented reality in early childhood education. [IJMA]. *The International Journal of Multimedia & Its Applications, 10*(6), 47. doi:10.5121/ijma.2018.10605

Milgram, P., & Kishino, F. (1994). A taxonomy of mixed reality visual displays. *IEICE Transactions on Information and Systems, 77*(12), 1321–1329. https://www.researchgate.net/publication/231514051_A_Taxonomy_of_Mixed_Reality_Visual_Displays

Moyer-Packenham, P. S., & Bolyard, J. J. (2016). International perspectives on teaching and learning mathematics with virtual manipulatives. In P. S. Moyer Packenham (Ed.), *Revisiting the definition of a virtual manipulative* (pp. 3–23). Springer., https://digitalcommons.usu.edu/cgi/viewcontent.cgi?article=3398&context=teal_facpub

Muxiddinovna, A. Z. (2022). The Place and Importance of Steam Educational Technology in Preschool Education. *Journal of Pedagogical Inventions and Practices, 11*, 3–5. https://zienjournals.com/

National Association for the Education of Young Children & National Council of Teachers of Mathematics (NAEYC & NCTM). (2010). *Position statement. Early childhood mathematics: Promoting good beginnings.* www.naeyc.org/resources/position_statements/psmath.htm

National Association for the Education of Young Children (NAEYC). (2010). *Early childhood mathematics: Promoting good beginnings.* https://www.naeyc.org/files/naeyc/file/positions/psmath.pdf

National Council of Teachers of Mathematics (NCTM). (2000). *Principles and standards for school mathematics.*, doi:10.5951/TCM.7.1.0026

Nikolopoulou, K. (2022). Online education in early primary years: Teachers' practices and experiences during the COVID-19 pandemic. *Education in Science, 12*(2), 76. doi:10.3390/educsci12020076

OECD. (2017). *PISA 2015 results (Volume V). collaborative problem solving.* OECD Publishing. https://dx.doi.org/ doi:10.1787/9789264285521-en

Oranç, C., & Küntay, A. C. (2019). Learning from the real and the virtual worlds: Educational use of augmented reality in early childhood. *International Journal of Child-Computer Interaction, 21*, 104–111. doi:10.1016/j.ijcci.2019.06.002

Özarslan, Y. (2013). *Genişletilmiş gerçeklik ile zenginleştirilmiş öğrenme materyallerinin öğrenen başarısı ve memnuniyeti üzerindeki etkisi.* (Publication No. 331054) [Doctoral dissertation, Anadolu Üniversitesi] Yükseköğretim Kurulu Başkanlığı Tez Merkezi. https://tez.yok.gov.tr/UlusalTezMerkezi/

Özdamlı, F., & Karagözlü, D. (2018). Preschool teachers' opinions on the use of augmented reality application in preschool science education. *Croatian Journal of Education, 20*(1), 43–74. doi:10.15516/cje.v20i1.2626

Özel, C., & Uluyol, Ç. (2016). Bir arttırılmış gerçeklik uygulamasınınn geliştirilmesi ve öğrenci görüşleri. *Türkiye Sosyal Araştırmalar Dergisi, 20*(3), 793-823. https://dergipark.org.tr/tr/pub/tsadergisi/issue/31706/347481

P21. (2009). *P21 Framework Definitions.* https://files.eric.ed.gov/fulltext/ED519462.pdf

Pan, Z., López, M., Li, C., & Liu, M. (2021). Introducing augmented reality in early childhood literacy learning. *Research in Learning Technology, 29*. Advance online publication. doi:10.25304/rlt.v29.2539

Pitchford, N. J., & Outhwaite, L. A. (2016). Can touch screen tablets be used to assess cognitive and motor skills in early years primary school children? A cross-cultural study. *Frontiers in Psychology, 7*, 1666. doi:10.3389/fpsyg.2016.01666

Rambli, D. R. A., Matcha, W., & Sulaiman, S. (2013). Fun learning with AR alphabet book for preschool children. *Procedia Computer Science, 25*, 211–219. doi:10.1016/j.procs.2013.11.026

Rasalingam, R. R., Muniandy, B., & Rass, R. (2014). Exploring the application of augmented reality technology in early childhood classroom in Malaysia. *Journal of Research & Method in Education, 4*(5), 33–40. doi:10.9790/7388-04543340

Redondo, B., Cózar-Gutiérrez, R., González-Calero, J. A., & Sánchez Ruiz, R. (2020). Integration of augmented reality in the teaching of English as a foreign language in early childhood education. *Early Childhood Education Journal, 48*(2), 147–155. doi:10.100710643-019-00999-5

Rittle-Johnson, B. (2017). Developing mathematics knowledge. *Child Development Perspectives, 11*(3), 184–190. doi:10.1111/cdep.12229

Rohibni, R., Rokhmawan, T., Sayer, I. M., & Fitriyah, L. (2022). The variety of mathematics learning media for early childhood in improving basic mathematics ability. *Bulletin of Science Education, 2*(3), 102–114. doi:10.51278/bse.v2i3.427

Safar, A. H., Al-Jafar, A. A., & Al-Yousefi, Z. H. (2017). The effectiveness of using augmented reality apps in teaching the English alphabet to kindergarten children: A case study in the State of Kuwait. *Eurasia Journal of Mathematics, Science and Technology Education, 13*(2), 417–440. doi:10.12973/eurasia.2017.00624a

Schacter, J., & Jo, B. (2016). Improving low-income preschoolers mathematics achievement with Math Shelf, a preschool tablet computer curriculum. *Computers in Human Behavior, 55*, 223–229. doi:10.100713394-017-0203-9

Shelton, B. E., & Hedley, N. R. (2002). Using augmented reality for teaching earth-sun relationships to undergraduate geography students. *The First IEEE International Workshop Agumented Reality Toolkit Bildiri Kitapçığı, 8*.

Sin, A. K., & Zaman, H. B. (2010). Live solar system (LSS): Evaluation of an augmented reality book-based educational tool. *2010 International Symposium on Information Technology*, (pp. 1-6).

Slavin, R. E., & Lake, C. (2008). Effective programs in elementary mathematics: A best-evidence synthesis. *Review of Educational Research, 78*(3), 427–515. doi:10.3102/0034654308317473

Somyürek, S. (2014). Öğretim sürecinde z kuşağının dikkatini çekme: Artırılmış gerçeklik. *Eğitim Teknolojisi Kuram ve Uygulama, 4*(1), 63–80. doi:10.17943/etku.88319

Stotz, M. (2018). *"Creature Counting": The Effects of Augmented Reality on Perseverance and Early Numeracy Skills*. (Publication No. 10813679) [Doctoral dissertation, Lehigh University]. ProQuest Dissertations & Theses Global https://www.proquest.com/docview/2049753987

Sundqvist, P. (2022). Teaching technology in a play-based preschool—views and challenges. In P. J. Williams & B. von Mengersen (Eds.), *Applications of Research in Technology Education: Helping Teachers Develop Research-Informed Practice* (pp. 219–232). Springer., https://link.springer.com/book/10.1007/978-981-16-7885-1

Tomi, A. B., & Rambli, D. R. A. (2013). An interactive mobile augmented reality magical playbook: Learning number with the thirsty crow. *Procedia Computer Science, 25*, 123–130. doi:10.1016/j.procs.2013.11.015

Tuli, N., & Mantri, A. (2021). Evaluating usability of mobile-based augmented reality learning environments for early childhood. *International Journal of Human-Computer Interaction, 37*(9), 815–827. doi:10.1080/10447318.2020.1843888

Ulutas, I., Kilic Cakmak, E., Akinci Cosgun, A., Bozkurt Polat, E., Aydın Bolukbas, F., Engin, K., . . . Ozcan, S. (2022). Digital Storytelling in Early Mathematics Education. In STEM, Robotics, Mobile Apps in Early Childhood and Primary Education (pp. 393-413). Springer.

Verbruggen, S., Depaepe, F., & Torbeyns, J. (2020). Effectiveness of educational technology in early mathematics education: A systematic literature review. *International Journal of Child-Computer Interaction, 27*, 1–17. doi:10.1016/j.ijcci.2020.100220

Weiss, I., Kramarski, B., & Talis, S. (2006). Effects of multimedia environments on kindergarten children's mathematical achievements and style of learning. *Educational Media International, 43*(1), 3–17. doi:10.1080/09523980500490513

Wu, H. K., Lee, S. W. Y., Chang, H. Y., & Liang, J. C. (2013). Current status, opportunities and challenges of augmented reality in education. *Computers & Education, 62*, 41–49. doi:10.1016/j.compedu.2012.10.024

Yılmaz, R. M. (2016). Educational magic toys developed with augmented reality technology for early childhood education. *Computers in Human Behavior*, *54*, 240–248. doi:10.1016/j.chb.2015.07.040

Yilmaz, R. M. (2018). Augmented reality trends in education between 2016 and 2017 years. In N. Mohamudally (Ed.), State Of The Art Virtual Reality And Augmented Reality Knowhow, (pp.81-97). InTechOpen. https://dx.doi.org/ doi:10.5772/intechopen.74943

Yılmaz, R. M., & Göktaş, Y. (2018). Using augmented reality technology in education. *Cukurova University Faculty of Education Journal*, *47*(2), 510–537. doi:10.14812/cuefd.376066

Yılmaz, R. M., Küçük, S., & Göktaş, Y. (2016). Are augmented reality picture books magic or real for preschool children aged five to six? *British Journal of Educational Technology*, *48*, 824–841. doi:10.1111/bjet.12452

Yuen, S., Yaoyuneyong, G., & Johnson, E. (2011). Augmented reality: An overview and five directions for AR in education. *Journal of Educational Technology Development and Exchange*, *4*(1), 119–140. doi:10.18785/jetde.0401.10

Yuksel-Arslan, P., Yildirim, S., & Robin, B. R. (2016). A phenomenological study: Teachers' experiences of using digital storytelling in early childhood education. *Educational Studies*, *42*(5), 427–445. doi:10.1080/03055698.2016.1195717

Zarzuela, M. M., Pernas, F. J. D., Martínez, L. B., Ortega, D. G., & Rodríguez, M. A. (2013). Mobile serious game using augmented reality for supporting children's learning about animals. *Procedia Computer Science*, *25*, 375–381. doi:10.1016/j.procs.2013.11.046

Zhou, F., Duh, H. B. L., & Billinghurst, M. (2008, September). Trends in augmented reality tracking, interaction and display: A review of ten years of ISMAR. *7th IEEE/ACM International Symposium on Mixed and Augmented Reality* (pp. 193-202). IEEE.

Zhu, Y., Yang, X., & Wang, S. J. (2017). Augmented reality meets tangibility a new approach for early childhood education. *EAI Endorsed Transactions on Creative Technologies*, *4*(11), 1–8. doi:10.4108/eai.5-9-2017.153059

Chapter 4

Developing Digital Collaboration Skills of Elementary School Pre-Service Teachers of English Using Bloom's Taxonomy

Tetiana Holovatenko

Borys Grinchenko Kyiv University, Ukraine & University of Minnesota, USA

ABSTRACT

Lockdown due to COVID-19 has rapidly increased the level of digitalization of higher education. The chapter dwells on the way how the TPACK framework enhanced by the development of digital skills and Bloom's taxonomy influence pre-service elementary school teacher's academic success rate, as well as their perceptions of preparedness to implement digital collaboration instructional strategies in teaching elementary school students. The study was set at Borys Grinchenko Kyiv University (Ukraine) in 2020-2022 academic years. Pre-service elementary school students (n=64), enrolled in two courses participated in the study. The study is mixed-method sequential explanatory design. The quantitative analysis of grades was followed by qualitative analysis of students' self-assessment and feedback. The data shows an increase in the student success rate and their interest towards implementing the digital technologies in their own practice. Further work needs to be done to disseminate an effective complex of activities for developing pre-service teachers' collaboration skills using specific digital tools.

INTRODUCTION

Since 2020 Ukrainian higher education has undergone major changes due to the COVID-19. There was a growing interest and societal expectations from pre-service teachers, employers, and other stakeholders towards the digitalization of Education. Universities have introduced mandatory online education during the lockdown. This has significantly facilitated the digital development of universities, stipulated further

DOI: 10.4018/978-1-6684-7015-2.ch004

interest in developing online courses (Chan, Bista, & Allen, 2021), instructional design (Smith, Traxler, & Elgar, 2022) and professional development of instructors to acquire the necessary skills for teaching online. For two consecutive years Ukrainian educational institutions have been constantly moving on the continuum between synchronous, asynchronous and hybrid learning modes depending on the health advisories in the region and the situation in academic groups.

Best practices of implementing online learning at higher educational institutions across Ukraine were further re-actualized and implemented with the introduction of the Martial Law due to the Russian invasion into Ukraine in 2022. The Martial law was introduced on February 24, 2022, and entrusted local authorities with creating safe conditions for civilians (Order of the President of Ukraine No 64/2022 On the Introduction of the Martial Law, 2022). As a response to its introduction, Ministry of Education and Science of Ukraine has recommended all educational institutions to stop the educational process and introduce the spring break (Ministry of Education and Science, 2022). It was resumed mid-March amidst the wartime when large territories of Ukraine were still occupied (In most oblasts of Ukraine the educational process resumed – Minister Shkarlet, 2022). It was possible due to the implementation of the experience of organizing the distance learning during lockdowns. Educational institutions unrolled distance learning full-scale across the country in less than three weeks from the full-scale invasion.

However, Kavytska and Drobotun claim that back in March 2020 the overall preparedness of instructors and instructional design support was inconsistent (2022), due to the lack of institutional guidance, technical support, and low digital literacy of participants of the educational process. As Kim concludes, one of the major drawbacks of training students online was their fatigue and lack of real authentic reasons for discussion and communication online due to reasons related to lack of familiarity with online learning and feeling "as if they talk to the screen" (Kim, 2021). It is important to add, that in 2022 the situation is contrary to the one in 2020 and it is necessary to disseminate best practices meanwhile accumulated by educational institutions.

Scholarly research has consistently shown that one of the major drawbacks of online learning is students' fatigue, distress, lack of communication with peers (Balta-Salvador, et al., 2021; Kim, 2021; Mosleh, et al., 2022; Salim, et al., 2022; Shanahan, et al., 2022; Yeh & Tsai, 2022). Lack of opportunities for the development of communication skills is a serious problem for those students, whose primary job responsibilities will include communication and community outreach. Teachers need well-developed communication skills to organize effective communication with students, colleagues, and students' families. Teachers also play an important role in building strong relations between the school and the community they serve. Among the school community outreach events are community service events, parent-teacher conferences, local events, etc. All the above mentioned requires excellent communication aptitude of teachers. However, pre-service primary school teachers are in disadvantage with the introduction of online learning due to lack of chances to actively participate in face-to-face communication and practice organizing outreach events. Moreover, the introduction of online learning has posed additional responsibility on teacher trainers. The core of the issue is that the quality of education could not be compromised when compared to brick-and-mortar campuses. Additionally, the approaches to implementing digital tools will be perceived as a model of instructional design by future teachers.

Aiming to enrich the previous research on the topic of developing online collaboration skills of pre-service teachers, the study was conducted to outline the system of developing pre-service teachers' skills of digital collaboration. The study aims to address the following research questions:

- How does the change of instructional strategies to developing digital collaboration skills influence pre-service elementary school teachers' academic success rate?
- What are pre-service teachers' perceptions of their ability to organize online collaboration activities of elementary school students after participating in the experiment?

In this paper, the author makes an attempt to triangulate the data by grounding research in the TPACK framework, the development of digital collaboration skills and Bloom's taxonomy of learning. The TPACK framework is calibrated to facilitate the development of digital collaboration skills. The content and pedagogical approach is designed to form higher order thinking skills of pre-service teachers based on the Bloom's Taxonomy of learning. Together these items create a background for the formation of digital skills using various programs and websites.

In the following section the author briefly reviews relevant theoretical background of the research, and introduces the methodology, the results and considers practical implications of the study.

THEORETICAL BACKGROUND

The TPACK Framework

Much research on the on e-learning has been conducted within the technological pedagogical content knowledge framework (hereinafter – TPACK framework) (Hunter, 2015; Tao & Ma, 2022; Wang & Zhao, 2021). This study is deeply rooted in the TPACK framework, which establishes the overall principles for implementing technologies using approaches tailored to the needs of the course content. Research by Tømte et al. affirms that teacher education programs have a favorable outline for developing the digital competence of pre-service teachers and instructors. However, this potential is used insufficiently and needs more comprehensive approach to its analysis and dissemination (2015). There is a need to frame the classroom experiences of teachers and students with technology in a way that enhances the alignment of teaching goals and the content area.

Current research on the usage of technology in education is primarily focused on the implementation of either TPACK or SAMR framework and various variations of models built on their basis. The TPACK framework, developed by Mishra and Koehler (2006), makes an attempt to integrate pedagogical, technological and content knowledge in education. On the contrary, the SAMR framework, developed by Puentedura, seeks to explain ways to rethink the educational process and enrich it with technology in a meaningful way (Puentedura, 2013).

The TPACK framework is to a large extent built on the idea of a balanced approach to teaching with the use of technology. However, it is necessary to look at the individual components of the framework and the way they all contribute towards the comprehensive approach in tailoring instructions to the needs of students. According to Mishra and Koehler (2006), the TPACK framework consists of three major blocks: pedagogical knowledge (how to teach), technological knowledge (what technology to use) and content knowledge (what to teach). The intersection of the two major areas creates a combination of technological pedagogical knowledge (how to teach and what technology to use), technological content knowledge (what technology to use to teach the content) and pedagogical content knowledge (how to teach specific content). The intersection of the three components makes a technological pedagogical content knowledge framework. These components are valid only if analyzed and implemented in the context (students' prior knowledge, classroom composition, school, and wider society). This framework is comprehensive and represents all the parts of the educational design. However, Rosenberg and Koehler stimulate the discussion of the importance of representing the notion of context in current TPACK framework (Rosenberg & Koehler, 2015, p. 188).

In this research, the author implements the TPACK framework in the pre-service teacher training context. Next, the author outlines the alignment between the framework and its implementation in this research. The pedagogical knowledge corresponds to the instruction provided to students; the technological knowledge covers the use of the technology to facilitate collaboration; and the content knowledge includes the subject specific information to be taught. At the same time, it should be mentioned that implementing technology in teacher training implicitly teaches pre-service teachers ways to incorporate it in their own practice. Thus, the basic hypothesis of this research is that students, who have experienced the TPACK framework approach, are implicitly more inclined to use technology in their future practice even prior to getting formal instruction.

Previous research has demonstrated the effectiveness of the TPACK framework in various settings. Wang and Zhao did the research proving the mediating role of ICT perception, perceived ICT competence and ICT self-efficacy in teacher training (Wang & Zhao, 2021). Tao and Ma used quantitative analysis to prove that TPACK provides guidance towards effective usage of online teaching tools (2022). Research on the implementation of the TPACK framework shows science teachers perceive themselves to be more proficient in content and pedagogical knowledge, than in technological knowledge (Muhaimin, et al., 2019). Durdu and Dag argue that courses build around the TPACK framework positively influence pre-service teachers' preparedness to implement technology in education (Durdu & Dag, 2017).

The author agrees on the importance of incorporating the TPACK framework into the teacher training process not only as course content to be taught, but also as an actual approach implemented by the instructor and experienced by students as participants.

In this research, the author aims at identifying ways to develop digital collaboration skills of pre-service teachers, which makes a comprehensive implementation of the TPACK framework more suitable to the needs of this research.

The Role of Digital Collaboration Skills in Teacher Training

According to TPACK framework, implementation of technology is one of the means to enhance the content taught and develop a broader set of skills for students. Recent research has shown a growing interest towards the development of online collaboration skills of pre-service teachers, which is considered to be a useful asset in developing academic, team-working and higher-order thinking skills (Aufa et al., 2021; Sjølie et al., 2019; Son, 2018).

To the author's knowledge, previous research on collaboration provided the structure of the collaboration skills, developed by individual authors and tailored to the needs of their research. For instance, Aufa (2021) adopted the following indicators for measuring the level of the development of online collaboration skills: working effectively with different team members (productive work); being flexible in order to achieve team goals (respectful attitude; compromise); taking responsibility for individual work and team work as well (responsibility together) (Aufa et al., 2021).

However, the development of such classifications leads to the lack of unified understanding of the notion of collaboration skills and insignificant representativeness of some components of the online collaboration. It also leads to lack of structured approach and understanding the importance of every sub-skill, thus leading to the development of collaboration skills.

In the attempt to provide a structured approach towards the development of the digital competence, the European Commission has developed the Digital Competence Framework for citizens. This framework includes five broad competence areas, which to large extend are practical and applicable to pre-service teacher training as well. These competence areas include Information and Data Literacy; Communication and Collaboration; Digital Content Creation; Safety; and Problem-Solving (European Commission, 2022, p. 7). Although these competence areas are interconnected, our primarily focus is to identify the structure of collaboration skills.

The broad competence area of Communication and Collaboration includes the following sub-competences: interacting and sharing through digital technologies, engaging citizenship through digital technologies, collaborating through digital technologies, netiquette, and managing digital identity (European Commission, 2022, pp. 15-26). In the following paragraphs, the author analyses the structure of each sub-competences.

The European Commission states that interacting through digital technologies includes the skills of using a variety of digital resources to communicate with other people, the ability to select digital technologies and identify appropriate communication means, showing others the most appropriate digital communication means for a given context, adapting digital technologies to the needs of communication, demonstrating the ability to guide others through digital technologies, creating solutions to solve complex problems related to interaction and digital communication (European Commission, 2022, p. 15). The author agrees that interaction is one of the key competences that instructors develop in students. As the author conducts this study with pre-service teachers who learn English as a Foreign Language and English Teaching Methodology, it is important to substitute real-life classroom communication with the digital one. The interaction plays an important role in teaching English as a foreign language to pre-service teachers. Ur (2012) argued that involvement in purposeful, genuine interaction is one of the keys to succeed in acquiring language skills (pp. 228-234).

However, the author would like to add that teaching interaction skills online from the instructor's perspective should include such intermediate steps as the choice of the appropriate digital technology and teaching how to use this technology effectively. The advanced level of formation of this competence includes proposing different digital tools and technologies for collaborative processes in the field (European Commission, 2022, p. 15). It means that the earlier pre-service teachers learn how to use digital technologies and implement them in the educational process, the more prepared they are to work with "digital natives" in primary schools and collaborate with their colleagues.

The competence of sharing information and files using digital technologies includes the ability to share data, information, and content with others using appropriate digital technologies. It also includes assessment of the most appropriate digital technologies to solve specific professional tasks and creating solutions to solve professional problems through digital technologies (European Commission, 2022, p. 15). To the author's opinion, it is important to introduce pre-service teachers to the range of various tools aiming at sharing the content and collaborating on it. This competence is targeted at the usage of technologies rather than pedagogical implications of sharing information digitally. Teaching students how to use digital technology with the learning objective is regarded by the Cabero (2014) as an important task for teacher trainers. The author also agrees with the importance of preparing pre-service teachers to implementing digital technologies in education.

Engaging citizenship through digital technologies includes identification of appropriate digital technologies to empower and participate in society as a citizen, discussion of appropriate digital technologies, as well as guiding others in choosing digital services. It also includes integration of knowledge to contribute to professional practices and knowledge and guiding others in engaging in citizenship through digital technologies (European Commission, 2022, p. 19). Previous research indicates the scope of the notion of the digital citizenship is perceived by pre-service teachers as rather vague. Karaduman (2017) suggested implementing a more comprehensive approach towards improving digital citizenship education within social studies teacher training programs. However, the development of the digital citizenship competence is beyond the scope of research questions for this paper, as the study is grounded in the development digital collaboration skills through the tasks levelled according to the Bloom's Taxonomy within the TPACK framework implemented in two courses for undergraduate students (The Foreign Language and Teaching Methodology and Modern Technologies of Teaching Foreign Languages to Young Learners).

Collaborating through digital technologies includes the selection of the most appropriate digital tools and technologies for collaborative processes, as well as selecting various approaches of their use and proposing new ideas and processes to the field (European Commission, 2022).

Collaboration skills are complex, and their formation is closely connected with interactive teaching of the subject content. It is very important to teach pre-service teachers effective techniques of initiating and keeping collaboration going. The process of collaboration is also facilitated by the implementation of the netiquette. The competence of netiquette means awareness of behavioral norms and know-hows while using digital technologies and interacting in digital environments. This competence is demonstrated through the ability to discuss, differentiate, clarify, express, describe and apply into practice behavioral norms and know-hows, communication strategies and generational diversity aspects to consider in digital environments as well as adapting to the given context and audience (European Commission, 2022).

The last competence included in the Communication and Collaboration competence area is managing digital identity. It includes identifying, displaying, and managing various digital identities; describing, explaining, discussing, applying, and guiding others through specific ways to protect their reputation online; recognizing, describing, manipulating, using, changing and integrating the data produced by users (European Commission, 2022).

This comprehensive list of competences addresses the needs of a broad cohort of the public. At the same time, in an attempt to identify specific indicators for the formation of the Communication and Collaboration competence, the author has adopted the following indicators based on the Digital Competence Framework for citizens (Table 1).

Table 1. A set of indicators for the collaborating through digital technologies competence

Domain	Indicators
Knowledge	Aware of the advantages of using digital tools and technologies for remote collaborative processes. Understands that in order to co-create digital content with other people, good social skills are important to compensate for the limitations of online communication.
Skills	Knows how to use digital tools in a collaborative context to plan and share tasks and responsibilities within a work team (e.g., digital calendar, planners etc.). Knows how to use digital tools to facilitate and improve collaborative processes, for example through shared visual boards and digital canvases (e.g., Mural, Miro, Padlet). Knows how to engage collaboratively in a wiki (e.g., negotiate opening a new entry on a subject that is missing from Wikipedia to increase public knowledge). Knows how to use digital tools and technologies in a remote working context for idea generation and co-creation of digital content (e.g., shared mind maps and whiteboards, polling tools). Knows how to evaluate the advantages and disadvantages of digital applications for making collaboration effective (e.g., the use of online spaces for co-creation, shared project management tools).
Attitudes	Encourages everyone to express their own opinions constructively when collaborating in digital environments. Acts in trustworthy ways to achieve group goals when engaging in co-construction of resources or knowledge. Inclined to use appropriate digital tools for fostering collaboration between the members of a team while, at the same time, ensuring digital accessibility.

Source: developed by author based on (European Commission, 2022, pp. 15-26)

Teacher educator's usage of digital technologies in preparing pre-service primary school teachers plays a crucial role in both framing students' user experience with technologies and teaching them pedagogically effective instructional techniques (Kotenko et al., 2020). However, pre-service training of primary school English teachers involves not only digital tools, but also teaching the language itself and the language teaching methods. Hence, the instructors should align the suggested framework to the language needs of their pre-service teachers.

The adaptations may be adjusted within the Cognitive Load Theory. The Cognitive Load Theory is built on the idea that working memory of learners has a limited capacity and thus instructional design should focus on reducing the workload to raise the effectiveness of the instruction (Skulmowski & Xu, 2021). Hence, the content, digital tools and instructions should be aligned with the idea of "bite-sized learning", meaning tasks are not time-consuming and have a well-defined learning objective. In terms of defining the cognitive load on students, the idea of lower level and higher level thinking skills fits the research objective.

Bloom's Taxonomy of Learning

Bloom has developed a comprehensive approach towards organizing cognitive processes of learning into several domains. The scholar has compiled a taxonomy of educational objectives for knowledge-based goals, skill-based goals and affective-based goals (Bloom, 1956). It has later been revised into what today is commonly referred as Bloom's Taxonomy of learning. Its domains are organized according to the level of abstraction involved during the task performance: remembering, understanding, applying, analyzing, evaluating, and creating (Anderson & Krathwohl, 2001). In this study the author incorporates Bloom's Taxonomy within the tasks suggested to pre-service teachers to develop their digital collaboration skills.

Every level of the Taxonomy is manifested through specific actions students are required to do. Remembering includes students showing their knowledge of the previously memorized material by recalling basic notions. Understanding of the material by students is demonstrated through identifying the main idea, comparing and organizing idea according to specific criteria. Applying the learnt material includes solving problems under instructor's supervision. Analyzing the material includes identifying the internal structure of the information and links between it. Evaluating the material learnt requires students to make judgements on the information and ideas based on the defined set of criteria. Creating involves combination of the material in a new way or suggesting alternative solutions of the issue (Anderson & Krathwohl, 2001). Analyzing, creating, and evaluating is considered to be a higher-order thinking skill.

The extension of the Bloom's Taxonomy is a detailed table with action verbs used for tasks at each of its level. This table helps to align the instructional design at different levels of the Taxonomy with the specific learning objective the instructor sets (Table 2).

Table 2. Action verbs for the bloom's taxonomy of learning

Level of the Taxonomy	Action verbs
Creating	Adapt, build, change, combine, compile, compose, construct, create, delete, design, develop, discuss, elaborate, estimate, formulate, happen, imagine, improve, invent, modify, plan, predict, propose a solution
Evaluating	Agree, assess, choose, compare, conclude, assess according to the criteria, criticize, decide, deduct, defend, determine, disprove, estimate, evaluate, explain the importance, interpret, justify, measure, prioritize, prove, rate, recommend, select, support
Analyzing	Analyze, assume, categorize, classify, compare, make a conclusion, contrast, discover, distinguish, divide, examine, infer, inspect, list, motive, simplify, survey
Applying	Build, construct, develop, experiment with, identify, interview, make use of, model, organize, plan, select, solve
Understanding	Classify, compare, contrast, demonstrate, explain, extend, illustrate, infer, interpret, outline, relate, rephrase, show, summarize, translate
Remembering	Choose, define, find, label, name, omit, match, list, select, recall, relate, spell

Source: Anderson & Krathwohl, 2001.

Instructors and scholars have consistently worked on implementing the Taxonomy into the educational process. Ogeyik (2022) studied which domains of learning are developed better using the webcast education. The scholar has empirically proved that the development of higher-order skills was not successful in case of the lack of opportunities to interact between participants (Ogeyik, 2022). The most likely explanation of these results is that students learn more from collaborative type of tasks involving solving complex problems. In this chapter, the author aligns various activities suggested to students with the idea of solving them collaboratively. This idea is also aligned with TPACK framework to teaching digital and content skills together with pedagogical approaches to skill formation.

Morze has developed an approach to prepare pre-service teachers to work in the ICR classroom. The approach is grounded into the use of digital tools, inquiry-based learning, and collaboration of students (Morze et al., 2020). According to scholars, this approach is effective in preparing pre-service students to STEAM education. Scholars also agree on the importance of the implementation of the Bloom taxonomy in the organization of teaching using LMS (Morze et al., 2021).

Verenna et al. has empirically proved that success of students at the lower level is a predictor of their success at the higher level of Bloom's Taxonomy, which includes analysis, evaluation, and creation

(2018). In this chapter, based on previous scholarly research, the author presents the way to incorporate the idea of the Bloom's Taxonomy levels into the instructional design.

The Approach to the Development of Digital Collaboration Skills

Teaching students the subject matter and developing their digital collaboration skills is a complex task. It comprises the provision of the instruction, explaining the procedure, pre-teaching basic functions of the program or resource, as well as providing students the general overview of the program layout and reinforcing the expected online behavior (netiquette). The instructional approach is based on building a sequence of activities presented within the TPACK approach, where students are encouraged to use digital tools to collaborate on a task involving higher-order thinking skills in two different courses – a general English course and teaching English course.

Next, the author presents a step-by-step instructional approach to teaching the digital collaboration skills (Figure 1). One of the first steps in starting online collaboration is clarifying the objectives for the course, module, practical class, and the specific assignment. The objective should include an action verb for the type of task students are expected to perform, the collaboration mode they are working in and the digital tool they are supposed to use. This type of specification of the learning objective is aligned with the TPACK framework and allows students to focus on the task itself, rather than identifying ways to do it. Previously suggested action verbs categorized into the levels of the Bloom's taxonomy are the starting point for planning the task (Table 2).

Figure 1. Instructional approach to teaching the digital collaboration skills

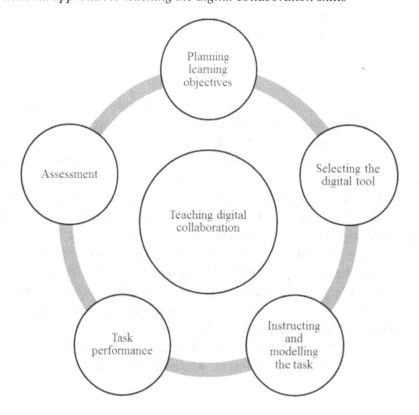

One of the keys to the effective organization of group collaboration is choosing the right web-conferencing tool. In the first few months the author has tried Skype, Google Meet, and Zoom for holding online classes. Using these tools has received rather contradictory feedback from students. Among the difficulties students have mentioned, there are joining the meeting, inability to watch the video recording of the class, and lack of possibilities for collaboration. To address these issues, the instructor sets the meeting via the Google Calendar and posts the link to the e-learning course; selects the video conferencing programs with the possibility of recording the meeting and the option to organize breakout rooms for working in groups.

Additionally, the instructor posts all necessary links, QR codes in the LMS online course. Typical structure of the course includes individual modules organized in blocks and a progress bar for students to see their progress in finishing the course. The typical structure of the course module includes recommendations to the module, module roadmap, forum, and assessment criteria. The next major block is lectures with comprehension check questions, seminars, tasks for practical tasks, additional resources, module tests, exam tests. There is also a section for links to external resources, where the instructor adds the links to resources to be used for collaboration.

The next step of the instructional design is choosing digital tools that enhance students' performance of the task. The choice of the digital tool should be conditioned by the accessibility and a user-friendly design of the tool. Prior to implementing the specific tool, the instructor should check if the tool is cybersafe and make sure that students know the interface and how to use it. Teaching interface and effective ways of using the technology needs an instructor to allocate instruction time to explaining it to their students. Table 3 provides a checklist the author has developed for choosing the digital tool for collaboration.

Table 3. Task planning checklist to organize the development of digital collaboration skills

Task Planning Checklist	
Identification of learning objectives	What is your broad course aim? What is you lesson objective? What is your desired outcome of the activity?
Selection of digital tools	Does the digital tool require sharing of personal details? Will this tool support students' acquisition of content and development of collaboration skills? Are students familiar with the interface of the digital tool?
Providing instruction and modelling of the task performance	Do students know the task? Is the instruction short and clear? Did you model the activity in the open pair? Do students know what netiquette they are supposed to use?
Task facilitation	What are you going to do when your students do the activity? What are your possible interventions in the groups work? How are you going to correct the mistakes students make?
Assessment	What kind of rubric do you want to use to provide feedback to your students? What kind of formative /summative assessment is performed?

Source: compiled by author

The third step in teaching digital collaboration skills is providing proper instruction and modeling the task. In terms of pedagogical design, this step is an important factor influencing the effectiveness of the activity performance. It is a good idea to start gradually developing collaboration skills with lower-level tasks in the Taxonomy and using simple technology. Examples of tasks implemented withing a study by the author are outlined in Table 4. Starting with lower level tasks will lower the Affective Filter of students (Yuan, 2018). When designing the lesson plan, the instructor provides for the activity to meet the learning objectives in terms of the content, decides if the selected technology will ensure the objective is met, and the implemented pedagogical approach facilitates collaboration. Moreover, a great importance is also given to the context of the course, student's background knowledge and teaching them netiquette.

Table 4. Model tasks levelled according to the bloom's taxonomy

Bloom's Taxonomy	Example of the Task
Creating	C1: Imagine, collage in a board, and describe the teacher's capsule wardrobe.
	C2: Work in a group and in a shared document design an English micro-lesson for Grade 3-4 students using the gamification technology
Evaluating	C1: Work in a group using a board, look at different teacher's outfits, assess how comfortable they are for primary school teachers and give suggestions on improving them.
	C2: Work in a group using a board, watch the lesson presentation, and provide critical feedback according to the protocol.
Analyzing	C1: Work in a group, compare teacher's outfits using the comparison vocabulary. Write your ideas in the chat.
	C2: Work in a group using Google Docs, watch the lesson and categorize its parts into the lesson plan framework.
Applying	C1: Work in pairs, identify 10 items of a teacher's outfit and write the list in Jamboard.
	C2: Work in pairs, in Google Docs plan the content of the sequence of activities for teaching new vocabulary to Grade 2 students.
Understanding	C1: Work in pairs, give 3 reasons and explain why … is a good piece of clothes for a teacher.
	C2: Work in pairs, outline a general sequence of activities for teaching vocabulary for Grade 2 students.
Remembering	C1: Work in pairs, in Jamboard one of you adds 7 pictures of items of clothes and the other should label it. The first student then checks the answers.
	C2: Work in pairs in breakout rooms, one of you should describe 5 cases of activities and their aims and the other should identify the stage of the lesson where activities best fit.

Source: compiled by author

The instructor should model the task performance using the specific digital tool. At this step, it is a good idea to provide a comprehensive rubric for the assessment of the task performance. The rubric should include guidelines on the task performance (content), the effectiveness of group work, the effectiveness of the usage of the digital tool as well as student's use of netiquette. After that, the instructor facilitates the collaboration and provides the feedback, formative and/or summative assessment. Below the author provides a rubric (Table 5) used as a guidance of teacher's expectation, a tool for self-assessment, and instructor's evaluation. When modelling the task for students, it is a good idea for the instructor to outline the rubric for assessment, which will ensure a comprehensive explanation of the task to students.

Table 5. A Sample rubric for assessing the collaborative group work

	Above Expectations	Meets the Expectations	Does Not Meet Expectations
Task performance	Demonstrate creativity and accurate use of language/ methods/ approaches.	Demonstrate the imitation of the model task to some extent.	Demonstrate a simple way to perform the task by following the model.
Group work	Cooperate effectively; demonstrates willingness to help others; generally, display positive attitude, ability to listen thoughtfully, respectfully share their opinion and stay focused on the task.	Sometimes cooperative and willing to help others; sometimes displays positive attitudes, sometimes listens thoughtfully, at times respectfully share their opinion and stay focused on the task.	Show limited or no willingness to cooperate and help others; demonstrate passive or negative attitude towards working with others; do not contribute towards the group work.
Usage of a digital tool	Demonstrates appropriate choice and usage of the technology and ability to share data; act in trustworthy ways to achieve group goals; ensure digital accessibility and cybersecurity.	Demonstrate the ability to select well-defined and routine digital tools and technologies for collaboration; know how to share data and it most times does it correctly; mostly ensure digital accessibility and cyber security.	Choose a simple digital to technologies for collaborative processes; do not know how to share data securely; do not ensure digital accessibility and cybersecurity.
Netiquette	Accurately applies a variety of behavioral norms while using digital technologies and interacting in digital environments.	Demonstrate the knowledge of a limited number of behavioral norms and know-hows while using digital technologies, and use them inconsistently.	Demonstrate the knowledge of simple behavioral norms and know-hows while using digital technologies and interacting in digital environments and their seldom usage.

Source: created by author

During the task performance online, students use additional tools, specified by the instructor or of students' choice (e.g., Zoom annotation tool, breakout rooms, collaborative board, chat box, etc.). If the task provides for the work with one file and does not cover reporting the results of the group work to all students, the students can use the annotation tool to collaborate on the task in pairs. If the task, students are asked to perform, includes reporting to the rest of the group and sharing the access with the rest of the group, it is worth working with collaborative boards (Zoom Whiteboard, Padlet, Miro, Google Jamboard etc.). One of collaborative boards with simple and intuitive interface is Google Jamboard. It can be used as a canvas, a handout, and an assessment task (Holovatenko, 2022, pp. 19-31). The above-mentioned tools might be paired with using the video conferencing chat tool. The chat might be used to give peer feedback, to collaborate on the writing task, or as a way to document the brainstormed ideas.

A great importance after the task performance is given to assessment. The teaching methodology includes formative and summative assessment. The author believes that within the Bloom's Taxonomy, the lower-level tasks should be assessed with formative assessment and the higher-level task should be assessed both with formative and summative assessment. The rubric outlined in Table 5 provides opportunities for formal assessment and peer assessment of students. At the same time, it can be used as a way of summative assessment by an instructor as well.

Next in this paper the author outlines the study and analyses the results of formative and summative assessments of tasks mentioned before.

METHODOLOGY

Design of the Study

The aim of the study is to identify effective instructional strategies for preparing pre-service elementary school teachers to collaborate online and further be able to implement digital collaboration in their practice. The author first did the literature review and designed the instructional approach to be implemented in two courses for undergraduate students at Borys Grinchenko Kyiv University, a municipal university in Ukraine.

Both courses are offered for Elementary Education students within the curriculum tailored to prepare specialists in elementary education, who are able to independently solve complex specialized tasks and practical problems in the process of pedagogical activity in general educational institutions; to form professional competencies in implementing the concept of "New Ukrainian School" reform, teaching elementary school children educational branches outlined in the State Standard of Elementary Education, at the level corresponding to academic and professional qualifications, carrying out professional functions in the process of inclusive education (Curricula, 2022).

The Foreign Language and Teaching Methodology course (12 credits) is aimed at developing general English skills of students and teaching the foundations of teaching English as a world language. Students were introduced to a set of collaborative online activities. The topics chosen for this study are centered around The Character of the Contemporary Educator (Appearance, Behavior, Feelings and Emotions, Character) and The Contemporary Educator's Image (Clothes and Social Norms, Fashion, Image of a Teacher). The other course (Modern Technologies of Teaching Foreign Languages to Young Learners,12 credits) aims at deepening the topics discussed in the previous course by learning about various approaches and methods of teaching English as a world language. For this study, we have focused on 2 modules of this course (Gamification and Task-Based Learning in Teaching English to Young Learners).

This study is built on the mixed-method sequential explanatory design (Ivankova, Creswell, & Stick, 2006). The results of quantitative and qualitative data are analyzed in complex. In order to explore the issue from all feasible perspectives, triangulation approach to data analysis is used. Grades students received as a part of their work serve as a quantitative way to analyze artifacts (lesson plans, activities etc.). Students' self-assessment and the end-of-course students' assessment feedback serves as a qualitative way to identify students' perception of the preparedness to develop digital collaboration skills of elementary school students.

The hypothesis of the research is that students, who have experienced pre-service preparation based on the TPACK framework, the Bloom's Taxonomy and The Digital Collaboration Skills approach, are implicitly prepared to use technology in their classrooms without getting formal instruction. To test this hypothesis the author has deliberately chosen 2 modules in each course, which are not directly related to preparing pre-service teachers to the implementation of technology in education.

Data Collection

The courses in focus of the study were taught by the author. The longitudinal study has started in September, 2020 and lasted until May, 2022. The participants ($n = 64$) (Table 6) were second- and third-year students, who studied 2 modules of The Foreign Language and Teaching Methodology course (12 credits) and Modern Technologies of Teaching Foreign Languages to Young Learners (12 credits). The first course covers the general English course and English teaching methodology. The second course is focused on teaching pre-service teachers intensive teaching methodology course with focus on learning technologies. Hereinafter, these courses are referred as Course 1 (C1) and Course 2 (C2). In 2020/21 academic year participants, enrolled in the course were considered to be a control group and in 2021/22 – the experimental group.

To prove there is no statistical significance between the number of participants in the control and experimental group, the author uses Pearson's criteria (χ^2) in the inbuild equation in the MS Excel. The χ^2_{emp}. for control group (n=29) and the experimental group (n=35) equals 0.578125. The χ^2_{cr} ($\alpha = 0.01$) = 6.6348 and χ^2_{cr} ($\alpha = 0.05$) =3.8414. Based on the result, the author accepts the zero hypothesis of participant samples being similar.

Table 6. Participant information

Academic year		2020/21 academic year		2021/22 academic year	
Total number of participants (N=64)					
Number of participants per year		29 – control group		35 – experimental group	
Courses		C1	C2	C1	C2
Year of studies		2 year	3 year	2 year	3 year
Gender	Male (% of total)	0 (0%)	1 (1%)	1 (1%)	0 (0%)
	Female (% of total)	11 (17%)	17 (27%)	16 (25%)	18 (29%)

Findings

How does the change of instructional strategies to developing digital collaboration skills influence pre-service elementary school teacher's academic success rate?

Organization of the educational process with the use of digital tools imposes a challenge on instructors, as tasks suggested for learners should foster both content acquisition, development of digital collaboration skills and higher-order skills. Students' activities are fundamental for the quantitative analysis of this study. Table 7 illustrates the mean scores and standard deviation for the summative assessment of all activities, which students did within the suggested modules.

Table 7. Results of summative assessment of collaboration tasks of participants

Course, Module	Mean	Standard deviation
Control group		
Course 1, Module 1-2	7.02	2.65
Course 2, Module 1-2	7.6	2.61
Experimental group		
Course 1, Module 1-2	8.2	1.64
Course 2, Module 1-2	7.51	4.02

The analysis of the table 7 allows the author to conclude that in the experimental group, students scored higher in course 1 and their grades were more consistent throughout the modules. Students of course 2 slightly underperformed compared to the control group, and their grades were less consistent due to the number of outliers (students with no attempt on the task got 0 for the task). However, if we look at the distribution of grades in course 2 (Table 8), a significant share of students scored top points. The increase in the share of students getting higher scores informs on the overall better performance of students.

Table 8. The distribution of grades in course 2 (control and experimental group)

Control Group		Experimental Group	
0	11 (9.2%)	0	55 (21.8%)
7	30 (25.2%)	7	2 (0.7%)
8	21 (17.6%)	8	23 (9.1%)
9	43 (36.1%)	9	25 (9.9%)
10	14 (11.7%)	10	147 (58.3%)

The grading system in the course included the assessment of activities on the scale from 0 to 10. Students awarded with 9 – 10 fall in the category of high level of proficiency (outstanding), 7 – 8 fall in the category of those with sufficient knowledge (good), 5 – 6 – low pass, 1 – 4 low failure and 0 either a failure or absent or unattempted.

Figure 2. The course 1 grade dynamics for control and experimental group

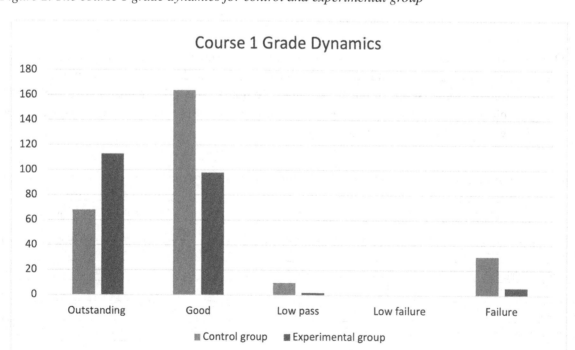

A chi-square test was performed to examine the difference in the empirical distribution of the results in the control and experimental group. The relation was significant, χ^2 (3, N = 498) = 44.6501, p = .00001. The result is significant at p < .05. The results of the experimental group show the significant difference between the achievements of students in the group, where digital collaboration instructions were implemented.

Figure 3. The course 2 grade dynamics for control and experimental group

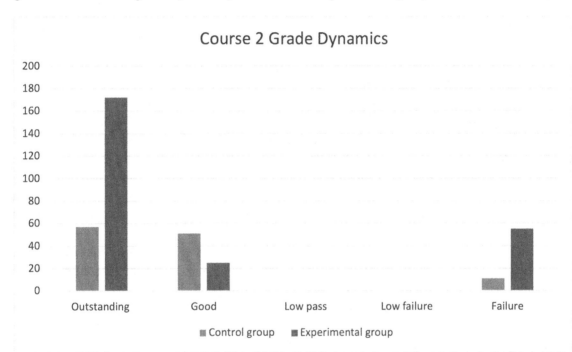

A chi-square test was performed to examine the difference in the empirical distribution of the results in the control and experimental group. The relation was significant, χ^2 (2, N =371) = 55.4226, p < .00001. The result is significant at p < .05. The results of the experimental group show the significant difference between the achievements of students.

Besides the survey the author has administered, every year the University and students assess the overall usage of e-learning courses by the instructor in terms of activity in the course, gradebook usage and the student assessment of the e-course (Table 9).

Table 9. The student satisfaction rate with the e-learning courses

Criteria	2020		2021		
	Course 1	Course 2	Course 1	Course 2	
Activity of course participants (%)	90	100	80	100	
Using gradebook (%)	100	100	100	100	
Student evaluation (%)	100	100	100	80	
Mean	96.6	100	93.3	93.3	

The results in the Table 9 indicate the overall content of students with the system of working with e-learning courses. The decrease in the satisfaction of students with these courses might be due to the distance learning fatigue documented in numerous research (Kim, 2021; Yang, 2021).

Statistical data shows the overall difference in the summative assessment of students. This finding supports the idea that integration of TPACK framework, digital collaboration skills, and levelling tasks according to the Bloom's Taxonomy increases interest of students in the subject matter and their success rate. However, the analysis of quantitative data does not allow us to make a conclusion that students implicitly learn how to use technology and will be able to implement it in their instruction with elementary school students.

Hence, it is also necessary to analyze the qualitative data with students' opinions on the course.

What are pre-service teachers' perceptions of their ability to organize online collaboration activities of elementary school students after participating in the experiment?

After students study the two modules, the instructor provided students with a survey on their experience in the course and the overall perceptions of their ability to implement the techniques they experienced as users in their practice. In addition to that, the university has also conducted student teaching assessment.

Students agree that the use of the LMS, which was the initial point of access to the collaboration activities, was effective (97%). However, the top two difficulties they mentioned were the level of difficulty of tasks and their volume. One of the students writes: *"... if you do tasks during the class without the instructor, you lack time to do all of them. [...] Overall, it is very interesting to work on the suggested tasks, there was a lot of practice, and you can improve communication skills, reading in English and learn quite a lot of new words"*.

Among the things students liked in the course there is a variety of instructional strategies, interactivity of the classroom, where they had plenty of opportunities to collaborate: *"... content, methods, technologies, ways of working with us. Especially that it was all preserved in distance education and implemented"*, *"working in groups, implementing gamification and using Quizlet"*, *"I liked that there was enough communication, we did not only listen to instructor, but also expressed our opinion and improved our English skills"*, *"Working in pairs was very exciting and effective"*, *"well-chosen materials to work with Jamboard and mind map, as well as group work"*, *"Practical activities and group work"*, *"Creative tasks, working in pairs, communication with the instructor"*, *"Interactive work: possibility to work with Jamboard and in pairs in breakout rooms"*.

The other recursive topic in the replies of students was applicability of the material and approaches into their own teaching practice. 99% of students agree that the syllabus topics focus on topics related to their professional activities. Students wrote: *"I liked that I can apply acquired knowledge into practice"*, *"The thing I liked most is that after this course I have really acquired a solid foundation (of the subject matter – author), which will be useful in my professional activities and personal development"*.

As students mentioned Jamboard often, the author has asked how likely they are to use it in their work with elementary school students. On a scale from 1 to 5, 14 students out of 18 third-year students in the control group have chosen agree and strongly agree answer. Students write *"Jamboard is a useful resource that helps to change the ordinary board in working with children"*, *"Google Jamboard is really great to be used in group activities, where every group has a slide they work on or when brainstorming ideas"*, *"It helps to develop team-working in distance learning"*, *"I liked working in Jamboard, because it gives me the feeling I am not online, but in a brick-and-mortar classroom with my groupmates. Together we did tasks, and everyone was accountable for the work. It was a true teamwork. It was fun!"*.

Some students notice this was their first time working with Jamboard and the experience at first was frustrating: *"At first it was difficult to work with Jamboard, because it was something new for me and I didn't quite understand how to use it. However, in some time I have noticed progress in learning and still remember the information we wrote on the board [...]. I am going to use it not only for teaching my students, but to structure information I learn at university and beyond"*.

The analysis of qualitative data shows a good match between the increase of awareness on specific digital technologies, which students use for collaboration, and their perceived attitude towards trying these technologies for promoting collaboration of their elementary school students.

DISCUSSION

In this paper, the author studied how the change of online learning instruction to be grounded in TPACK framework, digital collaboration and levelling tasks according to the Bloom's Taxonomy changed students' success rate in the course. The hypothesis of the study is that students, who have experienced the instructional approach the author suggested, are implicitly more inclined to use technology in their future practice even prior to getting formal instruction. The qualitative and quantitative provides evidence on how the developed instruction influenced the success rate and perceptions of participants. The results demonstrate that the TPACK framework, digital collaboration skills development and the Bloom's taxonomy enrich students not only with content knowledge, but implicitly shows students the example of the organization of online instruction. The findings are in line with Wang and Zhao, who revealed that ICT self-efficacy was a strong predictor of pre-service teachers' TPACK (Wang & Zhao, 2021). The participants in this study perceived the instruction provided within the course as an example of the implementation of applied strategies in their own work. However, comparing the results of this study with the results of previous study makes it necessary to mention that this study was centered around two courses, but the scale of the study of Wang and Zhao extended to three normal universities (Wang & Zhao, 2021).

Previous study on how TPACK influences the use of online teaching tools shows positive effects (Tao & Ma, 2022). However, in this study, the author suggests enhancing the framework with structured approaches on developing digital collaboration skills and Bloom's taxonomy of learning. Hence, the overall effectiveness of the approach for pre-service teachers is confirmed, yet there are some differences in the way the TPACK framework was implemented for students.

Among the difficulties of TPACK framework, participants often mentioned lack of knowledge or experience of specific digital tools. This is in line with one of the research results of Muhaimin (Muhaimin, et al., 2019). It justifies the importance of the complex implementation of the TPACK framework. The results obtained by Durdu and Dag also in line with the results of this study and previous studies. The author supports the idea of developing more courses, where students have to develop computer-based activities for their lessons (Durdu & Dag, 2017).

The findings of this study have a number of limitations, namely, the summative assessment grades covered all activities during the class build within all levels of Bloom's taxonomy. Thus, it is impossible to identify if some specific task or digital collaboration resource influenced the perceived idea of pre-service teachers' ability organize online collaboration of elementary school students.

CONCLUSION

The objective of this paper is to identify if the enhanced approach based on the TPACK framework will influence students' successful acquiring of material. The author presents five step model of the development of digital tools covering both preparation of the task, task performance and assessment. It is developed to take into account the triangulation of the theoretical frameworks and their practical implications. This paper has underlined the importance of a complex approach towards developing pre-service teachers' collaboration skills using digital tools. The author has grounded the development of digital collaboration skills into the TPACK framework, the development of digital collaboration skills and Bloom's taxonomy of learning. Both quantitative and qualitative findings proved the increase in the success rate of students and their perceptions of preparedness to implement digital collaboration strategies in their future work with elementary school students.

The approach implemented by the author is applicable to any course taught to pre-service teachers. It enables implicit pre-teaching them to the instructional strategies to develop online digital collaboration enhanced by TPACK and levelled with the Bloom's taxonomy.

This study is the first step towards enhancing our understanding of the role of organization of digital collaboration skills in preparing pre-service teachers. More quantitative research into the perception of efficacy of pre-service teachers in the TPACK framework is still required. Further work needs to be done to disseminate an effective complex of activities for developing pre-service teachers' collaboration skills using specific digital tools.

ACKNOWLEDGMENTS

This study was made possible with the informational support of libraries of the University of Minnesota Twin Cities, where the author is a Visiting Scholar. The author would like to gratefully acknowledge the help provided by the editor of the present book and anonymous reviewers for their feedback and enormous amount of trust in the very first draft of the paper. In addition, I also wish to express my gratitude to my sister, who has freed a substantial amount of my time for writing this paper.

REFERENCES

Anderson, L. W., & Krathwohl, D. R. (2001). *A taxonomy for learning, teaching, and assessing, Abridged Edition*. Allyn and Bacon.

Aufa, M., Hadi, S., Syahmani, Hasbie, M., Fitri, M., Saputra, M. A., & Isnawati. (2021). Profile of students' critical thinking, creativity, and collaboration skills on environmental pollution material. *Journal of Physics: Conference Series*, *1760*(1), 1–6. doi:10.1088/1742-6596/1760/1/012027

Balta-Salvador, R., Olmedo-Torre, N., Pena, M., & Renta-Davids, A. (2021). Academic and emotional effects of online learning during the COVID-19 pandemic on engineering students. *Education and Information Technologies*, *26*(6), 7407–7434. doi:10.100710639-021-10593-1 PMID:34108843

Bloom, B. S. (1956). *Taxonomy of educational objectives, handbook I: The cognitive domain*. David McKay Co Inc.

Cabero, J. (2014). Formación del profesorado universitario en TIC. Aplicación del método Delphi para la selección de los contenidos formativos formativos para el profesorado en TIC. *Educ. XX1, 11*, 111-132. doi:10.5944/educxx1.17.1.10707

Chan, R., Bista, K., & Allen, R. (2021). *Online teaching and learning in higher education during Covid-19: International perspectives and experiences (Routledge studies in global student mobility)*. Routledge., doi:10.4324/9781003125921

Coşgun Ögeyik, M. (2022). Using Bloom's Digital Taxonomy as a framework to evaluate webcast learning experience in the context of Covid-19 pandemic. *Education and Information Technologies*, *27*(8), 11219–11235. doi:10.100710639-022-11064-x PMID:35528755

Curricula. (2022). Borys Grinchenko Kyiv University. https://kubg.edu.ua/images/stories/Departaments/vstupnikam/pi/op_bak_po_en.pdf

Durdu, L., & Dag, F. (2017). Pre-service teachers' TPACK development and conceptions through a TPACK-based course. *The Australian Journal of Teacher Education*, *42*(11), 150–171. doi:10.14221/ajte.2017v42n11.10

European Commission. Joint Research Centre, Vuorikari, R., Kluzer, S., Punie, Y. (2022). *DigComp 2.2, The Digital Competence framework for citizens: with new examples of knowledge, skills and attitudes*, Publications Office of the European Union. https://data.europa.eu/doi/10.2760/115376

Holovatenko, T. (2022). Ways of Implementing Google Jamboard in Pre-Service Primary School Teacher Training to Using Modern Technologies of Foreign Languages Teaching. *Electronic Scientific Professional Journal. OPEN EDUCATIONAL E-ENVIRONMENT OF MODERN UNIVERSITY*, (13), 19–31. doi:10.28925/2414-0325.2022.132

Hunter, J. (2015). *Technology integration and high possibility classrooms: Building from TPACK*. Routledge., doi:10.4324/9781315769950

In most oblasts of Ukraine the educational process resumed – Minister Shkarlet. (2022, March 14). *Radio Svoboda [Radio Freedom]*. https://www.radiosvoboda.org/a/news-osvita-vidnovlennya/31752216.html

Ivankova, N., Creswell, J., & Stick, S. (2006). Using Mixed-Methods Sequential Explanatory Design: From Theory to Practice. *Field Methods, 18*(1), 3–20. doi:10.1177/1525822X05282260

Karaduman, H. (2017). Social studies teacher candidates' opinions about digital citizenship and its place in social studies teacher training program: A comparison between the USA and Turkey. *The Turkish Online Journal of Educational Technology, 16*(2), 93–106.

Kavytska, T., & Drobotun, V. (2022). Online Teaching Writing to University Students: Negative Stereotypes Ruined. In C. Giannikas, Transferring Language Learning and Teaching From Face-to-Face to Online Settings (pp. 67-87). IGI Global. doi:10.4018/978-1-7998-8717-1.ch004

Kim, J. (2021). Implications of a Sudden Shift Online: The Experiences of English Education Students' Studying Online for the First-Time During COVID-19 Pandemic in Japan. In J. Chen (Ed.), *Emergency Remote Teaching and Beyond.* Springer., doi:10.1007/978-3-030-84067-9_10

Kotenko, O., Kosharna, N., & Holovatenko, T. (2020). Pre-service Primary School Teacher's Foreign Language Training by Means of Using Innovative Technologies. In I. G. Papadopoulos (Ed.), *International Perspectives on Creativity in the Foreign language Classrooms* (pp. 257–280). Nova Press Publishing.

Ministry of Education and Science. (2022). *On the organization of the educational process.* AUC. https://auc.org.ua/sites/default/files/kerivnykam_06_03_org_osvit_procesu.pdf

Mishra, P., & Koehler, M. J. (2006). Technological Pedagogical Content Knowledge: A new framework for teacher knowledge. *Teachers College Record, 108*(6), 1017–1054. doi:10.1111/j.1467-9620.2006.00684.x

Morze, N., Boiko, M., Vember, V., & Dziabenko, O. (2020). Report 3. Methodological and technical design of innovative classroom. *Electronic Scientific Professional Journal of Open Educational E-Environment of Modern University*, 1-119. doi:10.28925/2414-0325.2020spv3

Morze, N., Varchenko-Trotsenko, L., Terletska, T., & Smyrnova-Trybulska, E. (2021). Implementation of adaptive learning at higher education institutions by means of Moodle LMS. *Journal of Physics: Conference Series, 1840*(1), 12062. doi:10.1088/1742-6596/1840/1/012062

Mosleh, S., Shudifat, R., Dalky, H., Almalik, M., & Alnajar, M. (2022). Mental health, learning behaviour and perceived fatigue among university students during the COVID-19 outbreak: A cross-sectional multi-centric study in the UAE. *BMC Psychology, 10*(1), 47. doi:10.118640359-022-00758-z PMID:35236395

Muhaimin, M., Habibi, A., Mukminin, A., Saudagar, F., Pratama, R., Wahyuni, S., & Indrayana, B. (2019). A sequential explanatory investigation of TPACK: Indonesian science teachers' survey and perspective. *Journal of Technology and Science Education, 9*(3), 269-281.

Order of the President of Ukraine No 64/2022 On the Introduction of the Martial Law. (2022). President. gov. https://www.president.gov.ua/documents/642022-41397

Puentedura, R. R. (2013). *SAMR: Moving from enhancement to transformation.* Ruben R. Puentedura's Blog. http://www.hippasus.com/rrpweblog/archives/2013/05/29/SAMREnhancementToTransformation. pdf

Rosenberg, J., & Koehler, M. (2015). Context and Technological Pedagogical Content Knowledge (TPACK): A Systematic Review. *Journal of Research on Technology in Education, 47*(3), 186–210. do i:10.1080/15391523.2015.1052663

Salim, J., Tandy, S., Arnindita, J., Wibisono, J., Haryanto, M., & Wibisono, M. (2022). Zoom fatigue and its risk factors in online learning during the COVID-19 pandemic. *Medical Journal of Indonesia, 31*(1), 13–19. doi:10.13181/mji.oa.225703

Shanahan, L., Steinhoff, A., Bechtiger, L., Murray, A., Nivette, A., Hepp, U., Ribeaud, D., & Eisner, M. (2022). Emotional distress in young adults during the COVID-19 pandemic: Evidence of risk and resilience from a longitudinal cohort study. *Psychological Medicine, 52*(5), 824–833. doi:10.1017/ S003329172000241X PMID:32571438

Sjølie, E., Francisco, S., & Langelotz, L. (2019). Communicative learning spaces and learning to become a teacher. *Pedagogy, Culture & Society, 27*(3), cc. 365-382.

Skulmowski, A., & Xu, M. (2021). Understanding cognitive load in digital and online learning: A new perspective on extraneous cognitive load. *Educational Psychology Review, 34*(1), 171–196. doi:10.100710648-021-09624-7

Smith, M., Traxler, J., & Elgar, E. (2022). *Digital learning in higher education: Covid-19 and beyond.* Edward Elgar Publishing., doi:10.4337/9781800379404

Son, J.-B. (2018). Activity-Based Approach. In J.-B. Son, Teacher Development in Technology-Enhanced Language Teaching (p. 133-156). Palgrave Macmillan, Cham. doi:10.1007/978-3-319-75711-7_8

Tao, Y., & Ma, J. (2022). Effects of the TPACK Levels of University Teachers on the Use of Online Teaching Technical Tool. *International Journal of Emerging Technologies in Learning, 17*(20), 188–199. doi:10.3991/ijet.v17i20.35135

Tømte, C., Enochsson, A., Buskqvist, U., & Kårstein, A. (2015). Educating online student teachers to master professional digital competence: The TPACK-framework goes online. *Computers & Education, 84*(84(May)), 26–35. doi:10.1016/j.compedu.2015.01.005

Ur, P. (2012). Classroom interaction. In P. Ur (Ed.), *A course in English language teaching* (2nd ed.). Cambridge University Press. https://doi-org.ezp3.lib.umn.edu/10.1017/9781009024518 doi:10.1017/9781009024518.016

Verenna, A., Noble, K., Pearson, H., & Miller, S. (2018). Role of comprehension on performance at higher levels of Bloom's taxonomy: Findings from assessments of healthcare professional students. *Anatomical Sciences Education, 11*(5), 433–444. doi:10.1002/ase.1768 PMID:29346708

Wang, Q., & Zhao, G. (2021). ICT self-efficacy mediates most effects of university ICT support on preservice teachers' TPACK: Evidence from three normal universities in China. *British Journal of Educational Technology, 52*(6), 2319–2339. doi:10.1111/bjet.13141

Yang, C. (2021). Online Teaching Self-Efficacy, Social-Emotional Learning (SEL) Competencies, and Compassion Fatigue Among Educators During the COVID-19 Pandemic. *School Psychology Review, 50*(4), 505–518. doi:10.1080/2372966X.2021.1903815

Yeh, C., & Tsai, C. (2022). Massive Distance Education: Barriers and Challenges in Shifting to a Complete Online Learning Environment. *Frontiers in Psychology*, *13*, 928717. doi:10.3389/fpsyg.2022.928717 PMID:35859848

Yuan, F. (2018). An English language multimedia teaching model based on Krashen's theory. *International Journal of Emerging Technologies in Learning*, *13*(8), 198–209. doi:10.3991/ijet.v13i08.9051

ADDITIONAL READING

Janssen, N., Knoef, M., & Lazonder, A. (2019). Technological and pedagogical support for pre-service teachers' lesson planning. *Technology, Pedagogy and Education*, *28*(1), 115–128. doi:10.1080/1475939X.2019.1569554

Kim, H., Yi, P., & Hong, J. (2020). Students' academic use of mobile technology and higher-order thinking skills: The role of active engagement. *Education Sciences*, *10*(3), 47. doi:10.3390/educsci10030047

Kotenko, O., Kosharna, N., & Holovatenko, T. (2020). Pre-service Primary School Teacher's Foreign Language Training by Means of Using Innovative Technologies. In I. Papadopoulos, E. Griva, & E. Theodotou (Eds.), *International Perspectives on Creativity in the Foreign language Classrooms* (pp. 227–280). Nova Press Publishing.

Lambert, J., & Gong, Y. (2010). 21st Century Paradigms for Pre-Service Teacher Technology Preparation. *Computers in the Schools*, *27*(1), 54–70. doi:10.1080/07380560903536272

Moodley, T., & Aronstam, S. (2016). Authentic learning for teaching reading: Foundation phase pre-service student teachers' learning experiences of creating and using digital stories in real classrooms. Reading & Writing. *Journal of the Reading Association of South Africa*, *7*(1), 1–E10. doi:10.4102/rw.v7i1.129

Niess, G.-W., Angeli, N., Margaret, G.-W. Henry, & Angeli, C. (2019). Handbook of research on TPACK in the digital age (Advances in educational technologies and instructional design). IGI Global.

Niess, G.-W., Niess, M., & Gillow-Wiles, H. (2021). Handbook of research on transforming teachers' online pedagogical reasoning for teaching K-12 students in virtual learning environments (Advances in mobile and distance learning). IGI Global.

Prince, J. (2014). *A Case Study of English Language Learners in a Digital Classroom: Exploring the Experiences of Students and Teachers Using IPads for Linguistic Development and Content Knowledge Acquisition.*

Tondeur, J., Scherer, R., Siddiq, F., & Baran, E. (2020). Enhancing pre-service teachers' technological pedagogical content knowledge (TPACK): A mixed-method study. *Educational Technology Research and Development*, *68*(1), 319–343. doi:10.100711423-019-09692-1

KEY TERMS AND DEFINITIONS

Bloom's taxonomy: This is a framework for hierarchical ordering of cognitive skills from those requiring lower-level cognitive skills (remembering, understanding, applying) to those requiring higher-level skills (analyzing, evaluating, creating).

Collaborative learning: This is one of learner-centered teaching approaches aiming at empowering individuals to work in a pair or a small group to contribute towards group task performance.

Digital collaboration: This is cooperation between people using digital tools and technology as means to perform the task.

Digital Competence Framework: This is an adopted within EU digital skills strategy framework of competence for citizens covering knowledge, skills and attitudes in five broad domains (Information and Data Literacy; Communication and Collaboration; Digital Content Creation; Safety; and Problem Solving). It aims at enhancing digital skills and competences for the digital transformation while fostering the development of a high-performing digital education system.

Netiquette: This is a set of online etiquette rules to create a safe and welcoming professional environment for all participants.

Pre-service teachers: These are teacher candidates who undergo a special training at a higher educational institution, which covers theoretical, practical training and certification to obtain a diploma and/or license to become an in-service teacher.

TPACK framework: A theoretical framework suggested by Mishra and Koehler (2006) as a way to integrate technology, pedagogical approaches and the content knowledge in the classroom setting.

Chapter 5
Checking Students' ORAs:
Oral Assessments With Butler, Kesey, and McBride

Matthew S. Macomber
Murray State University, USA

Whitney N. Chandler
Murray State University, USA

ABSTRACT

Online technology tools eliminate the need for teachers to bend to the strictures of traditional essays during assessments. Inspired by a shift in teaching and assessment needs during the pandemic, the authors experimented with requiring students to submit oral responses to novel studies in their high school English classrooms. The benefits of the digital oral reading assessment persist even as pandemic learning restrictions loosen, and the authors have since incorporated oral reading assessments into their classrooms as a matter of routine. Recommendations are provided in structuring prompts, creating rubrics, and collecting filmed responses, and solutions are offered to the problems of teacher time constraints, student testing anxiety, and the relative ease of student plagiarism. The authors provide the reader with three oral reading assessment prompts for texts of literary merit, including Octavia Butler's Kindred, Ken Kesey's One Flew Over the Cuckoo's Nest, and James McBride's The Color of Water, along with rubrics that can be adapted for use with any novel.

CHECKING STUDENTS' ORAS: ORAL ASSESSMENTS WITH BUTLER, KESEY, & MCBRIDE

Like many other teachers in the world, in early 2020 we found ourselves teaching through it was a unique challenge. Your authors, secondary teachers Matthew and Whitney, didn't know how to flip seamlessly from face-to-face instruction to virtual environments. However, we did know that we didn't want to give up our plans for teaching novels and other long reads. Although we were inexperienced visitors to the instructional landscape of teaching via videoconference, especially as recent advancements in commu-

DOI: 10.4018/978-1-6684-7015-2.ch005

nications and online technology have greatly impacted the direction of digital education (Kocdar et al., 2018), when it came to using novels, we were on firm ground. Whether we were teaching annotation skills to sophomores, introducing juniors to critical theories, or guiding seniors through comparative responses, we were confident in our texts, not only for the pedagogical opportunities they afforded us, but for the opportunities they provided for students to discover engaging meanings, connections, and value in their readings (Blau, 2003).

Unexpectedly being thrown into online teaching let us consider numerous aspects of our own instruction that needed updating. Due to technological advancements in many professions and corners of society, students' overall educations need to evolve to better train and prepare young people for future roles (Nieveen & Plomp, 2018). To gain confidence in any digital area, students should receive more opportunities to practice using online information and communication technologies (Peñarrubia-Lozano et al., 2021). Online assessments utilizing a variety of digital tools offer students continued discovery of authentic situations in which they are more likely to find themselves in the future (Akimov & Malin, 2020; Darling-Aduna, 2021; Theobold, 2021). Overall, to be successful in their future schools and careers, no matter their paths, students need to communicate confidently and skillfully, and much of this is likely to take place online (Akimov & Malin, 2020). Ironically, even though the majority of our post-graduate education learning has been online, giving our students the needed digital exposure and practice has been a struggle. And as we transition into a newer model of education with updated goals and digital priorities, it is important not to entirely dismiss everything that has been successful in traditional teaching (Nieveen & Plomp, 2018).

As literature teachers intent on not abandoning novel studies, online instruction with our students raised a major concern for us that we weren't quite sure how to solve: Were our students actually reading these books that we were working so hard to teach? Our fears of our students not reading the literature are not unique. For instance, one recent longitudinal study found the rates of students seemingly either not reading or grossly misunderstanding the literature triple in just a few years (Smith, 2021). Remote or not, we were not interested in supporting this trend.

ASSESSMENT OPTIONS FOR ONLINE INSTRUCTION: WADING THROUGH THE LITERATURE

To help us track if our students were reading the full texts, we explored our assessment options. There are four categories of assessment from which to choose: selected response, written response, performance assessment, and personal communication (Chappuis & Stiggins, 2020). Selected response assessments include multiple-choice, true or false, matching, and fill-in-the-blank questions. Written response includes both short and extended responses. Performance assessments include creative demonstrations and student-developed products. And personal communication includes interviews and conferences, student journals and reading logs, participation in discussions, and oral examinations.

In order to choose the most effective type of assessment for the digital landscape, we needed to consider which method would yield the best evidence for our desired results (Wiggins & McTighe, 2005). Pandemic learning forced us to rethink traditional assessment strategies and consider how, or whether, those would translate to an online environment with which we–and our students–were just becoming familiar. Because cheating and plagiarism are common concerns with online assessment (Akimov & Malin, 2020; Fisher et al., 2020; Kocdar et al., 2018), we wanted to ensure that we selected an assessment type which was as valuable for us as possible, while minimizing the probability that students' were not authentic.

Even in the traditional classroom, the smartphone in the palm has replaced the three-by-five note-card in cheating students' pockets (Lang, 2013). Naturally, the reliance on tech as a tool for cheating only intensified when we moved our classrooms online. Our students used technological difficulties conveniently from Day 1 online: Out students had video and audio malfunctions at suspicious times, or found reasons to be in the other room or offline as their peers worked. They created group chats to share links, keys, and other answers. They trawled Quizlet for ready responses to teachers' questions. And traditional strategies for preventing cheating during assessments, such as closely monitoring students as they work and putting them in different seating placements (Miller et al., 2013) were not valid solutions for us in our new digital landscape. In our experience, there were no such things as closed-book or phoneless exams during remote learning. We were struggling with a new normal in education. With the ever-growing technological tools available online, unmonitored student assessments are increasingly common (Lin et al., 2022). As if we didn't have anything else to worry about during a global pandemic and a complete upending of our personal and professional lives, we knew we'd have to work differently to stymie cheating, because working harder wasn't possible.

For our goal of determining if students were actually reading the assigned literature, we knew that we could not rely on selected response assessments: There was simply nothing that could stand in the way of students using Google to find answers, or communicating with classmates to share answers. That realization led us to consider written responses. We could choose essay questions or timed writes. Because essays offer students more flexibility in their responses, they are a good option for not only targeting student knowledge, and when teachers construct prompts successfully, they also target specific instructional goals and student learning outcomes (Miller et al., 2013). In theory, replacing multiple-choice and short-answer quizzes and tests with essay exams would improve our ability to determine if our instructional goals, including determining whether students were actually reading the novel, were being met. However, we also had to consider constraints such as class size, teaching load, and how much time it would take us to grade all our students' work.

According to the most recent numbers from the National Center for Education Statistics, the average classroom size in secondary public schools in the United States is twenty-three (United States Department of Education, 2018). Though this number is lower than what we see in our own rosters, it is a useful ballpark calculation: Offering effective feedback on twenty-three essays, multiplied across three or more separate sections, takes considerable time. If we followed a recommended time limit of five minutes while commenting on students' essays (Theobold, 2021; Williams, 2003), we would be spending nearly two hours per class commenting on their work. This does not include the time it would take to actually read what they had written, nor to communicate with the students who shared with us a private link to their writing or who mistyped our email addresses while sharing. Considering our desire to see the sun and our families once or twice a week, it was clear that this time commitment was not realistic for us. And anyhow, we were already assessing students' writing in the compositions they were completing alongside their readings for each unit. We liked the possibilities that the written assessments offered, but the fact remained that we could not commit enough time to reading and scoring them.

We still had performance assessments and personal communication up for consideration. With both of these types of assessments, students receive specific tasks for demonstrating knowledge and understanding (Chappuis & Stiggins, 2020). Because our goals in teaching novels included assessing both knowledge and reasoning targets, selecting personal communications as our mode of assessment made the most sense and aligned with the purposes we had previously established for teaching the text (Chappuis & Stiggins, 2020). When it came to using this method of assessment, we knew that individual interviews and conferences would be difficult to schedule, especially remotely, and that the minimum time commitment to meet and converse with each student would far exceed five minutes. Whole-group discussions are difficult to both facilitate and assess, with many students nervous to participate and reluctant to turn on their microphones and cameras. That left one strategy whose benefits the pandemic, digital teaching, and technological advancements only bolstered with renewed potential: the oral examination.

ORAL EXAMINATIONS: THE VALUE

We were attracted to the possibilities that prompts offered more to our students and required more of them intellectually than multiple choice questions. Rather than capturing students' knowledge of the details of the novel, more complex assessment prompts yield more complex and valuable data from students (Miller et al., 2013). Though they do not ask students to share written responses to be graded, oral assessments are constructed using the same process as traditional essays (Chappuis & Stiggins, 2020). Assigning a prompt as an oral examination provides a solution to our aforementioned time constraints. Instead of students spending lots more time writing and us spending lots more time reading and giving feedback, our students would be speaking directly to us, and we could provide our feedback orally as well. Furthermore, with oral evaluations we could hold our students to high standards without requiring holding them to a uniform type or specific structure (Golden, 2020; Theobold, 2021).

In order to gain experience with 21st century skills, students need assessments which charge them with understanding the material rather than being able to reproduce facts, and this shift in prioritization can be supported through the use of assessments such as oral responses (Nieveen & Plomp, 2018). Oral assessments also excite the traditional classroom environment, providing students with a fresher, more interesting and less limiting way to share their thoughts. Teachers who have assigned a standard essay to a group of students have probably heard the same complaints we have heard. The task transforms students into emotional actors ("Oh no, I hate writing essays") with physical complaints ("I'm not done, but my hand hurts"), and daydreamers ("I ran out of steam and took a nap instead") concerned with mundane details ("I'm worried I'm going to fail because I'm bad at spelling"). These concerns are irrelevant when using oral reading assessments. Furthermore, by eliminating the traditional pen-and-paper modality and inviting an accessible and personalizable device into the process, students with a variety of disabilities and health concerns can better show their learning without losing points for distractions like formatting, handwriting, or being out sick on the day of the essay. Some students earn much stronger grades when they struggle to express their understanding of the literature in writing (Theobold, 2021). When allowed to choose, research suggests students with a variety of accommodation and modification needs enjoy the opportunity to display their learning outside of traditional tests and summative assessments (Waterfield & West, 2006).

For many students, regardless of ability, pressing a pen to paper complicates the task and often muddles their voice in traditional assessment responses. The act of thinking then translating those thoughts to words which are then arranged according to syntactical rules and scholarly expectations can raise questions of audience and formality in students. Though many students have never been assessed with oral responses in their academic career (Theobold, 2021), adopting digital oral assessments handily solves these problems. Students can speak their mind without worrying about capturing it in writing perfectly, as there are rarely punctuation or spelling issues when speaking aloud. Through students' voice and body language, oral responses offer insightful opportunities to evaluate both their understanding and misconceptions of the literature (Theobold, 2021).

As high school teachers who are pressed for time but intent on skill-building, we find oral reading assessments to be an indispensable part of today's reading and writing course. And the magic isn't lost on students, either. Kang et. al (2018) write of their college students who prepared for oral midterm examinations that they "did not pinpoint one learning outcome in particular, [but instead] speak to the retention of the collective learning outcomes: 'To this day, I remember the questions, and the answers to the questions. It truly made me learn the concepts and not short-term memorize them'" (p. 8). Students report that their learning flourishes in no small part because oral examinations are less stressful than pen-and-paper ones and because they encourage an understanding of the material that is so deep that conversation about it flows naturally from the student's mouth, rather than being memorized and repeated. Students will not be successful on oral assessments if they only worry about memorizing key facts and details rather than concentrating on understanding (Theobold, 2021). Though the unfamiliarity of oral assessments may produce new anxieties in some students, it is the same anxieties and fears of failure that propel many to prepare more than they would for a familiar, traditional assessment (Huxham et al., 2012).

Oral assessments aren't a newfangled idea bookended by the era of pandemic learning; they have been used in secondary and post-secondary classrooms for many years. In certain academic fields and course levels, such as the "comps" PhD students sit for or the clinical examinations medical students are familiar with, oral assessments are customary (Huxham et al., 2012; Kang et al., 2018). And for any instructional situation, oral assessments offer multiple benefits for students and teachers because they strengthen students' oral communication skills, boast greater levels of inclusivity, yield more authentic results, allow teachers to assess understanding and critical thinking, and discourage plagiarism (Huxham et al., 2012). Additionally, oral responses allow students greater freedom in their responses than written responses (Sparfeldt et al., 2013) while also allowing their answers to the prompt to better convey their personal emotions and attitudes towards the reading (Huxham et al., 2012). Compared to our initial options in assessing students' readings, oral assessments have been shown to heighten both critical and reflective thinking when compared to traditional written assessment methods (Kang et al., 2018). Especially during the pandemic, encouraging critical thinking and reflection felt very important.

No matter the context in which they are used, a strength of oral assessments is that they meet students where they are. Because all students approach the readings and summative prompts with a variety of experiences and abilities, assessments should support students' personal growth rather than compare one student's performance to another's, nor should they expect all students to reach the same standards (Brimi, 2011; Golden, 2020). With oral response assessments, we are able to assess growth in specific areas without the interference of unwanted data. Students' reading and analytical abilities are not married to their writing mechanics, such as grammar or spelling, and assessments that impact the score of the former by taking off points for the latter are unfair to developing writers (Bean, 2011). Instead, the ORA approach allows students to display their understanding and engagement with the literature in broader ways than traditional assessments (Bean, 2011). When prompts require deeper readings than online summaries can support, students must interpret the texts for themselves, and in doing so become the authority on their perspective; it is in this level of reading–one that supports students' engagement and reflection with the text—that students and teachers will find the most value (Blau, 2003). Because students' self-value improves when they perform well on tests and assessments (Spencer-Waterman, 2005), it's important for teachers to fairly assess all students, from developing readers to the most gifted in the room. When these responses are assigned and scored, emphasizing students' current abilities in analyzing their reading, organizing their thoughts, evaluating their texts, and expressing themselves creatively, there is clear value attached to these skills for all students (Miller et al., 2013). Watching them across time gives insight into better academic performance and communication skills of student rather than a random collection of responses to questions (Theobold, 2021).

Despite these benefits, oral assessments are used considerably less in secondary and post-secondary classrooms today, largely owing to the amount of time required to assess all students in the traditional instructional environment (Fisher et al., 2020; Huxham et al., 2012; Kang et al., 2018). Additionally, some students' test anxiety can be heightened in response to the unfamiliar format of oral assessments (Huxham et al., 2012; Kang et al, 2018.; Sparfeldt et al., 2013). However, during the early days of our remote learning experience, we began using the video recording tool Flipgrid, which now calls itself Flip. Students were able to record themselves individually using the site, which saved us time, and they could re-record until they were satisfied with their response, increasing their comfort. In this way, the two most common complaints about oral assessments faded from our minds, and we felt confident enough to try this assessment style (Fisher et al., 2020).

The Process: Tools, a Job Description, and Examples

Flip.com

Even before remote learning became the norm in 2020, secondary and post-secondary classrooms have experienced increased access to mobile devices and online technology in recent years (Roblyer & Hughes, 2019). One such online technology is Flip.com. Flipgrid initially launched in 2014, was acquired by Microsoft in 2018, and has continued to offer the service to students and teachers for free ("Introducing Flip," 2022; Spachuk, 2020). According to its website, "Flip is a video discussion app, free from Microsoft, where curious minds connect, share short videos, and build community" and is used in "more than 190 countries around the world" ("About Flip," 2022). Many teachers have already discovered the benefits and advantages it affords teachers.

Flip.com engages students while removing barriers to teaching and learning. It can be used both on computer and mobile devices, and many young learners find the digital and interactive platform more attractive than traditional instructional methods (Yeon & Shepherd, 2020). It allows students to practice their presentation and communication skills (Iona, 2017). Teachers can save student responses to watch and score at the most convenient times and not worry about following a specific timeline, such as scoring them during class, or carrying home a stack of paper soon to be stained by coffee and flecks of Sunday's dinner (Fisher et al., 2020). Flip allows teachers to provide individualized feedback and to differentiate prompts for students as needed by allowing them to create different groups and to make public various videos within each group (Yeon & Shepherd, 2020).

Though any students with access to Flip will also have the means to create audio recordings for their assessment on the same device, Flip allows teachers to not only hear responses, but also to observe their body language, communicating much that the written word cannot, such as the conviction of students in their responses (Kuhnke, 2016). There is usually no way to know if students truly believe in their multiple-choice answers, but in an oral response, the students' reasoning is more clearly on display. But if body language and conviction is not a major element of a teacher's interest, he or she can increase the speed of students' video during replay, in order to reduce the time spent scoring each response. In our experience, most students' responses can be sped up without suffering any loss of understanding and comprehension. And because Flip videos are recorded and stored online, it is easy to highlight evidence from the video as needed for exemplification, explanation, remediation, and reflection, making follow-up with students easy and much more concrete than the conversations we're used to having with students, which force us to come up with examples on the spot.

In developing their oratory skills and camera faces, students exercise a range of high level thinking and problem solving processes (Sharon & Nurlaily, 2022). When the concern for plagiarism is reduced, recent studies suggest that moving from a traditional in-class evaluation method to an unmonitored online assessment had very little impact on students' performance (Lin et al., 2022). While students may feel averse to recording themselves, especially earlier in the year, a lack of confidence in front of the camera is common (Sharon & Nurlaily, 2022). And ultimately, through using Flip.com with our students, we allow our students a more comfortable environment in which to respond, rather than being confined to the classroom or a desk at home (Lin et al., 2022), as well as much quicker grading process and more time to relax for ourselves (Theobold, 2021).

All the options Flip makes available to educators and students alike made it the most attractive method for us as we sought to understand our students' diligence in completing the readings we assigned, but it also provided them flexibility in showing their comprehension of the literature. It allows students to review, edit, filter, add simple visuals, and re-record their responses as needed, and as such, it saves teachers considerable time as they are only watching and evaluating students' final, best versions of the assessment. With Flip, teachers are able to set a predetermined length to student responses, and they absolutely should take care to set a number they've arrived at thoughtfully. We set our student responses to a manageable five minutes, constructed our initial prompt and rubric, and the Oral Reading Assessment (ORA) was born.

Constructing the Prompts

The construction of ORA prompts is neither novel nor mysterious, as it is largely the same process that teachers take when they formulate written short answer and extended response prompts (Chappuis & Stiggins, 2020). In writing these prompts, the paramount concern is articulating what students are being asked to do and how they are expected to do it. To achieve the most valid and reliable assessment results, it is essential to create not only a challenging and more secure method of student assessment, but also create an equitable prompt that aids students in understanding the task and provides insight on students' progress and growth to both teachers and students (Spencer-Waterman, 2005).

We constructed ORA prompts using Chappuis and Stiggins's (2020) *Classroom Assessment For Student Learning*. The text recommends that in order for prompts to be clear, they should be written in the simplest language possible, in order to avoid letting complicated phrasing or sentence structure hinder students' comprehension of the question, and therefore, their ability to properly demonstrate their learning. To achieve this clarity, Chappuis and Stiggins (2020) recommended three necessary steps. First, teachers should set a clear and specific context. Second, teachers should indicate what students are to describe or explain. And third, teachers should point the way to an appropriate response without giving away the answer.

In pursuit of the first step, Chappuis and Stiggins (2020) suggested that "it is helpful to remind students of the specific body of knowledge they are to use when framing their responses" (p. 187). The goal is for students to immediately understand the purpose and logic of the assignment. The first half of the prompt should make apparent the framework and topic of the discussion, whether it be regarding the protagonist's growth or postcolonialism criticism or narrative structure or anything else students are learning and practicing while reading the literature. Prompts should remind students of the discussion and learning surrounding the text and their class's investigation of it.

The second step in Chappuis and Stiggins's (2020) prompt construction calls for a clear explanation of what students are being asked to discuss and explain. Prompts should use clear active verbs, such as "explain," "describe," or "identify." Furthermore, prompts should use specific language pertaining to what or who they are discussing. Teachers should aim for clear and concise directions that thoroughly explain to students their task in the fewest words possible.

Finally, the third step of Chappuis and Stiggins's (2020) guide in composing extended responses is to provide additional targets and guidelines for students to consider when formulating a response. In this section of the prompt, it should be apparent to students what will be required to respond completely and appropriately. As a goal for quality prompt construction, the authors advocate directions that allow "students who know the material [...] to answer well, and students who don't know it [to not] be able to bluff their way through with generalities" (p. 188). Successful prompts explain how students should display their knowledge without offering students who are prepared a blueprint for fibbing their way through the assessment.

Figure 1. Flip Prompt: Desktop

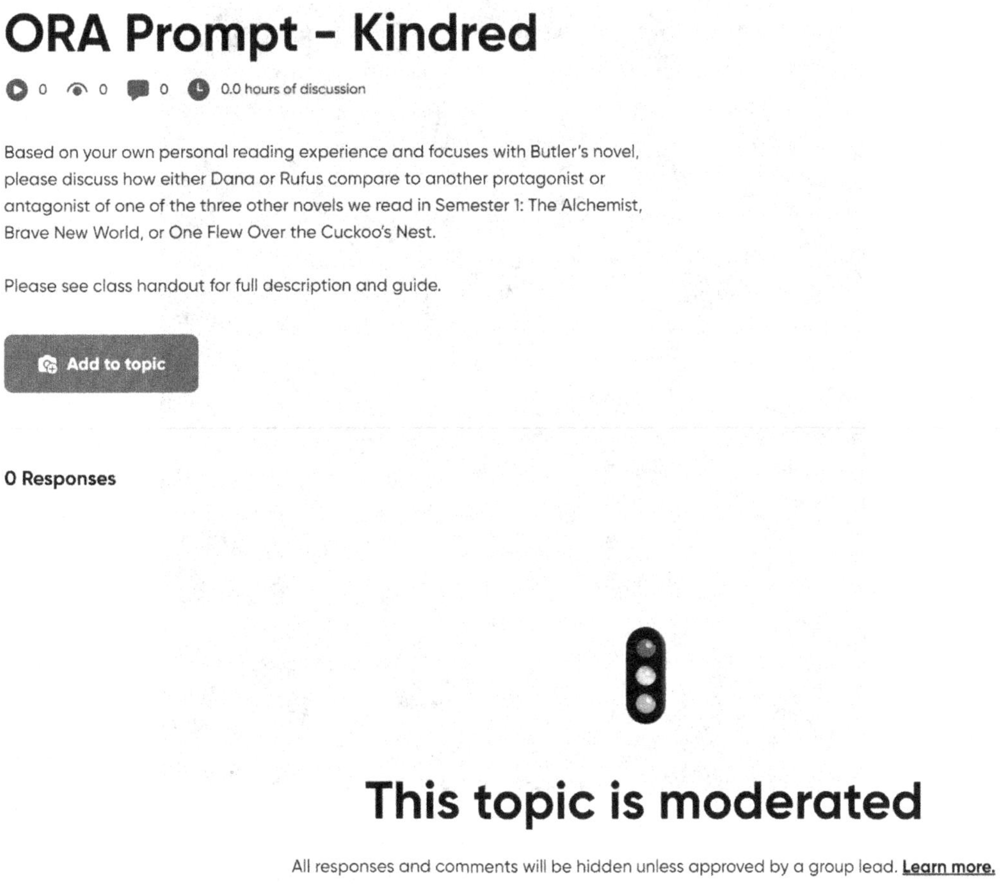

ORA Prompt - Kindred

▶ 0   👁 0   💬 0   🕒 0.0 hours of discussion

Based on your own personal reading experience and focuses with Butler's novel, please discuss how either Dana or Rufus compare to another protagonist or antagonist of one of the three other novels we read in Semester 1: The Alchemist, Brave New World, or One Flew Over the Cuckoo's Nest.

Please see class handout for full description and guide.

[⬡ **Add to topic**]

0 Responses

This topic is moderated

All responses and comments will be hidden unless approved by a group lead. **Learn more.**

Figure 2. Flip Prompt: Mobile

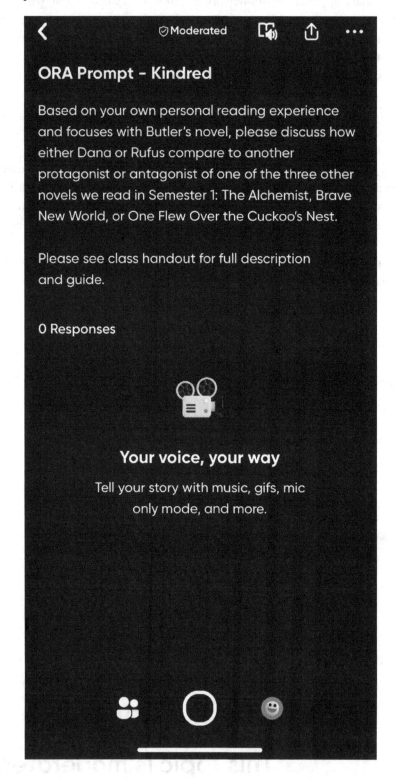

ORA Prompts and Classroom Contextualizations: Butler, Kesey, and McBride

Octavia Butler's Kindred (Matt)

Octavia Butler's time traveling novel introduces many of our students to literature concerning the antebellum history of African Americans and the lives and experiences of many slaves in the United States. Traumatic events in our history, such as the enslavement of African Americans in the U.S., often lack accurate depictions, as the survivors of these events have been irreparably harmed and transformed by them (Tettenborn, 2005). *Kindred* (1979) allows students to read beyond dates, facts, and recorded testimony of slaves and witnesses of slavery; instead, it allows students to become the witnesses themselves.

Butler's novel uses time travel to display the dangers of overlooking our past and failing to understand the consequences on both our contemporary world and future (Adèbìsì, 2022). *Kindred* serves as Butler's own endeavor to understand her personal social experiences attending university in the 1960s and living through such events as the assassinations of Martin Luther King Jr. and Robert Kennedy and the social rise of the Black Panther Party. In doing so, she explores how notions of race and social attitudes evolve over time (Adèbìsì, 2022). For students, it is also a novel which can inspire explorations of their own families' histories (Tettenborn, 2005).

As my high school juniors and seniors read the time-traveling slave narrative *Kindred* in a dual-credit English composition course through a local university, they focused their compositional responses around *Kindred's* place in either the time travel genre or the American slave narrative genre, holding the work up to other examples in the selected genre. While students explored multiple titles within either genre, what they eventually wrote about did not require a complete reading of the novel. In their written work, students' prompts were wide open: they had total control over where they wanted to take their analyses of the genre and the text. With the ORA, however, they needed familiarity with protagonist Dana's or antagonist Rufus's entire story. To avoid answers to the prompt being easily found online, students were tasked with comparing the entire character arc of either Dana or Rufus to another protagonist or antagonist's arc from other novels we read that semester.

Prompt: In this sequence, we have been exploring Octavia Butler's *Kindred* and discussing the different literary genres this work employs and occupies, as well as comparing it to other titles in the chosen genres. What we have not discussed much, however, is how this novel relates to a different reading this year. Let's change that.

Based on your own personal reading experience and focuses with Butler's novel, please discuss how either Dana or Rufus compare to another protagonist or antagonist of one of the three other novels we read in Semester 1: *The Alchemist*, *Brave New World*, or *One Flew Over the Cuckoo's Nest*.

In your response, be sure to:

- Explicitly state the two characters being discussed and the reason for the comparison.
- Provide specific passages from throughout *Kindred* which reinforce your conclusions and analysis of Dana or Rufus.
- Feel free to provide specific passages from your second novel, but this will not be a requirement, nor will scores be lowered for not making use of direct passages from a second novel. This is an assessment for *Kindred*, but please know what you're talking about with your second character/novel.

- For a more sophisticated response, consider more than the obvious, surface layer connections. Think about the authors. Think about the contexts in which the works were written. Think about the intended audience and outcomes of the novels. Think of how well the books have been received (all of these books are classics). Think.

Ken Kesey's One Flew Over the Cuckoo's Nest (Matt)

Kesey's first published novel (1962) offers archetypal characters and stereotypes who grow into distinct individuals with whom students relate and empathize (Schreck et al., 1999). While being critical of contemporary psychiatric treatments in the United States (Rutten et al., 2012), students meet characters whom they are very unlikely to ever interact with in real life (Schreck et al., 1999). Upon the release of the novel, readers were shocked at the treatment received by these characters and patients in general in mental health institutions (Stripling, 2009).

Set in the 1960s, *One Flew Over the Cuckoo's Nest* serves as an artifact of the counterculture and socially conscious sentiments in the United States at the time (Rutten et al., 2012). Regardless of the academic and professional fields students hope to pursue, reading about developments in modern medicine and patient treatment aids students' understanding of larger ideas about society and humanity (Stripling, 2009). Providing a window into the evolution of identification and treatment of mental disorders in the United States, Kesey's novel displays the power and potential of laughter and comradery for those in critical need of support with depression and other maladies of the mind (Stripling, 2009).

During the reading of *One Flew Over the Cuckoo's Nest* in class, my students' compositional efforts focused on parody and its application. Final compositions—parodies in the style and medium of a student's choice—did not need to relate to the novel at all. While we explored a variety of ways the novel has been parodied, the aims of student composition were not connected to their reading. Because I knew I would be using the ORA to assess student reading, their writing projects were free to explore completely different areas. While multiple students ended up focusing their parody projects on the novel, they did so only for their own interests.

Prompt: In this sequence, we have been exploring Ken Kesey's *One Flew Over the Cuckoo's Nest* and have been discussing and focusing on a variety of perspectives through which to understand the actions of Bromden, McMurphy and everyone else. Based on your own personal reading experience and focus with Kesey's novel, please explain the meaning, significance and/or relevance of the ending of the novel.

In your response, be sure to:

- Explain what you feel the ending of the novel is (this is dependent on who you feel the protagonist is).
- Provide specific passages from the novel which reinforce your conclusions and analysis of the ending of the novel.
- Discuss Kesey's work in its entirety. Do not only discuss the ending scene(s). Your discussion should make use of relevant information from throughout the novel to explain the ending.
- For a more sophisticated response, consider any relevant outside information needed to better understand the motivations of Kesey and/or his characters.

James McBride's The Color of Water (Whitney)

A beloved memoir that calls to mind questions of community and race as it reminisces on growing up in a rambunctious family of fourteen, McBride's story of his mother's and his own life prompts students to examine their own identity and to think about what it means to belong. The text provides a backdrop against which students can make thematic connections, and it provides ample opportunities for them to learn about voice, style, and syntax. The cast of characters in McBride's stories–siblings, mother, father and stepfather, ancestors, teachers, friends, boyfriends and girlfriends, and pets–are ignorant of and then all too aware of the constructs of race and religion and how society uses those constructs as tools and as weapons. For teachers looking for extension activities for gifted or high-achieving learners, the book complements a study of Foucauldian objectification, power struggle, and spatial significance (Kai, 2011).

This prompt is the assessment I used with eleventh grade students during our first semester study of narrative writing, theme, and the ways authors use rhetorical choices to connect plot with syntax. Because of our writing lessons' focus on transitional phrases at that time, I required students to use those phrases in their oral responses. I taught students that transitions are a natural feature of conversation, and I provided a video example of a poorly phrased, choppy, shallow response on Flip, which I marked public, making it viewable by students as many times as they found necessary. Video responses for this assessment were set to a maximum length of 5 minutes, and I found that the students whose responses were closer to that mark fared better on the rubric in that their responses were more detailed and more conversational than students whose responses simply jumped from one quote to the next.

Prompt: In this unit, we have been exploring narrative writing and the structure of a story, from prologue to chapters to epilogue. Based on your own personal reading experience, explain how the quotes in the "quote banks" below (see Appendix) are developed throughout McBride's story and how they link to other ideas. In your response, follow these guidelines:

- DON'T simply reword the quote, or stop with "what the author is saying"—I can read and understand the words myself. Instead, spend your time explaining its significance to Ruth's life or James's life.
- DO provide specific examples of how the theme on display in the quote you're referencing is carried throughout the book, including specific page citations.
- DO discuss McBride's book in its entirety. This doesn't mean you need to talk about every single chapter (after all, your video is only 5 minutes long). But do not only offer ideas from Chapter 1, as an example.
- DO try for a more sophisticated response. Talk to me by knitting together the quotes you're choosing from each bank. For example, for sophistication, DO NOT say to me, "Okay, now I'm going to talk about James's quote, and I picked the one that says…". Being able to transition gracefully between ideas without announcing your next move is an important writing skill. Watch my Flip video for an example of what not to do.

Theoretical Approach of ORAs

With our prompts and assessment tasks, we approach our ORAs through a cognitive theory lens. Using a cognitive theory approach, we aim to offer the correct activity and assessment to target the cognitive skills we are evaluating (Roblyer & Hughes, 2019). With cognitive theory, new information is individually and internally processed and uniquely applied for all students, and teachers serve as their experienced guide and mentor (Kirylo, 2016). Unique variables in every student will help or hinder the acquisition of new knowledge and the understanding of new material (Harasim, 2012). Students grow not necessarily when information is first presented to them but rather when that information is meaningfully connected with other personal experiences, both old and new (Kirylo, 2016). Cognitive theory, in part, studies if students gain new understanding and what that is if they do (Harasim, 2012). Within an educational and pedagogical taxonomy, our assessment targets students' cognitive domains, as we hope to assess their growth with "knowledge outcomes and intellectual abilities and skills" (Miller et al., 2013, p. 55). One of our roles as teachers and lesson designers is to decide which learning material is appropriate and best suited to achieve instructional goals and build towards mastery of targeted skills (Harasim, 2012). Through our ORA prompts, we target a variety of analytical and reading skills, as well as novel comprehension.

ORA Rubrics

For our extended-response ORAs, we employ an analytic scoring rubric in order to assess three specific aspects of students' responses (Miller et al., 2013). In our evaluations, we grade students on the insight and logic of their discussion, the quantity and quality of details and passages used as support, and the confidence, structure, and body language of their presentation. While holistic rubrics are plausible for ORAs, we want students to receive feedback on these specific categories so they can understand why and where their response is weak or strong (Chappuis and Stiggins, 2020).

In our rubric, we provide three scoring categories and various levels of quality (see Figures A & B). While the points can be scaled to any value, our rubric is based on ten points. As we can leave detailed comments on Flip.com, our aim is to provide students helpful descriptions summarizing their work comprehensively. We also want to emphasize the specific skills we are targeting, such as students incorporating specific passages and details from their texts and creating thoughtful discussions on their interpretations of what they read. Students review the rubric when prompts are assigned.

Building a prompt with a corresponding rubric and creating a topic on Flip where students can upload videos are all easy enough. But just as students may experience some anxieties about the new assessment style, so too do many teachers. When we started thinking about implementing ORAs, there was one major question we had yet to ascertain: How exactly is this going to go?

Table 1. Sample ORA Rubric (created by Matthew)

Pts	Discussion – Scoring Descriptions	Score
4	Response presents an exceptionally well-explained and logically concluded argument. Response goes beyond topics discussed in class. Avoids over-summarization of text.	
3	Response presents a well-explained and logically concluded argument. Although it might make use of topics and examples presented in class, it presents a thoughtful discussion of text.	
2	Response accurately discusses text and provides at least a somewhat concluded argument. While there may be large gaps in understanding present, there is a discussion of the novel present.	
1	Response is just bad. Let's be honest: You weren't really sure what you were doing, but you submitted something. You felt good about putting your name on it and hitting submit, but it was bad. Let's talk separately, because there's a chance that the kind of Bad you are bringing to this response isn't predictable enough to capture in words here.	
Pts	**Support – Scoring Descriptions**	**Score**
4	Response is exceptionally supported. All arguments are well-supported with direct passages from the novel.	
3	Response is thoroughly supported. Most arguments are supported with direct passages from the novel.	
2	Response offers some support, but more would strengthen the overall argument.	
1	It's as if you were offended by the very notion of using another's words in your response here. I'm sorry, but there are better authors in the world than you, and the author we just read is one of them. Use their words a little bit more in your response and it would have been better.	
Pts	**Presentation – Scoring Descriptions**	**Score**
2	Response was delivered confidently with a logical structure and easy flow.	
1.5	Response was delivered confidently with a logical structure and/or easy flow.	
1	Response was presented unconvincingly **or** presented with a confusing and ineffective structure.	
0.5	Yeah, I'm not sure. Maybe you were just having a rough few minutes and the world went gray and fuzzy for a little bit? Because the "You" that was in that video isn't the "You" with that bright smile and authoritative voice.	

Table 2. Sample ORA Rubric (created by Whitney)

Pts	Textual References – Scoring Descriptions	Score
7	You referenced three quotes. There was one from Ruth and one from James, and you connected those two characters' words to a thematic "big idea" supported by a third quote.	
5	You referenced two quotes. There was one from either Ruth or James, and you connected that person's words to a thematic "big idea" supported by a second quote.	
3	You referenced two quotes. There was one from Ruth and one from James. You didn't connect either of them to a thematic "big idea."	
1	You referenced only one quote. You didn't connect it to a thematic "big idea."	
Pts	**Sophistication – Scoring Descriptions**	**Score**
1	You spoke without announcing your transitions; it feels like we're having a conversation, in that you are anticipating what I might be wondering. You speak with fluency, and there's a flow to your response that makes sense.	
0	You announced your transitions, so that it felt like you were speaking in bullet points. It might have sounded something like this: "Ruth said *x*, and James said *y*, and that connects to the big idea *z*."	
Pts	**Presentation – Scoring Descriptions**	**Score**
2	You sound well-prepared and confident, with no awkward fumbling.	
1	You messed up some of the key details of the book, which made me wonder whether you read it closely, or the flow sounded awkward or illogical.	
0	You really, like.... took your time to say what you meant, or whatever... and it was, like... cringey for me, like, to listen to, umm... because I was like, "I don't think they know what they're talking about!")	

A Sort-of First Timer's Reflection (Whitney)

The Color of Water (McBride, 1995) is a student favorite. It's approachable and relatable, and many of the chapters are episodic in nature, lending themselves easily to one lesson and helping us move toward an understanding of the book as a whole. Its approachability is tricky for students, though: Because it doesn't feel like they're doing complicated reading, they can be deceived into a false sense of security in two ways. First, they may decide to simply not read it, or to skim it. Second, they may think that if it feels easy to read, it must be easy to ace the test at the end of the unit.

When it came time for a final assessment of students' reading in the spring of 2021, I knew an ORA would be the best fit. I had experimented with it in the spring of 2020 to great success, although many of my students were not attending class at all during this time due to my school's pandemic learning policy. So, I was anxious to see how that experience translated into a larger setting with stricter grading norms. Since pandemic learning continued, about two-thirds of my class were taking it digitally at this time, which meant that the students in my classroom and I connected live with the online students via Zoom. Although both sections of my class made good use of the native chat feature on that app, I knew that the students also had a group text thread, and most of the students were members of it. So, of course, I spent a lot of time that year making my assessments "uncheatable." Gone were the multiple choice tests with which we'd all grown familiar. Cheating on an essay was, at least, a little tougher–sure, students could Google, but I could, too. And it was usually not very hard to pick up on writing from two different students that sounded too similar. It only took a few revelations of plagiarism for me to thrash that idea out of them. Then, the common refrain at the beginning of each unit became, "Ugh, do we have to write an essay about this, too?" When I assigned students the ORA, I knew I could answer, "No!"

I designed an assessment that asked students to pick quotes from *The Color of Water* from a quote bank and to trace those quotes throughout the book. How did the characters speak to that idea? How did the narrative develop it? How did the author, James McBride, make his position clear? For full credit, students had to trace three quotes, one from each bank, connecting them to the characters and to one of the book's "big ideas," or themes. Because I was concerned that students would video themselves saying things like, "I picked quote number three because…", I asked them to work on transitioning between quotes without announcing themselves doing so. I found it helpful to film myself on Flip presenting an exemplar which was then marked public within the class, so that we could all watch it as many times as needed. The ability to re-watch filmed instructions is a perk of Flip that cannot be overstated.

When I introduced the assignment, students seemed satisfied with it, happy to not be writing another essay, if a bit hesitant to film themselves talking about a book. They asked thoughtful questions, mostly having to do with the particulars: how many points the assessment would weigh, is this a good example of a transition, can I do extra quotes from Ruth but skip James, and so on. I added some "dos and don'ts" to my assignment handout in addition to the rubric to quell students' anxieties and to make the assignment a bit clearer, as this was the first oral assessment many of my students had ever taken. And with that, we were off. Students used instructional time in class for a few days, consulting me as they gathered evidence and pondered thematic connections. I gave them plenty of time to film and re-film themselves. They were cheered when I announced that the videos they submitted would be marked private and that others wouldn't be watching them (a decision I made to stymie cheating).

At the end of that week, the videos I received were fairly accurate representations of what students actually knew. The assessment correctly sniffed out who had been reading and who hadn't. I was able to tell who hesitated because their thoughts were moving so quickly and those who hesitated because they inexplicably didn't know the main character's name. I could tell who only read the beginning of the book, which we had read aloud during class time, and who read the whole thing, based on the quotes they chose and the way they knit those ideas together with others. The funny thing is, it's easier to show you an example of what I mean than to tell you–to pull up the video of a student whose body language makes it obvious that they weren't engaging with the reading all along. But that's precisely the idea behind an ORA. Students' body language, verbal flow, eye contact, enunciation, and other factors can help them show us what they understand in many different ways, whereas essays force them to use words to figure out how to best tell us.

DISCUSSION: ASSIGNING ORAS TO STUDENTS

After we assign and discuss the prompt, we give students at least one week to consider, record, and submit their responses. During this time, students are also attending to other lessons: composition, rhetoric, grammatical skill practice, critical readings, etc. If the teacher has written an effective prompt, the majority of the effort and time going into the ORA will originate with the students, rather than teachers. While ORAs take time to review and score, they are much more flexible to grade than traditional assessments. Few other assignments can be faithfully graded while on a walk, for instance. Most importantly, there is nothing to read, as we assess their writing elsewhere.

We use ORAs to directly target students' knowledge and understanding of what we read. By hearing it rather than reading it, we are not distracted by tangential elements to the final product, such as grammar, spelling, or overall neatness of work. At the same time, ORAs give teachers the flexibility to assess students in different areas. Depending on how the prompt is written, an ORA could require students to talk about the book, using close reading skills, while focusing (for example) on parallel structure in their verb choices, thereby incorporating writing and language skills.

Recommendations

When assigning oral response assessments, we recommend having students respond to a single prompt. While we support the idea behind offering a collection of prompts from which students select, evaluating and scoring work responding to a sole prompt will consume less time, affording teachers the ability to provide deeper analysis on each response (Miller et al., 2013). No matter whether students are given only one prompt or a variety from which to select, however, prompts should allow students to make connections with other material from the course and, ideally, beyond it (Bean, 2011). Allowing time and space in class for students to discuss these potential connections will help increase their confidence in their responses overall. Furthermore, pairing oral response assessments that focus on reading and analytical skills with other assessments targeting writing skills increases the merit of student compositions (Bean, 2011).

Before students are asked to record their own responses, they should become familiar with the rubrics and scoring guides which detail the expected performance levels that will be used on their submitted work (Chappuis & Stiggins, 2020). While our own rubrics have evolved, what has remained the same is our decision to give the students the rubric with the prompt and discuss the different categories and descriptions of performance. By being provided with effective modeling and examples of what is expected of them, students feel less anxious about the prospect of oral examinations (Kang et al., 2019).

In addition, students should have multiple opportunities to practice and receive feedback on sample oral responses—those allowing students to learn without having their grade impacted—before they create longer submissions for summative grades (Sparfeldt et al., 2013; Chappuis & Stiggins, 2020).

We also recommend employing prompts that vary in rhetorical situations. If prompts allow students to respond with created scenarios, then students who are developing, proficient, or gifted in analytical reading can incorporate their own creativity into their work (Spencer-Waterman, 2005). For instance, asking students to instruct a hypothetical new reader is a great way to increase the rigor and critical thinking of students in their responses; in doing so, students can feel less anxious about their response as they are explaining their material to an audience who knows much less about the text, rather than writing for their teacher, who is likely to have more experience and understanding of the reading (Bean, 2011). As these assessments are meant to be assigned routinely throughout the course, there are ample occasions to experiment with more creative prompts than other tests, examinations, or essay questions traditionally presented to students.

Our final recommendation is to task students with creating a portfolio of all their recorded performances and reflecting on them at the end of the instructional term. This allows students to better understand their growth as both readers and presenters throughout the course (Spencer-Waterman, 2005; Chappuis & Stiggins, 2020). Portfolios, in the English class and in other subjects, are a way for students to think beyond simple measurements of growth in their abilities, providing them with a place to meaningfully connect and reflect on new learning (Estrem, 2004). Properly constructed portfolio assignments shift the burden of assessment from teacher to student, helping students develop proficiency with valuable skills they will use in other academic and career pursuits (Yaghoubi & Mobin, 2015). Because portfolios are a common tool employed by instructors from entry-level to graduate courses, our students benefit from gaining experience with them before leaving our secondary classrooms (Estrem, 2004). As Flip.com allows videos to be downloaded, our oral response assessments make it easy for students to curate and review their videos at the end of the course. Reviewing cumulative portfolios in final oral response assessments is another way to grant students more control over their learning in our classes (Estrem, 2004).

CONCLUSION

Oral reading assessments created and assessed online harness the power of digital learning but eliminate the dangers of tech, while playing to students' strengths and minimizing the drudgery and hassle of assessment for teachers and students alike. By highlighting the learner's voice, facial expressions, and body language, they ensure that students are personally engaged in the reading process and creating meanings and connections for themselves (Blau, 2003). They enable students to show their teachers what they have learned, rather than rely on their ability to simply tell us about it. And as teachers, we appreciate being able to step away from traditional and emphasized types of assessment. Inauthentic assessment can leave many unsatisfied. For teachers, the amount of time and energy that goes into catering to some assessments, such as standardized testing, convinces some educators to leave the career (Levine et al., 2022).

In our classrooms and online, when we communicate our learning verbally, we add our voices to a cavalcade of learners. We become a learning community. And now, tech tools and the digital landscape are an inescapable part of that community. But snaps disappear; stories expire; tweets get lost in the endless scroll. The internet boasts billions or trillions of bytes of information. Our connections are what we remember—what sticks are the stories we respond to because *hey,* we've been to that same restaurant, the hashtag we follow because *whoa,* we have that hobby too! As such, the modern teacher's quest is to encourage the permanence of knowledge in students' minds, to contribute something just as loud, or louder, than the dull roar of the internet in our students' minds.

A recent study found that assessment prompts like those we use for ORAs focusing on student interpretations and interests in their learning led to the inclusion of more diverse authors and topics on the reading list (Levine et al., 2022). And when we communicate about what we've learned verbally, no matter what it is we are reading, and especially if we can communicate it powerfully by harnessing visual technologies, the knowledge and the experience sticks with us longer. Online ORAs offer teachers and students a new way to connect, to make meaning together, and to form a community where we see *and* hear each other.

REFERENCES

Adèbìsì, F. (2022). Black/African science fiction and the quest for racial justice through legal knowledge: How can we unsettle Euro-modern time and temporality in our teaching? *Law, Technology, and Humans, 4*(2), 24–37. doi:10.5204/lthj.2507

Akimov, A., & Malin, M. (2020). When old becomes new: A case study of oral examination as an online assessment tool. *Assessment & Evaluation in Higher Education, 45*(8), 1205–1221. doi:10.1080/0260 2938.2020.1730301

Bean, J. C. (2011). *The professor's guide to integrating writing, critical thinking, and active learning in the classroom* (2nd ed.). Jossey-Bass.

Blau, S. D. (2003). *The literature workshop: Teaching texts and their readers.* Heinemann.

Brimi, H. M. (2011). Reliability of grading high school work in English. *Practical Assessment, Research & Evaluation, 16*(17), 1–12. doi:10.7275/j531-fz38

Butler, O. E. (1979). *Kindred.* Doubleday.

Chappuis, J., & Stiggins, R. (2020). *Classroom assessment for student learning: Doing it right—using it well.* Pearson.

Darling-Aduana, J. (2021). Development and validation of a measure of authentic online work. *Educational Technology Research and Development, 69*(3), 1729–1752. doi:10.100711423-021-10007-6 PMID:34092984

Estrem, H. (2004). The portfolio's shifting self: Possibilities for assessing student learning. *Pedagogy: Critical approaches to teaching literature, language, culture, and composition, 4*(1), 125-127.

Fisher, D., Frey, N., & Hattie, J. (2020). *The distance learning playbook: Grades K-12.* Corwin.

Flip. (2022). *About Flip.* Flip. https://info.flip.com/about.html

Flip. (2022, June 28). *Introducing Flip.* Flip Product Updates. https://info.flip.com/blog/product-updates/flip-rebrand-features.html

Golden, N. A. (2020). Organizing for meaningful assessment. *English Journal, 109*(6), 16–19.

Harasim, L. (2012). *Learning theory and online technologies.* Routledge. doi:10.4324/9780203846933

Huxham, M., Campbell, F., & Westwood, J. (2012). Oral versus written assessments: A test of student performance and attitudes. *Assessment & Evaluation in Higher Education, 37*(1), 125–136. doi:10.10 80/02602938.2010.515012

Iona, J. (2017). Flipgrid. *School Librarian, 65*(4), 211.

Kai, I. (2011). Space/place and situationality/situatedness of identity: Reading James McBride's *The Color of Water. Journal of General Education Tainan University of Technology, 10*(1), 203–219. doi:10.6780/ JGETUT.201101.0205

Kang, D., Goico, S., Ghanbari, S., Bennallack, K. C., Pontes, T., O'Brien, D. H., & Hargis, J. (2018). Providing an oral examination as an authentic assessment in a large section, undergraduate diversity class. *International Journal for the Scholarship of Teaching and Learning, 13*(2), 1–14. doi:10.20429/ ijsotl.2019.130210

Kesey, K. (1962). *One flew over the cuckoo's nest.* Viking Press.

Kirylo, J. D. (2016). *Teaching with purpose: An inquiry into the who, why, and how we teach.* Rowman & Littlefield.

Kocdar, S., Karadeniz, A., Peytcheva-Forsyth, R., & Stoeva, V. (2018). Cheating and plagiarism in e-assessment: Students' perspectives. *Open Praxis, 10*(3), 221–235. doi:10.5944/openpraxis.10.3.873

Kuhnke, E. (2016). *Body language: Learn how to read others and communicate with confidence.* Capstone.

Lang, J. M. (2013). *Cheating lessons: Learning from academic dishonesty.* Harvard University Press. doi:10.4159/harvard.9780674726239

Levine, S., Moore, D. P., Bene, E., & Smith, M. W. (2022). What if it were otherwise? Teachers use exams from the past to imagine possible futures in the teaching of literature. *Reading Research Quarterly, 58*(1), 5–24. doi:10.1002/rrq.488

Lin, L., Foung, D., & Chen, J. (2022). Assuring online assessment quality: The case of unproctored online assessment. *Quality Assurance in Education, 31*(1), 137–150. doi:10.1108/QAE-02-2022-0048

McBride, J. (1995). *The Color of Water.* Penguin Group.

Miller, M. D., Linn, R. L., & Gronlund, N. E. (2013). *Measurement and assessment in teaching* (11th ed.). Pearson.

Nieveen, N., & Plomp, T. (2018). Curricular and implementation challenges in introducing twenty-first century skills in education. In E. Care, P. Griffin, & M. Wilson (Eds.), *Assessment and teaching of 21st century skills: Research and applications* (pp. 259–276). Springer. doi:10.1007/978-3-319-65368-6_15

Peñarrubia-Lozano, C., Segura-Berges, M., Lizalde-Gil, M., & Bustamante, J. C. (2021). A Qualitative Analysis of Implementing E-Learning During the COVID-19 Lockdown. *Sustainability*, *69*(3317), 1–28. doi:10.3390u13063317

Roblyer, M. D., & Hughes, J. E. (2019). *Integrating educational technology into teaching: Transforming learning across disciplines* (8th ed.). Pearson.

Rutten, K., Roets, G., Soetaert, R., & Roose, R. (2012). The rhetoric of disability: A dramatic-narrative analysis of O*ne flew over the cuckoo's nest. Critical Arts*, *26*(5), 631–647. doi:10.1080/02560046.201 2.744720

Schreck, M. K., Lewandowski, S., Green, J., & Hart, C. A. (1999). What's the best novel you've ever taught? *English Journal*, *89*(2), 30–32. doi:10.2307/822136

Sharon, J. H. K., & Nurlaily, N. (2022). Students' perceptions of vlog as speaking assessment technique at senior high school. *IDEAS: Journal of Language Teaching & Learning. Linguistics and Literature*, *10*(2), 2036–2043. doi:10.24256/ideas.v10i2.3218

Smith, C. H. (2021). The teaching zone: Square pegs in round holes. *Teaching English in the Two-Year College*, *48*(4), 413–435.

Spachuk, K. (2020, February 1). *Charles Miller, co-founder and partner GM of Flipgrid at Microsoft.* The University of British Columbia. https://virtual.educ.ubc.ca/wp/etec522/2020/02/01/charles-miller-co-founder -and-partner-gm-of-flipgrid-at-microsoft/

Sparfeldt, J. R., Rost, D. H., Baumeister, U. M., & Christ, O. (2013). Test anxiety in written and oral examinations. *Learning and Individual Differences*, *24*, 198–203. doi:10.1016/j.lindif.2012.12.010

Spencer-Waterman, S. (2005). *Handbook on differentiated instruction for middle and high schools.* Routledge.

Stripling, M.Y. (2009). Teaching literature and medicine: Ken Kesey's *One flew over the cuckoo's nest. Teaching American Literature: A Journal of Theory and Practice*, *3*(1), 61-68.

Tettenborn, E. (2005). Teaching imagined testimony: *Kindred, Unchained memories*, and the African burial ground in Manhattan. *Transformations*, *16*(2), 87–103.

Theobold, A. S. (2021). Oral exams: A more meaningful assessment of students' understanding. *Journal of Statistics and Data Science Education*, *29*(2), 156–169. doi:10.1080/26939169.2021.1914527

United States Department of Education. (2018). *Average class size in public schools, by class type and state: 2017–18.* [Table]. NCES. https://nces.ed.gov/surveys/ntps/tables/ntps1718_fltable06_t1s.asp

Waterfield, J., & West, B. (2006). *Inclusive assessment in higher education: A resource for change.* University of Plymouth.

Wiggins, G. P., & McTighe, J. (2005). *Understanding by design* (2nd ed.). Pearson.

Williams, J. D. (2003). *Preparing to teach writing: Research, theory, and practice* (3rd ed.). Lawrence Erlbaum Associates. doi:10.4324/9781410607461

Yaghoubi, A., & Mobin, M. (2015). Portfolio assessment, peer assessment and writing skill improvement. *Theory and Practice in Language Studies*, 5(12), 2504–2511. doi:10.17507/tpls.0512.10

Yeon, S. H., & Shepherd, D. (2020). Transform your language instruction with Flipgrid. *Dialog on Language Instruction*, 30(1), 73–76.

APPENDIX

Quote Bank for McBride's *The Color of Water* ORA (Whitney)

Explain as many <u>quotes from Ruth</u> as you need to achieve the grade you want from the list below:

1. "Hurry up and get this interview over with. I want to watch Dallas" (1).
2. "If it doesn't involve you going to school or church, I could care less about it and my answer is no whatever it is" (27).
3. "[My father]'s marriage was a business deal for him. He only wanted money. That and to be an American. Those were the two things he wanted, and he got them too, but it cost him his family, which he ran into the ground and destroyed" (41).
4. "I still know all those verses, but I learned them out of... not out of love for God, but just out of... what? I don't know. Duty. My father was a rabbi, right?" (61-62).
5. "If you throw water on the floor it will always find a hole, believe me" (135).

Explain as many <u>quotes from James</u> as you need to achieve the grade you want from the list below:

1. "The question of race was like the power of the moon in my house. It's what made the river flow, the ocean swell, and the tide rise, but it was a silent power, intractable, indomitable, indisputable... and thus completely ignorable" (94).
2. "[My classmates] went wild, but even as I sat down with their applause ringing in my ears, with laughter on my face, happy to be accepted, to be part of them, knowing I had pleased them, I saw the derision on their faces, the clever smiles, the laughing at the oddity of it, and I felt the same ache I felt when I gazed at the boy in the mirror. I remembered him, and how free he was, and I hated him even more" (105).
3. "I used to look at [Daddy, my stepfather] and wonder, *What is his problem? Doesn't he know how goofy he looks?* But it never seemed to bother him in the least. Race was something he never talked about. To him it was a detail that you stepped over, like a crack in the sidewalk" (125).
4. "My anger at the world had been replaced by burning ambition" (184).
5. "As I stepped onto the bus, she squeezed a bunch of bills and change into my hand. 'It's all I have,' she said. I counted it. Fourteen dollars. 'Thanks, Ma.' I kissed her and got on the bus quickly to hide my own tears. I felt I was abandoning her—she hated Delaware and I had talked her into staying there, and now I was leaving [for college]. Yet she wanted me to go. As I sat down on the bus and looked for her through the window, it occurred to me that since I was a little boy, she had always wanted me to go. She was always sending me off someplace, to elementary school, to camp, to relatives in Kentucky, to college. She pushed me away from her just as she'd pushed my elder siblings away when we lived in New York, literally shoving them out the front door when they left for college. She would not hear of it when they applied to schools that were near home. 'If you stay here, you'll fool around,' she'd say. 'Go away and learn to live on your own.' […] She always cried when they left, though never in front of us" (189-190).
6. "I can clearly remember saying to my black college roommate in my freshman year, 'Racism is a problem that should end just about the time we graduate'" (204).

Explain as many <u>"big ideas"</u> as you need to achieve the grade you want from the list below:

1. "There's such a big difference between being dead and alive, I told myself, and the greatest gift anyone can give anyone else is life. And the greatest sin a person can do to another is to take away that life. Next to that, all the rules and religions in the world are secondary, mere words and beliefs that people choose to believe and kill and hate by" (written by James, p. 229).

2. "Sometimes without conscious realization, our thoughts, our faith, our interests are entered into the past, [my birth father Dennis] wrote. We talk about other times, other places, other persons, and lose our living hold on the present. Sometimes we think if we could just go back in time, we would be happy. But anyone who attempts to reenter the past is sure to be disappointed. Anyone who has ever revisited the place of his birth after years of absence is shocked by the differences between the way the place actually is, and the way he has remembered it. He may walk along old familiar streets and roads, but he is a stranger in a strange land. He has thought of this place as home, but he finds he is no longer here even in spirit. He has gone on to a new and different life, and in thinking longingly of the past, he has been giving thought and interest to something that no longer really exists. This being true of the physical self, how much more true it is of the spiritual self" (written by Dennis, p. 250).

3. "Her photos are horrible, heads cut off, pictures of nothing, a table, a hand, a chair. Still, she shoots pictures of any even that's important to her, knowing that each memory is too important to lose, having lost so many before" (written by James about Ruth, p. 283).

4. "I realized then that whoever had said kaddish for Mommy—the Jewish prayer of mourning, the declaration of death, the ritual that absolves them of responsibility for the child's fate—had done the right thing, because Mommy was truly gone from their world. In her mind, she was a guest here. 'I don't have this left in me anymore,' she remarked at one point" (written by James about Ruth, p. 284).

5. "While she never sought to capitalize on the fame engendered by the best-selling book, she got to meet a number of prominent people, including former President George H.W. Bush and his wife, Barbara. Ruth and her son James spent a couple of days with the Bushes at their Houston home and the Bush Library in 1990, and the two families exchanged notes for years afterward. When she and her son left Houston, Barbara Bush told James, 'Your mother is my hero.' James, who is the author of other books, is a well-regarded musician, bandleader, composer and screenwriter. Another son, Dr. Andrew Dennis McBride, director of health for the city of Milford, Conn., told a story that reflected his mother's down-to-earth nature: When the Bushes showed off their indoor swimming pool and bragged that Barbara used it every day, Ruth asked, 'What do you do about your hair?' 'Oh, that is a problem,' Barbara Bush acknowledged" (written by John Morrison of the Philadelphia Daily News, in Ruth's obituary).

Chapter 6
Improving the Key Competences in K12 by Collaborating in an Active Learning Environment Online

Lamia Büşra Yeşil
The Ministry of National Education, Turkey

ABSTRACT

The purpose of this action research is to transform the quality of teaching decisions and actions by adopting an active learning approach. The implementation was carried out as an eTwinning project for eight months in the 2021-2022 educational year with the first and second-grade 28 students in primary schools, aged six to nine, in Germany, Greece, and Turkey. Action research data collection techniques were used such as experiencing (by observing), enquiring (by asking), and examining (by using records of the poll questions answered by the pupils) and the results were reported with descriptive analysis. Learning was enriched with an emphasis on collaborative teaching and learning, active participation, and decision-making of learners. Learning methodologies such as inquiry-based, project-based, blended, and game-based learning increased learning motivation and engagement. Science, technology, engineering, and mathematics (STEM) helped foster the development of a range of competencies. Digital technologies contributed to capturing the multiple dimensions of learner progression.

INTRODUCTION

Throughout some parts of teaching careers, pedagogy was generally done by standing at the top of the class and 'talking at' the children. That was what we thought teaching was all about. When thinking about how to reshape our teaching practices, has brought us the notion of replacing ourselves from being a sage on the stage to being a guide on the side (King, 1993). As is stated in the famous quote of Trenfor, "The best teachers are those who show you where to look but don't tell you what to see." That is why teachers want to improve their teaching practice and subsequently student learning. The chalkboard, pencil, and

DOI: 10.4018/978-1-6684-7015-2.ch006

paper tasks and direct instruction do not make any interest to the students anymore in the digital era we live in. Teachers need to reshape their school practice for themselves with a lot of student engagement. Therefore, it is believed that the way to change student learning is to change instructional practice, and the researchers in this paper plan to use collaborative scenarios to make students attend the lesson and learn effectively as international teams. Through school projects that can be carried out online, it is possible to work in pairs not only with the ones sitting next to them but also with pairs living abroad.

Two researchers of this paper with the same ambitions and intentions met online on the eTwinning platform and designed an international school project. One more teacher from another country joined as well and they started a digital learning and collaboration journey together which is explained soon in detail. The main purpose of this project is to transform the quality of teaching decisions and actions to enhance student engagement and learning by adapting an active learning approach.

Every year eTwinning platform announces a theme for teachers to work together. Teachers and students are invited by eTwinning to reinvent their schools and consider the components that make their learning environment attractive and sustainable in 2022. "Our future beautiful, sustainable, together: Schools and the New European Bauhaus" is the campaign's recurring theme for the year (European School Education Platform, 2022). To achieve it, the researchers decided to design collaborative scenarios on the themes of sustainability, first aid, and children's rights along with tech integration in the project they have created. Discussions, problem-solving, case studies, role plays, and other methods are used actively to engage students with course material in an active learning environment.

The way to change student learning is to change instructional practice. Instead of giving children language skills tasks such as reading aloud assignments or filling the blanks according to what you hear type listening activities, the objective was to link the main courses with other disciplines and assess the effect of the designed activities on key competences for lifelong learning. The research questions are as follows:

1) How can we reshape our school practice with a lot of student engagement?
2) What is the impact of setting up collaborative scenarios via eTwinning on our students' learning in class? Does technology help to achieve it?
3) What is the effect of collaboration on the key competences for lifelong learning?

BACKGROUND

What is eTwinning?

Initiated in 2005 as the primary intervention of the eLearning Program of the European Commission, eTwinning has been co-funded since 2014 by the European Education, Training, Youth and Sports Program Erasmus+. European Schoolnet, an international partnership of 34 European Ministries of Education, operates as its Central Support Service to develop learning for schools, educators, and students throughout Europe. 38 National Support Services further support eTwinning at the domestic level (Etwinning.net, 2019).

eTwinning is the virtual place where active learning meets with technology. Effective use of technology in online learning environments may result in more interaction between teachers and students, as well as more collaboration among students (Bower, 2019; Gonzalez et al., 2020; Ku et al., 2013). Blasco-Arcas et al. (2013) report a positive association between students" interaction and active learning, which also results in higher learning performance. The platform allows students to engage in meaningful creative activities and explore their potential via international group works and innovative pedagogies.

It is a journey that can be used for building a transformative and collaborative knowledge culture. Students, teachers, and administrators learn from each other. Collaborative creativity among teachers is also essential for designing and implementing new learning environments and pedagogies as a way to respond to contemporary learning requirements and societal needs (Richardson, 2020). By participating in eTwinning, schools can enrich the learning and motivation of pupils and staff. Moreover, it provides professional development opportunities through learning events, webinars, and annual teacher workshops (Yeşil, 2020).

One of the participating classes in this project is in Germany and the founder teacher of the project delivers the native language lessons in Germany which are voluntarily taken by the bilingual kids. Students stay at the school after their daily schedule ends and they attend the language course for two hours once a week. There are some mixed-group classes that contain students from different grades. Formative assessment is used during the year. The course teacher wants her students to take responsibility for their own learning and engage them with tasks along with improving their 21st-century skills and key competences for lifelong learning so that they can become active agents during the lesson.

The other participating class in this project is in Greece and the founder teacher delivers the courses provided by the Greek syllabus for first graders. These are Greek language, Mathematics, Environmental Studies, and Skills Labs (a new course, added in September 2021 to the syllabus). In first grade in Greece, students' assessment is formative and descriptive. The course material could be more attractive to pupils and the teaching methods have to be renewed. So, researchers tried to renovate their teaching through the project described below, for their students to develop skills that are difficult to evolve through traditional teaching and traditional courses.

Before designing this sample project, the founder teachers had created different projects and worked together in previous years. While they continued to process their own course curriculum with their own students, they also worked to enrich the educational environment with school projects as they were technologically competent. No support was received from the school administration for these projects, and the projects were designed and carried out entirely by the free administration of the teachers.

What Is Active Learning?

As stated in Fitzsimon (2014), active learning is said to provide students with the key skills that employers look into. Aligning competency-based education with eTwinning, the aim is to give each student an equal opportunity to master necessary skills and become successful adults. Active learning, according to Bonwell and Eison (1991), is any learning technique that involves "students doing things and thinking about what they are doing." (p. 2). As suggested by Barkley (2010) and Prince (2004); small group discussion, peer questioning, cooperative learning, problem-based learning, simulations, journal writing, and case-study teaching are some of the instructional techniques that promote active learning, as well.

A variety of active learning instructional strategies and pedagogies are implemented in this research. Students engage the material they study through reading, writing, talking, listening, reflecting, creating, communicating, collaborating, and interacting with each other with the use of technology. Active learning changes the learner's role from that of a passive receiver to that of a 'maker,' which improves the learner's focus and attention, interpersonal communication skills, motivation for critical thinking skills, learner inventiveness, and many other factors, all of which help everyone achieve the course objectives (Habib, 2017).

What Are the Key Competencies of Lifelong Learning?

Key competences are defined as a combination of knowledge, skills, and attitudes (European Commission, 2018). According to "The Reference Framework" as shown in Figure 1 below, there are eight key competences: Literacy competence, Multilingual competence, Mathematical competence and competence in science, technology, and engineering, Digital competence, Personal, social, and learning to learn competence, Citizenship competence, Entrepreneurship competence, Cultural awareness and expression competence (The Council Of The European Union, 2018).

Figure 1. Key Competences by European Commission

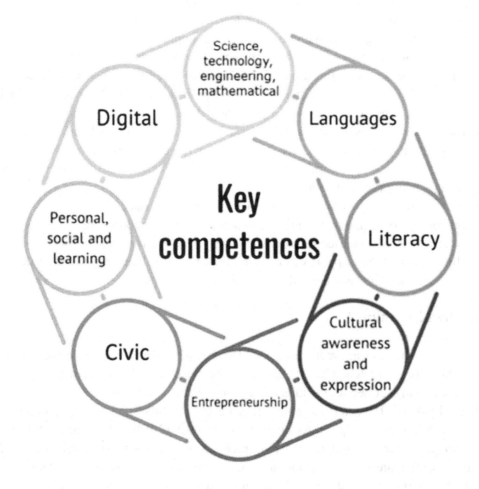

The key competences are all considered equally important; each of them contributes to a successful life in society. Key competences are those that all individuals need for personal fulfillment and development, employability, social inclusion, sustainable lifestyle, successful life in peaceful societies, health-conscious life management, and active citizenship. They are developed in a lifelong learning perspective, from early childhood throughout adult life, and through formal, non-formal, and informal learning in all contexts, including family, school, workplace, neighborhood, and other communities. In this school project, activities are designed in the beginning considering one of the key competences. Here is the explanation of what to understand from each of the headlines:

- **Literacy Competence**

Literacy competence involved the knowledge of reading and writing and a sound understanding of written information and thus required an individual to know vocabulary, functional grammar, and the functions of language. It also implied the ability to communicate and connect effectively with others, appropriately and creatively (European Commission, 2018).

- **Languages Competences**

Language competences integrated a historical dimension and intercultural competences. It relied on the ability to mediate between different languages and media, as outlined in the Common European Framework of Reference (2018). As appropriate, it could include maintaining and further developing mother tongue competences, as well as the acquisition of a country's official language(s).

- **Mathematical Competence and Competence in Science, Technology, and Engineering**

Mathematical competence was the ability to develop and apply mathematical thinking and insight in order to solve a range of problems in everyday situations (European Commission, 2018). Competence in science referred to the ability and willingness to explain the natural world by making use of the body of knowledge and methodology employed, including observation and experimentation, in order to identify questions and draw evidence-based conclusions (European Commission, 2018). Competence in science, technology, and engineering involved an understanding of the changes caused by human activity and responsibility as an individual citizen. It also included the ability to use and handle technological tools and machines as well as scientific data to achieve a goal or to reach an evidence-based decision or conclusion (European Commission, 2018). Competence included an attitude of critical appreciation and curiosity, a concern for ethical issues, and support for both safety and environmental sustainability, in particular as regards scientific and technological progress concerning oneself, family, community, and global issues

- **Digital Competence**

Digital competence involved the confident, critical, and responsible use of, and engagement with, digital technologies for learning and participation in society. It included information and data literacy, communication and collaboration, media literacy, digital content creation (including programming), safety (including digital well-being and competences related to cybersecurity), intellectual property-related questions, problem-solving and critical thinking (European Commission, 2018).

- **Personal, Social, and Learning to Learn Competence**

Personal, social, and learning to learn competence was the ability to reflect upon oneself, effectively manage time and information, constructively work with others, remain resilient, and manage one's own learning and career. It included learning to learn by knowing one's preferred learning strategies, knowing one's competence development needs, and various ways to develop competences (European Commission, 2018). For successful interpersonal relations and social participation, it was essential to understand the codes of conduct and rules of communication generally accepted in different societies and environments.

- **Citizenship competence**

Citizenship competence was the ability to act as responsible citizens and to fully participate in civic and social life, based on an understanding of social, economic, legal, and political concepts and structures, as well as global developments and sustainability (European Commission, 2018).

- **Entrepreneurship competence**

Entrepreneurship competence refers to the capacity to act upon opportunities and ideas and to transform them into values for others. It was founded upon creativity, critical thinking and problem solving, taking initiative and perseverance, and the ability to work collaboratively in order to plan and manage projects that were of cultural, social, or financial value (European Commission, 2018).

- **Competence in cultural awareness and expression**

Competence in cultural awareness and expression involved having an understanding of and respect for how ideas and meaning were creatively expressed and communicated in different cultures and through a range of arts and other cultural forms. It involved being engaged in understanding, developing, and expressing one's own ideas and sense of place or role in society in a variety of ways and contexts (European Commission, 2018).

THE PROJECT'S METHODOLOGY

In this action research project, the implementation was carried out as an eTwinning project for eight months in the 2021-2022 Educational Year with the first and second-grade 28 students in primary schools, aged 6 to 9, in Germany, Greece, and Turkey. The project was designed as part of formal school and classroom planning and implemented the activities once a week. The curriculum objectives and content were incorporated into the project work and activities, as well. The research project was divided into three main modules. To achieve a sustainable New European Bauhaus, it was emphasized natural resources, recycling, and reducing litter in the first module. In the second module, kids were taught how to provide first aid to a human being. In the last module, kids defended human rights by using some drawings and singing as a form of art to express themselves. Each theme was chosen according to the curriculum by considering the key competences, as well. Collaborative teaching and learning online were emphasized as well as active participation, and the decision-making of learners. All the material used was either copyright free or the source was acknowledged in terms of e-safety issues.

Implementation Process

The project started in October 2021. In September, teachers in Greece and Germany met online to collect materials and organized the project's possible schedule. In October, students started taking part in warm-up activities such as avatar creation and introducing themselves by recording their voices. A mobile app "Gradient" was used to create a cartoon-like image based on a real photo. Students took a selfie and the app transformed them into a cartoon.

Then, these photos were used in the "Chatterpix" app to make a short voice recording. Pupils introduced themselves in a minute so that we could appsmasch by combining two different content in the final product. All the videos that were created by the students were uploaded in a Padlet so that national country teams could view and comment on them.

Next, project logo options were created with the tool "Canva" and pupils voted for the best choice online. The project mascot was voted to catch student interest and a kick-off meeting was organized to meet with all project students. During the meeting, countries played a digital game about the countries' geography. The game was prepared by teachers using the questions about countries in the forum, written by the kids. As a final output of warm-up activities, a collaborative countries video was created and shared with the pupils in the class.

Figure 2. Module 1

MODULE 1	SPECIFIC OBJECTIVES	ASSESMENT CRITERIA	ASSESSMENT TYPES	ACTIVITIES	COMPETENCES	AREAS
KIDS SAVE THE ENVIRONMENT	-To identify natural resources. -To understand how natural resources are used. -To explain why people can conserve and protect natural resources by reducing, reusing and recycling. -Recognize of life.	-To analyze real situation. -To plan strategies and ideas to favour the improvement in environment. -Self determination, self regulation. (Personal Awareness and Responsibility)	1. Formative Assessment 2. Authentic Assessment: The task that students are ultimately completing have real world applicability. 3.Digital Content Assessment	-Natural Resources Lesson Online -Presentation of our countries' recycle bins -Recycling games together online -Online meeting for the European Week for Waste Reduction and Kahoot quiz solving.	Competence in Linguistic Communication. (CLC)	Arts&Crafts Social science Language ICT Environmental Education •
	- To reflect on the resources allocated to environmental protection	-Reflect, Collaborate to carry out and review (Communication)		-Recycle challenge where partners have to complete tasks -Sending recycle messages	Digital Competence (DC)	
	-Raising awareness of children on issues of vital importance, concerning both our man-made and natural environment and the protection of our planet.	-Develop and design, analyze and critique, question and investigate (Critical Thinking)		-Collaborative scenario creation for transnational pairs and collaborative presentation on reducing litter.	Learning to Learn. (L2L)	
	-To promote the search for problem search or possibilities of improvement.	Contributing the community and caring for environment. (Social Responsibility)		-Collaborative ecology game	Social and Civic Competences. (SCC)	
	To be aware of possible issues of burdening the environment in the wider school and town area.				Sense of Initiative and Entrepreneurship. (SIE)	
COMPETENCES		(CLC).(DC).(L2L).(SCC).(SIE)				
RESOURCES		Digital websites, presentation game by the Greek recycling Organisation, smart appliances' applications				
SOCIAL AGENTS		Humanitarian Organisation	Greek Recycling Organisation provides a ppt game (which we tranform to play online altogether). The organisation will be part of the European Week for Waste Reduction.			
COLLABORATIVE PRODUCTS		Recycle bins presentation, Natural Resources Lesson, Iconic Supermarket Video, Ecology Game, EWWR Kahoot, Recycling Challenge.				

As shown in Figure 2 above, the first selected topic was the environment and sustainability. The first module started with an online collaborative lesson about Natural Resources in which all students responded and contributed using technological devices during a videoconference. Students had to brainstorm, watch content, circle the correct option about it, draw together, solve a quiz together, and even use VR (virtual reality) to check out some landscapes. The perfect tool for this kind of collaborative activity is "Nearpod". It was amazing for pupils to be able to see simultaneously what the other country was working on online. Students played together online recycling games at the next meeting which were simply created in Powerpoint but answered altogether during the Zoom conference.

As part of this project work, a video was created together about environmental messages. The countries proposed to each other online recycling games to play in the classroom. Some collaboration tools were preferred to organize the scenario of an iconic supermarket which was another collaborative product where the students talked with each other to show which was the product that produced less litter. A design and collaboration were created in such a way that a student from Greece, who wanted to buy wooden toys, would be responded to by a student from Germany.

The project products created by one school were integrated with the project products of the other partner school. In this way, all recorded videos had a mission to complete the other partner's tasks. The final videos were combined in the tool "Canva" again collaboratively so that the workload was divided equally among project teachers. While working on the theme of sustainability pupils managed to act in the same video. As the last activity for this module, the researchers created a scavenger hunt game about ecology in which all partners participated and used technology as an assessment tool.

Figure 3. Module 2

MODULE 2	SPECIFIC OBJECTIVES	ASSESSMENT CRITERIA	ASSESSMENT TYPES	ACTIVITIES	COMPETENCES	AREAS
KIDS SAVE A HUMAN LIFE	-To be better prepared and more confident in situations that may require first aid. -To identify any first aid skills you already have. -To learn about and practice the recovery position. -To become more aware of the contents and uses of a First Aid Kit. -To identify common items found in a First Aid Kit by working in national groups. -To understand why it's important to keep a first aid kit and to make it accessible. -To teach integrated STEM education. -To become comfortable with iteration and learn from failure. -To be exposed to and learn about the jobs of the future. -Understand the need to follow certain rules for dealing with emergencies	-To make questions about general interesting topics which important for children. -Generating ideas, Developing ideas (Creative Thinking) -Connect and engage with others. (Communication) -Question and Investigate (Critical Thinking) -Well being, self determination, self regulation (Personal Awareness and Responsibility)	1. Formative Assessment 2. Authentic Assessment: The task that students are ultimately completing have real world applicability such as first aid scenario. 3.Digital Content Assessm	-First Aid model creation -Playing CPR games online -Live meeting in order to demonstrate the defibrillator and group CPR with our handmade first aid models. -Watch2gether a video of the CPR procedure and discuss the steps in the chat. -Practice the recovery position. -Collaborate online with Greek humanitarian organization "Kids Save Lives". -Creation of a collaborative multilingual first aid manual with audio recordings about CPR. -Forming transnational teams and write a scenario together. -Shooting five short movies about CPR for teams. -First aid kits presentation and games. -Robot scenarios and filming -Reflections with KWL Chart and Slido.	Competence in Linguistic Communication. (CLC) Competence in Mathematics, Science and Technology. (CMST) Digital Competence (DC) Learning to Learn. (L2L) Social and Civic Competences. (SCC) Sense of Initiative and Entrepreneurship. (SIE)	Language Social Science Values Art&crafts Robotics
COMPETENCES	(CLC), (CMST), (DC), (L2L), (SCC), (SIE)					
RESOURCES	Digital websites.					
SOCIAL AGENTS	Greek Humanitarian Organisation:					
COLLABORATIVE PRODUCT	First Aid Multilingual Audio Guide, First Aid Kits Presentation, First Aid Movies as transnational teams (5 movies)					

As shown in Figure 3 above, the second selected topic was first aid. The countries helped each other to understand the steps of CPR watching together and analyzing a relevant video. The tool named "Watch-2gether" let different people work on the same content with the chat function. Kids demonstrated to their partners what they already knew for them to learn (defibrillator demonstration, peer-to-peer learning). Most of the activities were experiential, so children learned during the activity. The Greek Recycling Company provided educational materials and the Greek humanitarian organization provided CPR mannequins and an educational defibrillator. The classes also had a Zoom video conference meeting with them to attend a CPR scenario together.

Partner students created questions and implemented them in a Flipgrid session. Flipgrid was a tool in which different people could work on the same subject via recording short videos. All responses were collected in a virtual class. All teams answered their partners' questions using this tool. The tool had the QR code option for the answers. When demonstrated in class, even parents could see the videos by scanning the QR codes with their mobile phones. Pupils also reviewed partners' answers using these QR codes which were the outputs of the Flipgrid.

For this module, partner schools created a collaborative multilingual first aid manual where students contributed photos, videos, and voice recordings by using the tool "Genial.ly". Genial.ly web tool had the option to work collaboratively online and add as many materials as possible such as photos, videos, etc. with beautiful templates liked by the kids. Short movie scenarios were created and students were assigned certain scenes. Five transnational teams were created to achieve this task. Each team's scenes were composed of a short movie in which children of all countries participated. A collaborative presentation was created to show the first aid school kits and simple games created for the students to play containing pictures of different first aid kits in schools. Finally, each team assigned a scenario to the other in order to execute it with their educational robot set. The majority of the activities were collaborative, using collaborative ICT tools. Students had the opportunity to reflect and share their opinions after each activity.

As shown in Figure 4 above, the last selected topic was human rights. In the last module, each team selected some rights from the Convention on the Rights of the Child (United Nations, 1989). The students drew them, and then all teams uploaded their drawings on a Wakelet board and they guessed what rights were depicted in each drawing. During a videoconference, kids drew the rights online and created a flashcard set with an international partner. Peardeck's Flashcard Factory tool was used for this activity. Each student took part in a different transnational team and it was one of their favorite activity. Next, kids sang a song about the rights, and a video clip was created in which all pupils were shown singing in a common video. Students used the app called "Animaze". As one of the final outputs of the topic, the students created avatar animations and recorded themselves speaking to the partner schools about the rights they had. Students managed to speak Greek, German and Turkish to create a video, and students managed to learn what needed to be taught by creating a product rather than reading loud alone and later memorizing the sentences for an exam.

Figure 4. Module 3

MODULE 3	SPECIFIC OBJECTIVES	ASSESMENT CRITERIA	ASSESSMENT TYPES	ACTIVITIES	COMPETENCES	AREAS
KIDS DEFEND HUMAN RIGHTS	-Recognize that every child has rights and understand why there is a need for children's rights -Identify some children's rights -Understand that some children do not enjoy the same rights	-Come up with plans and take action to support children's rights. -Valuing diversity. (Social Responsibility) -Collaborate, carry out, and review (Communication) -Develop and design (Critical thinking) -Relationships and cultural context (Positive personal and cultural identity.)	1. Formative Assessment 2. Authentic Assessment: The task that students are ultimately completing have real world applicability. 3.Digital Content Assessm	-The rights of the children presentation and drawings. The other teams had to guess what right is depicted. - Creation of a flashcard set along with that right's number according to the convention of UNESCO. -A common singing video about the Rights of A Child with a certain division of work. -A common rights video in which students talk the language of their partners about the rights they have. -Module 3 Reflections	Competence in Linguistic Communication. (CLC) Multilingual Competence (MC) Digital Competence (DC) Citizenship Competence (CC) Entrepreneurship Competence (EC) Cultural Awareness and Expression Competence (CAEC)	Language Social Studies Language Art Values Art&crafts
COMPETENCES	(CLC), (MC),(DC), (CC), (EC), (CAEC)					
RESOURCES	Digital websites.					
SOCIAL AGENTS				My Rights Song		
COLLABORATIVE PRODUCT	Common Rights Video, Common Singing Video, Flashcard Set.					

DATA COLLECTION

Action research data collection techniques were used in this research such as experiencing (by observing), enquiring (by asking), and examining (by using records of the poll questions answered by the pupils). Observation and informal interviews, audio and video recordings, and photographs were taken during the activities. Students' reflections, preferences, and satisfaction with the project activities were all considered effective outcomes. Students' self-reports of whether they learned during active learning teaching were also included in the teacher reports. Formative assessment, authentic assessment in which the task that students were ultimately completing had real-world applicability such as first aid scenario and digital content assessment was implemented. This action research used mixed methods of qualitative and quantitative data in different modules of the project and the results were reported with descriptive analysis. Quantitative data included predetermined questions and assessments of work, completed by the teachers.

Here are the tools which were used in Module 1. Data Tool 1: Nearpod. The tool was used to make a collaborative online session. Data Tool 2: Wakelet. The web tool was used to collect the impressions on Natural Resources live lesson. Data Tool 3: Answergarden. The tool was used to spot the most commonly liked object for future messages. Data Tool 4: Twinboard. The tool was used to collect reflections about the final iconic supermarket activity. Data Tool 5: Goosechase. The tool was used to create a collaborative ecology game and the results were collected during the treasure hunt game. In this treasure hunt game students created and attended online about ecology, the questions and missions were suggested by the kids. Data Tool 5: Google Forms. To evaluate Module 1, the students used a Google form survey where they expressed their preferences by selecting the appropriate emoji. Students chose from the options: I liked it a lot ! 💝 / I liked it! 😊 / Not so sure 😕.

In Module 2, different tools were used to collect data. Data Tool 1: KWL Chart. One of the active learning techniques was called the KWL chart in which students reflected on what they already knew about the subject in the beginning, what they wanted to learn during the process, and what they learned at the end of the module. Data Tool 2: Pre-test and post-test about "how confident they feel about dealing with an emergency?" Data Tool 3: Twinboard Reflection for the First Aid Game. Data Tool 4: Twinboard Reflection for the Greek Humanitarian Organization. Data Tool 5: Twinboard Reflection: For the First Aid Quiz Games. Data Tool 6: Twinboard Reflection for the Robot Movies. Data Tool 7: Flipgrid. Data Collection Tool 8: Slido. The survey tool was used to spot the favorite activities by a ranking poll.

In Module 3, students defended the children's rights and they took action by creating common videos talking in the language of the partner countries. Data Tool 1: Google Sheets. The chart was used to exchange information about the foreign language and for the decision of sentences. Data Tool 2: Peardeck. Flashcard Factory Tool. Data Tool 3: Twinboard. Overall reflections were collected. Data Tool 4: Getacquainted. Five questions were asked to the students to get all-inclusive feedback about the whole project.

DATA ANALYSIS

- **Module 1**

According to the starter poll in Module 1, 75% know a little about Natural Resources. During the session, students joined many different activities such as drawing a line matching the natural resource to the item people make from it and matching the waste to the problem it causes. Student groups drew a line from each item to the correct recycling box. They had a chance to discuss together how to reduce the use of natural resources in their homes. Activities were completed successfully. When asked about how they feel about their ability to explain ways to conserve and protect natural resources, students 50% responded as very confident. It was observed that students both actively engaged in the lesson and loved the process of being part of an international team.

Data Tool 2: Some impressions written on Wakelet were as follows:

Student A: "Most people around me seem to be unaware of recycling. Thanks to these lessons, I learn that recycling is very important. We need to teach them too".

Student B: "I like this subject and I learn many things about what natural resources are. I like painting together".

Student C: "Our lesson is very enjoyable. I like making video conference and playing with partner schools".

Student D: "I like giving votes, painting, and VR. It is great to have lessons at the same time with other countries".

Student E: "We have to protect our natural resources! What an amazing lesson!"

According to the poll, implemented by using Answergarden, students chose the items among the ones in which they personified some objects and recorded voice messages by using their facial expressions. Plastic bottles, batteries, TV, bins, papers, a pencil case, a lamp, and different boxes were chosen by the kids. Following were some sample sentences recorded by the students on the app "Earthspeakr:

"Make our planet a cleaner place to live".

"Please don't forget to put me in the recycling bin after you finish drinking me".

"We can't protect our planet without recycling".

According to the reflections written by the students about the iconic supermarket activity, here were some student responses:

"I realized how much rubbish we make when we shop!".

"It was a very useful activity! From now on I'll shop only for environmentally friendly products!".

"I love playing both the customer role and the sales officer role. We make practice before recordings and I like this activity a lot".

In the treasure hunt activity, students created and attended the online game about ecology by using their devices. The kids completed missions and answered questions such as "Take a video of your team saying the word "recycling" in your language"; "The batteries cannot be recycled. Right or wrong?"; "Take a photo of a recycle bin in your school!"; "Write something that cannot be recycled"; Say "protect our forests" in your language." Students responded by taking videos, photos, and some thumbs-up/down reactions. This final activity of Module 1, it was aimed to elaborate the lesson with some outside activities, underlining the importance of natural resources and recycling. By adding some gamification elements such as time, points, and achievement tasks to the inquiry-based learning design, kids extremely enjoyed involving in the process and they actively took part in their learning process. Game tasks engaged students by making real-world connections through exploration and high-level questioning. It was the students' responsibility to solve the tasks and they successfully managed to work together as a team. Natural elements such as trees, pine cones, and flowers were the main focus and it was emphasized as a vision to protect and preserve these elements. By carrying out this activity, the students practiced their multilingual and digital competence, the personal, social, and partners that they actually could do for the environment, and realized that protecting nature was achievable. The questions also served as a consolidation and evaluation tool of the previous activities. The points, the photos, and the students' curiosity to see their partners' answers were powerful motives in order to complete the activity. Students learned, consolidated, evaluated themselves, shared, and had fun, all at the same time.

According to the Google Forms Report, "Earthspeakr Videos" was the favorite activity of the module with 84,6% of the students replying "I liked it a lot!" along with the activity "Creating talking avatars & TwinSpace profiles with text and drawings" and the rest of the students selecting "I liked it!"."Goosechase-Collaborative Ecology Game" took the second place with 80,8% replying they liked it a lot!.

Figure 5. Survey Results for Module 1

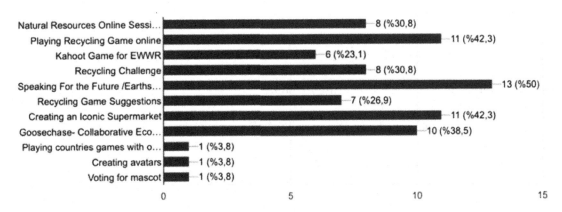

Which activity is your favorite?

26 yanıt

Natural Resources Online Sessi...	8 (%30,8)
Playing Recycling Game online	11 (%42,3)
Kahoot Game for EWWR	6 (%23,1)
Recycling Challenge	8 (%30,8)
Speaking For the Future /Earths...	13 (%50)
Recycling Game Suggestions	7 (%26,9)
Creating an Iconic Supermarket	11 (%42,3)
Goosechase- Collaborative Eco...	10 (%38,5)
Playing countries games with o...	1 (%3,8)
Creating avatars	1 (%3,8)
Voting for mascot	1 (%3,8)

As shown in Figure 5, the results indicated that students liked the Earthspeakr activity the most in which they actively took part in the decision-making processes and created final products. The second one was the playing recycling game online activity in which students met online during a videoconference and actively played with partner countries. The third one was an iconic supermarket in which the kids worked together with an international pair.

- **Module 2**

According to the KWL Chart used in Module 2, at first, students reflected on their ideas about what they already knew about first aid. Here were some sample answers about the current situation:

"The ambulance arrives to save a patient".

"The doctors save lives".

"Teachers know some things about first aid and they can help us when we need it".

"Only adults know about first aid".

"I know that we call 166 for the ambulance to arrive".

"If one of our friends falls and hurts her knees, we use the first aid kit in our classroom and help her before her mom comes to pick her up".

"In our school, we sometimes fall and get injured. The teachers on duty help us use the materials in the first aid cabinet".

In the beginning, it was also asked what they want to learn. Here were some sample questions:

"We are children, can we do first aid?"

"Which number should we dial to call an ambulance?"

"I haven't heard about a defibrillator. What is it?"

"Does it hurt the injured person while giving first aid?"

"What should we do to find out whether the injured is alive or not?"

"How can I help someone who is not breathing?"

"What is in the school's first aid kit?"

As understood from the raised questions above, the students were eager to take action for saving someone's life and wanted to take an active part in our selected topic by heart. In the end, their opinions were collected again about what they learned at the end of this module. Here were some sample answers:

"I learned how to save a human life. Also, I learned that we should have also masks and blankets in our first aid kit".

"I learned when to call 112. Also, I learned that many things are missing from our school's first aid kit".

"I learned how to make chest compressions when someone is not breathing!"

"I learned what priority is for people who need urgent help. I will check the breath of the person who needs help first".

"I learned that in an emergency, I should call 112 without panic and ask for help".

"I learned what the coma position does. I learned to put the injured person into a recovery position".

"I played a rescuer role in the short movie. I learned that when an accident happens, we are all responsible for our lives and take action".

In this module pre-test and post-test were implemented about "How confident do they feel about dealing with an emergency situation?" by using Data Tool 2: Twinpoll as shown in Figure 6 below.

Two images showed that the demonstrations and practice worked with the kids in a significant way. Their personal strengths and abilities were improved and their personal choice was that kids could save lives by behaving correctly in an emergency situation. Making these pre-tests and post-surveys was useful for the teachers as well to be able to evaluate the process.

Figure 6. Twinpoll Results

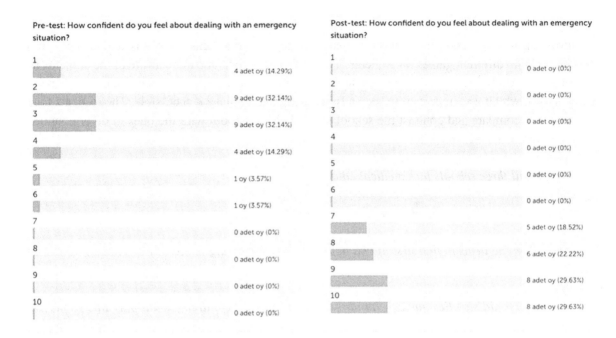

In the next activity, a mobile game was chosen for students to play in class. Most games demand quick thinking from the players. Additionally, users must use logic to anticipate three steps ahead in order to solve difficulties and finish stages. This is fantastic because it aids youngsters in later life as they grow in reasoning, precision, and the capacity to problem-solve quickly and creatively. In this case, kids learned how to stay safe and protect themselves from danger, check if a patient is unconscious, calmly call Triple Zero (000), speak correctly to the operator and emergency service, inspect a casualty's Airway for foreign material, look, listen and feel for signs of breathing on a person, carefully and correctly place a patient in the life-saving recovery position (St John Ambulance Victoria, 2018). Some sample students' reflections after playing the game were as follows:

"It was the most exciting game I've ever played. Because I was excited about trying to save a child who needed help".

"It was great to save his life. I wish an accident won't happen but if it happens, everyone can save lives".

"I haven't played a CPR game before. I loved it".

When asked for reflections about the online meeting, organized to collaborate with the Greek Humanitarian Organization, some sample responses were as follows:

"I liked all of our meetings with Greece and Turkey. I liked watching the presentation".

"It was exciting to have guests in our Zoom meeting this time. We watched him on Youtube. Then he was in front of us. Amazing!"

During the module, a presentation was prepared about the first aid kits in schools, and the items were transformed into different games for students. The aims were to become more aware of the contents and uses of a First Aid Kit, to identify common items found in a First Aid Kit by working in national groups, to understand why it was important to keep a first aid kit, and to make it accessible. The students found the chance to compare and contrast the school kit in their classroom with the ones in other countries, and their comments were as follows:

"I think that all three schools lack medical equipment".

"We should also have a rescue blanket, like Germany!"

"I haven't seen the items in that first aid kit before. It was surprising to me. If we get hurt, we will use them".

"We played first aid supplies games with my friends. I think all children should play this game. That was so fun".

As a next activity, we integrated robotics into our lessons. Robotics activities could enhance students' three-dimensional thinking skills, facilitate their development of technological literacy (Bers, 2008), and attract them to technology-related careers (Nugent et al., 2010). In this sense, some educational robots were used to help kids to save lives. The robots were used as a medium to display kids' ideas and thinking. It was also aimed to teach integrated STEM education, to teach computational thinking, to become comfortable with iteration and learning from failure, and to be exposed to and learn about the jobs of the future. To achieve those aims; at first, a collaborative sheet was used to design some scenarios and each country wrote a scenario for the other partner country to execute with a robot. After the activity, students reflected on the process as follows:

"I loved playing with clay. I liked putting tiles together in order for Sandy to move".

"I found coding very easy and I loved this lesson".

"I acted as the one who started coughing and Dash helped me to survive. I liked the activity so much. I liked the legos as well".

"It was funny how our robot rolled like a ball. Our robot was very clever".

"I liked it when our robot was reading the tiles. I loved the outcome. The robot was doing what we told them".

"I liked it when I found the mistake in the code!"

For the next activity, Data Collection Tool 7 was used which was Flipgrid. For the Flipgrid session, eleven topics were created and students answered the topics via videos. Question 1: How can we help a person with an object in the respiratory passage? Question 2: How do we check the breathing of an injured person? Question 3: What is the first thing we should do when we see an injured person? Question 4: How should we lay an injured person on the ground? Question 5: Where should we call to help an injured person? Question 6: What are the children playing? Have you played something similar? Show it to us! Question 7: What are the children making? Maybe you have made something similar! Show it to us! Question 8: How do you say "defibrillator" in your language? Question 9: Do you have a first aid kit in your school? Show it to us! Question 10: How long should you check for breathing? Question 11: Can kids save lives? The results helped us to cover the subjects which were studied together and proved that students could easily answer when asked to.

As a Data Collection Tool 8, the Slido tool was preferred. As shown in Figure 7 below, the most chosen activity was the mobile game. The second one was the first aid video movies in which kids acted some roles as transnational teams. The third one was the robot scenario where teams exchanged some scenarios and played with an educational robot set.

Figure 7. Slido results

Which one is your favorite?

1. Playing First Aid Action Heroes Game — 4.68
2. Collaborative First Aid Movie/Video — 3.36
3. Our robot scenarios and a movie — 3.25
4. Making a CPR model from bottles and clothes — 3.07
5. First Aid Quiz Games about the First Aid Kits — 2.75
6. Making a Group CPR Online — 2.11
7. Practicing Recovery Position — 1.79
8. Creating Flipgrid Video questions&responses — 1.71
9. Creating a multilingual audio First Aid Manual — 1.43

- **Module 3 and Overall Poll**

According to the overall Getacquainted poll results, 80% percent of our kids were very happy about the project work. 22 out of 25 pupils thought that they could save the environment. 16 students thought they could save a human life, while the rest loves learning about their rights. 19 kids loved learning about their rights. 90% percent of our group wanted to join an eTwinning project next year.

RESULTS AND DISCUSSION

1. How could we reshape the school practice with a lot of student engagement?

Cross-discipline learning allowed for strengthening the connectivity between the different subjects in the curriculum. Learning methodologies such as inquiry-based, project-based, blended, arts- and game-based learning increased learning motivation and engagement as well as science, technology, engineering, and mathematics (STEM) helped foster the development of a range of competences. Learning was enriched with an emphasis on collaborative teaching and learning and active participation and decision-making of learners.

Furthermore, this project work proved that learning was not bounded by the four walls of the school building. A new teaching and learning environment could be founded for improving active learning. This vision was also supported by the Future Classroom Lab, created by European Schoolnet with its six learning spaces as Present, Exchange, Interact, Investigate, Create, and Develop (European Schoolnet, 2021). Students who took part in this research had the chance to implement the subject by interacting with each other, exchanging information, creating presentations, and eventually managing active participation in their own learning.

2. What was the impact of setting up collaborative scenarios via eTwinning on our student's learning in class? Did technology help to achieve it?

The design of activities promoted working together to create products or achieve the missions collaboratively. The collaborative eTwinning work offered meaningful learning during the process. Teamwork and collaboration increased, thus fostering respect and mutual help among classmates and progressively increasing their autonomy and personal self-esteem by acquiring self-confidence. They had substantially improved their handling of technological devices by performing most of their activities through these media, as well as their language skills. Digital technologies contributed to capturing the multiple dimensions of learner progression.

3. What was the effect of collaboration on the key competences for lifelong learning?

The researchers adopted competence-oriented approaches based on active learning that can be used in all education, training and learning settings throughout life and we successfully created some activities to improve the key competences of our project. A significant evolution of the students' competences was observed, among which Linguistic Competence, Social and Civic Competences, Learning to Learn, and Digital Competence stood out directly.

Here was the correlation between the competences and their relations to the project activities, carried out to achieve the set objectives.

- **Literacy Competence**

During the activities, students had the chance to interpret concepts, their feelings, facts, and opinions in both oral and written forms, Visual, sound/audio, and digital materials across disciplines and contexts were used to communicate and connect effectively with project partners.

- **Languages Competences**

In Module 1, students completed some missions in the Goosechase game by recording some sentences in their native languages. In Module 2, a multilingual audio first aid manual was created collaboratively by recording voices in English, Turkish, Greek, and German. In Module 3, students recorded their voices while talking about their rights, and they spoke their sentences in the language of the partner countries. Besides, the project mascot was used to speak in the native language to announce the module's objective at the beginning of each module. These activities were implemented for the ability to use different languages (speaking, writing, reading, listening) appropriately and effectively for communication, as well.

- **Mathematical Competence and Competence in Science, Technology, and Engineering**

Coding and programming were included in this project to create a movie about the scenario written by a partner country. Through the lesson about natural resources, virtual reality experimentation was integrated into the task for kids to observe in the Nearpod session. Students observed nature during the scavenger hunt game and willingly worked for the recycling challenge. In these Skillslabs, the sustainability issues were underlined and the researchers managed to raise awareness.

- **Digital Competence**

These Skillslabs promoted gaining digital competences via the creation of collaborative digital content, e-safety precautions, and problem-solving activities such as iconic supermarket common video and first aid common movie. At the end of the project, it was evident that digital technologies supported communication, creativity, and innovation, and the kids were aware of their opportunities, limitations, effects, and risks.

- **Personal, Social, and Learning to Learn Competence**

For successful interpersonal relations and social participation, it was essential to understand the codes of conduct and rules of communication generally accepted in different societies and environments. With the collaboration maintained during the project, students' choices were respected and underlined the code of conduct was with the project rules. It was managed to set up a positive attitude toward their personal, social, and physical well-being and learning. Through the first aid and CPR activities, the importance of first aid was underlined. Aligning with the sustainability module, it was revealed that not only humans but also plants, animals, and the planet could be saved by the kids.

- **Citizenship competence**

To achieve the New European Bauhaus, as beautiful, sustainable, and together, it underlined the importance of natural resources, recycling, and reducing litter and created some messages for the future. The project partners contributed to the multi-cultural and socio-economic dimensions of European societies, and how national cultural identity contributed to the European identity by creating an iconic supermarket altogether and promoting the zero waste movement. Students from different countries engaged effectively with others in the common interest, including the sustainable development of society by taking responsibility for the environment.

- **Entrepreneurship competence**

Entrepreneurial skills were founded on creativity which included imagination, strategic thinking and problem solving, and critical and constructive reflection within evolving creative processes and innovation. They included the ability to work both as an individual and collaboratively in teams, to mobilize resources (people and things), and to sustain activity. The iconic supermarket activity created for a zero-waste movement could be given as an example of entrepreneurship skills.

- **Competence in cultural awareness and expression**

During the last module of the project, kids defended human rights by using some drawings and they managed to express themselves. Kids took part in the flashcard creation process and communicated with their partners during a videoconference. The art of design as a form of expression helped improve competence in cultural awareness.

SOLUTIONS AND RECOMMENDATIONS

Project activities are successfully designed to improve the key competences of our project. The researchers adopt competence-oriented approaches that can be used in all education, training and learning settings throughout life. Cross-discipline learning also allows for strengthening the connectivity between the different subjects in the curriculum. Learning methodologies such as inquiry-based, project-based, blended, arts- and game-based learning increased learning motivation and engagement as well as science, technology, engineering, and mathematics (STEM) help foster the development of a range of competences. Digital technologies contribute to capturing the multiple dimensions of learner progression.

As shown in Table 1 below, there is an assessment of some students who takes part in the project from Greece, written by the project teacher, showing the improvement for each student.

As shown in Table 2 below, there is an assessment of each student who takes part in the project from Germany, written by the project teacher.

Table 1. Students evaluations in greece

Participant	Evaluation
Student 1. (A.) from Greece	Her literacy competence is high. She fully understands what she reads and she uses vocabulary and grammar according to her age. She communicates effectively with others. She seems to use greetings in English effectively. She has cultivated her language competences through the use of the defibrillator both in English and Greek. She has developed her mathematical competence by spotting mistakes in our robot code. She is capable to observe things and draw conclusions. She has raised environmental awareness and succeeded in changing things for the better in school life. She created digital content with no difficulty. She can formulate ideas about sustainability and carry them out. She has effectively learned with no effort how to develop mechanisms in order to conquer knowledge. She is now competent to help other people and protect the environment as a 6-year-old kid. She is brilliant at working in a team. She decisively expressed herself through art to defend kids' rights.
Student 2. (T.) from Greece	She had slight difficulty reading and concentrating. Through this project, she got better and that's because her self-confidence was raised through collaborative activities. She seemed to enjoy contributing to solutions and group outcomes. She learned how to greet in English. She hesitated to express herself during the robotics activities and she didn't seem to understand coding so well. But she quite understood her role in the short movie and was sure she knows how to be a useful citizen. She loves drawing and she expresses her ideas effectively. She also made progress in critical thinking.
Student 3. (K.) from Greece	He participates with enthusiasm in every activity. Although he is very bright he doesn't seem to understand every time what he has to do. Usually, he needs more than two efforts to achieve the desired result. His digital literacy is very high and he constructs knowledge fast. He is not much of a team player but he worked on it and he did really fine. He is definitely ready to put into practice what he learned about environmental protection and saving human lives. The convention of children's rights really caught his interest and couldn't decide which right to draw, though he is not a perfect painter. He decided that he will have a supermarket when he grows up like the one we created during the project.
Student 4. (V.) from Greece	She understands quite well all instructions. Her reading and writing are at a very high level. This project helped her improve her language competences as she is a bilingual child. She effectively contributed to every problem-solving activity though she found coding a bit difficult. Module 2 activities boosted her curiosity and performed everything with great detail. She handled well web 2.0 tools and loved the collaboration with foreign partners. Every day she grabs every opportunity to realize what she has learned during the project.
Student 8. (K.) from Greece	He is a boy with low literacy and language competences. The project allowed him to try more and be competitive. He is not a team player but the activities were designed in such a way that he had to collaborate and he did it successfully. His lack of concentration made it difficult for him to achieve from the beginning but his persistence won every time in the end. He also had a hard time coding and he almost did not participate in this activity. But he loved crafting and drawing activities. We have to work more on problem-solving, and social and citizenship competence.

Consequently, skills such as problem-solving, critical thinking, the ability to cooperate, creativity, and computational thinking are more essential than ever before in our quickly changing society. They are the tools to make what has been learned work in real-time, in order to generate new ideas, new theories, new products, and new knowledge. The researchers hope that their project will become an investment for improving basic skills and competences and it establishes good practices for the future. By considering the project objectives to encourage active learning and improve key competences for lifelong learning, the researchers would judge the implementation to have been successful. The methodologies and collaborative lesson scenarios would be recommended to other teachers. For the other colleagues who want to implement these activities in this project, it is recommended to be prepared beforehand and become familiar with the digital tools.

Table 2. Students Evaluations in Germany

Participant	Evaluation
Student 1. (M.) from Germany	She is the one who has the most strong personality for her age. Very smart, and good at all linguistic skills, and her natural talent is extended by meeting with active learning strategies and innovative pedagogies. The project helped her improving ICT skills. According to the Reference Framework, I observe that mostly citizenship competences improved her because she has become an active defender of sustainability.
Student 2. (E.) from Germany	He has medium-level linguistic skills. Her Turkish is good at speaking but he is unable to read well and writes slowly. The project mostly helped him to improve his literacy, language, and digital competences.
Student 3. (Y.) from Germany	He is good at entrepreneurship as well as linguistic skills. He immediately acts on the related part and encourages his friends to take part in the role play, as well. His personal, social, and learning to learn competence are extended mostly during the project.
Student 4. (B.) from Germany	He has difficulty in speaking skills and stammers in many cases during the project work. At the end of the project, he is much better at linguistic skills and expresses himself better. He takes responsibility for the activities that we designed for citizenship competence.
Student 5. (EG.) from Germany	One of the most hard-working and clever students in their class. She is good at decision-making, and actively takes part in main outputs such as supermarket activity in module 1, the first aid short movies in module 2, the common rights video in module 3, and other interactive activities. The most surprising effect of the project work between her and me is the positive relationship between us. After recording first aid videos, based on the scenario, she hugged me for the first time. Because she was so much happy for taking part in this activity.
Student 7. (E.) from Germany	She is the oldest in her group and the most hardworking and enthusiastic one. We carried out Fliprigrid sessions mostly with her. Genial.ly voice recordings also are mostly her contribution. Considering key competences, the competences mostly developed in her case are language and entrepreneurship skills.

FUTURE RESEARCH DIRECTIONS

This research only describes the activities carried out around three main themes. However, when a teacher designs a course with web tools, it is possible to use them in all branches. As a continuation of this study, it is possible to carry out studies in different fields with different web tools. Technology integration alone can be a new field of study when using different disciplines together.

CONCLUSION

This sample project can be assessed as creative and innovative in terms of its methods, practice, and production. Through project work, the teachers use different pedagogical methods such as game-based learning (first aid quizzes, recycle games, scavenger hunts), inquiry and project-based learning (iconic supermarket), peer-to-peer method (the recovery position practice, the defribrilator case), mobile learning (Earthspeakr, First Aid Action Heroes), STEM and scenario-based learning (robot scenarios and first aid short movies). 5E Method is followed in the natural resources lesson, integrating it with VR, as well. Flipgrid's QR codes raise interest among students. The techniques are effective by asking questions to motivate students, organizing collaborative teamwork, and allowing students to choose how they access and display information online. Pupils are simply not in a position to follow through on the teacher's ideas. Kids can implement their own ideas.

Throughout this partnership, everyone learns from each other and creates one of the best learning places for their students. The researchers assess all students in this project as shining stars. Each of them has something best inside and the project has extended what is hiding there behind.

ACKNOWLEDGMENT

This research received no specific grant from any funding agency in the public, commercial, or not-for-profit sectors.

REFERENCES

Appleby, R. (2021). *Developing Creative Thinking with Intentional Teaching Practices in Academic Subjects for Early Childhood Classrooms*. SOPHIA. https://sophia.stkate.edu/maed/437

Barkley, E. (2010). *Student engagement techniques: A handbook for college faculty*. Jossey-Bass.

Bers, M. U. (2008). Engineers and storytellers: Using robotic manipulatives to develop technological fluency in early childhood. In O. N. Saracho & B. Spodek (Eds.), *Contemporary perspectives on science and technology in early childhood education* (pp. 105–125). Information Age.

Blasco-Arcas, L., Buil, I., Hernández-Ortega, B., & Sese, F. J. (2013). Using clickers in class: The role of interactivity, active collaborative learning, and engagement in learning performance. *Computers & Education*, *62*, 102–110. doi:10.1016/j.compedu.2012.10.019

Bonwell, C., & Eison, J. (1991). ASHE-ERIC Higher Education Report: Vol. 1. *Active learning: Creating excitement in the classroom*. The George Washington University, School of Education and Human Development.

Bower, M. (2019). Technology-mediated learning theory. *British Journal of Educational Technology*, *50*(3), 1035–1048. doi:10.1111/bjet.12771

European Commission. (2018). *Commission Staff Working Document Accompanying the document Proposal for a Council Recommendation on Key Competences for Lifelong Learning {COM(2018) 24 final}*. Europea. https://eur-lex.europa.eu/legal-content/EN/TXT/PDF/?uri=CELEX:52018SC0014&from=EN

European School Education Platform. (2022). Etwinning weeks 2022. *ESEP*. https://school-education.ec.europa.eu/en/group/etwinning-weeks-2022

European SchoolNet [EUN]. (2021). *Future Classroom Lab*. EUN. https://fcl.eun.org/about

Fitzsimon, M. (2014). Engaging students' learning through active learning. *Irish Journal of Academic Practice*, *3*(1), 9–18.

Gonzalez, T., De La Rubia, M. A., Hincz, K. P., Comas-Lopez, M., Subirats, L., Fort, S., & Sacha, G. M. (2020). Influence of COVID-19 confinement on students" performance in higher education. *PLoS One*, *15*(10), 1–23. doi:10.1371/journal.pone.0239490 PMID:33035228

Habib, R. B. (2017). Students teaching students: An action research project incorporating active learning at language classroom. *Journal of Education and Human Development*, *6*(2), 182–199.

King, A. (1993). From sage on the stage to guide on the side. *College Teaching*, *41*(1), 30–35. doi:10.1080/87567555.1993.9926781

Nugent, G., Barker, B., Grandgenett, N., & Adamchuk, V. I. (2010). Impact of robotics and geospatial technology interventions on youth STEM learning and attitudes. *Journal of Research on Technology in Education*, *42*(4), 391–408. doi:10.1080/15391523.2010.10782557

Prince, M. (2004). Does active learning work? A review of the research. *Journal of Engineering Education*, *93*(3), 223–232. doi:10.1002/j.2168-9830.2004.tb00809.x

Richardson, C. (2020). Supporting collaborative creativity in education with the i5 framework. *Educational Action Research*.

St John Ambulance Victoria. (2018). *First aid action hero - The game. St John Ambulance Australia (VIC) INC - Saving lives through first aid*. St John Ambulance Victoria. https://www.stjohnvic.com.au/community-programs/action-hero/

The Council Of The European Union. (2018) *Key Competences For Lifelong Learning A European Reference Framework*. Brussels: Official Journal of the European Union. https://eur-lex.europa.eu/legal-content/EN/TXT/PDF/?uri=CELEX:32018H0604(01)&rid=7

United Nations. (1989). *Convention on the Rights of the Child*. UN. https://www.ohchr.org/en/instruments-mechanisms/instruments/convention-rights-child

Yeşil, L. B. (2020). Shaping School Culture With Technology: Impact of Being an eTwinning School on Its Climate. In M. Durnali (Ed.), *Utilizing Technology, Knowledge, and Smart Systems in Educational Administration and Leadership* (pp. 259–278). IGI Global. doi:10.4018/978-1-7998-1408-5.ch014

KEY TERMS AND DEFINITIONS

AppSmashing: It involves combining together content created in various apps and "smashing" them together into one finished product. In this context images created by the Gradient app are used in the Chatterpix app to create a final video for students' introduction.

eTwinning: Since 2014, the European Education, Training, Youth, and Sports Program Erasmus+ has co-funded eTwinning, as the main intervention of the European Commission's eLearning Program.

Flip: A free video discussion and sharing program from Microsoft designed for classrooms and beyond is called Flip (formerly known as Flipgrid).

Game-based learning: A method of active learning called "game-based learning" makes use of games to enhance student learning.

Key competences: They are defined as a combination of knowledge, skills, and attitudes by European Commission.

Project-based learning: (PBL) A teaching strategy known as project-based learning (PBL) involves having students actively participate in projects that are both personally and practically relevant.

Virtual Reality: (VR) Pose tracking and 3D near-eye displays are used in virtual reality (VR) to provide users an immersive sense of a virtual world.

Chapter 7
Empathy Through Textual and Dialogic Engagements:
A Classroom Narrative Study

Jason D. DeHart
University of Tennessee, Knoxville, USA

Kate Cimo
North Coventry Elementary, USA

ABSTRACT

In this chapter, the co-authors explore the power of children's and youth literature as high-quality materials for building connections online during the pandemic. Both authors note their experiences, as well as texts that provided a range of connections. The chapter is a narrative case study of the first author's experiences, while the researcher/co-author includes experiences that line up both practically and theoretically. The difficulty of pandemic teaching, as mitigated by some steps in instruction, is a theme of the chapter.

INTRODUCTION

Flexibility is a term that teachers know well. Educators at all levels have to be able to change course on a dime for all sorts of reasons, including the individualized needs of learners (Corley, 2005) and times of trauma (Crosby et al., 2020). Sometimes a lesson completely fails because the technology educators expected to be able to use suddenly fails to work, or teachers have to rethink how to teach a lesson because the students are not ready to learn it as envisioned. Being flexible is just part of our job and being able to adapt to whatever changes are necessary is also something that teachers have learned to do daily. In sum, educators are always responding. Burns and Botzakis (2016) noted that responsive teaching is purposeful and considers "learners' identities *and* academic needs" (p. 12). The 2020-2021 school year certainly gave students, teachers, and families many challenges. Because of the essential nature of teacher voice, the narrative study (Clandinin & Connelly, 2004) presented in this chapters highlights the

DOI: 10.4018/978-1-6684-7015-2.ch007

experiences of the teacher/co-author. The experiences of the researcher/co-Katelign with this teacher's stories of classroom practices that been illuminated by interactions in online spaces, and his notes form a background for the chapter, as well, in terms of practical and theoretical alignments.

WHEN TEACHING CHANGED (AGAIN)

When the pandemic hit, teachers were expected to be flexible in ways that seemed impossible – and sometimes were – leading to the need for both reflection and self-care (Vanderhill & Dorroll, 2022). A lot has happened in the last few years in classrooms, both virtual and in-person; we hope never to revisit many of the events from this year. Surprisingly, there have been some changes that have occurred in the 2020-2021 context that have been ideas we will continue to use moving forward. This article is focused on the practices of a middle grades teacher (Jason), who made instructional decisions to foster online community through literacy practices during the pandemic. For Jason, the most surprising of all has been that the need to be flexible has led to empathy in my classroom and school community. We have been humbled over and over again this year and together with our students have realized a lot about community. Through social-emotional learning, or SEL, (Denham et al., 2003; Katzman & Stanton, 2020), we have grown and we have had to be incredibly flexible in our classroom community. This experience has made us have a deeper and more empathetic understanding.

In the course of the researcher/co-author's experiences as a middle grades educator, schooling seemed to be in a constant state of flux. There were standards changes, textbook changes, and personnel changes at both the school and district levels that seemed to be continuous. This called for constant reading and refreshing of materials, and changes in lesson plans. Additionally, classroom practices changed in response to the growing world of technology. When the researcher began teaching, his classroom was stocked with a few tattered books and a whiteboard. By the time he moved to post-secondary education, nearly all of his students carried cell phones and a large digital screen decorated the learning space. This digital accenting of the traditional brick-and-mortar space was arguably reversed or expanded in the 2020-2021 teaching context.

Notably, teachers found themselves attempting to make connections with students across distance, using digital platforms and video conferencing to maintain some sense of community, as well as steps toward learning. This was a pedagogical and communal reality that varied in contexts, from struggles with making Internet connections to increased linking with learners and even authors to demonstrate literacy practices (Buchholz et al., 2022). Many educators were striving to make the connections and invite the participation that is a hallmark of responsive environments (Maskiewicz & Winters, 2012). As Buchholz et al. (2022) further noted, engagement around children's literature was a nexus point for learners. The teacher/co-author in this chapter illuminates their practices with this phenomenon further through the use of texts for empathy building.

THEORETICAL FRAMEWORK: SOCIAL/EMOTIONAL LEARNING IN MIDDLE GRADES LITERACY

A number of frameworks exist for social-emotional learning, a topic that has proliferated and been pushed back on in the pandemic context (Blad, 2020). We are particularly drawn to frameworks and approaches which firmly position literacy and engagement with texts and composition for thinking about the ways that teachers work with students. We also agree that an SEL framework should be integrated "throughout the school's academic curricula and culture, across the broader contexts of schoolwide practices and policies, and through ongoing collaboration with families and community organizations" (CASEL, n.d., n.p.). We also note, at a practical level, the much-needed nature of SEL as a hallmark of teaching literature as children encounter characters who both share and extend known and familiar experiences and views, as well as a general hallmark of teaching that responds in the moment to the needs of the learner.

The roots of SEL can be found in cognitive and psychology and a focus on competencies (Jones et al., 2019). Garcia and Dutro (2018) noted that SEL approaches should be read across perspectives, disciplines, and theories "for dialogue and debate," through tensions, and with a focus on "how English teachers and teacher educators address issues of trauma and healing in our classrooms" (p. 377). Such an approach is textual, communal, dialogic, and can take place in virtual spaces, as well as in face-to-face settings, depending on the public health need or the trauma that is being processed. High quality children's literature can so often stimulate critical and thoughtful conversations (Hawkman et al., 2022; Husbye et al., 2019).

LITERATURE REVIEW

Building community connections in the context of the pandemic has been a focus of literature over the past two years, including studies in teacher preparation (Wells, 2021) and a renewed/emerging awareness of the disparities in access to digital resources and the inequity that is both a cause of consequence of such disparities (Evans-Amalu, & Claravall, 2021). Researchers have also reported on the ways in which children maintained social connections in this time of distance and public health concern (Quinones & Adams, 2021).

The importance of the connections that can be made in and across digital spaces is not a new area of study. Burnett et al. (2006) reported on the ways in which digital storytelling and composing created avenues for exploration with young children, and Tobin (2000) noted the responses and reflections of young children viewing media products. A number of studies have also focused on the digital practices and connections of secondary students (McLean, 2010; Michikyan & Suárez-Orozco, 2016; Stornaiuolo & LeBlanc, 2014). Major et al. (2018) explored the connective threads between digital technology and classroom dialogue, including discussion processes that were assisted or mediated by digital devices, the use of interactive whiteboard technologies, blogging, and computer applications and software located on a range of devices. Hennessy (2011) pointed to interactive technologies like digital whiteboards, as well as digital artifacts, as connection points for learners in online environments. Additionally, the researcher/co-author (DeHart & Densley, 2022) has co-written about the impact of exploring children's literature and middle grades novels in the pandemic context.

As Stornaiuolo and LeBlanc (2014) pointed out, this work is hardly easy: "The complex relationships involved in such exchanges require literacy teachers and scholars to take into account both people's local histories and cultures and the broader ideological systems in which they are rooted" (p. 192). Literacy practices which tend to foster SEL connections include shared reading and dialogic reading (Doyle & Bramwell, 2006), and have focused on younger readers (Figueroa-Sánchez, 2008; Harper, 2016). Harper (2016), in particular, noted the role of emotion in responses and development, and stated, "Sharing high-quality literature with young children provides a range of language to help them identify, label, and express emotions" (p. 81).

CLASSROOM NARRATIVE AND CONTEXT

We next turn to the classroom context. In this section and following sections, Kate adopts the first-person pronoun to tell their story. In this way, as part of the narrative work, their story is centralized, while Jason has shared the context for the study, including the grounding in the literature. Jason has also included some of the experiences that has found prevalent in classroom environments online as a connection point for both practice and theory. The classroom teacher's narrative is an essential area of consideration when thinking about pandemic education and both the social and emotional challenges and needs that have presented during this time.

The role of the teacher as both co-Katend primary voice is a unique affordance of drawing upon Clandenin and Connelly's (2000) narrative study methodology. By taking this approach, their words are left intact in this report, rather than filtered through my (Jason's) way of evaluating, rewording, and understanding these events and experiences.

Our collaboration began around a common interest in reading aloud with older readers, and works toward the research question: In what ways do/did teachers engage students in literacy instruction in the pandemic context?

Methods

Our collaborative work together began with an invitational/open-ended interview in winter 2020, and our common interest in middle grades literacy was formed on the basis of an article that was published about teaching practices, which inspired Jason to reach out to find more information.

Over the course of a year, the co-authors worked together at different points to fashion a narrative through revisions and shared stories in Google Doc format. Each aspect of Kate's experiences were shared with Jason in this form, and the words that reflect this teacher's experience has been retained without edits from the researcher/co-author. This is an attempt to honor the primacy of the experience, as well as the first-hand knowledge and authentic voice of this teacher.

Kate's Position(ality)

As an English Language Arts and social studies teacher to 6th graders, I was really thrown off course this year when I found out right before school started that I would be teaching in a completely virtual classroom and that I would be teaching all subjects. This isn't necessarily a huge surprise since I am an elementary teacher, but it felt like an overwhelming load to take on--especially as someone who likes to get all their ducks in a row in advance. I suddenly didn't know how to make my lessons and routine work in a virtual environment. So much of my normal day with my students involves small groups and conversation and in-person work where I can have back and forth dialogue with my students.

How would this be as effective in a Google Meet? I decided that my very first mission, if I were to have any hope of my students feeling safe and even vulnerable enough to grow in my classroom, was to do everything I could to build up our virtual community. Zhang and Quinn (2017) have reported about the social-emotional development and potential for literacy growth that occurs in a routine morning meeting, but the online environment presented a series of challenges. Nevertheless, we needed to get to know each other and we needed to find ways to connect in this awkward environment.

THE IMPORTANCE OF FLEXIBILITY

This is where a lot of flexibility on my part became necessary. I had to experiment a lot with how to create situations where students connected with each other and with me without putting them too far outside of their comfort zone. Finding the right balance between students being willing to participate in our game or activity and completely closing off (camera off and muting the entire time) turned out to be an incredible challenge for me and very delicate work. In response, administrators required teachers to have a morning meeting for 20-30 minutes. I decided to make the goal for our meetings "connection," whether that meant connecting with ourselves by journaling, connecting with friends by playing games in small groups, or working as a whole class to solve something like a mystery.

This morning meeting, I believe, ended up being the key piece to making my students comfortable enough to make growth academically this year. This is the first place where I witnessed that unexpected empathy that stemmed from flexibility. It was teaching that extended beyond survival or routine response to responsive community building. Interactions, even online, fostered a sense of belonging that is essential for middle school students (Booker, 2018).

Once students started hearing their peers respond to prompts or seeing their responses on a Padlet, they began to find things they had in common. I also used feedback from my own middle school-aged kids who were also learning virtually to know what might help. One of the best tips they gave me was about how to create effective breakout rooms. Students said two people in a room can be awkward because there is too much pressure to talk, and that can be scary, whereas four or more can be hard because there are too many people. They reported that three was the magic number. I combined that advice with giving my students surveys to form breakout groups. To improve student learning experiences, I give these surveys fairly frequently and also leave spaces for them to write in comments, suggestions, or general feedback. In these small breakout rooms, I would go in and very quickly learned that students could use some direct instruction on good manners as well as problem solving those awkward situations.

Again, this took a lot of flexibility on my part as well as the students' because these were all unexpected challenges we had to overcome this year. In addition, it created so many pathways toward building empathy because we all started to realize that each of us was having a hard time with this format in one way or another, but each of us was also able to help out in some way.

Once I saw that my students were making connections with each other, I decided to take on the second major component I wanted to tackle this year which was how to make my read aloud time work well in this virtual format. It might seem silly to think that read aloud--something I only spend about 15 to 20 minutes a day doing--would take so much precedence this year, but I really believed that it would be a keystone to the students showing growth in ELA and social studies in general. This piece of my teaching also took on flexibility because I needed to figure out how to make it as meaningful in our new circumstances. In normal years, this part of the school day was so easily infused wherever it fit because I had already created a great base of books and had a good list of discussion starters for them. All I needed was the pocket of time, the students, and the book and everything else just fell into place beautifully. The conversation flowed naturally, the students and I could all see each other and react to each other's body language, and I could readily tell how engaged students were or were not so I could figure out how to draw them in. This year, with cameras off and many students nervous about participating, it made conversations much more difficult; I was only getting responses from the same small group of students, while others remained silent. Instead of being something that created a community and a sense of belonging, it felt isolating and frustrating.

Jason notes a similar feeling of frustration and tension, largely due to concerns for family members and students. This feeling of tension and difficulty was compounded as instructional spaces began to open up and many of the researcher/co-author's colleagues and students began to experience more symptoms of COVID. Navigating this environment, from online-only to hybridized spaces has been an emotional process. A belief in and passion for teaching has held the focus of the researcher/co-Kates much as possible, as well as interest in digital environments and virtual learning engagements and literacy.

Building Community and Empathy through Read Alouds

While shared reading and dialogic reading have been mentioned as salient for SEL instruction in literacy, this teacher found the link they were looking for with virtual classroom read alouds. Cunningham and Allington (2015) have noted that reading aloud is a practice that is more common with younger teachers, both of us have found that well-chosen books create powerful connections even into the middle school years.

I reflected a lot on how to adapt my practices. I found that each time I made a minor change, I would see corresponding improvement. Examples of this included more participation and chatting from students, including times when these responses were not prompted. Another change I made was to really be careful about my read aloud selection so that I would hopefully be choosing something that personally engaged a larger group of students. The first time I tried this was for a nonfiction read aloud. Instead of reading a longer book that might have been a little harder to understand over multiple days, I chose a new book of very brief, exciting true stories. There were so many that I decided to make a list of all of them and let the students choose which ones they wanted to hear.

This ended up being a really engaging way to include them. The next book I chose was going to be a fiction story with great characters who go through a lot of change. One of the themes in the book was specifically on how to trust and be vulnerable which I thought fit perfectly with the pandemic. This book was incredibly engaging and the kids begged me to keep reading every day. Some even stayed on our Meet after I dismissed them for the day to continue talking about it. And others gave me suggestions for prompts for their Writing about Reading assignment. This was the reason I had wanted read aloud to work this year and I finally felt like I reached it at this point. Once I had that momentum going, I could keep adding on how I engaged them in their reading. We were able to use the stories in our other lessons as well and in our real-life conversations. Being able to connect with the characters created a great shift in their empathy because they could apply those connections to their own lives and to each other. And, quite simply, just having that experience of sharing a book we all loved so much with each other made our relationships stronger and more natural.

DISCUSSION AND IMPLICATIONS

In considering the responses of students in these online spaces, the choice to stay and opt in for further engagement indicates a particular connection with learning. Jason took further steps to include student voice in the process of co-constructing a classroom environment, democratizing the process and thereby creating buy-in. This sense of buy-in and engagement was evident in student requests, and students' growth in empathy was gauged informally in their responses to texts, as well as more formally as part of their journal writings. The power of literature as a vehicle for and reflection of human experience is a potentially relevant point here, as we continue to make connections about our historical and very present experiences, as well as difficult questions that we must explore as thoughtful and active citizens and members of teaching and learning communities. Though often less commonly found in secondary classrooms, the use of read aloud with texts was, quite literally, a way of sharing voice and providing opportunities for connections and dialogue.

Further instructional steps included composing responses and gamifying learning, as well as engaging in communal morning meetings to focus on making connections in a time of distance. None of these instructional moves were scripted or prompted by an outside source; rather they were the product of the teacher's reflections, consideration of students' needs and voices, and constant process of tailoring and augmentation. This sense of responsiveness is a central element for both authors as the experiences, health, and interests of students continued to be the focus of classroom decision-making and were active ingredients in shaping the learning environment. Responding in these environments, for Jason, was also a process of collaborating with colleagues to support one another in times when Internet access was difficult, or when health needs or other needs arose.

While further narrative work and case study examinations will be helpful for grappling with the reality of the pandemic classroom, a number of instructional implications stem from this work.

Engagement with Texts Online and In-Person Have Communal Potential

As noted in Kate's descriptions, classroom read alouds became an avenue for building engagements. In a time when students could have just as easily tuned out and turned on another screen, the use of read aloud fostered a sense of engagement that led to further dialogue. This teacher described the enthusiasm of students as they engaged in the read aloud, requesting time for more reading from the teacher.

Negotiating connection and instruction across digital spaces and through learning at a distance, this educator was able to leverage the power of texts, including *A Long Walk to Water* (Park, 2011). What is more, this teacher indicated that this was a part of their instructional routine well before the pandemic, and situated this passion for reading aloud in their personal literacy history and family engagements. The person a teacher is in terms of seeing themselves as a reader and learner has potential implications for the ways in which texts are taken up for instructional purposes.

Additional texts that the researcher/co-author has used in digital community contexts include Sara Varon's *My Pencil and Me* (2020), *I Am Every Good Thing* by Derrick Barnes and Gordon C. James (2020), *Rick Riordan Presents Tristan Strong Punches a Hole in the Sky* by Kwame Mbalia (2020), and *Guts* by Raina Telgemeier (2019). Each of these books were showcased in different contexts, from an online clinical literacy space to a graduate level online course, to a small group clinical book club, to an undergraduate methods course. The affordances these texts offered included a focus on the power of creativity, voice, and agency; the poetic nature of picture books with poetic connections to personal experiences; the power of fantasy to show us hard truths about reality; and the necessity of therapy and processing difficult experiences.

Digital Dialogic Processes Build Community

Student journals served as an additional space for checking in with student voices and making sure that questions and needs were addressed as much as could be in distance learning. Tools like Padlet proved to be additional spaces for engagement and encouragement, not simply as end in themselves but as digital communities where students could see one another's reactions to content. These spaces could be accessed asynchronously, allowing for dialogue to continue outside of a particular time. In the researcher/co-author's experience working with both university-level students and with children online during the pandemic, Padlet spaces and other such online community gatherings could be a link to processing and continuing conversation well beyond the boundaries of a particular class meeting time, and allowed for creative extensions of drawn/illustrated and poetic responses to content and the changing context.

In addition to the read aloud, the teacher's choice to foster connection and community arose through the communal oral literacy practice of the morning meeting. In what could have simply been perceived as a mandate, this teacher chose to take up the morning meeting as an opportunity, rather than as an obligation, and center connections. Once more, we note the centrality of children's literature for building connective threads of experience to maintain human interactions, but also to make dialogue possible.

Responsive and Reflective Teaching Matters

Finally, this is the teacher's own story of their work in a classroom that was intended to be an in-person experience, but was instead transposed to a virtual environment. This pivot has presented challenges for teachers at all levels. By returning to a personal sense of values, as well as what this teacher valued in their literacy pedagogy, the virtual classroom became a thread of theoretical and practical connection.

The teacher's flexibility and focus on empathy through textual experiences served as a foundation for possibility in instruction; what is more, this instructional routine highlighted important social and emotional needs for learners. It is likely the case that further research is needed to focus on even more stories of the pandemic as we work collectively to make sense of this time together. It is also the case that research into emotional processes and support will likely prove beneficial as the world continues to shift, and we adjust to what is hopefully as post-pandemic context.

CONCLUSION

In our pedagogy at the secondary and post-secondary levels, we commit to continuing to be flexible and finding many ways to create empathetic connections. At the beginning of the year, Jason felt the pressure of teaching in a difficult time. They were mindful of important steps in self-care. But as the year went on, they found themselves following the same advice that they gave to their own students: to make small, achievable goals and then build from there.

In sum, Kate thinks this advice kept them flexible in a positive way so that they could focus on what was really important for both students and the teacher: Empathy for one another.

REFERENCES

Barnes, D., & James, G. C. (2020). *I am every good thing*. Nancy Paulsen Books.

Blad, E. (2020). There's pushback to social-emotional learning. *EdWeek*. https://www.edweek.org/education/theres-pushback-to-social-emotional-learning-heres-what-happened-in-one-state/2020/02

Booker, K. (2018). The high tide raises all ships: Middle grades teachers' perspectives on school belonging in early adolescence. *RMLE Online: Research in Middle Level Education, 41*(8), 1–15. doi:10.1080/19404476.2018.1505402

Buchholz, B. A., Jordan, R. L., & Frye, E. M. (2022). "Can we see ur dog [?]": Co-constructing virtual author visits in the chat. *The Reading Teacher*. https://ila.onlinelibrary.wiley.com/doi/full/10.1002/trtr.2142

Burnett, C., Dickinson, P., Myers, J., & Merchant, G. (2006). Digital connections: Transforming literacy in the primary school. *Cambridge Journal of Education, 36*(1), 11–29. doi:10.1080/03057640500491120

Burns, L. D., & Botzakis, S. (2016). *Teach on purpose! Responsive teaching for student success*. Teachers College Press.

Clandinin, D. J., & Connelly, F. M. (2004). *Narrative inquiry: Experience and story in qualitative research*. Jossey-Bass.

Collaborative for Academic, Social, and Emotional Learning (CASEL). (n.d.). *What is the CASEL framework?* CASEL. https://casel.org/fundamentals-of-sel/what-is-the-casel-framework/

Corley, M. A. (2005). Differentiated instruction: Adjusting to the needs of all learners. *Focus on Basics, 7*, 1–6.

Crosby, L. M. S. W., Shantel, D., Penny, B., & Thomas, M. A. T. (2020). Teaching through collective trauma in the era of COVID-19: Trauma-informed practices for middle level learners. *Middle Grades Review, 6*(2), 1–6.

Cunningham, P., & Allington, R. L. (2015). *Classrooms that work: They can all read and write*. Pearson.

DeHart, J. D., & Densley, E. (2022). What Messages or Symbols Make You Feel Empowered?" A Virtual Book Experience with Tristan Strong. *The Journal of Literacy and Technology, 23*(1).

Denham, S. A., Blair, K. A., DeMulder, E., Levitas, J., Sawyer, K., Auerbach-Major, S., & Queenan, P. (2003). Preschool emotional competence: Pathway to social competence? *Child Development, 74*(1), 238–256. doi:10.1111/1467-8624.00533 PMID:12625448

Doyle, B. G., & Bramwell, W. (2006). Promoting emergent literacy and social–emotional learning through dialogic reading. *The Reading Teacher, 59*(6), 554–564. doi:10.1598/RT.59.6.5

Evans-Amalu, K., & Claravall, E. B. (2021). Inclusive online teaching and digital learning: Lessons learned in the time of pandemic and beyond. *Journal of Curriculum Studies Research, 3*(1), i–iii. doi:10.46303/jcsr.2021.4

Figueroa-Sánchez, M. (2008). Building emotional literacy: Groundwork to early learning. *Childhood Education, 84*(5), 301–304. doi:10.1080/00094056.2008.10523030

Garcia, A., & Dutro, E. (2018). Electing to Heal. *English Education*, *50*(4), 375–383.

Harper, L. J. (2016). Using picture books to promote social-emotional literacy. *Young Children*, *71*(3), 80–86.

Hawkman, A. M., Tofel-Grehl, C., Searle, K., & MacDonald, B. L. (2022). Successes, challenges, and surprises: Teacher reflections on using children's literature to examine complex social issues in the elementary classroom. *Teachers and Teaching*, *28*(5), 1–19. https://www.tandfonline.com/doi/abs/10.1080/13540602.2022.2062747. doi:10.1080/13540602.2022.2062747

Hennessy, S. (2011). The role of digital artefacts on the interactive whiteboard in supporting classroom dialogue. *Journal of Computer Assisted Learning*, *27*(6), 463–489. doi:10.1111/j.1365-2729.2011.00416.x

Husbye, N. E., Buchholz, B. A., Powell, C. W., & Vander Zanden, S. (2019). Death didn't come up at center time": Sharing Books about Grief in Elementary Literacy Classrooms. *Language Arts*, *96*(6), 347–357.

Jones, S. M., McGarrah, M. W., & Kahn, J. (2019). Social and emotional learning: A principled science of human development in context. *Educational Psychologist*, *54*(3), 129–143. doi:10.1080/00461520.2019.1625776

Katzman, N. F., & Stanton, M. P. (2020). The integration of social emotional learning and cultural education into online distance learning curricula: Now imperative during the COVID-19 pandemic. *Creative Education*, *11*(9), 1561–1571. doi:10.4236/ce.2020.119114

Major, L., Warwick, P., Rasmussen, I., Ludvigsen, S., & Cook, V. (2018). Classroom dialogue and digital technologies: A scoping review. *Education and Information Technologies*, *23*(5), 1995–2028. doi:10.100710639-018-9701-y

Maskiewicz, A. C., & Winters, V. A. (2012). Understanding the co-construction of inquiry practices: A case study of a responsive teaching environment. *Journal of Research in Science Teaching*, *49*(4), 429–464. doi:10.1002/tea.21007

Mbalia, K. (2020). *Rick Riordan presents Tristan Strong punches a hole in the sky*. Disney Books.

McLean, C. A. (2010). A space called home: An immigrant adolescent's digital literacy practices. *Journal of Adolescent & Adult Literacy*, *54*(1), 13–22. doi:10.1598/JAAL.54.1.2

Michikyan, M., & Suárez-Orozco, C. (2016). Adolescent media and social media use: Implications for development. *Journal of Adolescent Research*, *31*(4), 411–414. doi:10.1177/0743558416643801

Park, L. S. (2011). *A long walk to water*. HMH Books for Young Readers.

Quinones, G., & Adams, M. (2021). Children's virtual worlds and friendships during the COVID-19 pandemic: Visual technologies as a panacea for social isolation. *Video Journal of Education and Pedagogy*, *5*(1), 1–18. doi:10.1163/23644583-bja10015

Stornaiuolo, A., & LeBlanc, R. J. (2014). Local literacies, global scales: The labor of global connectivity. *Journal of Adolescent & Adult Literacy*, *58*(3), 192–196. doi:10.1002/jaal.348

Telgemeier, R. (2019). *Guts*. Scholastic.

Vanderhill, R., & Dorroll, C. (2022). Teaching, self-care, and reflective practice during a pandemic. *PS, Political Science & Politics*, *55*(3), 1–5. doi:10.1017/S1049096521001918

Varon, S. (2020). *My pencil and me*. First Second.

Wells, M. S. (2021). Preparing teachers during a pandemic: Virtual practicum in an undergraduate literacy course. *Teacher Educators'. Journal*, *14*, 61–82.

Zhang, C., & Quinn, M. F. (2018). Promoting early writing skills through morning meeting routines: Guidelines for best practices. *Early Childhood Education Journal*, *46*(5), 547–556. doi:10.100710643-017-0886-2

KEY TERMS AND DEFINITIONS

Empathy: The skill or ability to develop an understanding of someone else that goes beyond sympathy.

Morning meeting: A school practice of gathering students prior to the school day to share thoughts, ideas, feelings, and other matters of daily business. The morning meeting has been a practiced site of community building.

Read aloud: A classroom practice in which the teacher reads from the primary text. Students often do not have a copy of the text.

Responsive pedagogy: The practice of shaping and refining teaching in response to the particular needs of a group of students.

Shared reading: A classroom practice in which teachers and students share a copy of the text during reading. Teacher and/or students may read.

SEL: The abbreviation for social/emotional learning.

Text: Any written or digital product that conveys meaning.

Chapter 8

Integrating Collaborative ICT Tools in Higher Education for Teaching and Learning:
A Modest Proposal for Innovation in Digital Instructions

Niroj Dahal

Kathmandu University School of Education, Nepal

ABSTRACT

In this chapter, the author will discuss his experiences working collaboratively to teach and learn in order to create an engaged pedagogy by subscribing action research methodologies in various semesters that involves his (PGD, Master, and MPhil) students of 2019-2021 batches in techno-pedagogy and its trend in learning. This chapter presents the ongoing learning of research conducted within the context of the researcher's teaching practice. The author will provide examples of some of his PGD, Master, and MPhil students' technological learning collaborative activities (i.e., LMS, Google Apps, and other open sources), including forum discussions, choices, managing quizzes, lesson study, workshops, and Google Docs activities (Doc, PowerPoints, and Jamboard), which are created for on-campus, online, and distance teaching and learning in Nepali universities (namely, Kathmandu University and Nepal Open University).

INTRODUCTION

The revolution in information and communication technologies has made the world a small, interconnected community (Can & Bardakci, 2022; Lavidas et al., 2022). Higher education is increasingly dependent on digital platforms and tools. In Nepal, where online courses are common, facilitators use collaborative tools for course delivery and evaluation. Jamboard, Google Apps Documents, workshops, chat rooms, comment sections, wikis, and the forum discussion are frequently being used in the teaching and learning

DOI: 10.4018/978-1-6684-7015-2.ch008

activities. Due to the prevalent use of ICT tools in online education can now support collaborative and cooperative learning. Although each student is responsible for his or her own learning, that aligned with the knowledge is socially constructed forms the basis of collaborative learning (Alafodimos et al., 2009). In this line, Vygotsky argued that social interaction can increase a person's learning capacity. Motivating and maintaining effective student interactions is possible, but not straightforward. So, curriculum, teaching methods, and technology need to be planned, coordinated, and put into action in teaching and learning processes. On the contrary, the university with the most course options, teachers who have too many assignments, and big class sizes could all be to blame (Kikilias et al., 2009). This chapter aims to reduce the amount of time needed to evaluate students' submission on a given assignment(s) by integrating collaboration tools in Moodle, Google docs and other applications.

Next, by valuing autonomy and engagement over technology, this chapter further aims to advance pedagogy, learning, and learner empowerment. The purpose of this chapter is to compel higher education instructors to support their students' quality engagement even when they are teaching on-campus and/or remotely. This chapter serves as one of the teachers' (though not the only ones') guiding principles when managing the material online or in any other format. This circumstance has provided teachers with several opportunities while also posing a number of challenges when integrating ICT tools (Dahal & Dahal, 2015; Cassibba et al., 2021). The strategy presents opportunities for educators to hone their skills, knowledge, and competencies.

This philosophy asserts that cooperative learning activities should be incorporated into the curriculum and pedagogy to facilitate the completion and evaluation of student assignments (Katsaris & Vidakis, 2021). The collaborative tools, specific to teaching and learning, are investigated through action research in this chapter (Dahal & Pangeni, 2019; McNiff, 2013). Based on the author's prior integrating collaborative assessment strategies, this chapter showcase and examine the collaborative tools that are most useful (Dahal, 2022; Dahal & Pangeni, 2019). One of the chapter's other key strengths is how well collaborative teaching scenarios can help with learning and assignments. The learning opportunities in higher education could be improved with the aid of innovative ICT tools and techniques by creating numerous collaborative tasks using various tools. Facilitators with the knowledge and skills to develop a unique, innovative online program are unquestionably required to efficiently use collaborative tools. In this perspective, the capacity of collaborative teaching scenarios to facilitate student activities and assessments is highlighted along with other crucial features. After taking into account how the group effort reduces the amount of time required for manual evaluation by course facilitators. This innovation enhances learning opportunities in higher education by enabling and designing numerous collaborative projects for learning and assessment using various collaboration tools. In many other learning activities as well, integrating technology is seen as a motivating strategy for students (Kim & Park, 2012).

As so many people use ICT, there are many ways for online education to support collaborative and cooperative learning. On the other hand, it can be hard, but not impossible, to get and keep students interacting in a good way. Increased technological integration and student-centered instructional strategies are positively correlated with higher education (Kim et al., 2013). Additionally, the ICT revolution has made the world a small, interconnected village. The digital learning platforms and tools are important parts of higher education. Course facilitators have used a range of collaborative tools to deliver and evaluate courses in developing nations like Nepal. A few of the resources and/or ICT tools included were wikis, Google Apps (docs, slides, and Jamboard), workshops, chat rooms, and comment sections (Dahal, 2022). The researcher decided to utilize the aforementioned tools, including Moodle and Google apps. These materials and/or tools assist facilitators in creating and evaluating student work (Alafodimos et al., 2009). Moodle and Google apps are used in this study to script collaborative learning scenarios. Improving learning outcomes, higher education can now design a variety of collaborative tasks using a variety of collaborative tools. Collaboration is common in academia, especially at the university level (Lazarinis et al., 2022). It has many benefits, such as immediate and objective feedback, a quick assessment, and many others (Karakose et al., 2022). Most often, collaborative learning is appropriate for group projects (Nugroho et al., 2022).

Nepali universities are integrating online programs (example, PGD, Master's, MPhil, and doctoral degree) collaboratively for leaning and assessment. The use of these tools allows facilitators to produce and assess student work. It is now possible to create a variety of collaborative tasks in higher education using a range of collaborative tools, which enhances learning outcomes. Most often at the university level, academics participate in collaborative learning. These platforms offer numerous advantages, such as quick evaluation and immediate, factual feedback. In this scenario, some unanswered questions, such as, how teachers can support online and distance learning by using new ICT tools? what fresh perspectives on utilizing ICT tools, techniques, and methodologies do educators and practitioners need to cultivate in light of the rapidly changing situation? how are ICT resources used, along with methods of instruction? what specific ICT tools are additionally needed to carry out activities that are part of the regular teaching process? These questions pave the foundation of the collaborative teaching and learning scenario in higher education.

To address these issues, meticulous planning, coordination, and implementation of curriculum, pedagogy, and technology are required. Although there are a few potential reasons for this, some of them include the university with the broadest selection of courses, overworked professors, and sizable class sizes. In order to close the gaps and address the unresolved issues raised above, this chapter looks into potential ICT tools that will make instruction possible for any grade level. Due to the gaps and reasons, the guiding questions for this chapter are which collaboration tools, such as those in Moodle, Google Docs, and other programs, support the students' learning and evaluations? and what specific ways does the group project reduce the time required for the manual evaluation of the course facilitators? I chose the aforementioned tools, including Google apps and Moodle, to fill the gap and meet the current demand of integrating collaborative tools.

LEARNING MANAGEMENT SYSTEM: A REVIEW

Learning systems are often used to help students finish the tasks that facilitators have set up for them. Learning Management Systems (LMS) can work well as e-learning systems (Dahal et al., 2020). Students use LMS to submit learning tasks, assignments, and communicate with teachers and peers. Teachers use it to create and grade submissions on the courses (Karakose et al., 2021). Further, Moodle and Google Apps are popular open-source LMSs for group projects(s). Facilitators are still needed, but collaborative tools make it easier and help with the management of learning tasks. Kathmandu University School of Education (KUSOED) facilitators use the Moodle platform and Google apps to support learning. In many ways, this system makes it harder for students to participate in educational activities.

The LMS has proven to be a good way to help teachers and students in the classroom. As was said at the beginning, Moodle is one of the most popular and well-known free learning management systems. The Moodle learning platform was made so teachers, administrators, and students could make their own learning environments in a safe, reliable, and integrated way. In the literature, there are a lot of problems with LMSs, especially the Moodle system. These issues came up because Moodle was used to improve face-to-face teaching or online (Kuk et al., 2011). Because of this, a number of researchers have looked into how student evaluations that work with Moodle can help with making assignments, self-evaluation, and formative assessments (Dahal, 2019; Dahal, 2021).

More research has been done on the growth of commercial LMS and their move to open-source platforms. The group evaluations in Moodle are the focus of these in-depth analyses. Even though Moodle is used a lot in Nepali universities and schools and has many benefits for teachers and students "to learn and develop collaborative tasks, there are some things that can't be done with it" (Dahal et al., 2020, p. 18). For this system to be fully useful for group learning, it needs to be improved (Dillenbourg et al., 2001). The people who made Moodle were researchers, developers, and instructional designers. The system has been improved by adding more services that let new capabilities to be added. These works have been tried out with students and teachers at different educational institutions all over the world (Mazza & Milani, 2004; Dahal et al., 2022). Learners can improve their learning skills while working from home, though, by using online collaboration tools. A good online collaboration tool ensures that everyone collaborates on a particular project and decreases the chances that significant events will be missed. The benefits of working with others are solving hard problems, learning new things, improving communication, coming up with new ideas, and making work more efficient and productive (Dahal et al., 2022).

COLLABORATIVE TOOLS ON MOODLE

In this section, the collaborative tools included in all versions of Moodle are reviewed.

Forum

Learners and facilitators take part in the forum discussion by posting comments. Facilitators or other students may grade forum posts, and different types of forum categories are in practice (see more at https://www.umass.edu/it/support/moodle/add-a-forum-activity -moodle#Forum%20Types). Therefore, a forum can significantly aid in the development of a community and effective online communication. Even in academic environments, forums can be used for a number of creative purposes. Figure 1 below demonstrates how a forum can be used for collaborative learning and assessment.

Figure 1. Responses to forum

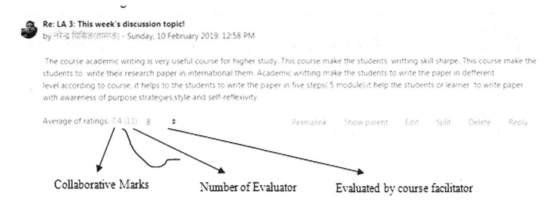

Workshop

There are several options for this peer evaluation exercise. Students can either attach their work or use an online text editor to turn in their work. A student gets two grades: one for the assignment itself and another for how it was turned in as an assignment. Students can also read peer reviews of their own work and the work of other students. See Figure 2 about the final grading of the learning evaluation.

Figure 2. Evaluation of peer work

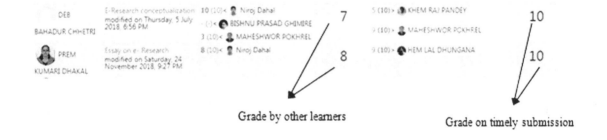

Chat

An additional tool for group learning is this one. Students can communicate with other Moodle course participants and instructors in real-time using the module's chat feature.

Chat rooms are useful for learning new viewpoints on a subject because they function very differently from asynchronous forums. There are many tools available for managing and reviewing chat conversations in the chat room. See Figure 3 below for interface of chat.

Figure 3. Chat user interface

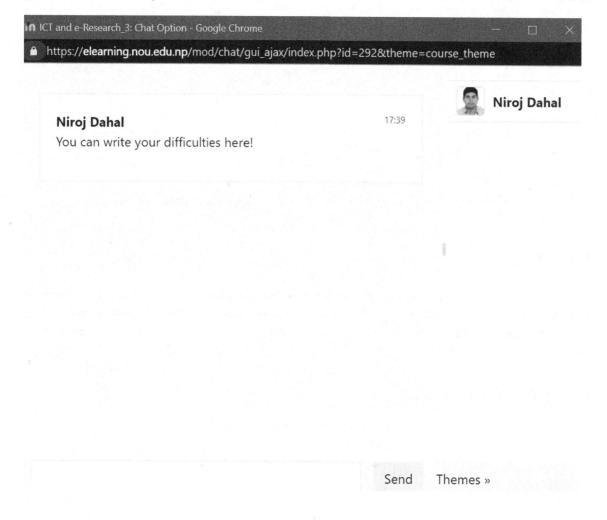

Comment

This is yet another teamwork tool that Moodle offers. Students can post queries, worries, and fixes for various problems. Using the following summary, it will be simpler to understand. See Figure 4 for the participation of students in the comment section.

Figure 4. Participation of students in the discussion on comments

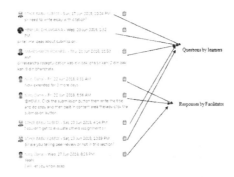

Wiki

The term "wiki" refers to a website that allows multiple people to edit content at the same time. A wiki page is a type of shared website that any student in the class can make at any time using a web browser. A wiki's first page is called the "front page." Every student can add to the Wiki by making new pages or links to pages that haven't been made yet. The explanation below will help you understand what's going on in the passage. See Figure 5 and 6 for Wiki activities.

Figure 5. Wiki activity

Learning and Collaborative Activities

 LA 1: Planning Document

> This is a collaborative planning document (Wiki) where you will combine ideas of GIS at the very first day of the course. Feel free to add, edit and (where appropriate) delete contributions. But bear in mind everyone's actions are recorded.

So, Wiki could be a good way for groups to work on projects together. Students, teachers, and anyone involved in the session can collaborate on a single document in real time.

Figure 6. Multiple attempts by learners

How do you define GIS?

Created: Friday, 22 February 2019, 8:29 PM by Niroj Dahal

Diff	Version	User		Modified	
•	14		Darshana Shrestha	8:26 AM	29 May 2019
•	13		Avashree Shakya	6:20 AM	6 March 2019
	12		Subekshya Sherchan	9:01 PM	5 March 2019
	11		Shyamhari Budhathoki	8:38 PM	5 March 2019

COLLABORATION TOOLS ON GOOGLE APPS

A list of the collaborative tools found in Google apps is presented in this section.

Jamboard, Docs, Slides, and Sheet

Dahal et al. (2022) state that "real-time task collaboration includes the ability to create, edit, and share documents online, as well as the ability to access them and track changes made to documents of all types as necessary" (p. 285). It's also simple for the whole group to collaborate on revising the same document as the session's final deliverable. It's also possible to give each student their own copy and have them collaborate in real time with the instructor and fellow students. See Figure 7 for jamboard, docs, slides and sheet logs.

Figure 7. Jamboard, Docs, Slides, and Sheet logs

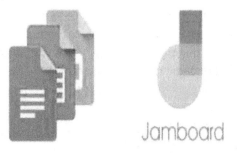

OTHER TOOLS THAT FACILITATE COLLABORATIONS

Students can talk about what they know, understand, and can do in face-to-face, online, or distance learning situations. One of the most important skills for students to learn in the 21st century if they want to get better and keep growing. Students need help from their teachers, peers, and friends during the learning process to finish different learning tasks and improve their knowledge and skills. For students to understand the social constructivism learning theory (Vygotsky, 1978), they need to talk to each other and work together (Habermas, 1972). When learning happens in person, students can take part in group discussions, do their homework, and give presentations. But how is that possible when students learn or teach from far away? Are there any good ICT strategies, tools, or techniques that students can use to work on group projects together? If they exist, how do they help teachers and students? Different technology-based platforms are needed to help teachers and students work together and talk with each other in virtual and remote learning environments. Teachers can use these resources and/or tools to help their online students work in groups, talk about topics, come to conclusions, and present what they have learned. Both teachers and students seem to get a lot out of these resources and/or tools because they can talk about the assigned topic or issues and share what they know. The collaborative learning and teaching platform uses a number of ICT tools to do the same things that groups do in person. Some of these tools can be useful. The functions are made possible by these synchronous and asynchronous media. Some of the tools learners and/or facilitators can use are, Flipgrid, Padlet, Google Meet and Zoom (for break-out sessions). Google Site, Google Jamboard, and Google Docs. Some examples are Google Chat, Evernote, MOODLE, and Microsoft's virtual whiteboards, blogs, and microblogs. Because they have free or low-cost features, these tools can be useful and helpful for teaching from a distance and working in collaborative project.

As was already stated, the resources and/or tools are great for teachers to use when giving students tasks that require them to work together, talk to each other, and talk about what they are doing. Students can organize their thoughts, questions, and ideas into groups during the teaching and learning process. This helps them learn more and come up with new ideas. Most of these tools let students and/or teachers record what students do, so teachers can use them again in the future. As an alternative, teachers can also make videos and put them on YouTube. You can also find some of these tools online (showing the face). When there is a strong internet connection, these helpful tools work great. This means that both teachers and students can work without interruptions. It also makes learning worth it by highlighting the benefits of social interaction and learning with others. Even peers and teachers can, when it's appropriate, congratulate their partners and students. With these ICT tools, students will be encouraged to learn and take an active role in the process. The goal is to give them as much virtual encouragement as possible.

CREATIVITY-ENCOURAGING TOOLS

Creativity is evident when students come up with novel ideas and produce something unique using the materials at hand (Songkram et al., 2021). Creative ideas and thoughts can occasionally be expressed in this way. However, the capacity for original thought and the production of intriguing tangible goods can be regarded as creative abilities. It is the capacity of a person to contest an established or ongoing system or set of practices (a material). Regarding education, being creative in the classroom means coming up with creative solutions to problems that exist in the world. Real-world problems require a person to have exceptional problem-solving skills in order to be solved. In addition, creative problem-solving is essential when dealing with complex issues. Numerous innovative teaching strategies are successful in encouraging students' original thoughts.

Addressing students' creativity while having them complete tasks and activities in a virtual learning environment is not easy when teaching remotely. It may be challenging for teachers to encourage their students to engage in activities, use their imaginations, and complete tasks. Additionally, students working on online projects and assignments that test their capacity for innovation may find it challenging to follow virtual instructions. However, it is the duty of the teachers to highlight the creative endeavors of the students by making use of a variety of online and ICT-based platforms. For this situation, there are some tools available. MovieMaker, Audacity, iMovie, PowerPoint online, Snagit, Storybird, Bitmoji, and emojis are a few examples of tools for creating audio and video. SketchUp, Pixabay, Unsplash, Canva, and PowerPoint are tools for image creation. Camtasia and Screencastify are programs for screencasting. These are a few tools that can be used to instruct students on how to be more imaginative while working with individual or collaborative project(s).

TOOLS FOR CREATING CONTENTS FOR COLLABORATIVE LEARNING

Some of the tools that can be found online or in applications and used to create unique learning activities based on pre-existing content include Adobe Spark, PlayPosit, EdPuzzle, Quizlet, and Canva. Because they take time to make, it is best to add more complex activities to a website or learning management system that already exists. It's much better to encourage students to develop their own ideas. Adobe Systems made a set of media production apps called Adobe Spark that can be used on mobile devices and the web. Using the online tool PlayPosit, teachers can create and edit interactive video tests with uploaded or streamed content. Teachers send in an audio clip or video from well-known websites like YouTube and Vimeo to make an interactive movie or bulb. With just one video, teachers can engage every student using Edpuzzle's user-friendly platform. Users of the straightforward educational tool Quizlet can learn anything. It supports the creation of educational resources like games, flashcards, and tests that evaluate students' understanding of ideas.

METHODS FOR GETTING THE LIVE REACTIONS

Mentimeter, Crowdsignal, Poll Everywhere, and Google Forms are examples of online tools. These tools let instructors deliver online courses for quick feedback, feedback collection, and interaction tracking while keeping an eye on student progress. Crowdsignal is a mobile app that lets you take surveys and quizzes without using the internet. By syncing surveys and tests made on https://crowdsignal.com with this program, teachers can get information from their students. With Poll Everywhere, shy or hesitant students can respond openly with their friends, and everyone can respond at the same time on their own devices. Mentimeter is a simple web tool for getting feedback from people online. Teachers can use Mentimeter to make presentations that are fun and interesting. Google Form is a web-based survey and questionnaire tool that lets people work together in real time and gives them a lot of ways to customize surveys and/or online questions.

COLLABORATION TOOLS: AN ADVANTAGES

As a teacher, I enjoyed seeing how students collaborated on projects. Because the assignment is so engaging, every student interprets its significance uniquely. This prompted the researcher to conduct a survey, interview, solicit the students' feedback, and have them evaluate the quality of their classmates' work in light of the criteria set forth. Also, all the students agreed that having their peers look over their group projects was a good way to learn. It was thought that peer review was a better way for students to make changes to their group project work and get those changes back (s). The students all agreed that doing this activity together made them want to talk to and/or give feedback to their peers in order to encourage a culture of sharing ideas.

In the beginning, completing the tasks was exciting and challenging, and teamwork was essential. It was difficult to defend their illogic in light of the rules for submission and evaluation. As a result of worrying that their group members would criticize their grades, some students reported difficulty assigning grades to their group project partners. All of the students had to put in twice as much effort into a single project. While you may have already completed and submitted the majority of your traditional course assignments, this procedure requires you to evaluate the work of at least two of your classmates.

CONSIDERING WORKSHOP AS A COLLABORATIVE TOOLS

The teachers gave the students a group project that they had to turn in and have their peers review. The student will have to turn in their work and give their peers' work a grade. Through this process, students could see how strict the rules were. Comments and criticism were also very important in this situation. On the other hand, some students didn't seem to care about the rules for judging. Not only did they give a grade, but they also gave feedback and comments that didn't meet the standards of the course facilitator (s). When the students looked at their grades, comments, and feedback, they didn't think about the rules for peer evaluation (Machado & Tao, 2007). In this activity, it would be very important for one student to grade, comment, and give feedback to the other students in a fair way.

Once each option has been carefully put together with all of its parts, the course leaders must set up the first phase according to the different stages of collaborative tools and activities. During the submission phase, students turn in their work on time so that they can use the evaluation criteria to look at the work of their peers. As the last step of the phase, the course facilitator had to approved and confirmed the final grades with final remarks. During the activity phases, students helped each other look over what they had done, grade it, comment on it, and give feedback. So, collaborative tools are a set of tools that both students and teachers need to help them teach and learn. Using these tools to make learning part of the assessment could also help change the way students learn in higher education (Dahal & Pangeni, 2019; Dahal, 2019).

The task of developing, coming up with, and executing collaborative activities should fall to the facilitator. The facilitator will need more time to conceptualize and develop the activity's technological components. The planned collaborative activity includes all necessary elements, including guidance and evaluation, allowing the facilitators to fulfill their duties completely (Martin et al., 2008). A manual review that necessitates careful consideration might be necessary for the collaborative activity. Maintaining grade records, grades, comments, and feedback obviously reduces the facilitator's workload. The manual workload of the course facilitator might be decreased if such activities are implemented.

FINAL THOUGHTS

The author concludes that a collaborative learning course design might get more students involved in group activities. The main action goal of the chapter was to help students with their assignments and tests by putting collaborative tools into classrooms. This chapter shows how Moodle and Google apps can help teachers and students work together. Using technology to create collaborative classroom learning strategies, students can improve their skills, knowledge, and abilities. Students have numerous opportunities to move from receptive to productive learning during class discussions. Google and Moodle offer an alternative to the standard methods of online instruction by allowing students to work together on projects and incorporate teacher feedback into their own learning. Because these programs were easy to understand, most students liked using them.

The usability and critical thinking of these apps also make teachers' jobs easier and get students involved in the learning process by letting them read and evaluate the work of their peers. Even though this study was done based teaching and learning online and/or on-campus, I integrated a variety of tools for teaching and learning with others, like "forums", "comment boxes", "chat", "Sheets", "Jamboard", "Google Docs", "workshops", "Slides" and "Wiki" (Dahal et al., 2020, p. 21). The lessons learned from these experiences allow readers to see how Google and Moodle can be used to make teaching and learning more innovative.

ICT tools significantly impact the many facets of education. ICT tools enable teachers to support the students' quality engagement on-campus and even when they are teaching remotely, by bridging the gap between the various approaches to teaching and learning. Teachers now struggle to convey the subject matter in a clear and concise manner due to the shift from paper to digital pedagogy (Dahal et al., 2020). This chapter offers a variety of options for teachers who want to conduct online lessons and collaborative teaching in higher level and/or school level. Several information and communication technology (ICT) tools, including the development of interactive learning quizzes, the provision of online learning resources, the evaluation of formative feedback, and the collection of real-time responses from students, were discussed as potential means to this end. However, educators must be free to select the ICT tools that best match their pedagogical strategies. If teachers want to use both currently available and future technologies effectively, they must change how they view ICT's role in instructions.

ACKNOWLEDGMENTS

PGD, Master, and MPhil students from 2019-2021 batches who participated in the research are gratefully acknowledged. I would also like to thank the anonymous reviewers who helped me rewrite this book chapter. The Kathmandu University School of Education's research-based environment, guidance, and support are much appreciated. I have learned more with these supports. Last but not least, I want to acknowledge all who directly and/or indirectly support me.

REFERENCES

Alafodimos, C., Kalogiannakis, M., Papadakis, St., & Papachristos, D. (2009). Adult Education and Lifelong Learning: The case of GSAE (General Secretary for Adult Education) in Greece. In D. Guralnick (ed.) Proceedings of the *International Conference on E-Learning in the Workplace* (ICELW-09), 10-12 June 2009, New York: Kaleidoscope Learning (CD-Rom).

Can, Y., & Bardakci, S. (2022). Teachers' opinions on (urgent) distance education activities during the pandemic period. *Advances in Mobile Learning Educational Research*, 2(2), 351–374. doi:10.25082/AMLER.2022.02.005

Cassibba, R., Ferrarello, D., Mammana, M. F., Musso, P., Pennisi, M., & Taranto, E. (2021). Teaching mathematics at a distance: A challenge for universities. *Education Sciences*, *11*(1), 1. doi:10.3390/educsci11010001

Dahal, B., & Dahal, N. (2015). Opportunities and challenges to use ICT in Nepalese mathematics education. In *Proceedings of Second National Conference on Mathematics Education* (pp. 102-106).

Dahal, N. (2019). Online assessment through Moodle platform in higher education. *ICT Integration in Education Conference, 19-21, 2019,* Kathmandu, Nepal.

Dahal, N. (2021). Workshop activity in online courses of mathematics education: Insights for learning and assessment. The *14th International Congress on Mathematical Education,* Shanghai, China.

Dahal, N. (2022). Understanding and uses of collaborative tools for online courses in higher education. *Advances in Mobile Learning Educational Research*, 2(2), 435–442. doi:10.25082/AMLER.2022.02.012

Dahal, N., Luitel, B. C., & Pant, B. P. (2022a). Exploration of the Workshop activity for peer assessment in online courses of mathematics. *Advances in Mobile Learning Educational Research*, 2(2), 475–482. doi:10.25082/AMLER.2022.02.016

Dahal, N., Luitel, B. C., Pant, B. P., & Rajbanshi, R. (2022b). Enhancing student-teachers assessment skills: A self-and peer-assessment tool in higher education. *International Journal of Education and Practice*, 10(4), 313–321. doi:10.18488/61.v10i4.3173

Dahal, N., Luitel, B. C., Pant, B. P., Shrestha, I. M., & Manandhar, N. K. (2020). Emerging ICT tools, techniques, and methodologies for online collaborative teaching and learning mathematics. *Mathematics Education Forum Chitwan*, 5(5), 17–21. doi:10.3126/mefc.v5i5.34753

Dahal, N., Manandhar, N. K., Luitel, L., Luitel, B. C., Pant, B. P., & Shrestha, I. M. (2022c). ICT tools for remote teaching and learning mathematics: A proposal for autonomy and engagements. *Advances in Mobile Learning Educational Research*, 2(1), 289–296. doi:10.25082/AMLER.2022.01.013

Dahal, N., & Pangeni, S. K. (2019). Workshopping in online courses: Insights for learning and assessment in higher education. *International Journal of Multidisciplinary Perspectives in Higher Education*, 4(1), 89–110. doi:10.32674/jimphe.v4i1.1275

P. Dillenbourg, A. Eurelings, & K. Hakkarainen (Eds.). (2001). European perspectives on computer-supported collaborative learning. *Proceedings of the First European Conference on Computer-Supported Collaborative Learning*. University of Maastricht.

Habermas, J. (1972). *Knowledge and human interest*. Heinemann.

Karakose, T., Ozdemir, T. Y., Papadakis, S., Yirci, R., Ozkayran, S. E., & Polat, H. (2022). Investigating the Relationships between COVID-19 Quality of Life, Loneliness, Happiness, and Internet Addiction among K-12 Teachers and School Administrators—A Structural Equation Modeling Approach. *International Journal of Environmental Research and Public Health, 19*(3), 1052. MDPI AG. Retrieved from doi:10.3390/ijerph19031052

Karakose, T., Polat, H., & Papadakis, S. (2021). Examining Teachers' Perspectives on School Principals' Digital Leadership Roles and Technology Capabilities during the COVID-19 Pandemic. *Sustainability, 13*(23), 13448. MDPI AG. doi:10.3390/su132313448

Katsaris, I., & Vidakis, N. (2021). Adaptive e-learning systems through learning styles: A review of the literature. *Advances in Mobile Learning Educational Research, 1*(2), 124–145. doi:10.25082/AMLER.2021.02.007

Kikilias, P., Papachristos, D., Alafodimos, N., Kalogiannakis, M., & Papadakis, St. (2009). An Educational Model for Asynchronous E-Learning: A case study in a Higher Technology Education. In D. Guralnick (ed.) *Proceedings of the International Conference on E-Learning in the Workplace* (ICELW-09). Kaleidoscope Learning (CD-Rom).

Kim, C., Kim, M. K., Lee, C., Spector, J. M., & DeMeester, K. (2013). Teacher beliefs and technology integration. *Teaching and Teacher Education, 29*, 76–85. doi:10.1016/j.tate.2012.08.005

Kim, Y., & Park, N. (2012). Development and application of STEAM teaching model based on the Rube Goldberg's invention. In Yeo, SS., Pan, Y., Lee, Y., Chang, H. (Eds), Computer science and its applications: (Lecture Notes in Electrical Engineering, vol 203). Springer, Dordrecht. doi:10.1007/978-94-007-5699-1_70

Kuk, K., Prokin, D., Dimić, G., & Stanojević, B. (2011). New approach in realization of laboratory exercises in the subject programmable logic devices in the system for electronic learning: Moodle. *Facta Universitatis-series. Electronics and Energetics, 24*(1), 131–140.

Lavidas, K., Apostolou, Z., & Papadakis, S. (2022). Challenges and Opportunities of Mathematics in Digital Times: Preschool Teachers' Views. *Education Sciences, 12*(7), 459. MDPI AG. doi:10.3390/educsci12070459

Lazarinis, F., Karatrantou, A., Panagiotakopoulos, C., Daloukas, V., & Panagiotakopoulos, T. (2022). Strengthening the coding skills of teachers in a low dropout Python MOOC. *Advances in Mobile Learning Educational Research, 2*(1), 187–200. doi:10.25082/AMLER.2022.01.003

Machado, M., & Tao, E. (2007). Blackboard vs. Moodle: Comparing user experience of learning management systems. *The 37th ASEE/IEEE Frontiers in Education Conference.* Milwaukee.

Martin, L., Martinez, D. R., Revilla, O., Aguilar, M. J., Santos, O. C., & Boticario, J. G. (2008). Usability in e-Learning Platforms: Heuristics comparison between Moodle, Sakai and dotLRN. *The 7th Europian Conference on e-Learning*, Agia Napa, Cyprus.

Mazza, R., & Milani, C. (2004). GISMO: A Graphical Interactive Student Monitoring Tool for Course Management Systems. *International Conference on Technology Enhanced Learning*, Milan.

McNiff, J. (2013). *Action research: Principles and practice.* Routledge. doi:10.4324/9780203112755

Nugroho, S. A., Trisniawati, T., & Rhosyida, N. (2022). Developing powerpoint-based interactive multimedia of mathematics learning multiples and factors materials for elementary school. *Advances in Mobile Learning Educational Research, 2*(2), 411–420. doi:10.25082/AMLER.2022.02.009

Songkram, N., Songkram, N., Chootongchai, S., & Samanakupt, T. (2021). Developing Students' Learning and Innovation Skills Using the Virtual Smart Classroom. *International journal of emerging technologies in learning, 16*(4).

Vygotsky, L. (1978). Interaction between learning and development. *Readings on the Development of Children, 23*(3), 34–41.

Chapter 9
A Systematic Review of the Literature on Digital Citizenship

Pelin Yolcu
University of Dicle, Turkey

ABSTRACT

It can be called "digitalization" to first convert all kinds of data such as voice, text, document, image into computer bits consisting of 0 and 1 and then send it to another place with the help of telecommunication technology. The lifestyles of individuals and societies have started to become digital thanks to the whole of the data produced in the digital environment or later transferred to the digital environment. Technological developments in the information age we live in have changed the lifestyles of individuals along with the opportunities they provide. One of these technological developments, especially the internet, has rapidly increased its place in the lives of individuals since the 1990s, and has become effective in many areas such as education, communication, health, politics, industry, and media. Individuals share their feelings and thoughts in online environments, exchange information, and quickly become aware of events taking place in various parts of the world.

INTRODUCTION

In its traditional sense, citizenship refers to membership in a nation (Fischman and Haas 2012: 170). Since the first time this concept emerged, it has reached the present day by crossing different regions and cultures in a dynamic state. The concept of citizenship was used to express a citizen who believed in political participation, freedom and equality in the city-states of Athens, a person living under the auspices of the dominant structure in the medieval feudal state, and people who adopted the same ideology in the Soviet Union (Parlak & Kaftan, 2010). On the other hand, events affecting societies fundamentally have transformed the understanding of citizenship. In the historical process, the increase in population, new inventions, geographical discoveries, and developments in science and technology bring about a transformation in the understanding of citizenship (Gutas, 2011).

With the transition from an industrial society to a scientific society, the development in science and technology has been reflected in every aspect of life and integrated with daily life. At the end of this

DOI: 10.4018/978-1-6684-7015-2.ch009

integration, concepts such as digital citizenship began to take their place in social life (Akgün et al, 2011). Therefore, since communication between citizens has started to take place in the digital environment and with technological tools, a good citizen and a good digital citizen should be able to act safely, consciously and effectively when using technology in real life and the virtual environment.

The development of information and communication technology has made the tools in which these technologies are used widespread. As a result of these developments, it has become easier to access information with these tools without the limitation of time and place, and it has become possible for each individual to communicate with citizens living in another world's geography. At this point, the concept of digital citizenship, which has emerged with the elimination of borders in the point of communication and communication of the Internet and with globalization, can correctly use technology and the tools included in human life, respect personal rights and ethical rules on digital platforms, and use digital tools responsibly and security awareness. Refers to the person (Mossberger et al., 2007).

Digital citizenship is the individual's effective use of communication tools and displaying the responsibilities expected from her daily life in the virtual environment. According to Farmer (2010), digital citizenship is defined as education aimed at raising people who access information in the virtual environment effectively and use this information positively, both socially and individually. Therefore, digital citizenship is the problematic, safe, legal and ethical use of the individual's channels of access to information and the Internet (Bailey & Ribble, 2007).

Considering the common point of the definitions made for digital citizenship, it comes to the fore that digital citizens participate effectively in online environments. In addition, it is seen that digital citizens use communication and information technologies in a responsible, safe, legal and ethical manner. In addition, digital citizens need to be aware of the risks experienced in online environments and combat these risks. However, this alone is not enough. In addition, digital citizens must create safe communities and environments, be aware of how to organize their personal information, and become competent in Internet use. Technological developments in the information age we live in have changed individuals' lifestyles and the opportunities they provide. One of these technological developments, especially the Internet, has rapidly increased its place in the lives of individuals since the 1990s and has become influential in many areas, such as education, communication, health, politics, industry, and media. Individuals share their feelings and thoughts in online environments, exchange information and quickly become aware of events occurring in various parts of the world. Topics such as face-to-face communication, face-to-face education, shopping in stores, reading on paper, searching for information from the library, social networks, course software, virtual shopping sites, newspaper applications, and search engines have begun to be carried out online environments.

For users of the digital world, it is no longer enough to use the computer well, and the importance of maintaining an effective and correct existence in this environment is increasing daily. Many jobs such as receiving news, communicating, shopping and researching over the Internet have forced individuals to use information and communication technologies effectively. In line with the technological developments, whose effects we see in all areas of life, individuals from all age groups have come to use these resources as a necessity beyond entertainment. This virtual world, which is used so effectively, has carried the roles of individuals in real life to these environments and has made the transition to digital citizenship a necessity. While individuals with limited resources were influential in the past, it has become essential to raise individuals who have developed digital citizenship behaviours, know how to access primary resources by using technology well, and can use applications such as e-government (Greenhow & Robelia, 2009). The state and its devices use communication channels, which are a necessity of democracy, to meet the demands and needs with the help of their developing technologies. It uses digital technologies to learn and meet (Altincik, 2022).

BACKROUND

Digital Citizenship

It is seen that digital citizenship is defined as the standards associated with the appropriate use of technology (Ribble, 2007). From a broader perspective, it has been stated that digital citizenship is to implement behaviours that ensure the legal, safe, ethical and responsible use of information and communication technologies in the online environment (ISTE, 2007). In another definition, digital citizenship is described as being able to use technology competently, understand and interpret digital content and determine its reliability, research, create content, communicate with appropriate tools, think critically about ethical issues, be safe, respectful and responsible online (A Common Sense Media White Paper, 2011). Vizenor (2013) defined the concept of digital citizenship as the use of technology for the individual's social, social and political activities.

Digital citizenship is a concept beyond being able to use digital technology but also includes using digital tools and applications correctly and effectively. Understanding this concept is also essential in understanding the effects of today's information age on our real life. Mossberger, Tolbert, and McNeal (2008), the reasons behind why the concept of digital citizenship has come to the fore and discussed in recent years:

- Positive effects of information technologies on society and economy,
- Provide equal economic opportunities for Internet access and use,
- Supporting citizens' active participation in society and democracy,
- They state that Internet access and use policies create inequality for individuals with low income and education levels and minorities.

The users of a digital world that affects and shapes individuals in society in terms of psychological, physical and social relations have been called "digital natives" and "digital immigrants" by Prensky (2001, p. 1). The digital natives' group, which is intertwined with the digital world, prefers easier and faster access; Digital immigrants born before the web age, on the other hand, have difficulty using digital media tools. They prefer to read from the text instead of the figure, to first look at the printed resources and then the Internet to get information and to read the user guide instead of practising to learn how to use the program (Prensky, 2001). Although digital immigrants have difficulties using digital resources, with the increase in the spread of the digital world, digital natives and digital immigrants have been able to conduct their business faster by connecting to online environments.

The online community of digital natives and immigrants has also taken on the roles of digital citizens. Mossberger, Tolbert, and McNeal (2008) examined three aspects of the online community. These; are forms of communication with its regular and effective use, the effect of the Internet on the participation of individuals as democratic citizens and the effect of the Internet on equality of opportunity. In this context, digital citizens are expressed as people who frequently use technology at work to fulfil their civic duties and for economic gain. Digital citizens are described as individuals who can look critically, predict ethical dimensions, and display correct attitudes while using information and communication technologies (Mercimek, Yaman, Kelek, & Odabaşı, 2016).

Similarly, a digital citizen is defined as an exemplary citizen who can criticize while using information and communication resources, is aware of the ethical consequences of online behaviours, does not harm others while using technology, exhibits the right attitude in his sharing and cooperation, and encourages others in this direction (Çubukçu & Bayzan, 2013). Banko and Babaoğlan (2014) stated that there is a digital age process in which digital citizens, whose numbers are increasing daily, become individuals who follow the developments through mobile devices. Digital citizenship, which affects the lives of individuals and societies, also constitutes a key point for the family, the minor institution that makes up society.

The results in Table 1.1 were reached by examining the X, Y, and Z generations in a digital context in the study, where it was mentioned that especially the mothers and fathers who are involved in the Internet environment to follow their children find themselves more actively in the digital world as a result of observations and experiences (Banko & Babaoğlan, 2014).

Table 1. The results in Table 1.1 were reached by examining the X, Y, and Z generations in a digital context in the study, where it was mentioned that especially the mothers and fathers who are involved in the Internet environment to follow their children find themselves more actively in the digital world as a result of observations and experiences

Generation	Feature	Relationship with digital citizenship
Generation X	The generation born between 1965-1979	Later, they meet with digital tools and gradually try to adapt to the world of digital citizens.
Generation Y	The generation born between 1980-2000	They met with digital tools in their childhood or youth and adapted to the world of digital citizenship without difficulty.
Generation Z	The generation born after 2000	They have been intertwined with digital tools since they were born and have been innately digital are citizens.

As seen in Table 1, X, Y and Z generations have difficulty adapting to digital citizenship as their age increases. In this direction, it can be said that the number of digital citizens is increasing day by day and a growing digital world. This digital world, which has grown with the widespread use of portable technologies, emerges as an environment where digital citizens living in it not only consume information but also produce information and share it with others, and speed is at the forefront.

According to Hollandsworth, Dowdy, and Donovan (2011), digital citizenship encompasses a wide range of behaviours, each of which carries varying degrees of risk. Lack of digital citizenship awareness and education can lead to dangerous situations. If these problems are not addressed in the field of education, digital culture draws its direction, ignoring the potential for an efficient and long-term solution. According to Miles (2011), education is needed to create a culture of responsibility that enables individuals to become digital citizens and avoid the risks they face while using the Internet. In addition, it is stated that by training the experts working to protect children, they can be better equipped against our ever-changing digital world.

Dimensions of Digital Citizenship

In the literature, it is seen that different classifications have been made regarding the dimensions of digital citizenship. One of them is the classification made by Oyedemi (2012). Digital citizenship dimensions are in this classification; Citizenship and human rights, the ability to access and apply communication technologies, the regular use of technologies, and the policy that enables the applicability of these components are discussed in five dimensions. In the classification made by Choi (2016), digital citizenship is considered in four dimensions. These are defined as Media and Information Literacy, Digital Ethics, Participation, and Critical Resilience.

In the classification made by Choi (2016), the digital ethical dimension of digital citizenship; includes digital rights and responsibilities that include responsible and ethical behaviour in the digital environment, awareness of social, cultural and political problems arising from digital technologies, protection of personal information, prevention of cyberbullying (Ohler, 2012; Ribble, 2004; Winn, 2012). Media and information literacy dimension; includes understanding the need for information, accessing information, evaluating information, synthesizing information, and knowing online communication (Moeller et al., 2011). Participation dimension; It includes different types of online interaction, such as socio-economic, cultural and political participation. The critical resistance dimension includes more linear, innovative, hierarchical, and uncreative forms of participation, potentially involving deep digital interaction (Choi, 2016; Yalçınkaya & Cibaroğlu, 2019).

Although there are different classifications and explanations regarding digital citizenship in the literature, it is seen that the most widely used classification is the classification made by Ribble (2004, 2011). In this classification, as shown in digital citizenship; is based on nine dimensions: digital access, digital literacy, digital communication, digital rights and responsibilities, digital law, digital ethics, digital security and digital health. Nine dimensions of digital citizenship aim to raise a new type of citizen with a high level of information literacy. Digital citizenship dimensions can be accepted as among the characteristics that individuals should have today.

Digital Ethics

If digital ethics; can be defined as the rules that encourage proper behaviour in order not to harm others in the media developing with technology and to ensure the continuation of the system in good faith during all kinds of human actions performed on these platforms. Digital ethics aims to bring a moral framework to the behaviour and lifestyle of the individual in digital life, which has become a part of daily life. Acting by these rules, which are used when deciding on right and wrong, sometimes means doing what is appropriate for the situation. We need to develop a new theoretically based vision for this field, which we can also describe as cyber ethics. For example, buying a music CD from a store without paying the price is defined as theft; Unauthorized downloading of music on digital channels will also be considered theft (Bailey, 2008).

In a structure where digital technology and human values are evaluated together, digital ethics should be designed as a system where digital technology will develop and advance human values. Activities in this area should include, in particular, the formulation and justification of policies for the ethical use of digital media. Regarding the benefit it offers to the system, it is also possible to express digital ethics as integrating digital technology and human values (Rogerson, 2020). All our actions in daily life, whose boundaries are not defined by legal science, fall into the field of ethics. In today's mentality, where daily life habits are shaped and changed by digitalization, ethics should be digitalized simultaneously. However, the ethical atmosphere that has preserved its existence in the traditional world may be insufficient in evaluating the behaviours in the digital world. At this point, Rogerson (2020) offered some suggestions for current ethics that need to be developed, from providing digital education to children, adding new information messages about search engines and information resources, and limits drawn for situations where it is challenging to make ethical decisions (Rogerson, 1996).

Digital Technology; On the one hand, it can be used to benefit social events, as well as; On the other hand, it can lead to moral indifference along with the feeling of endless freedom and irresponsibility that individuals feel when using technological mass media. There may be situations in which acting contrary to moral rules is considered legitimate and normalized in the minds through various rationalizing ways. In addition to their main account in the virtual world, They can also exist with fake, bot and parody accounts. For this, the boundaries of "digital ethics" must be determined in the virtual world. Today's new technology offers channels where ethical violations can be easily carried out. It may be possible for harmful formations such as terrorism to become widespread and massive with the advantages of digitalization. Ethical problems in the field of information technologies have been discussed a lot, especially in the context of globalization. The difficulty of encountering real faces or actual actions, the increase in the production speed of virtual reality and privacy violations seem to be the most fundamental problems.

Studies on ethics can be traced back to Norbert Weiner, the founder of cybernetics. In his work published in 1950, Weiner; states that the developments in the field of information processing led to significant changes that require deep analysis of human society (Mingers & Walsham, 2010). In order to avoid the adverse effects of the Digital Age, it would not be correct to stay away from the digital world and not use its positive aspects. So what needs to be done is to create the ethical plane of digitalization as much as possible and not to condemn the truth of simulation in the virtual world.

On the other hand, artificial intelligence systems should be mentioned as the value that high technology brings to humanity. The primary purpose of artificial intelligence studies is to produce artificial systems with consciousness and the original qualities of human beings. This is impossible in today's conditions and is the subject of a long discussion. Artificial intelligence has a significant role in bringing the issue of ethics to the agenda; because human beings want to be sure about a future fiction that is faithful to their existence. Humanity lags behind artificial intelligence systems that it produces with its natural mind; however, these systems do not have the complex brain structure and emotional thinking structure of humanity that has evolved over the centuries. The human brain is not a program or software; it resembles a complex neural network that constantly configures itself (Kaku, 2016).

Modern worldview; It is the manifestation of science's understanding that social reality can be re-built and that everything can change in the contemporary world. On the other hand, one of the severe problems caused by modernity in human life is a technology and human relations. It is possible to know what exists on this subject; however, there is a disagreement between the traditionalists, who think that it cannot be changed, and the modern segment, who thinks that the knowledge of the natural and social can both be acquired and changed.

Digital Communication

Humanity, which has passed from an industrial society to an information society with the effect of technological developments, has met the phenomenon of globalization with worldwide interaction the widespread use of computer and Internet technologies brought along socio-cultural changes and economic effects. Today's information technologies, which have multiplied the knowledge produced throughout history, have developed in parallel with post-industrial transformation and digitalization.

Digital technology, which transforms all audio and visual information into binary codes with computer-based devices, has made information independent of time and space. Digitization, which enables all kinds of information to be used and transferred by electronic devices, started through digital codes (0 and 1) (Brennen and Kreiss, 2014). Digitization (and digitization), which started with analogue encoding information with passwords, was applied to all aspects of business and life, and the digital transformation began. Digitized information was transmitted to different environments in less than a second and could be reproduced. At the centre of this new era was the digitization of information and everything audio-visual. Digitalization has turned into a tool that allows social activities to be articulated and have a single communication infrastructure. So much so that a brand new "virtual civilization" emerged in parallel with the physical civilization (Schmidt & Cohen, 2014). Communication tools and media took their place at the top of the sectors most affected and transformed by the developments in the digital age.

With the technologies provided by the massage, there was a communication revolution in which the previous communicative ties were loosened, and the borders disappeared. A virtual communication atmosphere was built with the realization of information flow over the digital networks surrounding the world. The Internet, which formed the communication revolution's infrastructure and started the digitalization era, moved beyond the military borders, its starting point, to the centre of extraordinary information mobility. Parallel to technological developments, connections began to accelerate, information became digital, and information began to permeate everywhere (Castells, 2008). In contrast, the Internet has become wireless like the devices used, and innovative, fast and interactive communication tools have been put into use. Applications such as mobile communication, social media, e-government, e-commerce, robots and intelligent systems are among the digital technology products that change all sectors, such as communication, banking, health and manufacturing. The digital age, which affects and transforms people's lives and relationships, has also created its human type quickly. This term, conceptualized as "digital natives" (Prensky, 2001, 1-8), is used for new generations who become a part of the cyberculture by connecting to a network with Internet technologies. People involved in the cyberculture shaped by social media develop new interpersonal relationship methods, etiquette, social expectations and behaviour patterns.

The phenomenon of digitalization has deeply affected economic, social and cultural structures. In addition to the economic structures in which change is inevitable from the way of production to job and profession definitions, the social and cultural structure, which covers all areas from people's way of thinking to their life preferences, has been transformed. The increasing impact of digitalization has reshaped the social organization, revealing the transformation into a "network society" (Castells, 2010, p. 500). This conceptualization states that the social infrastructure has changed with the effect of communication networks. In addition to the economy, the digitalization of culture and its spread across national borders, removing obstacles to the circulation of all commodities and capital, accelerated globalization. In this process, knowledge and culture experienced a unique process of reproduction and diffusion with the help of digital technologies. New media platforms created through computers and the Internet have popularized digital culture, a new way of life and approach. With the digitalization of content, the change in the ways of producing, accessing, transmitting and storing information has deeply affected traditional media tools and all areas of social life. With the spread of the Internet and new communication technologies, the media began to be divided into technology-centred and started to be called traditional and new. The reshaping of media consumption trends, depending on technological developments, enabled the interest in traditional media to turn to digital. As the digital revolution regressed traditional media, it was not long before those who gave these tools a short lifespan were proven wrong.

Accordingly, traditional media had to disappear because of mobile phones, the increase in news and printing costs, the performance of e-readers, the rise of digital news platforms and advertising trends (Pfanner, 2013). However, communication and journalism continued to exist in essence. However, the ways of delivering content to consumers have changed. The emergence of new possibilities in distribution enabled the transition from print to digital and news producers' discovery of the Internet, tablets and smartphones. The speed brought by digital technology to communication tools, and the multimedia feature that brings together text, sound and image, led to significant changes in the production and presentation of the news and the reader's behaviour.

Traditional and digital communication tools, brought together by mobile communication, continuously improve information technology and increase the audience they interact with each passing day. Interactive newspapers are offered to readers with "Quick Response Code" and "Augmented Reality" applications. With the applications implemented in printed newspapers, a hybrid communication tool in which analogue and digital communication technologies are used together has been created (Aktaş, 2014: 145). Content published in print media is brought together with digital content in the online environment with the help of QR codes and augmented reality applications, and interactive environments are created via mobile devices. The static structures of traditional communication tools gain a dynamic structure with the hybridization of communication tools. The change experienced with the integration of traditional and new media leads to the reproduction of everything from the content to the language used and the way of presentation. Thus, in addition to carrying the message, the Internet is transformed into a communication network with more than one centre, and cultural codes are transmitted with hybridizing tools and new media. As the ways of accessing information diversify, the proliferation of communication channels and networks that connect individuals and societies is accelerating.

The views that mixed media will prevent the degeneration of traditional media and have an essential functionality for the democratization of society continue to be discussed (Strategic Developments, 1996). With Internet technology's elimination of physical boundaries, the differentiation in the target audiences of traditional and hybrid media has also become evident. Unlike traditional media, whose target audience is primarily homogeneous groups and contains messages for mass purposes, the messages of new communication tools target heterogeneous groups. Homogeneous messages have been replaced by a personalized publishing approach based on individual interests. Users independent of time and space are reached with unique content, and the effect of demassification is created (Aktaş, 2014; Pavlik, 2013). In this context, mixed media brought together by the communication technologies revolution and the Internet, described as intelligent technologies (Chatfield, 2013), have turned into actors that enable the spread of global culture and accelerate interaction worldwide.

In the early days, the idea that the Internet would save the masses from the passive culture of television with the utopia of unlimited freedom (Siberia) was very effective. However, this utopia ended with the discovery of the Internet, which started by connecting military and academic circles with commercial and political circles in a short time. The widespread use of mass media and social media applications has made it inevitable for local media to be connected to global communication networks to meet their needs, such as technology and content production. Global culture, which has become a commodity with the contribution of the media, which has gained functionality in the globalization process of local areas, has accelerated societies' dependence on the culture industry by being marketed through mediatic products. Internet and social media applications, which have become an integral part of today's daily life and whose usage intensity is increasing, have massified consumption and control (Maigret, 2011). The media, which markets the policies and cultural products produced by international companies, has become a convenient tool for societies to adopt new habits and value judgments. The global cultural pressure on the traditional culture of societies has given people a cultural shock that they have difficulty keeping up with the rapid social change around them (Toffler, 2011).

Digital Security

The emergence of new technologies and their spread to society have led to changes in living habits and the reshaping of social concepts. Information and communication technologies play an active role in the rapid change process towards becoming an information society; It has started to completely change our daily experiences in many fields, such as communication, banking, electronic signature, distance education, public services and e-government applications. This change also affected the production, communication, transportation, education and trade styles of societies (Karakaş, 2002). As a result of the increasing use of computer and mobile communication devices in our country, the amount of information produced in every field is increasing rapidly.

In the process of transformation into an information society, besides many conveniences in economic and social life, various risks and threats against information security also arise. The vast majority of people using these technologies are not aware of the risks and threats that may arise against information security (Özenç, 2007). These risks and threats can cause people to incur financial losses or undesirable situations such as changing, deleting or accessing their information without permission. Essential elements of information security; are confidentiality, integrity and accessibility (Fussell, 2005; McCumber, 2005; Schlienger & Teufel, 2001). Confidentiality is the inaccessibility of information by unauthorized persons; integrity ensures the accuracy and completeness of the information, its content not altered, deleted or destroyed; Accessibility is the availability of information by those authorized to use it at any time. These three essential elements are the components of information security that cannot be considered independently of each other.

The concept of information security has been expressed as ensuring the physical security of information in written and printed media until the 1990s. The great transformation and the increase in information transfer after the effective use of mobile phones, computers and the Internet in daily life have caused the definition of information security to change. Today, when the concept of information security is considered in terms of information technologies, the concept of digital data security comes to the fore. The security of digital data in electronic media has gained importance due to reasons such as data loss due to power cuts, protection and encryption of computers to prevent access to files from outside, privacy and copyrights. From this point of view, studies on information security have been evaluated within the scope of digital data security. Canbek and Sağıroğlu (2006) define digital data security as "all efforts to create a secure information processing platform to protect data or information from unauthorized access while keeping and transporting data or information in electronic environments" (p. 168).

In addition to the conveniences experienced as a result of the intensive use of computers and the Internet, many digital data security problems have emerged. Some of these problems are; computer viruses, technical problems, computer tricks, information theft, abuse of access authority, failure of power supplies, camera systems and telephone exchanges due to natural disasters, hardware-related problems and software threats. Perhaps the most crucial element that threatens digital data security is human-made threats. According to Tekerek (2008), these threats occur due to the user's unconscious and ignorant use of technology without adequate training or due to behaviours intended to damage the system. Canbek and Sağıroğlu (2007) defined the concept of social engineering, which has emerged as the point of deliberately damaging the system and has been frequently used in recent years to obtain the necessary information to access the system by using psychological and social tricks on legitimate users who use or manage the computer system that a hacker is interested in. described as techniques. Advances in information technologies, of course, make our lives easier.

On the other hand, digital data security risks are also increasing due to the inability to predict the risks that may arise due to the inappropriate and malicious use of these technologies and the ignorance of threats. The way to eliminate or minimize risks is to raise awareness among individuals. In this context, it would be appropriate to examine the concept of awareness, which is frequently used in daily life. Acar (2004) defined awareness as "the individual's awareness of what and how he/she experiences while coming into contact with all sense organs, another individual or his/her environment" (p. 56).

Digital Literacy

Traditionally, 'literacy' means that an individual can read and write the language shared in a particular culture, while digital (digital) literacy is digital literacy, with the process of accessing, organizing, analyzing, interpreting, evaluating, communicating and producing information using digital technologies. It also includes reading and writing texts (Akkoyunlu & Yılmaz Soylu, 2010). Digital literacy is not an alternative or a replacement for traditional literacy but an extension that contributes to the general literacy needed to work, learn and socialize in today's world (Churcill, Oakley, & Churchill, 2008). The definition of digital literacy in the literature varies, but most researchers agree that digital literacy requires some skills or skill sets that are interdisciplinary (Churchill, 2016).

Gilster (1997) stated that digital literacy is a special kind of mindset associated with mastering ideas, not just pressing buttons (Gilster, 1997). Gilster's view is based on three accepted principles of digital literacy: The first of these is the knowledge and ability to access and use various hardware devices and software applications, and the second; proficiency in understanding and critically analyzing digital content and practices, and third: the ability to create with digital technology (Media Awareness Network, 2010).

Based on these principles of Gilster, the European Commission, competencies related to digital literacy, solving problems, communicating, managing information, collaborating, creating and sharing content; knowledge, skills, attitudes (skills, strategies, values) required to use ICT and digital media in a practical, productive, appropriate, critical, creative, autonomous, flexible, ethical manner for work, leisure, participation, learning, socialization, consumption and awareness) (Ferrari, 2013; Murray and Perez, 2014: 86). Digital literacy has also been defined as "the ability to survive in the digital age" (Eshet-Alkalai, 2004). The indicator of an individual being digitally literate; is the adaptation to new or emerging technologies (Ng, 2012). Comprehensive definitions of digital literacy, beyond being skills-based, include the process of critical thinking and problem solving that encompasses the ability to solve problems effectively in a technology-rich environment.

According to Eshet-Alkalai (2004), the term "digital literacy" encompasses five types of literacy:

1-Visual literacy (learning from visuals, visual thinking skills),
2- Reproduction literacy (the ability to reproduce creatively using materials such as text, audio, video, and pictures),

3- Multi-literacy (the use of hypertext in the creation of a non-linear information environment and the ability to freely navigate among the displayed information)

4- Information literacy (critical thinking, ability to search and evaluate information effectively),

5- Socio-emotional literacy (managing online socialization's emotional and social aspects, avoiding pitfalls, fraud, etc.)

A model was developed by Wan Ng (2012) on the dimensions of digital literacy. According to this model, digital literacy is a combination of three dimensions (technical, cognitive and social-emotional): Having technical and operational skills in using computer communication technologies in daily activities; technical dimension, critical thinking in research and evaluating the cycle of acquiring digital information; cognitive dimension and using the Internet responsibly (protecting security and privacy) in communication, socialization and learning; is the social-emotional dimension (Ng, 2012).

Literacy is shaped in line with the current needs of the age. The concept of literacy, in its current meaning, is far beyond a literacy behaviour such as perceiving and deciphering the writings on paper; It has taken the form of meeting competence in a process where cognitive features such as meaning, interpretation, synthesis and translation predominate. Digital literacy is at the centre of these three dimensions; In the background of what is heard and seen, there is a 'critical evaluation' based on impartiality.

Digital Health

The digital health system, the set of complementary technologies, processes and structures in the digital health ecosystem, typically encompasses a large number of individual solutions and organizations (Digital Health, 2017). Within the scope of digital health applications, there are applications such as 3D printers (Branch, 2015), wireless mobile health (mHealth), wearable technologies, phone applications (Bhavnani et al. 2017). With the spread of these technologies, it has become easier to provide patient care in the field of health, to collect medical data related to health and to share this data with relevant persons, institutions or organizations. Digital health technologies provide benefits such as encouraging communication between patients and healthcare providers, enabling non-healthcare professionals to participate in preventive health activities, increasing patients' adherence to treatment requirements, and enabling them to manage the chronic disease process themselves (Lupton, 2013). It also shapes people's health behaviour by sharing real-time data with digital health technologies (Pagoto & Bennett, 2013).

E-Health is one of the popular health informatics topics of today, which provides great convenience for patients in the delivery of health services, both in accessing medical information and in shaping the health service to be provided to them, and in the diagnosis and treatment stages of the health service production process, on the other hand. EHealth scientists make many definitions. Eysenbach (2001), defined e-health as "a new field where medical informatics, public health and commerce meet health services and information delivered or developed through the Internet and related technologies. In a broader sense, the term characterizes not only a technical development but also a concept of mind, a way of thinking, an attitude, networking and global thinking to improve health services locally, regionally and worldwide using information and communication technologies" (p. 1). Toygar (2018) identified e-health as the new name of health in the age of technology. The eHealth system is not designed to exclude physicians and other health service providers from the system but to increase the performance of service providers with technological tools—innovation and flexibility (Kılıç, 2017).

The Internet, a vital health resource and contains much information, is an indispensable information access platform for individuals using health services. Individuals mostly use the Internet to access information on health issues, read the information they have accessed, decide whether to apply to a physician and make follow-up physician appointments (Andreassen et al., 2007). The eHealth practices help people increase their health literacy, provide preventive services, access services and personally manage their health (Drosatos et al. 2016). e-Health practices help increase health services' sustainability with limited resources (COCIR, 2015). The e in eHealth does not only have an electronic meaning. The 10-e, which reveals what eHealth is about, is stated below (Eysenbach, 2001).

1. Efficiency: eHealth promises to increase efficiency and reduce costs by avoiding repetitive or unnecessary diagnostic or therapeutic interventions.
2. Enhancing Quality of Care: With the increase in productivity, the costs are reduced, and the quality is increased. eHealth provides the opportunity to compare different service providers and increases the quality of health services by directing patient flows to those offering the best quality.
3. Evidence-Based: eHealth interventions realize effectiveness and efficiency in an evidence-based manner with scientific evaluations.
4. Empowerment of Consumers and Patients: eHealth opens new avenues for patient-centred healthcare delivery by enabling consumers to access knowledge bases of medical and personal electronic records over the Internet.
5. Encouragement: It encourages partnership between patient and physician in making joint decisions.
6. Education: Online resources provide educational opportunities to physicians and consumers.
7. Enabling information: It provides information exchange and communication between health institutions in a standardized way.
8. Extending the Scope of Healthcare: Extending the scope of healthcare beyond traditional boundaries.
9. Ethics: eHealth poses new challenges and threats to issues such as informed consent, confidentiality and equality with the new patient-physician interaction.
10. Equity: While eHealth promises to make healthcare more equitable, there is a digital divide in rural and urban populations, rich and poor, young and old, and many areas. In addition to these ten items, Eysenbach adds the features of e-health as easy to use, entertaining and exciting (Eysenbach, 2001).

Digital Commerce and Law

With the digital economy approach, the application of Internet-based digital technologies to the production and trade of goods and services has become an increasingly important part of the global economy (Bolwijn et al., 2019). "Digital economy" is generally defined as economic activities in the information and communication technology (ICT) sector, which includes telecommunications, Internet, information technology services, hardware and software (Chen, 2020). Another approach that emerged with digitalization is the concept of "Digital Commerce". Although there is no single known and accepted definition of digital commerce, there is growing consensus that it encompasses digitally enabled commerce transactions in goods and services that can be presented digitally or physically and involve consumers, firms and governments. That is, while digital technologies provide all forms of digital commerce, not all digital commerce can be delivered digitally.

It can also include commerce, goods and services that are digitally enabled but physically delivered, such as a book purchased online or a hotel reservation (OECD, 2019). In this context, digital platforms are becoming increasingly important to facilitate online activities, mainly by reducing transaction and information costs for businesses and consumers. These platforms exist in many areas, such as software operating systems, portals, media, healthcare and payment systems. Platforms create a two-sided market by connecting different end-user groups and generating network benefits (Ferracane et al., 2020). According to the OECD (2019) definition:

digital commerce is not only about services delivered digitally, but also about increasing the trade of goods and services – including the supply chain – provided through increased digital connectivity. However, the scale of operations and the emergence of new (and disruptive) players and business models are transforming manufacturing processes and industries, including those previously unaffected by globalization. (n.p.)

Using digital commerce transactions increases the speed at which business operations reach more stakeholders and respond to orders more effectively. Digital business activities also include cross-organizational activities, suppliers, distributors, partners, customers, etc., elements that effectively combine online relations on a global basis (Gökmen, 2012). Digitization increases the scale, scope and speed of commerce. It enables companies to bring new products and services to more digitally connected customers worldwide. It also enables businesses, tiny ones, to use new and innovative digital tools such as to overcome barriers to growth, help facilitate payments, enable collaboration, avoid investing in fixed assets through the use of cloud-based services, and use alternative financing mechanisms.

As there are rules to be considered in all digital environments, there are also rules to be considered, especially in the Internet environment. A digital citizen should act with the awareness that it is a crime to do all the criminal behaviours in real life on the Internet and should complain to the relevant authorities about those who commit crimes on the Internet. In this context, producing and sharing content with all three risk dimensions of the Internet can constitute a crime.

Digital Rights and Responsibilities

Digital Rights and Responsibilities refer to freedoms that extend to the digital world (Ribble, 2011). In other words, it means that everyone has the right to freely express themselves in the virtual world, which cannot be prohibited. For example, by expressing opinions in forms in the virtual environment, creating groups, and participating in discussion environments, etc. fundamental rights cannot be restricted (Şeremet, 2014).

Although the Internet has an important place among digital tools, most digital tools have started to offer Internet technology. While the Internet can be a medium where everyone can express themselves freely, it also constitutes the balance point of the online environment within the framework of rights and responsibilities, where this freedom of expression can be limited to the extent that it does not violate the personal rights of others. For example, when searching for information on the Internet, there are ways to use the information to be cited, intellectual and industrial rights on that information and online responsibilities within the framework of these rights. Similarly, a digital citizen has responsibilities against the injustice done on the Internet and illegal content on the Internet. At this point, we have rights and responsibilities towards all risk groups on the Internet.

Digital Access

Electronic participation in society is expressed as digital access (Ribble, 2011). In another definition, digital access is explained as the full participation of citizens in online environments (Aydemir 2019). Just as it is not possible to write on paper without pen and paper, it is not possible to be a digital citizen without access to information and communication technologies. In order to become a digital citizen, first of all, electronic access should be supported, and everyone should have equal access to electronic media (Aygün, 2019). However, the fact that technology offers different options to people in terms of interaction and communication prevents all individuals who make up society from having equal access to digital environments. Therefore, different people do not have equal access to technology due to various factors such as social and economic conditions and physical barriers (Ribble, 2011). This is also evident in the studies conducted in this context. In one of these studies, Zickuhr and Smith (2012) state that the increase in mobile connection and Internet usage has reduced the gaps in accessing technology in recent years, but digital differences persist for some groups. Another study found differences in digital access between different genders, generations and social groups. Eliminating these inequalities should be the main task of the following societies, and in this context, the inequality of opportunity in accessing technology should be eliminated, and no one should be left out of digital access (Aygün, 2019). Açıkgül (2011) summarized what needs to be done to increase digital access under four headings. These:

- State support and infrastructure services,
- Business investment and incentives,
- National education strategy,
- It is financial and price standardization.

It can be said that these efforts to increase digital access will increase digital citizenship behaviours.

CONCLUSION

According to the findings, although digital literacy levels are parallel with the use of technology, it is striking that the literacy level is behind. Although the adaptation of an individual to new technologies plays a vital role in determining whether he is digitally literate or not, a digitally literate person stands out as an individual who can actively access and maintain the digital information he needs in solving any problem, solves and evaluates the information he has reached for his use, and can add new ones to it. Skilful use of digital devices and spending more time in the digital world does not mean that users use technology wisely. Technology and digitalization have become a necessity rather than a request. It is seen that all this transformation has entered a new era and that, like every concept that changes and transforms in this new period, the perspective on citizenship has also changed, and the definition of the concept has been expanded by adding new competencies. Digital citizenship, which expresses the state of having the skills required by the digital age, shows that everyone has become a digital citizen in this period when technology is used in every field. In this new era, technology has peaked, and everyone has become a digital citizen. Digital people, more specifically mentioned in this world, are used to making it easier to deal with digital applications and not avoid real life with digital reach, communication and literacy pictures.

FUTURE RESEARCH DIRECTIONS

In this context, the works to be planned from now on includes:

- Data can be collected from higher education students on a departmental basis, and their digital citizenship awareness or experiences can be examined according to departments.
- Digital citizenship awareness or experiences of high school students, who are prospective higher education students of the future, can be examined according to high school types.
- Digital citizenship awareness or experiences can be examined using different variables.

REFERENCES

Acar, N. V. (2004). *How aware am I: Gestalt therapy (2. Baskı).* Babylon Publishing.

Açıkgül, E. (2011). *The effect of digital divide on pre-service science teachers' use of information and communication technologies in the scientific process.* [Unpublished Master's thesis. Adıyaman: Adıyaman University].

Akkoyunlu, B., Yılmaz Soylu, M. & ve Çağlar, M. (2010). Developing a "numericalcompetence scale" for university students. *Journal of Hacettepe University Faculty of Education (H. U. Journal of Education) 39*, 10-19. https://dergipark.org.tr/download/article-file/87452

Aktaş, C. (2014). *QR Codes and Hybridization of Communication Technology.* Kalkedon Publications.

Altincik, H. (2022). Evaluation Of Democracy, Civil Society And Lobbying. In *A Digital Context, İn: Individual, Society And Communication In The Context Of Digitalization* (pp. 187–195). Education Publisher.

Andreassen, H. K., Bujnowska-Fedak, M. M., Chronaki, C. E., Dumitru, R. C., Pudule, I., Santana, S., Voss, H., & Wynn, R. (2007). European citizens' use of Ehealth services: A study of seven countries. *BMC Public Health, 7*(1), 1–7. doi:10.1186/1471-2458-7-53 PMID:17425798

Aydemir, M. (2019). An examination of the renewed social studies course curriculum in terms of digital citizenship and its sub-dimensions. *International Journal of Contemporary Educational Research, 4*(2), 15–38.

Aygün, M. 2019. *Investigation of digital citizenship status of social studies teachers and social studies teacher candidates.* [Master's Thesis, Yıldız Technical University].

Bailey, D. (2008). *Cybercitizenship and cyper cafety: Cyber ethics.* Rosen Central. https://archive.org/

Banko, M., & ve Babaoğlan, A. R. (2014). *The effect of the digital citizen on the Gezi Park process.* Gezi Park. http://www.geziparkikitabi.com/

Bhavnani, S. P., Parakh, K., Atreja, A., Druz, R., Graham, G. N., Hayek, S. S., Krumholz, H. M., Maddox, T. M., Majmudar, M. D., Rumsfeld, J. S., & Shah, B. R. (2017). 2017 roadmap for innovation—ACC health policy statement on healthcare transformation in the era of digital health, big data, and precision health: A eeport of the American college of cardiology task force on health policy statements and systems of care. *Journal of the American College of Cardiology*, *70*(21), 2696–2718. doi:10.1016/j.jacc.2017.10.018 PMID:29169478

Bolwijn, R., Casella, B., & Zhan, J. (2019). International production and the digital Economy. In R. Tulder, A. Verbeke, & L. Piscitello (Eds.), *International Business in the Information and Digital Age*. Emerald Publishing.

Branch, C. (2015). 3D Printing in healthcare, the review. *Journal of Undergraduate Student Research*, *16*(3), 1–4.

Brennen, S., & Kreiss, D. (2014). Digitalization and digitization. *Culture Digitally*. https://culturedigitally.org/2014/09/digitalization-and-digitization

Broadband Commission. (2017). *Digital health: A call for government leadership and cooperation between ICT and health*. Broadband Commission.

Canbek, G., & Sağıroğlu, Ş. (2006). A review on information, information security and processes. *Journal of Polytechnic*, *9*(3), 165–174.

Castells, M. (2008). *The rise of the network society*. Bilgi University Press.

Castells, M. (2010). *The rise of the network society*. Wiley. https:// onlinelibrary.wiley.com/doi/pdf/10.1002/9781444319514.oth1

Chatfield, T. (2013). *How we adapt to the digital age*. Sel Publishing.

Chen, Y. (2020). Improving market performance in the digital economy. *China Economic Review*, *62*, 101482. doi:10.1016/j.chieco.2020.101482

Choi, M. (2016). A concept analysis of digital citizenship for democratic citizenship education in the internet age. *Theory and Research in Social Education*, *44*(4), 565–607. doi:10.1080/00933104.2016.1210549

Churchill, N., Lim, C. P., Oakley, G., & Churchill, D. (2008). Digital Storytelling and Digital Literacy Learning. In Readings in Education and Technology. [University of the Fraser Valley Press.]. *Proceedings of ICICTE*, *2008*, 418–430. http://www.icicte.org/ICICTE2008Proceedings/churchill043.pdf

COCIR. (2015). COCIR eHealth Toolkit: Integrated Care: Breaking The Silos (Fifth Edition). COCIR.

Common Sense Media. (2011). Digital literacy and citizenship in the 21st century. *Common Sense Media*. https://www.commonsensemedia.org/sites/default/files/uploads/pdfs/DigitalLiteracyandCitizenshipWhitePaper-Mar2011.pdf

IACR. (2007). *Communication technologies*. International Conference on Information Security and Cryptology. IACR.

Çubukçu, A., & ve Bayzan, Ş. (2013). The perception of digital citizenship in Turkey and methods to increase this perception with the conscious, safe and effective use of the Internet. *Middle Eastern and African Journal of Educational Research, 5*, 148–174.

Çubukçu, A., & ve Bayzan, Ş. (2013). The perception of digital citizenship in Turkey and methods to increase this perception with the conscious, safe and effective use of the Internet. *Middle Eastern and African Journal of Educational Research, 5*, 148–174.

Erdem, C. (2019). *Digital citizenship in South Africa.* [Unpublished PhD Thesis. Nigeria: Obafemı].

Drosatos, G., Efraimidis, P. S., Williams, G., & Kaldoudi, E. (2016). *Towards Privacy by Design in Personal e-Health Systems.* Proceedings of the 9th International Joint Conference on Biomedical Engineering Systems and Technologies (BIOSTEC 2016), (*vol. 5*, pp. 472-477). ScitePress. 10.5220/0005821404720477

Eshet-Alkalai, Y. (2004). Digital literacy: A conceptual framework for survival skills in the digital era. *Journal of Educational Multimedia and Hypermedia, 13*(1), 93–106.

Eysenbach, G. (2001). What is e-health? *Journal of Medical Internet Research, 3*(2), 1–2. doi:10.2196/jmir.3.1.e1 PMID:11720962

Ferracane, M., & Marel, E. (2020). Patterns of trade restrictiveness in online platforms: A first look. *World Economy, 43*(11), 2932–2959. doi:10.1111/twec.13030

Ferrari, A. (2013). *DIGCOMP: A framework for developing and understanding digital competence in Europe.* JRC Publications.

Fussell, R. S. (2005). Protecting information security availability via self-adapting intelligent agents. Military Communications Conference, (pp. 297). IEEE. 10.1109/MILCOM.2005.1606116

Gilster, P. (1997). *Digital literacy.* John Wiley.

Gökmen, A. (2012). Virtual business operations, e-commerce & its significance and the case of Turkey: Current situation and its potential. *Electronic Commerce Research, 12*(1), 31–51. doi:10.100710660-011-9084-2

Greenhow, C., & Robelia, B. (2009). Informal learning and identity formation in online social networks. *Learning, Media and Technology, 34*(2), 119–140. doi:10.1080/17439880902923580

Hollandsworth, R., Dowdy, L. ve Donovan, J. (2011). *Digital citizenship in K-12: It takes a village.* Springer.

Kaku, M. (2016). *Physics of the future. (Y. S. Oymak ve H. Oymak, Çev.).* METU Development Foundation Publishing.

Karakaş, Z. (2002). *Technology management.* [Unpublished Master's Thesis, Sakarya University Institute of Social Sciences, Sakarya].

Kılıç, T. (2017). e-Health, good practice; Netherlands. *Gumushane University Journal of Health Sciences, 6*(3), 203–217.

Lupton, D. (2013). The digitally engaged patient: Self-monitoring and self-care in the digital health era. *Social Theory & Health, 11*(3), 256–270. doi:10.1057th.2013.10

Maigret, E. (2011). *Media and communication sociology*. Communication Publications.

McCumber, J. (2005). *Assessing and managing security risk in IT systems*. CRC Press.

Media Awareness Network. (2010). *Digital literacy in Canada: From inclusion to transformation*. A Submission to the Digital Economy Strategy Consultation. http://www.ic.gc.ca/eic/site/028.nsf/eng/00454.html

Mercimek, B., & Yaman, N. D., Kelek, A ve Odabaşı, H. F. (2016). The new reality of the digital world: Trolls. *Trakya University Journal of Education Faculty, 6*(1), 67–77.

Mingers, J., & Walsham. (2010). Toward ethical information systems: The contribution of discourse ethics. *Management Information Systems Quarterly, 34*(4), 833–854. doi:10.2307/25750707

Moeller, S., Joseph, A., Lau, J., & ve Carbo, T. (2011). *Towards media and information literacy indicators*. UNESCO.

Mossberger, K., Tolbert, C. J., & ve McNeal, R. S. (2008). *Digital citizenship: The Internet, society, and participation*. MIT Press.

Mossberger, K., Tolbert, C. J., & ve McNeal, R. S. (2008). *Digital citizenship: The Internet*. MIT.

Murray, M. C. V. P. (2014). Unraveling the digital literacy paradox: How higher education fails at the fourth literacy. *Issues in Informing Science And Information Technology, 11*, 85–100. doi:10.28945/1982

Ng, W.NG. (2012). Can we teach digital natives digital literacy? *Computers & Education, 59*(3), 1065–1078. doi:10.1016/j.compedu.2012.04.016

Ohler, J. (2012). Digital citizenship means character education for the digital age. *Education Digest: Essential Readings Condensed for Quick Review, 77*(8), 14–17.

Oyedemi, T. D. (2012). *The partially digital: İnternet, citizenship, social inequalities, and digital citizenship in South Africa*. [Unpublished PhD Thesis. Nigeria: ObafemıAwolowo University]. https://scholarworks.umass.edu/dissertations/AAI3518402/

Pagoto, S., & Bennett, G. G. (2013). How behavioral science can advance digital health. *Translational Behavioral Medicine, 3*(3), 271–276. doi:10.100713142-013-0234-z PMID:24073178

Pavlik, J. V. (2013). *New media and journalism*. Phoenix Publications.

Pfanner, E. (2013). Peering into the future of media. *New York Times*.

Pool, C. R. (1997). A new digital literacy: A conversation with Paul Gilster: Integrating technology into teaching. *Educational Leadership, 55*(3), 6–11. http://www.ascd.org/publications/educationalleadership/nov97/vol55/num03/A-New-Digital-Literacy@-A-Conversation-with-Paul-Gilster.aspx

Prensky, M. (2001). Digital natives, digital immigrants. *Marc Prensky*. http://www.marcprensky.com/writing/Prensky%20%20Digital%20Natives,%20Digital%20Immigrants%20-%20Part1.pdf

Prensky, M. (2001). Digital natives, digital immigrants. *Horizon, 9*(5), 1–6. doi:10.1108/10748120110424816

Ribble, M. (2004). Digital citizenship: Addressing appropriate technology behavior. *Learning and Leading with Technology*, *32*(1), 6–11.

Ribble, M. (2007). *Digital citizenship in schools*. International Society for.

Ribble, M. (2011). *Digital citizenship in schools*. International Society for Technology in Education.

Rogerson, S. (1996). Preparing to handle dilemmas in the computing profession. *Organizations and People*, *3*(2), 25–26.

Rogerson, S. (2020). Re-imagining the digital age through digital ethics, invited position paper. In J. Arthur, T. Harrison ve G. Polizzi (Eds.), Promoting character education as part of a holistic approach to re-ımagining the digital age: Ethics and the Internet webinar (pp. 25-28). University of Birmingham Jubilee Centre for Character and Virtues.

Schlienger, T., & Teufel, S. (2001). *Analyzing information security culture: Increased trust by an appropriate information security culture*. University of Fribourg.

Schmidt, E., & Cohen, J. (2014). *New digital age*. Optimist Publications.

European Commission. (1996). *Strategic Developments for the European Publishing Industry towards the Year 2000. Europe's Multimedia Challeng: Main Report*. European Commission DG XIII/E.

Tekerek, M., & Tekerek, A. (2013). A research on students' information security awareness. *Turkish Journal of Education*, *2*(3), 61–70.

Toffler, A. (2011). *Shock future fear*. Corridor Publishing.

Tyger, R. L. (2011). *Teacher candidates' digital literacy and their technology integration efficacy*. [Unpublished Doctoral dissertation, Georgia Southern University]. http://digitalcommons.georgiaso uthern. edu/cgi/viewcontent.cgi?article=1557&context=etd

Hollandsworth, R. (2011). Digital Citizenship. *Techtrends: Linking Research & Practice to Improve Learning*, *55*(4), 37-47.

Vizenor, K. V. (2013). *Binary lives: Digital citizenship and disability participation in a use created content digital world*. ERIC.

Winn, M. R. (2012). Promote digital citizenship through school-based social networking. *Learning and Leading with Technology*, *39*(4), 10–13.

Yalçınkaya, B., & ve Cibaroğlu, M. O. (2019). Examining the perception of digital citizenship: An empirical evaluation. *Business & Management Studies: An İnternational Journal*, *7*(4), 1188–1208.

Zickuhr, K., & Smith, A. (2012). *Digital differences*. Pew Research Center.

KEY TERMS AND DEFINITIONS

Citizenship: Citizenship means being a part of the political institutions, usualla country. In constitutional countries, those living in that country must be boun to that country by citizenship in order to benefit from the rights promised by the state in the constitution. These people are called citizens.

Digital Citizenship: Digital citizenship (cyber citizenship or e-citizenship) refers to the ability regularly use information technology in an ethical, critical and secure manner.

Digital Immigrant: The digital immigrant refers to the generation that was born in the analogue world, encountered the technological culture later and tried to keep up with it.

Digital Native: It is a class that meets digital domestic technology as soon as it is born, grows up as a wolf of the Internet, knows computers and technologies like their mother tongue, manages and uses it.

Digital World: The digital world is the name given to a concept by former US vice president Al Gore in 1998 that describes a virtual representation of the world that is geo-referenced and linked to digital information archives of the world.

Chapter 10
Transmedial and Transformational Practices in Comics Work

Jason D. DeHart
University of Tennessee, Knoxville, USA

ABSTRACT

In this chapter, the author relates an analytic description of the composing practices of a digital comics maker, linking print processes and digital processes. This narrative case study includes a focus on the titles that have been salient for the comics maker, as well as the linking that this composer includes in their work across video games, toys, music, podcasts, and other types of texts. The chapter includes a focus on what teachers can learn about the interconnected and intertextual, digital world in which students live, act, and practice.

INTRODUCTION

In the fall of 2019, I was introduced to the self-published comics work of a comics artist (pseudonym: Miguel) and was informed that I should contact this author and artist as a recent graduate from our university. This meeting and interaction was delayed by the pandemic, but I managed to meet with Miguel online in the fall of 2021. The transmedial practices of this artist, particularly aligning punk rock/metal and comics work, form the basis of this interview and analysis. His work, in particular, highlights a number of affordances for the comics medium, which uniquely position it in relationship to this book and content:

1. Miguel uses both print and digital means to create work, as do a large number of comics artists in the current context of comics creation.
2. Miguel's inspirations hail from a number of sources, both in terms of traditional print and digital sources (including film and video games).

DOI: 10.4018/978-1-6684-7015-2.ch010

In terms of pedagogical implications, Miguel's story illustrates how a contemporary university school setting served as an inspiring nexus point, along with popular media (including film, music, and comics) to inspire comics and creative work. My purpose in this project has been to descriptively explore this author/artist/creator's first-hand account of his journey to creating and I give attention to both the centrality of educational practices and structures in his training and development, as well as the ways in which media and materials have shaped him. In terms of authorship, his role as a self-promoting and self-producing published author links to the power of inspiration and making as forces that are endemic to both artistry and fandom. As a literacy educator, my questions focus on the descriptions that this author/artist shares of his practices, and I inquire about the ways in which his literacy practices have been shaped for a continual engagement as an adult.

METHODOLOGY AND METHODS

This narrative case study draws upon the research of the primary author and the experience of Miguel as a co-author in an attempt to capture a visual and verbal rendering of literacy practices in adult education, as well as the creative responses that are made possible in a literacy/comics community. Clandinin's (2006) work on narrative analysis informs the presentation of this study, as does the materials that have been gathered (i.e., Miguel's work, interview materials) to form a case study bounded by this individual's experiences (Stake, 1995), an intrinsically built from his role as a creator, author, and artist.

Brandell and Varkas (2001) pointed to the efficacy of the narrative case study as a methodology for gaining close understanding on an individual and/or experience in descriptive terms. Miguel has first-hand knowledge of what it is to be a creator, as well as a member of fandom, while my experiences as author have only related to fandom itself, beyond research publications. His perspective is unique as an emerging author/artist in the comics medium, and his notes on his process and story position him as a voice for this chapter.

Specific methods included an interview housed in a virtual conferencing space, which generated a transcript. This transcript was then read, cleaned up for technical accuracy, and analyzed by the author. In terms of analysis, a focus on the origins of the author formed an initial thread of inquiry as I sought to locate those areas in which Miguel discussed his traditional schooling and unpack the kinds of descriptions he shared of these pedagogical spaces. As a secondary form of analysis, I located those times that Miguel talked about his creative processes. These processes included notions of collaboration and community, particular intertextual inspirations that were noted by titles, and a description of the process itself that this author/artist embarks on in his work.

FANDOM, COLLABORATION, AND COMMUNITIES

Chief among the content shared in this chapter is the role of comics in literacy. I use the term comics to denote the traditional form and juxtaposition of words and images, rather than to denote a particular type of material as a distinct format, either short or long, print or digital. The interview participant did not delineate his creating in this way, but spoke of comics as both a print and digital material. In alignment with this open-ended framing, I have embarked on this chapter with a similar approach.

Miguel's identity as a fan located his practices in a larger set of responses to cultural materials, including the edgier work published by Image Comics (Perren & Felschow, 2017). He noted the value that is placed on creator-owned work by this publisher, which has been a hallmark of Image since its development. de Kloet and van Zoonen (2007) located authenticity as a major feature of fandom, the notion of a "true fan" (p. 326). These researchers also noted the importance of the emic relationship of the fan to speak to the unique nature of fan community; in this case, Miguel speaks with an insider's knowledge of adult comics fandom, creativity, and musical insights that inform his visual preferences and reading choices. Hills (2017) noted the corollary of a community of fandom was non-authentic, or "non-communal" (p. 856). This notion of insider's knowledge is a kind of marker for those who truly know the material and engage regularly with a series of stories and well-known characters, including the universe building that is often a part of fantasy/comics narrative.

This presence of fandom and affinity spaces within the wider world of comics has been studied in relationship to family practices in blogging (Lewis, 2014), as well as in linking to poetry compositions with print-to-print material relationships (Kersulov & Henze, 2021). Lewis (2014) noted a commitment and sense of "dedication" to digital work, evidenced by "enthusiasm" and "time committed" (p. 71), and noted this digital work as a center of agency for young authors. The architecture of digital environments both creators and authors, regardless of age, issues into a sense of ownership and decision-making in crafting structures online and opening avenues of potential communication. Robbins (2017) considered the relationships between and among digital environments, fandom, and culture, noting the potential for presentations of "diversity and identity issues," as well as power and privilege (p. 212).

In terms of online authorship and creation, Black (2009) has written about the affordances for literacy that can be located in fanfiction, including the interactions that occur for participants across geographic borders. De Kosnik (2009) has written about the open-access/free nature of fan fiction, observing the role of commercialization in digital processes. Maldonado and Yuan (2011) linked notions of digital navigation and engagement with the creation of comics, and Bahl (2015) has noted the "overlaps and possibilities" when thinking about comics and digital environments (p. 179).

TRANSMEDIAL PRACTICES (WITH COMICS IN MIND)

Interwoven within in the comics practices evident in the subject's life and creative work is a sense of connectedness with gaming culture and music culture. Giacotto (2022) noted the role of comics in literacy as "much more than a happy distraction," suggesting, "The strong visual aspect [of comics] helps readers' imagination anchor expressions by not putting them in context but making the medium multimodal" (p. 20). In terms of video games, Gee (2003) has written about the affordances of video games for literacy development, with particular notes for learning in sciences. Gee (2003) noted that video games can serve as informational texts, offering content within a situated context, rather than in a space that lacks relevance or connection.

Steinkuehler (2010) suggested that video games exist in a wider "ecology" of materials that youth engage with as a routine part of daily life (p. 61), and noted the narrative qualities of games. Steinkuehler (2010) further noted that games carry the additional affordance of linking players to a sprawling online community. In spite of the relationships that are possible for gaming and literacy, the dissonance between academic/school life and gaming have been tenuous in Steinkuehler's view. Harvey (2015) links the idea of the critiquing fan with the assembly of media and images, including music, that is part of modern storytelling engagement as a viewer and listener, as well as from the role of a fan. This researcher further links fandom with notions of friendship and community in recounting seeing a film with a group of people with like interests. Pence (2012) further links transmedia concepts with teaching, including the ways in which stories are both retold and explored in further detail across forms of media, from film to digital constructions. Weaver (2013) has also noted the role of comics as a nexus or hub of interconnected transmedia storytelling, discussing the intricate worlds and storylines that form a thread through narratives across media.

A YOUTH OF COMICS, TOYS, AND COPYING

As a youth, Miguel "fell in love" with the work of Daniel Warren Johnson, calling work "insane," and noting the unity of thrash metal and drawing located in the work as a source of energy. This sense of insanity was considered a compliment as Miguel discussed the vivid nature of Johnson's work in comics. The activity was described as gestural and "super fun," an innovative sense of practice in which the artist could do whatever they wanted. Indeed, Johnson's style is unique and has been brought into mainstream universes (both Marvel and DC Comics) to take on classic characters. Johnson also explores stories that focus on science fiction characters of his own, as well as characters in the wrestling world. The term "fell in love" conveys an immediate avocation with the material, both in terms of creative choices (as in, ranges of topics) and style.

In addition to the other media that Miguel located as inspiration, he mentioned paying visits to KayBee Toys as a physical space of creative exploration and grounding sense of play from the 1990s. Miguel recounted the experience of finding a Spiderman action figure:

This red and blue figure was in this packaging, and of course it was Spiderman. After I rip open the packaging, this thing falls out, I have no idea what it is. And it was a Todd McFarland issue 306, Amazing Spider-Man, I think is what it was. I couldn't, couldn't read at the time but, man, I loved the pictures in it. And then that just started me just like copying images when I was a kid in my sketchbooks. Just copy, copy, copy all the time. And so yeah, and then fast forward years later. And then that love starts to come back and then the fire starts to come back a little bit. (personal communication, October 2021)

The author/artist notably tranforms to an active present tense when discussing this event, and describes finding the comic book inside in a way that brings to light both his delight and his emerging awareness of an artist and author who would later transform him yet again (McFarlane is one of the major figures at Image Comics, a publisher of Daniel Warren Johnson's work that is noted in the interview transcript). These relationships between makers and materials act as a kind of tradesman/fandom mentoring from afar, as readers encounter the work of artist they love for the first time and then seek to emulate these practices in their own creations.

In fact, Miguel noted that these early interactions with reading images and copying work led to the establishing of sketchbook practices in Miguel's middle school years, in addition to a developing affinity with music and skateboarding. Of further note, engagement with the comics pages preceded being able to read the words, providing a vivid and visual scaffold for engagement with the character, storyline, and style in a manner that was not a lock-step identification of a moment of literacy development, but rather an invitation to print concepts that did not rely on knowledge of the words and symbols used in the book (yet). Comics, toys, music, and even physical enactments were all part of Miguel's storyworld as a young person, expanding beyond traditional limits of what might count as literacy engagement as he navigated the world around him.

Within the context of college, Miguel encountered acrylic painting in a classroom space, as well as the art and video game design of a title, *Witcher 3*, merging physical and digital materials. Miguel recounted:

And then like finding out that concept art, you could get paid creating stuff for entertainment, like design-ing the worlds and whatever, even just the little things like nuts and bolts. People design that for gains and stuff, of course. It was like a light bulb for me, and I was like, Well, I don't want to be an electrician. I want to I want to draw stuff. I'd be awesome. So, I started diving into the research for that. And then with all the podcasts and stuff I was listening to, it was like visual storytelling was important aspects for concept artists and illustration. (personal communication, October 2021)

This move from digital material was one that led to self-reported research, and linked to this author/ artist's ideas about the role that he wanted to play in the larger world as a member of the work force. His statement about being an electrician demonstrates this interest in and involvement with a kind of making and creating that underscores his desire to link this work commercially as a means to earn a living. The linking between youthful or hobby-related affinities and agency in the adult world here is conveyed in the experience of discovering concept art as a venue for creation. Miguel notes the role of visual storytelling in his process, and further notes yet another media text that informed his practices and direction – the podcast, a form of text that has been examined in terms of youth identity and in terms of literacy practices (Bianchi-Pennington, 2018; Hennig, 2017; Wilson et al., 2012).

As an artist, Miguel is not limited to comics art. At the time of our interview, he was working on a portrait commission using the lightbox. He said, "I did a digital painting of it when I blew it up, printed it out and it's light box that. And now I'm pretty much just like matching the image as I go" (personal communication, October 2021). Endemic in this response is the notion that an artistic work takes on several steps and layers across media, a process that Miguel further described later in our interview. This work was done in addition to what Miguel called personal projects and "stuff on the side" (personal communication, October 2021) as the artist engaged with multiple projects, also including a card game with friends. The role of multitasking and managing multiple projects was one that was evident in our discussion as Miguel had a personal system for thinking about the projects in which he would engage and how they would unfold based on his priorities. The social practices of linking friendship with art and creation, as well as fandom was evident in this discourse, leading to collaboration. This sense of collaboration is woven into the fabric of the design process of many comics (Gray & Wilkins, 2016). This work also included a sense of visual development, and Miguel's practices linked with a writer who was his roommate at the time.

As part of their collaborative process, the team learns how to play music together and engaged in scripting. The platform Kickstarter was mentioned as a platform that the team was exploring. Alvermann's (2017) notion of multiliteracies was evident here as this writer/artist team located platforms in which to share their work with a wider audience and within the conext of collaboration. Miguel termed this "twenty-four hour seven-day fun." Engagements among this creative them including sequential art that was created and uploaded on YouTube, work that "fired up" Miguel in 2015. In addition to YouTube, the team edited a podcast about comics creation. The activity of the team was clearly not limited to the printed page or one particular avenue/medium of expression. This sense of engagement and being fired up was evident as Miguel discussed his individual and collaborative work, and as he noted his continuous involvement in creating and attempting to make a viable living as a comics maker/game designer.

Linking to Comics and Digital Interactions

Miguel commented on the affordances of the comics medium as an ideal way to merge his storytelling interests and avocations. He noted both the use of the image and likened this textual quality to the intensity of animation, making another connection to digital media. This merging of materials as a seamless series of texts holds implications for the ways in which educators and mix and mingle materials in a physical and digital/virtual collage approach in K-12 contexts, as well as undergraduate and graduate studies. Miguel noted that this inception into making comics had continued into a lifetime habit and the desire to pursue a career in the comics industry. In particular, Miguel mentioned Johnson's *Murder Falcon* (2019), as well comics featuring Godzilla – a character and storyline he merged with music. He further noted is interested in body horror as a genre of both film and material for making.

In terms of his initial comics work, Miguel chose to create a story in the western genre, inspired by the *Red Dead Redemption* game, stating that the story began to form in response to his love of the game. Linking once more to educational approaches and possibilities, Miguel found the space to create his graphic novel in an undergraduate art class. The instructor encouraged students to work on passion projects, creating open invitations for linking materials and inspiration together. Miguel also mentioned that part of his work was headed in a gamified direction and noted that he has a collaborator who is a game developer.

For Miguel, the sense of digital interaction did not stop at materials, but issued into the affordances of community that he found. He noted that he reads comments from readers, provide a real-time and instant sense of feedback about his work. The choice to launch his work in an online platform allowed for these interactions, and further noted the lifetime of the format as an avenue for seeing his own growth and development as an artist and creator. Awareness of his growth led to revisions in his subsequent work.

When discussing his process as a creator, the author/artist noted that he began with water color art and made a short comic. In terms of further steps in making process, Miguel noted that he draws upon a diverse range of materials and is always trying new things. I have retained his words below in chunks of dialogue, which additional annotations for analysis, indicated in brackets. He begins with a description of the ways in which he moves back and forth in processes, likening it attention deficit hyperactivity disorder as he uses some approaches, and then others, depending on the frame from which he seeks to work and share.

I.   I'm kinda just like ADHD, just switching up all the time. [alternating styles]
II.   I don't know. So, but majority is a, that's probably the most fun than I have in terms of doing comics and image-making, working with ink. [drawn a particular medium/style on the page]

Miguel notes the ways in which image and the page work in this section, and draws attention to his chosen medium of ink as one way of creating. This links to his artistic background and formal training in at least a print-based regard.

III. Because the process that I go through is these small, tiny little thumbnail sketches of trying to figure out the bigger picture. [initial steps]

For this author/artist, there is a drafting phase that allows him to envision the larger world of the project. In the typical sequence of composing, there is a similarity in beginning to work out the details of what will be shared, as noted in the work of Edwards-Groves (2011).

And then I'll usually, sometimes I'll blow it up on Photoshop and then just start going in with details and like fixing proportions and stuff and put an image together. [digital processing → moving print to digital]

And then there's other times where I'll, I will pencil out on paper and then ink it after that. [dynamic of print making processes]

But most of the time I'm penciling, digitally, printing it out on like a Bristol paper, 11 by 17 Bristol paper, and then inking it with India ink of some kind. [merged processes of print and digital making → movement from one medium to the next]

I have, it's ink that I got off Amazon because they're super cheap, but I use those pens that I'm forgetting the name of right now. But you refill and they're almost like a repeater, graphing pens, paragraphs, like ink for that, that I put in my brush pens and stuff. [notes on preferred physical materials and access to these materials]

It's very liquidy, you know, it just flows. [affordances of the chosen materials for physical making]

So, just to be cheap because I don't like to buy a whole bunch of stuff, so I just keep refilling my ink cartridges with that brush pens and go at it. [notes on preferred physical materials and access to these materials]

The author and artist discusses the access necessary, as well as the multiple steps in using materials in these statements. Such a range of materials carries a cost, and Miguel finds himself using what is reusable, easy to refill, and cost-effective for his work. Here, there is a sense of the perseverance and time spent in locating sensible materials in sensible ways, another indication of an involvement with making that overcomes boundaries that might otherwise be prohibitive.

I mean, it's a multi-step process. All of the steps. It's crazy how much work is put in to a comic. You don't realize it until you do it, I suppose, or, or watch someone do it. [summative process notes]

Miguel noted that the entire process usually takes roughly six months for the work to be complete for a 64-page comic book form. From locating materials, to navigating processes, to prioritizing projects, the account of this artist is one that speaks to the volume of work and dedication that is necessary, but also an aspect of one who identifies as a fan and creator. Later, he returned to his conversation of the digital processes that he employs:

I'll just put that in Photoshop. And then once I print it out and start doing the inking stage, I also letter like with, with the ink. But that, that may change for the next few projects coming up just to save a little bit more time.

Also in terms of comics, Miguel mentioned that he is creating a PDF in black and white, a project he hoped to complete by the end of October 2021. There is a sense of autonomy in designing projects and then determining ideal finish dates as an independent artist and consumer, a sense of making for both self and others. Commissions were part of this author/artist's life, while passion projects formed another avenue of creating and engagement. Miguel locates consuming in the way that he samples music and media as forms of authorial inspiration. The process is active and does not seem to arrive with ease; rather, there is a multi-fold sense of His agency is evident in finding and celebrating authors and stories that he likes, and that form a connective thread of continued inspiration for creating.

CONCLUSION AND IMPLICATIONS

As a creator who is a college graduate and adult, Miguel acts as a narrative case study model of literacy practices that unite media, and his links to education are notable for consideration. He is a creator who draws upon collaborative methods and engagements to shape his work, and seizes upon platforms to share and market his creations. Chiefly, he notes the affordance of making space for passion projects as part of instructional routines. This move to merge physical and digital media transcends a singular approach to making with one particular medium, or in a particular style. His interests subsume music, film, video games, and comics in a seamless stream of materials that is not bounded. There is no prioritizing of materials for this reader, viewer, and maker that was evident in our discussion, aside from particular titles that formed a part of his literacy history and spoke to his current work.

Miguel's notes about his inspirations speak to the interconnected nature of texts not only within a particular genre, or even medium, but as a free-flowing range of materials that can serve to inspire readers and makers. This comment centralizes the function of reading and engagement, along with film viewing, as a range of textual and literacy practices that can be part of the same routine for readers. What is more, the notion of "copying" so often discouraged in school practices is seen here as a means of moving to the next step as a creator.

Implications for educational practices include, but are not limited to, the role of teacher for creating spaces for invitational composing; the role of teachers and policymakers in acting as mediators of content and consumers of texts, rather than guardians of particular types of literacy engagement; and, the ways in which making and composing is valued as a part of classroom practices. Miguel notably did not mention canonical texts or curriculum as inspirations for his creative process, but spoke to the value and possibilities locating in everyday materials (e.g., action figures, video games, comics).

Educators might ask themselves: What practices can I locate in everyday practices to transform the ways I think about, talk about, and teach literacy concepts? Miguel's work demonstrates that there need not be a noticeable and substantive dichotomy between print and digital materials – it is the case that we are continually living and being in a world where "real life" and "digital life" are one and the same. By the same turn, this merging of realities entails a merging of practices as reading, writing, and composing can take place within traditional texts, as well as across a range of media with varying degrees of access, and with particular ties to areas of attention and interest from readers and creators.

REFERENCES

Alvermann, D. E. (2017). The M word: Dare we use it? *Journal of Adolescent & Adult Literacy, 61*(1), 99–102. doi:10.1002/jaal.665

Bahl, E. K. (2015). Comics and scholarship: Sketching the possibilities. *Composition Studies, 43*(1), 178–182.

Bianchi-Pennington, B. (2018). Designing literary discussion with podcasts. *Journal of Adolescent & Adult Literacy, 61*(5), 589–591. doi:10.1002/jaal.724

Black, R. W. (2009). Online fan fiction, global identities, and imagination. *Research in the Teaching of English, 43*(4), 397–425.

Brandell, J. R., & Varkas, T. (2001). Narrative case studies. The handbook of social work research methods, 293-307.

Clandinin, D. J. (Ed.). (2006). *Handbook of narrative inquiry: Mapping a methodology.* Sage Publications.

de Kloet, J., & van Zoonen, L. (2007). Fan culture: Performing difference. *Media studies: Key issues and debates*, 322-341.

De Kosnik, A. (2009). Should fan fiction be free? *Cinema Journal, 48*(4), 118–124. doi:10.1353/cj.0.0144

Edwards-Groves, C. J. (2011). The multimodal writing process: Changing practices in contemporary classrooms. *Language and Education, 25*(1), 49–64. doi:10.1080/09500782.2010.523468

Gee, J. P. (2003). What video games have to teach us about learning and literacy. [CIE]. *Computers in Entertainment, 1*(1), 20–20. doi:10.1145/950566.950595

Giacotto, S. (2022). Using comics to teach. *Language Magazine, 21*(11), 20.

Gray, B. C., & Wilkins, P. (2016). The case of the missing author: Toward an anatomy of collaboration in comics. In Cultures of Comics Work (pp. 115-129). Palgrave Macmillan, New York.

Harvey, C. B. (2015). Fantastic transmedia. In *Fantastic Transmedia* (pp. 12–39). Palgrave Macmillan. doi:10.1057/9781137306043_2

Hennig, N. (2017). Podcast literacy: Educational, accessible, and diverse podcasts for library users. *Library Technology Reports, 53*(2), 1–42.

Hills, M. (2017). From fan culture/community to the fan world: Possible pathways and ways of having done fandom. *Palabra Clave (La Plata), 20*(4), 856–883. doi:10.5294/pacla.2017.20.4.2

Johnson, D. W. (2019). *Murder falcon.* Image Comics.

Kersulov, M. L., & Henze, A. (2021). Where image and text meet identity: Gifted students' poetry comics and the crafting of "nerd identities.". *The Journal of Media Literacy Education, 13*(1), 92–105. doi:10.23860/JMLE-2021-13-1-8

Lewis, T. Y. (2014). Affinity spaces, apprenticeships, and agency: Exploring blogging engagements in family spaces. *Journal of Adolescent & Adult Literacy, 58*(1), 71–81. doi:10.1002/jaal.322

Maldonado, N., & Yuan, T. (2011). Technology in the classroom: from Ponyo to "My Garfield Story": using digital comics as an alternative pathway to literary composition. *Childhood Education*, *87*(4), 297–301. doi:10.1080/00094056.2011.10523197

Pence, H. E. (2011). Teaching with transmedia. *Journal of Educational Technology Systems*, *40*(2), 131–140. doi:10.2190/ET.40.2.d

Perren, A., & Felschow, L. E. (2017). The bigger picture: Drawing intersections between comics, fan, and industry studies. In *The Routledge Companion to Media Fandom* (pp. 309–318). Routledge. doi:10.4324/9781315637518-38

Robbins, M. A. (2017). *Confessions of a Fangirl: Interactions with Affinity Spaces and Multimodal, Multicultural Texts at Book Clubs and Fandom Events* [Doctoral dissertation, University of Georgia].

Stake, R. E. (1995). *The art of case study research*. Sage Publications.

Steinkuehler, C. (2010). Video games and digital literacies. *Journal of Adolescent & Adult Literacy*, *54*(1), 61–63. doi:10.1598/JAAL.54.1.7

Weaver, T. (2013). *Comics for film, games, and animation: using comics to construct your transmedia storyworld*. Routledge. doi:10.4324/9780240824055

Wilson, A. A., Chavez, K., & Anders, P. L. (2012). "From the Koran and Family Guy": Expressions of identity in English learners' digital podcasts. *Journal of Adolescent & Adult Literacy*, *55*(5), 374–384. doi:10.1002/JAAL.00046

KEY TERMS AND DEFINITIONS

Affinity space: An online or physical community in which fans can gather to share thoughts and work.

Comics: In this work, comics is a term that is used to define a particular mode of storytelling, aligned with a particular grammatical sensibility.

Fandom: The community or group that aligns themselves with a particular media-related avocation or interest (for example, comics fandom).

Fanfiction: A type of storytelling, often found in digital spaces, in which authors take up and transform characters they love to make their own stories in which they decide what happens inside or outside of canon.

Mode: A site of communication within a text (for example, movement or sound).

Multimodality: Communication practices that unite across modes, or methods of reproducing content.

Transmedia: The merging of stories and content across media, often with commercial purposes.

Chapter 11
The Struggle Is Real:
Teachers' Experiences With Recruiting Critical Digital Literacy to Their Practices

Vicki A. Hosek
Illinois State University, USA

Lara J. Handsfield
Illinois State University, USA

ABSTRACT

Digital environments offer opportunities and spaces for students to engage in critical literacy practices. This necessitates a teacher's critical understanding of the social structures at work in online environments while instructing students. In this chapter, findings are presented from a mixed-methods study of four practicing teachers who characterized themselves as having strong personal and pedagogical knowledge of critical digital literacies (CDL) and claimed to recruit that knowledge to their classroom practices. Data analysis of teacher surveys, lesson plans, classroom observations and interviews pointed to several obstacles the teachers faced with incorporating critical dimensions into their students' technology use. The obstacles include: school/district technology restrictions; a lack of in depth understanding of CDL, and limited modeling and opportunities during teacher education and teacher development programs to build and recruit CDL to their practices. Implications for teacher education and development and suggestions for future research are presented.

PURPOSE

Digital environments provide dialogic opportunities for students to engage in critical literacy practices (Pangrazio, 2016). This requires instruction founded on sociocultural awareness and teachers' critical understanding of digital environments (Hosek & Handsfield, 2019; Song, 2016; Watulak & Kinzer, 2013). However, there is an over-emphasis in teacher education and professional development on the technical aspects of integrating digital literacy practices into instruction (Philip & Olivares-Pasillas, 2016; Selwyn, 2016). This is particularly the case in work centered around technological pedagogical content

DOI: 10.4018/978-1-6684-7015-2.ch011

knowledge (TPACK) (Hosek, 2018; Koehler & Mishra, 2006, 2009). Less emphasis is devoted to the critical dimensions of digital literacy practices and development of a teacher's own critical digital literacies (CDL) (R. J. Chen, 2010; Philip & Olivares-Pasillas, 2016). This has led to digital literacy practices that are largely substitutive, resulting in superficial rather than meaningful student engagement in digital environments (Cuban, 2009; Author, 2018; Lim et al., 2013). In other words, such practices reproduce a functionalist frame, which "avoids ideological considerations (Marcuse, 1964), reflecting a positivist view that facts are separate from human values, thus avoiding explicit linkages between education and politics" (Edmondson, 2002, p. 113). This approach to and understanding of digital environments positions teachers and students as passive recipients of discourses present in those environments rather than active representatives of diverse perspectives.

In this paper, we share findings from a mixed-methods study investigating practicing teachers' beliefs about how they are prepared to critically integrate technology into their classroom practices and what led to and/or hindered their engagement in the critical dimensions of technology use in their teaching practices. Specifically, we explore the following question: What do practicing teachers who characterize themselves as having strong personal, pedagogical and technological knowledge of CDL identify as factors that support or hinder their abilities to engage CDL into their instruction? This research carries implications about both future research, such as pushing past functionalist frames (Edmondson, 2002) for technology use in educational settings, as well as the importance of connecting critical theory to digital literacy practices during teacher education and development programs.

RELEVANT LITERATURE

We reviewed literature in two areas: 1) studies concerning how the digital literacy and CDL practices of teacher candidates and practicing teachers has been conceptualized and measured; and 2) studies exploring how teacher candidates and teachers recruit a critical lens when integrating digital literacy tools into their instruction. In our review, we found a strong emphasis on the technical aspects of digital literacy practices in teacher education and professional development and less emphasis on the critical dimensions of teachers' digital literacy practices.

Measuring Digital Literacy and TPACK

There is an emphasis in the research on the technical aspects of digital literacy and the quantitative valuation of it. This is especially true of studies that rely on the Technological Pedagogical and Content Knowledge (TPACK) framework and TPACK measurement instruments (Chai et al., 2010; Hofer & Grandgenett, 2012; Koh & Divaharan, 2011; Neiss, 2011; Schmidt et al., 2009). The TPACK framework connects teachers' domains of knowledge whereby "technology, pedagogy, and content do not exist in a vacuum, but rather, are instantiated in specific learning and teaching contexts" (Koehler et al., 2013, p. 16). See Figure 1 and Table 1 for detailed explanations of each TPACK component. Complexity of the knowledge domains that comprise TPACK led to issues of reliability and validity in multiple studies (Archambault & Barnett, 2010; Banister & Reinhart, 2012; Chai et al, 2010; Koh & Divaharan, 2011; Pamuk, 2012). Importantly, these studies stop short of considering the role of critical theory in the development of digital literacy practices despite Koehler, Mishra, and Cain's (2013) emphasis on the importance of context when operating in digital environments. Missing is consideration of the socioeconomic affordances and barriers that accompany technology use; the power structures at work in digital environments; and the limited exposure of both students and teachers to diverse ideologies when participating in those environments (Chai et al., 2010; Hofer & Grandgenett, 2012; Koh & Divaharan, 2011; Schmidt et al., 2009; Young et al., 2012). In short, empirical research about how digital literacies are defined in teacher education and teacher development programs is largely functionalist (Edmondson, 2002) in emphasis, leaving little room for consideration of the critical dimensions of digital literacy practices and the development of teachers' personal CDL. This led us to consider literature that incorporated either a CDL framework and/or central components of CDL.

Figure 1. TPACK model
(Adapted with permission from "What is Technological Pedagogical Content Knowledge? by M.J. Koehler and P. Mishra, 2009, Contemporary Issues in Technology and Teacher Education, 9(1), p. 63. [Copyright 2009 by tpack.org]).

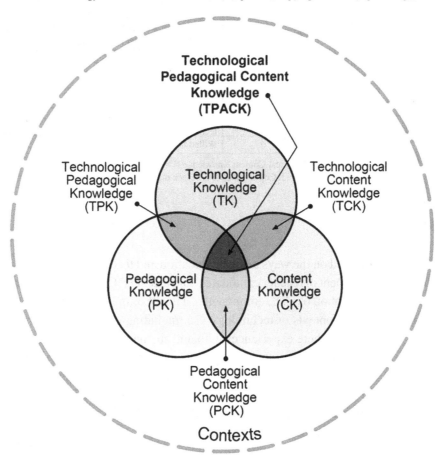

Table 1. Description of TPACK components

Component	Description
Content Knowledge (CK)	Knowledge about subject matter being taught and learned
Pedagogical Knowledge (PK)	Knowledge surrounding beliefs about how content should be taught and how students learn content; includes beliefs about the purpose of education and the methods and practices that support that purpose
Pedagogical Content Knowledge (PCK)	Knowledge of the conditions that promote learning discipline content including how curriculum, assessment and pedagogy are linked
Technology Knowledge (TK)	Broad understanding of technology and its applicability so as to improve productivity; knowledge that aids in the accomplishment of a variety of tasks; continually evolving and developing
Technology Content Knowledge (TCK)	An understanding of the impact of technology on practices and content of a specific discipline; knowledge of the affordances and constraints of technology in a discipline; how technology and content work together and/or constrain each other
Technological Pedagogical Knowledge (TPK)	Knowledge of how teaching and learning changes with the use of technology; knowledge of the affordances and constraints of a wide range of technologies and their impact on instructional design and strategies
Technological Pedagogical Content Knowledge (TPCK)	The understanding that emerges from the interactions of technology with pedagogy and content; meaningful and deeply skilled use of technology in a discipline

Note. Adapted from "What is Technological Pedagogical Content Knowledge?" by M.J. Koehler and P. Mishra, 2009, *Contemporary Issues in Technology and Teacher Education, 9*(1), p. 63. Copyright 2009 by tpack.org

CDL Studies

To identify research that focused on the ways teacher education and teacher development programs have been approaching the development of teacher candidates' and teachers' CDL practices, we utilized Watulak and Kinzer's (2013) description of CDL components. Those components include: 1) Understanding cultural, social, and historical contexts of technology use, including ethical and appropriate practices; 2) critical thinking and analysis where experiences with and surrounding technology use leads to more disciplined thinking that includes critical examination of social inequities; 3) reflective practice that shows an awareness of the social, cultural, and historical contexts in personal practices as well as how personal practices position others; and 4) functional skills with digital tools (Watulak & Kinzer, 2013). Our review revealed that researchers recognized the benefit of integrating digital environments into classroom communities and addressed certain components of CDL.

In his study of the online engagement of university students, Hughes' (2009) determined that students' online activities suggested a university focus on "ensuring they possess the skills and understanding to search, authenticate and critically evaluate material from the range of appropriate sources, and attribute it as necessary" (Hughes, 2009, p. 7). Notably, while critical examination is a component of CDL, Hughes (2009) concluded that the online activities stopped short of meeting the needs of the students due to the limitations imposed during instruction while engaging online. Van Laar et al. (2017) study highlighted a similar disconnect between students' needs and opportunities offered. As a result, they proposed that 21st Century Workplace Skills require the inclusion of a critical component when defining digital literacy.

Few literacy researchers would question the importance of engaging students critically in digital environments. Studies show that teacher-led critical engagement activities helps with student development of social awareness (W. Chen, 2013; Moran et al., 2011; Gil de Zúñiga et al., 2012; Riedl et al., 2013), networking skills, and collaboration resulting in a positive impact on learning (W. Chen, 2013; Gil de Zúñiga et al., 2012; Lim & Richardson, 2016; Riedl et al., 2013). Gil de Zúñiga et al. (2012) identified a positive relationship between students who used digital resources and an increase in participation in politics, discussion, and civic engagement (Gil de Zúñiga et al., 2012). Further, Gainer (2010) found that students "drew on their cultural resources and life experiences as they deconstructed, debated, resisted, and reimagined dominant narratives of urban students" (p. 372) while engaging in online assignments.

Choudhury and Share (2012) studied the role of social network sites (SNS) in student empowerment. Similar to Gainer (2010), they concluded that strong teacher guidance while participating on SNS led to a stronger presence of student critical thinking, and increased students' self-esteem and pride (Choudhury & Share, 2012). Kirschner's (2015) study of students' use of SNS showed that regardless of students' online experience in their personal lives, transitioning from personal to educational use requires guidance from educators. As evidenced in these studies, the teacher's role is pivotal in effectuating student CDL practices. This points to the importance of providing opportunities for teachers to develop understanding of CDL and CDL pedagogies which we examine next.

Digital Literacy Practices in Teacher Education and Teacher Development

Previous research shows that teachers' pedagogical beliefs impact their digital literacy practices (Anderson et al., 2011; Koehler & Mishra, 2009; Koh et al., 2014; Prestridge, 2017; Tondeur et al., 2013). In addition, specific exposure to modeling of content area digital literacy practices plays a key role in teachers' decisions surrounding instructional technology use (Goktas et al., 2009; Sutton, 2011). While there are limited studies exploring teachers' CDL practices, some research offers insight into the kinds of teacher development activities that support technology integration.

Earlier research illustrates that providing opportunities for teachers to examine their pedagogical beliefs in combination with technology integration methods leads to increased digital literacy practices (Ertmer et al., 2012; Koh et al., 2014; Overbay et al., 2010; Prestridge, 2017; Ruggiero & Mong, 2015). Liu et al. (2015) and Tondeur et al. (2013) found that teachers who observed other educators successfully adopting and integrating technology increased the likelihood that they would integrate it themselves. Studies also show that collaboration about ways to incorporate digital literacy practices to help meet content area standards led to increased technology use of those educators (Stanhope & Corn, 2014; Tondeur et al., 2013; Udesky, 2015).

However, the prevalent short workshop format for technology integration PD does not result in sustained instructional digital literacy practices (Battersby & Verdi, 2015; DuFour & Mattos, 2013; Louis & Wahlstrom, 2011). Darling-Hammond et al. (2009) pointed out that "While teachers typically need substantial professional development in a given area (close to 50 hours) to improve their skills and their students' learning, most professional development opportunities in the U.S. are much shorter" (p.5). Concerning technology integration, Gulamhussein (2013) reported that "...mastery comes only as result of continuous practice despite awkward performance and frustration in the early stages...When teachers are coached through the awkward phase of implementation, 95 percent can transfer the skill" (p. 37). In fact, researchers found that teachers benefited most from continual, practiced use of technology skills they learned (Liu et al., 2015; Ruggiero & Mong, 2016; Sutton, 2011; Tondeur et al., 2008; Topper & Lancaster, 2013).

These issues are consistent with research on teacher preparation and digital literacy practices. Studies show that education students do not feel they see enough real classroom application of technology, which negatively impacts their instructional digital literacy practices use (Goktas, et al., 2009; Ruggiero & Mong, 2015; Sutton, 2011; Topper & Lancaster, 2013). Furthermore, teacher candidates' self-efficacy regarding the use of technology is another strong factor in their decision to integrate technology as practicing teachers (Bandurra, 1977; Banister & Reinhart, 2012; R. J. Chen, 2010; Duffin et al., 2012; Holzberger et al., 2013). However, even if teachers are comfortable with technology integration, they may not do so in critical ways (Hosek & Handsfield, 2019). A missing critical approach to and engagement in digital environments is a missed opportunity for students to learn about, critically evaluate, engage with, and present diverse perspectives. As such, a focus on this missing critical "C" in the research and in teacher education is an important starting point.

THEORETICAL FRAMEWORK

Our theoretical framework for this study brings together two different areas of conceptual work related to technology, teacher development, and literacy: Technological, Pedagogical, Content Knowledge (TPACK) (Koehler & Mishra, 2006, 2009) and Critical Digital Literacies (CDL) (Watulak & Kinzer, 2013). These two areas of scholarship reflect distinct epistemological frameworks that reflect different ideological commitments regarding teaching, learning, and literacy. However, we bring them together into what we refer to as the C-TPACK framework, which re-centers the missing "C", or critical component, in the field of digital literacies and teacher education and development.

TPACK

Koehler and Mishra's (2006; 2009) TPACK framework informed our approach to this study by providing an understanding about how teachers' technology integration has been previously defined and studied in the research. Conceptually, TPACK appears to allow for the dynamic nature of technology knowledge by connecting it to the content and pedagogical foundational knowledge of pre-service and practicing teachers (Harris & Hofer, 2014, 2017; Niess, 2011). However, we believe that an essential component is missing to truly address the impact that contexts have on teacher decisions surrounding instructional use of technology.

The TPACK framework was originally envisioned to support the consideration of context and situated practice (Koehler et al., 2013; Davies & West, 2014). Koehler and Mishra (2006; 2009) warned that without context tied to a theoretical perspective, research "constrains our current educational uses of computers" and "seriously limits our vision of what might be accomplished with computer technology in a broader social, cultural, or educational context" (p. 119). This missing consideration of context is evident in research since the introduction of the TPACK framework (Chai et al., 2010; Hofer & Grandgenett, 2012; Koh & Divaharan, 2011; Schmidt et al., 2009; Young et al., 2012), which led us to consider the incorporation of a critical lens to ensure that attention is paid to the ideological underpinnings of digital environments.

The C-TPACK Framework

The C-TPACK framework draws on conceptualizations of previous researchers who have proposed a democratic instructional approach where critical analysis of content and context join with the creation and design of new content that represents students' voices (Burnett & Merchant, 2011; Garcia, 2013; Author, 2018; Watulak & Kinzer, 2013). Watulak and Kinzer (2013) explained CDL as having several components which include: "understanding cultural, social, and historical contexts of technology use; critical thinking and analysis; reflective practice; and facility with the functional skills and tools of digital technology production" (p. 128).

Importantly, the C-TPACK framework connects components of TPACK and CDL to ensure a critical component is considered when studying and understanding decisions and practices of teachers regarding instructional technology use. This framework: 1) prioritizes the recognition and critical analysis of the ideologies and social factors that are embedded in digital literacies; 2) considers necessary the inclusion of new technologies in the understanding and valuing of the development of student' literacy development; 3) recognizes the importance of connecting content, pedagogical, and technological knowledge to more meaningfully integrate technology; and 4) values the participatory and collaborative practices of digital environments that contribute to student literacy development.

METHODS

Again, the purpose of this study was to examine practicing teachers' beliefs about and engagement in the critical dimensions of digital literacy classroom practices. Our findings are based on analyses of a portion of data from a larger study (Hosek, 2018). This mixed methods study spanned one academic semester and included two phases of data collection. Phase 1 consisted of collection and analysis of online surveys regarding practicing teachers' understandings of C-TPACK. Survey results led us to invite a sub-set of those teachers who self-identified as having high C-TPACK to participate in Phase 2, resulting in four Phase 2 participants. During Phase 2, we collected and analyzed the teachers' lesson plans, completed observations of them teaching those lesson plans, and interviewed the teachers' post-observations.

Below, we describe the setting, participants, data sources and collection, and our analytical approaches to the data collected.

Setting and Participants

Participants were identified based on purposeful sampling of graduate education students at Middle State University (pseudonym). Only those who were also practicing teachers were considered for inclusion in this study. During Phase 1, 58 (n=58) graduate students at MSU (pseudonym) completed an online survey that contained demographic questions, C-TPACK likert-scale questions, and open-ended questions regarding technology integration experiences and CDL knowledge. Graduate students who were also practicing teachers and whose survey answers indicated a high level of C-TPACK (explained below) were recruited and agreed to further participate, resulting in four participating teachers (n=4) in Phase 2, which was qualitative. Those four teachers (all assigned pseudonyms) included: Andrew, a high school History teacher; Kate, a 7th/8th grade English Language Arts teacher; Diane, an 8th grade Physics teacher; and Sara, a high school Spanish teacher.

Data Sources

C-TPACK surveys, lesson plans, observation notes, and verbatim interview transcripts served as our data sources. Our survey was based on Schmidt et al.'s (2009) TPACK survey and included an additional section of questions created by Hosek (2018) with the purpose of understanding teachers' CDL knowledge. This resulted in eight sections of questions representing eight knowledge domains. The domains included: Digital and Critical Digital Literacies, Technology Knowledge (TK), Content Knowledge (CK), Pedagogical Knowledge (PK), Pedagogical Content Knowledge (PCK), Technological Content Knowledge (TCK), Technological Pedagogical Knowledge (TPK), and Technological Pedagogical Content Knowledge (TPCK).

Additionally, lesson plans that the teachers identified as including teacher and student use of technology were collected and analyzed. Observations of teachers conducting those lessons were made, and detailed notes were taken during the observations for analysis. Finally, post-observation interviews using a semi-structured format were conducted. Hosek (2018) conducted all data collection and had no prior interactions or relationships with the participants.

Data Analysis

Both quantitative and qualitative methods were used to analyze the 58 surveys collected. Descriptive statistics were generated from the likert-scale answers that included the mean, median, mode, minimum and maximum scores, range and variance. In addition, we calculated the overall C-TPACK score for each graduate student. Item responses were scored with a value ranging from "1" assigned for (strongly disagree), to "5" (strongly agree). For each section, the participant's responses were averaged. For example, the six questions under TK (Technology Knowledge) were averaged to produce one TK (Technology Knowledge) score. Those graduate students who scored the highest total C-TPACK scores were recruited for Phase 2.

We conducted qualitative analysis of the open-ended questions, lesson plans, observation notes, and verbatim interview transcripts using first and second cycle coding (Saldana, 2016). Throughout data analysis we used Descriptive Coding primarily for organizing the data into categories. In addition, we used In Vivo and Process Coding to analyze open-ended survey questions and interview transcripts while Process Coding was used for observation notes. We created construct tables for constant comparative analysis of the different data formats for each individual teacher and to complete cross-case analysis of the Phase 2 participants. Our construct table analyses was guided by the C-TPACK framework. In addition, both a social constructivist and constructivist grounded lens led to identification of themes within and between the data.

FINDINGS

The findings from this study contributed to our understanding of the difficulties teachers face with implementing CDL. As explained earlier, all teachers self-identified as having a high C-TPACK in the quantitative portion of the survey. However, all teachers indicated they had limited to no exposure to CDL and CDL modeling in their respective teacher education and professional development programs. Our analyses and triangulation of the survey short answers, lesson plans, observations, and interviews led us to identify patterns across the participants that pointed to factors that hindered the teachers' abilities to recruit CDL into their instruction. See Table 2 for a summary of each participants' data.

Table 2. General summary of participant data

Participant	Survey Results	Lesson Plan	Observations
Andrew - High school History teacher	High C-TPACK; example included personal and student CDL components	Personal CDL; no CDL in student activities	Personal CDL components present; students' online engagement limited
Kate - 7th/8th grade Language Arts teacher	High C-TPACK; no CDL components in example activity	Personal CDL; CDL in student activities	Personal CDL components present; students engaged in some CDL components
Diane - 8th grade Physics teacher	High C-TPACK; no CDL components in example activity	Personal CDL; no CDL in student activities	Personal CDL components present; students' online engagement limited
Sara - High school Spanish teacher	High C-TPACK; example included personal and student CDL components	Personal CDL; no CDL in student activities	Personal CDL components present; students' online engagement limited

CDL Recruitment in Instructional Practices

In the survey short answers, all teachers wrote that they believed they incorporated CDL in their instructional practices. Each provided an example of an instructional activity they had used with students that they believed showed recruitment of CDL. Using the CDL components (listed earlier; Watulak & Kinzer, 2013) as our guide, we found that only Andrew and Sara's examples included both their personal recruitment of CDL (e.g., in instructional design choices and selecting resources) and also opportunities for students to engage in the critical dimensions of technology use.

In all cases, the teachers' lesson plans showed that each did recruit CDL to prepare materials and activities for their classes. However, only in Kate's lesson plans did we find opportunities for students to engage in CDL. Kate's (7th/8th grade ELA) instructional practices with students reflected recruitment of some, but not all, components of CDL. Her lesson was housed within a unit entitled "Passion Projects." During her lesson, students were provided with a multitude of digital options for developing presentations that represented their passions. Throughout the lesson, students freely engaged in multiple digital platforms including Google Classroom, YouTube, and various presentation apps. Kate also engaged each student in discussion about their topic and digital platform choices. She did not engage her students further about critical examination of the ideological underpinnings of the resources and materials they chose and the platforms they engaged in.

In their surveys, Andrew (History teacher) and Diane (Physics teacher) indicated that they did not intentionally plan to incorporate critical dimensions into their planning and instruction. Sara (Spanish teacher) stated she did intend to, and Kate (Language Arts teacher) was unsure. This information was important as it aligned with Author 1's observations of Andrew and Diane, but did not align in the cases of Sara and Kate. Author 1 used the interviews to delve deeper into why this was the case and discovered that school technology policies (in the cases of Andrew, Diane, and Sara) and a lack of understanding CDL (in the cases of Diane and Kate) played strong roles in decisions made surrounding technology use during instruction. See Table 2 for compilation of the results of the survey, lesson plan analysis, and observations.

Difficulties and Barriers

The interviews greatly informed us about the reasons for the teachers' decisions highlighted above. Below, we explain the difficulties and barriers that the teachers identified which include: school policy technology restrictions, understanding of CDL, and limited teacher education and development opportunities to engage in the critical dimensions of digital environments.

School policy technology restrictions

Andrew and Diane explained that their schools had highly restrictive technology policies, particularly with respect to student use of the internet and social media platforms. This significantly impacted their decisions about opportunities for students to critically engage in technology during their lessons. Sara and Kate taught in schools with little technology restrictions for students. These less restrictive policies contributed to different decisions for these teachers. Sara chose to impose her own strong restrictions surrounding student technology use in her classroom because she worried about her students' lack of CDL. She explained that her students "don't have those skills and are not thinking critically." Kate chose to engage her students in projects that maximized their access and use of all digital platforms available.

While the observed classroom decisions of Andrew and Diane seemed to be similar regarding student technology use, there were important differences impacting the teachers' decisions that the interviews flushed out. In his interview, Andrew identified his pedagogical beliefs as grounded on critical theory and constructivism. He stated that he "pushed students to make connections and to understand how events were shaped by previous events and outcomes." Andrew also had a clear understanding of CDL. In his interview, he explained that when engaging in digital environments, "you've got to challenge the authority. You're questioning things." When asked about the digital resources he chooses, he stated "you have to understand that almost everything in it has some viewpoint they're trying to steer you towards."

Andrew saw the benefit of engaging students in critical examination of history content materials and resources; however, the digital platforms where he could provide those opportunities were continually and increasingly blocked due to his school district's restrictive policies. While he didn't provide opportunities for student development of CDL, he personally recruited CDL to critically examine ideologies and power structures at work in media and online resources, which was evident throughout his lesson. For example, when showing photos of soldiers and their spouses/girlfriends celebrating their send off, Andrew explained that "the government wanted to generate excitement about joining the war." Throughout the lesson, he continually asked the students to consider the source and the possible motives and agendas that were being represented in the images the public was shown. Despite using his own CDL to choose, reflect about and consider social, political, and historical contexts of media, Andrew strongly limited his students' technology use during the lesson resulting in functional and substitutive rather than transformative and critical engagements. This aligned with his survey answers.

Conversely, Diane did not see her school's restrictive technology policies as a problem as she worried that her students would "end up on inappropriate websites and not stay on track" with her lesson objectives. In addition, she was unsure about what CDL was and that it "is kind of something that's new to me." She also stated that she saw only a limited connection between CDL and science content: "...I have a tendency to think about critical literacy, um, related to social studies a lot more than say, science." This aligned with her survey responses to the Likert scale questions.

Regardless, Diane explained that the Next Generations Science Standards (NGSS) emphasized digital literacies, and she stated that she continually considered constructivist ways to integrate technology into her instructional technology use with her students. She believed technology "can play a vital role in the science classroom" and that she was hoping to incorporate "iQuests and virtual labs." While she saw the potential for more student-centered technology use, like Andrew, her decisions surrounding instructional technology use with her students reflected traditionalist and didactic practices.

Understanding of CDL

Sara and Kate did not face the same school restrictions as Andrew and Diane; however, each made very different instructional decisions about the opportunities they provided to their students for engaging in critical dimensions of technology use. Like Andrew, Sara had a strong understanding of CDL and her personal planning and use of technology throughout her lesson reflected recruitment of CDL. Interestingly, in her interview, Sara explained that it was her strong understanding and valuing of CDL that led her to restrict her students' technology use during her lesson because she believed her students "don't have those skills and are not thinking critically." She explained that she was unsure about how to help her students develop their CDL, which she believed was essential before giving them access to digital environments during her class. Regarding her students' CDL, she stated: "...that is something where I kind of have to guide the students...because they don't know where or what to look for." She also worried her opinion would "overly influence my students about how they should think about different things." Her beliefs resulted in traditionalist and largely substitutive decisions surrounding instructional student use of technology.

Unlike Sara, Kate was uncertain about what CDL meant and explained her understanding as limited to finding reliable resources. Until this study, she stated that she had not seen a connection between critical theory and digital literacy. This aligned with her survey answers. She explained that she highly valued student-centered opportunities for meaningful engagement in digital environments. This was supported in her lesson planning and lesson activities. It was also clear that she recruited CDL to her personal planning and technology use.

It was evident that technology was integral to all of the teachers' personal practices. In all cases, at least some component of CDL was present in their personal use of technology. In the case of Andrew, Diane, and Sara, students were not extended the opportunities to engage in the critical dimension of technology use. These teachers made conscious decisions to use technology in substitutive and traditional ways. In Kate's case, her instructional practices incorporated limited opportunities for students to critically engage in digital environments.

Limited Teacher Education and Development Opportunities

Combining the findings from the survey data with lesson observations and teacher explanations in the interviews, we identified another barrier that the teachers faced when recruiting CDL to their instructional practices: None of the teachers were provided with opportunities to engage in critical dimensions of technology in their teacher education and development programs. All teachers explained that their PD surrounding technology integration consisted of short workshops focused on learning about new technology apps. For example, Kate explained that her school's PD was "as short as possible" and that "I don't feel like we're that critical in our decision-making about the technology we learn." All teachers actively sought ways to integrate technology on their own time. They each stated that their self-directed PD was driven by their personal interests. However, none of the teachers sought out professional development opportunities that connected theory to technology integration.

DISCUSSION

By inductively moving from quantitative data to qualitative data, we gained a deep understanding of how these teachers' C-TPACK, perspectives, and practices worked together to inform their digital literacy decisions and practices. Equally important, we learned about the difficulties practicing teachers face in recruiting CDL to their instructional practices. The teachers provided information about their perceived personal CDL and their beliefs about their recruitment of CDL to their practices in their surveys. The lesson plans and observations gave us opportunities to see how and in what ways their self-identified beliefs aligned with their teaching practices. The interviews allowed us to delve into any disconnects and provided the teachers with opportunities to explain why they believed those disconnects were present. This information helped us to determine how they felt supported and/or hindered which led us to identify implications this study has for teacher education and development as well as future research.

First, the teachers had limited exposure to critical digital theory during teacher education coursework and professional development. Without knowing or learning about the critical dimensions of technology through study and practice, recruitment of CDL is unlikely (Ertmer et al., 2012; Koh et al., 2014; Overbay et al., 2010; Pangrazio, 2016; Prestridge, 2017). In this study, the teachers' instructional technology use did not fully reflect CDL, and, with the exception of Kate, they did not engage students in CDL practices during the lessons.

Second, uncertainty about their students' CDL and school policies surrounding student engagement in digital environments led three of the teachers to choose traditionalist and didactic teaching practices. Analyses of lesson plans and observations of three of the teachers showed that while their personal technology use and planning practices aligned with constructivist and CDL practices, they chose not to incorporate a critical component in their instructional student technology use. Consequently, student technology use was largely substitutional and strongly controlled. When asked during interviews, all teachers believed they included a critical dimension in their planning, and three teachers believed they included it during instruction. In actuality, only one teacher included a critical component in her technology use with students. All of the teachers expressed concerns about incorporating CDL practices due to a lack of confidence in the CDL of their students resulting in traditionalist and didactic practices in most cases.

Finally, the teachers explained that moving beyond substitutive technology use with students towards transformative and critical use requires considerable time and support which is not always available. While each believed using a critical lens when working in and learning about digital environments was important, their teacher education and development did not tie critical theory to technology and did not offer opportunities to develop their own CDL.

IMPLICATIONS

Importantly, there is a noted absence in educational technology research using theoretical frameworks that delve into the critical dimensions of the digital literacies of teachers (Avila & Pandya, 2013; Burnett & Merchant, 2011; Selwyn, 2012; Song, 2016; Watulak & Kinzer, 2013). This study supports the movement away from a functionalist approach towards a critical approach of understanding teachers' digital literacy practices. We propose the use of the C-TPACK framework to challenge functionalist frames by providing a way for researchers to study and analyze the critical dimension of digital environments. This study is an example of how the C-TPACK framework effectuated the combining of post-positivist and constructivist paradigms which deepened our understanding of teacher digital literacy practices.

Previous studies show that the TPACK framework lacks a critical lens and are largely predictive in nature (Chai et al., 2010; Koh & Divaharan, 2011; Pamuk, 2012; Paratore et al., 2016). In this study, the teachers' consideration of the missing "C" was instrumental to their decisions surrounding student use of technology. Examining the predictive component (through quantitative valuation) in light of the qualitative findings led us to deeper understanding of how and why teachers' C-TPACK may or may not be recruited into classroom practices. While constructivism and critical theory may be at the center of a teacher's pedagogical beliefs, as was the case in our study, a focus on functionalism in teacher education and development programs and educational research surrounding digital literacies practices can lead to traditionalist and didactic teaching practices.

This study also exposes a professional development need of practicing teachers for a stronger understanding of how to incorporate critical literacy into their practices with students in digital environments. Teacher education and development can provide optimal contexts to connect critical literacy to technology practices in instruction (Avila & Pandya, 2013; Song, 2016; Watulak & Kinzer, 2013). Changes to foundational beliefs through observation and hands-on practice in teacher education and professional development, combined with critical reflection about personal pedagogical beliefs, can lead to digital literacy practices that contain critical dimensions (Kim et al., 2013; Ertmer et al., 2012; Liu et al., 2015). Our hope is that this would also result in an increase in teacher C-TPACK.

When educators recruit a critical digital lens into their teaching practices, they support students' agency and critical literacy development. This study pointed out the difficulties teachers faced recruiting the critical "C" to their instructional practices calling for the re-centering of the critical component in digital literacies in future research and teacher education and development programs.

REFERENCES

Anderson, S. E., Groulx, J. G., & Maninger, R. M. (2011). Relationships among preservice teachers' technology-related abilities, beliefs, and intentions to use technology in their future classrooms. *Journal of Educational Computing Research*, *45*(3), 321–338. doi:10.2190/EC.45.3.d

Archambault, L. M., & Barnett, J. H. (2010). Revisiting technological pedagogical content knowledge: Exploring the TPACK framework. *Computers & Education*, *55*(4), 1656–1662. doi:10.1016/j.compedu.2010.07.009

Avila, J., & Pandya, J. Z. (2013). Traveling, textual authority, and transformation: An introduction to critical digital literacies. In J. Avila & J. Z. Pandya (Eds.), *Critical digital literacies as social praxis* (pp. 127–153). Peter Lang.

Bandura, A. (1977). Self-efficacy: Toward a unifying theory of behavioral change. *Psychological Review*, *84*(2), 191–215. doi:10.1037/0033-295X.84.2.191 PMID:847061

Banister, S., & Reinhart, R. V. (2012). Assessing NETS• T performance in teacher candidates: Exploring the way to find teacher assessment. *Journal of Digital Learning in Teacher Education*, *29*(2), 59–65. do i:10.1080/21532974.2012.10784705

Battersby, S. L., & Verdi, B. (2015). The culture of professional learning communities and connections to improve teacher efficacy and support student learning. *Arts Education Policy Review*, *116*(1), 22–29. doi:10.1080/10632913.2015.970096

Burnett, C., & Merchant, G. (2011). Is there a space for critical literacy in the context of social media? *English Teaching*, *10*(1), 41–57.

Chai, C. S., Koh, J. H. L., & Tsai, C. C. (2010). Facilitating preservice teachers' development of technological, pedagogical, and content knowledge (TPACK). *Journal of Educational Technology & Society*, *13*(4), 63–73.

Chen, R. J. (2010). Investigating models for preservice teachers' use of technology to support student-centered learning. *Computers & Education*, *55*(1), 32–42. doi:10.1016/j.compedu.2009.11.015

Chen, W. (2013). The implications of social capital for the digital divides in America. *The Information Society*, *29*(1), 13–25. doi:10.1080/01972243.2012.739265

Choudbury, M., & Share, J. (2012). Critical media literacy: A pedagogy for new literacies and urban youth. *Voices from the Middle*, *19*(4), 39–44.

Cuban, L. (2009). *Oversold and underused*. Harvard University Press. doi:10.2307/j.ctvk12qnw

Darling-Hammond, L., Wei, R. C., Andree, A., Richardson, N., & Orphanos, S. (2009). *Professional learning in the learning profession*. National Staff Development Council.

Davies, R. S., & West, R. E. (2014). Technology integration in schools. In *Handbook of research on educational communications and technology* (pp. 841–853). Springer New York. doi:10.1007/978-1-4614-3185-5_68

Duffin, L. C., French, B. F., & Patrick, H. (2012). The teachers' sense of efficacy scale: Confirming the factor structure with beginning pre-service teachers. *Teaching and Teacher Education*, *28*(6), 827–834. doi:10.1016/j.tate.2012.03.004

DuFour, R., & Mattos, M. (2013). How do principals really improve schools? *Educational Leadership*, *70*(7), 34–39.

Edmundson, J. (2002). Asking different questions: Critical analysis and reading research. *Reading Research Quarterly*, *37*(1), 113–119. doi:10.1598/RRQ.37.1.5

Ertmer, P. A., Ottenbreit-Leftwich, A. T., Sadik, O., Sendurur, E., & Sendurur, P. (2012). Teacher beliefs and technology integration practices: A critical relationship. *Computers & Education*, *59*(2), 423–435. doi:10.1016/j.compedu.2012.02.001

Gainer, J. S. (2010). Critical media literacy in middle school: Exploring the politics of representation. *Journal of Adolescent & Adult Literacy*, *53*(5), 364–373. doi:10.1598/JAAL.53.5.2

Garcia, A. (2013). Utilizing mobile media and games to develop critical inner-city agents of social change. In J. Avila & J. Z. Pandya (Eds.), *Critical digital literacies as social praxis* (pp. 107–125). Peter Lang.

Gil de Zúñiga, H., Jung, N., & Valenzuela, S. (2012). Social media use for news and individuals' social capital, civic engagement and political participation. *Journal of Computer-Mediated Communication*, *17*(3), 319–336. doi:10.1111/j.1083-6101.2012.01574.x

Goktas, Y., Yildirim, S., & Yildirim, Z. (2009). Main barriers and possible enablers of ICTs integration into pre-service teacher education programs. *Journal of Educational Technology & Society*, *12*(1), 193–204.

Gulamhussein, A. (2013). *Teaching the teachers: Effective professional development in an era of high stakes accountability.* Center for Public Education. http://www.centerforpubliceducation.org

Harris, J., & Hofer, M. J. (2014). The construct is in the eye of the beholder: School districts' appropriations and reconceptualizations of TPACK. In L. Liu & D. C. Gibson (Eds.), *Research highlights in technology and teacher education* (pp. 11–18). Association for the Advancement of Computing in Education.

Harris, J. B., & Hofer, M. J. (2017). "TPACK stories": Schools and school districts repurposing a theoretical construct for technology-related professional development. *Journal of Research on Technology in Education*, *49*(1-2), 1–15. doi:10.1080/15391523.2017.1295408

Hofer, M., & Grandgenett, N. (2012). TPACK development in teacher education: A longitudinal study of preservice teachers in a secondary MA Ed. program. *Journal of Research on Technology in Education*, *45*(1), 83–106. doi:10.1080/15391523.2012.10782598

Holzberger, D., Philipp, A., & Kunter, M. (2013). How teachers' self-efficacy is related to instructional quality: A longitudinal analysis. *Journal of Educational Psychology*, *105*(3), 774–786. doi:10.1037/a0032198

Hosek, V. A. (2018). *Locating the critical component in technological, pedagogical, and content knowledge (TPACK): An examination of how graduate students recruit TPACK and critical digital literacy into classroom practices* [Doctoral dissertation, Illinois State University]. ProQuest (10978267).

Hosek, V. A., & Handsfield, L. J. (2019). Monological practices, authoritative discourses and the missing "C" in digital classroom communities. *English Teaching*, *19*(1), 79–93. doi:10.1108/ETPC-05-2019-0067

Hughes, A. (2009). *Higher education in a Web 2.0 world*. Bristol, England: JISC. https://www.jisc.ac.uk/media/documents/publications/heweb20rptv1.pdf

Kim, C., Kim, M. K., Lee, C., Spector, J. M., & DeMeester, K. (2013). Teacher beliefs and technology integration. *Teaching and Teacher Education*, *29*, 76–85. doi:10.1016/j.tate.2012.08.005

Kirschner, P. A. (2015). Facebook as learning platform: Argumentation superhighway or dead-end street? *Computers in Human Behavior*, *53*, 621–625. doi:10.1016/j.chb.2015.03.011

Koehler, M. J., & Mishra, P. (2006). Technological pedagogical content knowledge: A framework for teacher knowledge. *Teachers College Record*, *108*(6), 1017–1054. doi:10.1111/j.1467-9620.2006.00684.x

Koehler, M. J., & Mishra, P. (2009). What is technological pedagogical content knowledge? *Contemporary Issues in Technology & Teacher Education*, *9*(1), 60–70.

Koehler, M. J., Mishra, P., & Cain, W. (2013). What Is Technological Pedagogical Content Knowledge (TPACK)? *Journal of Education*, *193*(3), 13–19. doi:10.1177/002205741319300303

Koh, J. H., Chai, C. S., & Tsai, C. C. (2014). Demographic factors, TPACK constructs, and teachers' perceptions of constructivist-oriented TPACK. *Journal of Educational Technology & Society*, *17*(1), 185–196.

Koh, J. H., & Divaharan, H. (2011). Developing pre-service teachers' technology integration expertise through the TPACK-developing instructional model. *Journal of Educational Computing Research*, *44*(1), 35–58. doi:10.2190/EC.44.1.c

Lim, C. P., Zhao, Y., Tondeur, J., Chai, C. S., & Tsai, C. C. (2013). Bridging the gap: Technology trends and use of technology in schools. *Journal of Educational Technology & Society*, *16*(2), 59–68.

Liu, S. H., Tsai, H. C., & Huang, Y. T. (2015). Collaborative professional development of mentor teachers and preservice teachers in relation to technology integration. *Journal of Educational Technology & Society*, *18*(3), 161–172.

Louis, K. S., & Wahlstrom, K. (2011). Principals as cultural leaders. *Phi Delta Kappan*, *92*(5), 52–56. doi:10.1177/003172171109200512

Marcuse, H. (1964). *One-Dimensional Man*. Beacon.

Moran, M., Seaman, J., & Tinti-Kane, H. (2011). *Teaching, learning, and sharing: How today's higher education faculty use social media*. Pearson Learning Solutions.

Niess, M. L. (2011). Investigating TPACK: Knowledge growth in teaching with technology. *Journal of Educational Computing Research*, *44*(3), 299–317. doi:10.2190/EC.44.3.c

Overbay, A., Patterson, A., Vasu, E., & Grable, L. (2010). Constructivism and technology use: Findings from the impacting leadership project. *Educational Media International*, *47*(2), 103–120. doi:10.1080/09523987.2010.492675

Pamuk, S. (2012). Understanding preservice teachers' technology use through TPACK framework. *Journal of Computer Assisted Learning, 28*(5), 425-439.Pangrazio, L. (2016). Reconceptualising critical digital literacy. *Discourse (Abingdon)*, *37*(2), 163–174.

Pangrazio, L. (2016). Reconceptualising critical digital literacy. *Discourse (Abingdon)*, *37*(2), 163–174. doi:10.1080/01596306.2014.942836

Paratore, J. R., O'Brien, L. M., Jiménez, L., Salinas, A., & Ly, C. (2016). Engaging preservice teachers in integrated study and use of educational media and technology in teaching reading. *Teaching and Teacher Education, 59*, 247–260. doi:10.1016/j.tate.2016.06.003

Philip, T., & Olivares-Pasillas, M. C. (2016). Learning technologies and educational equity: Charting alternatives to the troubling pattern of big promises with dismal results. *Teachers College Record*, (ID Number: 21616). Retrieved from http://www.tcrecord.org

Prestridge, S. (2017). Examining the shaping of teachers' pedagogical orientation for the use of technology. *Technology, Pedagogy and Education, 26*(4), 367–381. doi:10.1080/1475939X.2016.1258369

Ruggiero, D., & Mong, C. J. (2015). The teacher technology integration experience: Practice and reflection in the classroom. *Journal of Information Technology Education, 14*, 162–178. doi:10.28945/2227

Saldana, J. (2016). *The coding manual for qualitative researchers*. SAGE Publications Ltd.

Schmidt, D. A., Baran, E., Thompson, A. D., Mishra, P., Koehler, M. J., & Shin, T. S. (2009). Technological pedagogical content knowledge (TPACK): The development and validation of an assessment instrument for preservice teachers. *Journal of Research on Technology in Education, 42*(2), 123–149. doi:10.1080/15391523.2009.10782544

Selwyn, N. (2012). Making sense of young people, education and digital technology: The role of sociological theory. *Oxford Review of Education, 38*(1), 81–96. doi:10.1080/03054985.2011.577949

Selwyn, N. (2016). Digital downsides: Exploring university students' negative engagements with digital technology. *Teaching in Higher Education, 21*(8), 1006–1021. doi:10.1080/13562517.2016.1213229

Song, A. Y. (2016). Operationalizing Critical Digital Literacies: A Holistic Approach to Literacy Education in the Modern Age. *Talking Points, 28*(1), 17–24.

Stanhope, D. S., & Corn, J. O. (2014). Acquiring teacher commitment to 1: 1 initiatives: The role of the technology facilitator. *Journal of Research on Technology in Education, 46*(3), 252–276. doi:10.1080/15391523.2014.888271

Sutton, S. R. (2011). The preservice technology training experiences of novice teachers. *Journal of Digital Learning in Teacher Education, 28*(1), 39–47. doi:10.1080/21532974.2011.10784678

Tondeur, J., Kershaw, L. H., Vanderlinde, R. R., & Van Braak, J. (2013). Getting inside the black box of technology integration in education: Teachers' stimulated recall of classroom observations. *Australasian Journal of Educational Technology, 29*(3), 434–449. doi:10.14742/ajet.16

Tondeur, J., van Keer, H., van Braak, J., & Valcke, M. (2008). ICT integration in the classroom: Challenging the potential of a school policy. *Computers & Education, 51*(1), 212–223. doi:10.1016/j.compedu.2007.05.003

Topper, A., & Lancaster, S. (2013). Common challenges and experiences of school districts that are implementing one-to-one computing initiatives. *Computers in the Schools, 30*(4), 346–358. doi:10.1080/07380569.2013.844640

Udesky, L. (2015). Classroom coaches critical as teachers shift to common core. Retrieved from https://edsource.org/2015/classroom-coaches-critical-as-teachers-shift-to-common-core

van Laar, E., van Deursen, A. J., van Dijk, J. A., & de Haan, J. (2017). The relation between 21st-century skills and digital skills: A systematic literature review. *Computers in Human Behavior*, *72*, 577–588. doi:10.1016/j.chb.2017.03.010

Watulak, S. L., & Kinzer, C. K. (2013). Beyond technology skills: Toward a framework for critical digital literacies in prè-service technology education. In J. Avila & J. Z. Pandya (Eds.), *Critical digital literacies as social praxis* (pp. 127–153). Peter Lang.

Young, J., Young, J., & Shaker, Z. (2012). Technological Pedagogical Content Knowledge (TPACK) Literature using confidence intervals. *TechTrends*, *56*(5), 25–33. doi:10.100711528-012-0600-6

Chapter 12
Digital Citizenship and Digital Literacy:
An Evolving Trend

Fatima A. Al Husseiny
Lebanese International University, Lebanon

Jana M. Saab
Lebanese University, Lebanon

Maya H. Abdallah
Lebanese International University, Lebanon

Noura H. Wehbe
Al Ain University, UAE

ABSTRACT

The rapid development of technology and communication had given birth to a new world order that impacted all aspects of citizens' lives. This new world order was often known as a world driven by digital tools and innovations. In digital mobility, citizens' lives become faster so that the interaction among individuals has no boundaries. This resulted in the development of digital citizenship. The emergence of social media certainly disrupted citizens' behavior. Therefore, digital literacy was necessary for this era of disrupted society, so becoming a smart and good citizen would be someone's necessity, not a luxury.

INTRODUCTION

The 21st century was marked by a digital revolution that transformed the personal and academic life of learners. Every student uses at least one smart device daily. Therefore, it is inconceivable to imagine a classroom without technology. To achieve the competencies of the digital era, students must be actively engaged in and invested in their learning experience (Al Husseiny & Youness, 2023). There is a significant shift in teaching paradigms in modern learning experiences to support student-centered learning.

DOI: 10.4018/978-1-6684-7015-2.ch012

Students with all their needs and skill levels have to be involved in the instructional journey for better achievement on the academic level (Al Husseiny & Kaddoura, 2021a). With the growing demand for information and communication technologies (ICT) in higher education and their continuous progress, lecture-based classes are now outdated strategies in higher education. There is a significant shift in instruction, which is no more teacher-centered but student-centered to develop an active learner.

Maintaining an active learning environment focuses on learners' engagement in the process and enhancing their learning skills (Al Husseiny & Kaddoura, 2021b). Interactive technology in learning has increased student engagement by supporting constructivist approaches to creating an active learning environment. In the study, An approach to reinforce active learning in higher education for IT students, the results showed that student evaluation indicates that technology integration improves student comprehension and retention of learning material while increasing student motivation.

Furthermore, the Covid-19 pandemic compelled all educational institutions to go online. This change necessitated adapting instructional tactics to the new virtual setting. The teacher must go above and beyond to attract and retain students in the online class. As a result, new online tools are being sought. Online learning serves tech-savvy learners with on-demand life skills (Itani et al., 2022).

BACKGROUND

The emergence of digital technologies has influenced people's lives. The digital world has changed how we think about our lives. The increased use of the Internet has a significant role in developing various fields, such as education, medicine, business, communication, and more. This access has opened many opportunities for all people worldwide to look for contemporary research in a particular field of study (Coklar & Tatli, 2020). Therefore, this enhanced communication and socialization around the globe. Indeed, digitalization has contributed to developing educational opportunities for all students (Coklar & Tatli, 2020). Using the Internet and technologies has led to the evolvement of digital citizenship. In this realm, digital citizenship aims to guide the next generation in making intelligent choices in a wide range of digital contexts and situations (Buchholz et al., 2020; Harris & Johns, 2020; Lauricella et al., 2020; Nurhidayati & Ratnasari, 2020; Saputra & Siddiq, 2020; Tapingkae et al., 2020; Vlaanderen et al., 2020). This shows that digital citizenship paves the way for everyone to live better lives.

Furthermore, digital citizenship has a lot of benefits and positive impacts on society. Also, it is argued that the aspects of online citizenship need to be governed and streamlined (Saputra & Siddiq, 2020; Stone, 2020; Xu et al., 2019). The best way to protect people from the risks associated with online activity is to educate young people to become digital citizens (Gleason & von Gillern, 2018; Manzuoli et al., 2019). Imer and Kaya (2020) asserted that the increased use of the Internet had stimulated specialists to guide the young generation and educate them about the significance of digital citizenship education. Moreover, the Internet and technology are vital in life nowadays (Brodovskaya et al., 2020; Buchholz et al., 2020; Saputra & Siddiq, 2020). Additionally, using smartphones to communicate is necessary for the 21st century to exchange data (Lapsley & Segato, 2019; Ramachandran et al., 2020). Digitalization lets people stay updated with all news and share their ideas and feelings through social media platforms (Gleason & von Gillern, 2018; Jabeen & Ahmad, 2021). Online technologies have become essential during the COVID-19 pandemic, and students have begun to use them frequently (Ranchordas, 2020).

DIGITAL CITIZENSHIP

Before the definition of digital citizenship, it is crucial to know the meaning of citizenship. To be more specific, citizenship means belonging to a particular country or society and havening the nationality of that country. Indeed, citizenship encompasses duties, responsibilities, and rights (Ozturk, 2021). Therefore, digital citizenship is a set of rules of behavior related to technology use (Coklar & Tatli, 2020). For example, technology is highly used in education by teachers and students, which has become an integral part of the teaching and learning process (Bowser, 2017). Citizenship in the digital world is defined by one's ability to understand and use media and data (Imer & Kaya, 2020).

On the other hand, media literacy refers to identifying the need for information and acquiring, assessing, and constructing it. Understanding and applying data presented in various forms and sources via computers or the Internet (Aristeidou & Herodotou, 2020; Kim & Choi, 2018). This shows that understanding the use of media and the Internet helps to develop education.

The notion of digital citizenship is developed many years ago. Although there is a high usage of technology, there is an increased need to implement this concept in schools and teach students about security when using the Internet and technology (Coklar & Tatli, 2020). Moreover, one should have access to the Internet and knowledge in using it to be a contributing part of society and to have citizenship (Harris & Johns, 2020; Lauricella et al., 2020; Michaelsen, 2020; Nurhidayati & Ratnasari, 2020; Ramachandran et al., 2020; Stone, 2020). This shows the importance of learning about technology and its primary uses. Additionally, knowledge of the social media platforms (Facebook, LinkedIn, Instagram, and Twitter) is significant for full digital citizenship. This was a new viewpoint on improving skills and knowledge of contemporary digital technology, like laptops, cell phones, and Tablets (Heath, 2020; Lapsley & Segato, 2019; Tapingkae et al., 2020).

Furthermore, audios and visuals in modern media are an integral part of 21st-century knowledge. This is because of the enhancement in digital media and other media, like writing and reading (Simonofski et al., 2019). For more illustration, Coklar and Tatli (2020) asserted the nine features of digital citizenship. First, digital access encompasses the use of technology anywhere. Second, digital commerce is concerned with e-commerce and electronic sales. Third, digital communication enhances the exchange of information in the digital world. Indeed, digital ethics includes the social norms that should be applied when using electronic devices.

Moreover, digital literacy is also essential, and it involves technology literacy. It is significant for teachers and students to know how to use technology (Coklar & Tatli, 2021). Additionally, there is digital health that is concerned with physical and psychological health in the integration of technology. Digital law deals with the rules and regulations to protect social media users. Digital rights include the freedom that every person has digitally. In addition, digital security is vital to make students aware of viruses while using electronic devices (Ozturk, 2021). All in all, teachers should teach students about these aspects of digital citizenship.

DIGITAL LITERACY

The excessive flow of information influences social and educational features (Dewi et al., 2021). Many opportunities emerged with technology (Johnston, 2020). Because of the rapid advancement of communication and information technology, one medium has been combined with the other, resulting in the emergence of unique and more complex model systems (Dewi et al., 2021). The Internet has connected all people around the globe. The Internet is an inseparable part form adolescents' life. That's why they must know the primary Internet security skills (Dewi et al., 2021). In addition, students use social media for entertainment (Pangrazio, 2016).

Moreover, before creating online security information programs for young people and adolescents, it is critical to understand how they analyze and use digital technology, online communication, and dangerous or insecure attitudes (Pati & Majhi, 2019; Treglia & Tomassoni, 2019). It is important to note that digital literacy is related to the capability of processing data for students in an educational context. To illustrate, students benefit from online resources to do their assignments (Jan 2018; West, 2019). Therefore, students can recognize their ability to assess and analyze information.

Grammar, structure, writing skills, and the ability to create writing, photos, sounds, and styles employing technology are used to assess digital literacy. Digital literacy has at first been centered on technological skills. Still, with the rise of computers, the web, and the widespread use of social media, the focus of digital literacy has transitioned to smartphones (Chib et al., 2019; McDougall et al., 2018). The Internet makes long-distance interaction across boundaries of nationality and culture possible. As a result, media literacy has become more and more critical in forming a society. Digital literacy is comprehending and applying information from various sources via networked computers (Dewi et al., 2021). It is contended that "In digital literacy skills are divided into several core competencies, among another Internet searching, hypertextual navigation, content evaluation, and knowledge assembly (Alexander et al., 2016; Kim, 2019).

Searching expertise on the Internet refers to the capability to look for data and carry out various tasks on the Internet. Understanding of hypermedia and hyperlinks and how they work, the distinction between reading books and surfing the Internet, the way the web performs, and the ability to recognize the features of websites constitute hypertextual navigation competence (Anisimova, 2020; Kaeophanuek et al., 2019). Students need to be trained in the competencies of digital technology so that they can utilize them in the learning process. In this way, they can search for information easily and achieve high results. To add more, "Digital literacy learning must also involve understanding universal values that must be adhered to by every user, such as freedom of expression, privacy, cultural diversity, intellectual rights, copyright, and so on. Digital literacy allows people to interact well and positively with their environment" (Dewi et al., 2021, p. 427). This shows the significance of understanding the actual values when using digital technology. People will interact with each other via various digital platforms. Therefore, respecting the culture of others has a significant role in enhancing communication among people.

In a nutshell, digital citizenship and digital literacy are crucial, and students, parents, and teachers should have deep knowledge about them. Integrating technology into humans' daily life is necessary for the 21st century.

DIGITAL CITIZENSHIP AND EDUCATION

In the modern era of technology, most people need a social presence on digital platforms. Students, teachers, and parents must know how to use these platforms (Ribble, 2021). In addition, with the rise of the usage of technology, students can connect with their teacher only at school but also at home through digital devices. Parents are wondering about a suitable time for their children to use their smartphones. To illustrate more, the World Health Organization sets an ideal time for children between 3 and 4 years old, which is 60 minutes (World Health Organization, 2019). According to Anderson and Vogels (2020), a research study has proved that only 27% claim that online learning is more beneficial than in-person learning. Many things could be improved with the use of technology while learning online. In this case, curriculum designers and educators insisted on integrating technology into the curriculum. Another positive feature is that while classmates (22%) and instructional websites (18%) rank near the bottom in terms of providing advice, they still have a massive effect (Ribble & Park, 2019). This implies that students and teachers need to master technological literacy.

DIGITAL SKILLS

Individuals must be ready to switch occupations and flexible in learning new skills. The use of information and communication technology (ICT) in the workplace is widespread, and qualified ICT workers are in high demand. Many skill frameworks and definitions have been created in recent years to examine disparities in digital abilities and to develop treatments for skill improvements (e.g., 21st-century skills, digital skills, digital competence, digital literacy, e-skills, and internet skills). The concept of digital skills has evolved from a technical focus to a broader viewpoint that considers higher-order or content-related skills. (Claro et al., 2012). There are seven fundamental digital talents. Technological, informational, communication, collaborative, creative, critical thinking, and problem-solving are 21st-century digital skills. (Van Laar et al., 2017).

Digital information skills. ICT's increased access to information necessitates the development of search, evaluation, and information organization abilities in digital settings (Catts & Lau, 2008). The ability to detect digital information effectively and efficiently, accurately describe information needs, and select digital communication is a component of information management (Ananiadou & Claro, 2009).

Digital communication abilities. ICT has made it simpler to communicate quickly, widely, and at a distance with a large audience. People can speak with one another at any length of time and space, express themselves, and form relationships (Yu et al., 2010). ICT-based communication is viewed to foster social connections and solidify social bonds (Hwang, 2011). Employees must know how to use email, social networking sites, and instant messaging systems politely and successfully. (Lewin & Mc-Nicol, 2015; Wang et al., 2012).

Digital collaboration abilities. ICT is increasingly used to assist collaboration processes, which manage interdependencies over time to accomplish a common purpose. When teams need to share information and make choices across the company and national boundaries, ICT is beneficial (Wang, 2010). Colleagues can instantly share ideas, knowledge, and experiences by using collaboration software like chats (like Skype or WhatsApp).

Digital talents for critical thinking. Because people interact and resources are created in a global online environment with various objectives and competencies, critical thinking has been suggested as being particularly crucial. (Starkey, 2011).

Digital creativity. ICT may foster creativity in various ways, including concept development, idea creation, and idea realization. (Loveless, 2007).

Digital problem-solving abilities. In a society where knowledge is plentiful, issues can be framed in various ways, and there are several internet resources for answers. The drawback is that because there needs to be an integrated perspective, information to tackle problems may be online but ignored (David & Foray, 2002). As a result, to construct problems or identify approaches to find the best solutions, employees need to be able to solve problems online. They must use their knowledge in different contexts, solve complex problems, and find multiple solutions. (Van laar et al. 2020)

DIGITAL SKILLS IN HIGHER EDUCATION

Since digital skills are crucial abilities graduates should have before entering the profession, they should be included in the curriculum. Knowing the learners' abilities and the digital skills framework can help educators design appropriate learning objectives, activities, and assessments to support the learners' acquisition of these skills. Graduates will need various skill sets, including digital abilities, to take on challenges and stay relevant. They are renowned for giving the next generation the skills needed in the twenty-first century to ensure survival in an unfamiliar setting. People with these talents are, therefore, more employable, productive, and creative, and they will continue to be safe in the new digital industry landscape.

Consequently, it is essential to have digital abilities, which include the capacity to gather and handle information using digital tools, communication programs, and networks. (UNESCO, 2022). To fulfill this criterion, educators must introduce their pupils to digital literacy and ascertain the degree of that literacy before assisting the latter in creating materials that may be utilized to educate the former with the abilities. This is crucial since it can help them make appropriate evaluations and strategies to attain desired learning outcomes according to various disciplines or courses. Most significantly, the practice helps them better understand their pupils and develop lesson plans catering to their needs. Therefore, everyone who wishes to improve their digital skills must first learn how to use computers and other digital devices to gather information (Syed Aris et al., 2022).

DIGITAL SKILLS FOR ADULTS

With the advent of Internet-based services like e-health, e-government, e-learning, and others, the significance of digital literacy among older adults became clear because these services are seen as enablers that prolong the time during which the elderly can remain in their own homes before the need to move into retirement homes.

Along with socializing, digital skills are increasingly needed for practical tasks, including finding contacts, getting medical assistance, assessing medical indicators in e-health services, paying bills, and participating in democratic processes. Because most older adults did not have the chance to interact with modern digital technology or to acquire the knowledge necessary for practical use at the time when using the Internet became commonplace, the problem of older adults learning digital skills has its roots in the way they learned in their youth and during their professional lives.

Playing games could be a beneficial tool to help older folks learn how to operate a touchscreen device like a smartphone. Entertaining gaming experiences unquestionably aid in more successful, relaxed learning of digital device use, which speeds up the adoption of new skills. The elderly's expressed enjoyment of playing games helps them build good feelings about digital technology since it allays their worry that they will not be able to participate in modern society, which helps close the digital divide (Jerman, 2020).

DIGITAL SKILLS IN TIMES OF COVID–19

Distance learning relies on the resources of the digital field, as well as on the management of ICT and the advancement of digital skills, amid these times of world tragedy caused by the epidemic that created COVID-19. In the era of the COVID-19 outbreak, it was discovered that there was a strong correlation between the integration of ICT and digital skills since these abilities enable students to learn and master technical tools, making them compatible with online education. According to a study, compatibility plays a role in adopting and integrating ICT in teaching and learning. The emphasis here is on aligning the task's requirements with the technology. Consequently, Lin, Huang, and Chen (2014) suggested that technology advancements would be implemented, provided they were cost-effective and suited to the current scenario (Manco-Chavez et al. 2020).

ELEMENTS OF DIGITAL CITIZENSHIP

Documents, studies, and related articles all demonstrate aspects of digital literacy. It splits into two sections: The definition and components of digital literacy and the definition and connection between the characteristics of digital literacy and other forms of literacy.

The eight components that make up the digital literacy skill are as follows:

1. Access is the capacity to locate the information's origin and obtain, collect, and retrieve that information for recurrent use.
2. Manage, which is the capacity to employ a resource that is accurate and simple to evaluate
3. Integrate, or the capacity to connect with all other stakeholders. The term "digital literacy" also refers to the capacity to extrapolate from and analyze the content of information obtained through ICT equipment.
4. Evaluate, which involves determining the information's usefulness and timeliness.
5. Generate, which is the capacity to comprehend and use the benefit of the appropriate media-creating tools.
6. Communication, or the capacity to connect with and engage with another person in a digital setting.
7. Analysis, which is the capacity to comprehend the method, the reasoning, and the goal of the created media. This involves evaluating how each person's beliefs and actions.
8. Synthesis is the ability to mix facts to produce new understanding (Phuapan et al. 2015).

DIGITAL CITIZENSHIP IN THE AGE OF SOCIAL MEDIA

In June 2014, the terrifying tale of two Wisconsin preteens who stabbed their best friends 19 times in the wood shook many news organizations. Upon questioning, the females admitted that an online internet meme called "Slenderman" inspired them to do it as a way of "impressing" him (Gansner, 2017). In the wake of this horrible event, the topic of media literacy and responsible internet use is again making headlines worldwide. Multiple queries have arisen to question whether the girls' online behavior caused the lines between reality and fiction to blur and the best practices that would safeguard young people's digital citizenship.

Of these concerns, all parties that constitute the educational system, from decision-makers to educators, rushed to build a curriculum of formal education to instruct students on the best methods to develop skills necessary to engage in productive conversations and participate in notions with people from various backgrounds ethically and legally (Gleason & von Gillern, 2018). This curriculum instructs young internet users on multiple subjects, such as information literacy, cyberbullying, safety, and user privacy and security. This response came to secure students' safety, privacy, health, and well-being after realizing the significant amount of time kids spend online where they are prone to the dangers of online life, including physical and psychological threats (Gleason & von Gillern, 2018).

In this era of media, multiple scholars of education, political science, and communication highlighted the importance of social media platforms like Facebook, Instagram, YouTube, Twitter, LinkedIn, and others in supporting innovative approaches to citizenship stimulated by identity expression and connected to shifting conceptions of literacy (Bennett, 2008).

Although people use social media for a spectrum of reasons, including commercial and entertainment, politics dominates everyday life these days, reinforcing the idea that one's participation in social issues matters. Many young people in this global and digital age have expressed a desire to give back to their society. Compared to the options often provided in youth engagement organizations, social media offers a spontaneous response that seems more enticing, making it young people's resort to sharing opinions and engaging with their communities (Bennett, 2008).

Users' online participation could improve their civic and political involvement if they are politically interested. Social networking also takes a new form as users leverage their online engagement, or the act of "hanging out" online, to strengthen the civic networks that promote real-world political engagement in issues they are interested in (Isin & Ruppert, 2020).

The use of social media by young people promotes political participation in "digital citizenship"-related activities, such as civics discussions. This encourages both individual and group political participation, in addition to civic involvement, by giving communities a chance to share tales that, in turn, foster trust, connections, and a vision for communal growth. These activities combine offline and online behaviors and classroom and extracurricular activities and are examples of what educators' label as connected learning techniques (Isin & Ruppert, 2020).

For example, one main objective of education has always been encouraging students' civics participation. The International Society for Technology in Education also emphasized principles that support the idea of digital citizenship. It justified educators from all fields of study to get their students involved in civic engagement and digital citizenship-promoting activities. Through various in-class exercises and projects that link classroom learning to extracurricular activities, instructors can support students in developing their skills to communicate effectively online (Gleason & von Gillern, 2018).

In addition, dutiful and actualizing are two types of citizenship proposed by Bennett (2008). Faithful citizenship means students' actual participation in civic organizations. They are expected to vote, get involved with leading organizations, or address a formal figure through letters touching base on a particular social issue that interests them. However, actualizing citizenship involves using social technologies to organize civic activities through peer networks and promote individual expression (Bennett, 2018).

This signifies that although some people will not actively participate in a politician's campaign or volunteer for office, they can still acquire skills and build connections through the media by dropping their opinions, participating in conversations, or even producing content online. It is essential to mention that this notion is not limited to politics. Young users can participate in various broad social issues they feel passionate about. One example of this would be the "feminist movement" on Twitter a couple of years back, where women from around the world utilize their accounts to advocate for women's rights concerning gender equality.

DIGITAL LITERACY IN THE AGE OF SOCIAL MEDIA

As one type of communication media, social media is a user's portal into interactive dialogue. It is used not only to share information but also to inspire others, self-express, engage in personal branding, participate in political events, spread awareness on social issues, or simply chase quick entertainment.

The spread of information is no longer tied to dominant authority like mass media or mainstream press. Today's reality dictates that everyone has the chance to spread or obtain information regardless of what truth lies behind its identity. Internet and technology use is dominating people's lives, and their efficient use requires introducing a new type of literacy, commonly known as digital literacy. It includes a set of skills, including technical skills, that act as prerequisites people should master before using digital tools to delve deep into political participation and civic engagement with online communities (Li & Li, 2022).

The European Commission (2018) defined digital literacy as acquiring digital content, creating content, cooperating with online communities, protecting personal and others' privacy, and so on. Kazakov's (2019) perspective of digital literacy entitles locating and critically understanding information the person is interested in from the media, then engaging in purposeful media messages and content sharing. However, social media's ease of access intrigues several concerns for one's safety while navigating the social platform. Online social interactions had many people deeply concerned with understanding what it means to be a "good digital citizen" and how does "acceptable social behavior" look like because social hoaxes are viciously spread with no concern for logic (Gleason & von Gillern, 2018).

A study by Priwati & Helmi (2021) titled: "The manifestations of digital literacy in social media among Indonesian youth" revealed that people are used to receiving data and information from social media platforms and engaging in various activities after receiving a piece of information from the Internet. 26.5% of users forward the obtained information to others, 17% of users try to critique and confirm the data by referring to trustworthy sources who have the habit of presenting good news, and 16.3% tend to discuss the information with peers to decide on its validity (Priwati & Helmi, 2021).

Based on the research's results, participants showed expected behavior while presented with information from social media platforms. Users revealed that they forward information they think is valid and worthy of sharing with others. This happens after ensuring the data is correct; if not, they do further research to "double-check" or ensure it is real (Priwati & Helmi, 2021).

In addition, a higher degree of digital literacy is associated with people who are more acquainted with the Internet. As for personal characteristics, males, young people, and those with better education show higher degrees of digital literacy. Individuals with higher incomes and good health conditions are also positively associated with digital literacy (Li & Li, 2022).

As an ending note, adapting new digital literacy, or even media literacy that covers a wide variety of media messages, is necessary to raise users' critical evaluation while consuming, producing, or engaging with online content, whether it speaks to their interest. Triggering media messages cannot be stopped once they are within reach of the public, and the aftermath of their destructive tendencies is limitless - especially if it touches point with degrading, discriminating, or provoking gender-biased issues.

Reflecting on what has been said, the destructive nature of controversial social rumors implements a framework that promotes digital literacy competencies necessary to attain an inclusive digital society that encourages meaningful civic engagement.

CONCLUSION

The new mass media, unrestricted by any factor, allows users from around the globe to engage digitally with online communities on a spectrum of topics and social issues relevant to their experience and resonates with their interests. However, having an online presence comes attached to the responsibility of having digital citizenship that eases users' participation in political and civic activities. This new opportunity brings along a new type of literacy, known as digital literacy, related to the best practices and skills safeguarding one's privacy, the validity of data, and positively creating and presenting information that leaves a desired impact on social situations. While putting their digital citizenship to good use, users are expected to utilize their critical information processing and criticism skills and employ them in constructive discussions while considering the aftermath of positive and negative interactions with the online community.

FUTURE RESEARCH

Research in digital citizenship and literacy will be crucial to ensure that people can traverse the digital terrain responsibly and effectively. There is a need to investigate the relationship between digital citizenship and various forms of civic engagement. Also, developing practical methods for encouraging safe and responsible online conduct is another area that needs research. Moreover, another required critical analysis is diving into the impact of cultural factors on digital citizenship and literacy in a meaningful and beneficial way.

Other areas for research

- Developing and validating comprehensive measures of digital literacy and digital citizenship.
- Investigating the relationship between digital literacy and digital citizenship and various forms of civic engagement.
- Identifying effective strategies for promoting safe and responsible online behavior.
- Exploring the impact of digital literacy and digital citizenship on mental health outcomes.
- Examining the role of digital literacy and digital citizenship in reducing online hate speech.
- Investigating the impact of digital literacy and digital citizenship on financial decision-making.
- Exploring the impact of digital literacy and citizenship on social and emotional learning outcomes.
- Identifying the role of digital literacy and digital citizenship in promoting cultural competence.
- Examining digital literacy and citizenship's impact on political participation and engagement.
- Investigating the impact of digital literacy and digital citizenship on health literacy and health outcomes.
- Identifying effective strategies for promoting digital literacy and digital citizenship in older adults.
- Exploring the impact of digital literacy and digital citizenship on workplace productivity.
- Investigating the impact of digital literacy and digital citizenship on entrepreneurial success.

- Identifying effective strategies for promoting digital literacy and digital citizenship in low-income communities.
- Examining the impact of digital literacy and digital citizenship on academic success for students with disabilities.
- Investigating the impact of digital literacy and digital citizenship on cross-cultural communication.
- Identifying effective strategies for promoting digital literacy and digital citizenship in early childhood.
- Exploring the impact of digital literacy and digital citizenship on environmental sustainability behaviors.
- Investigating the impact of digital literacy and digital citizenship on media literacy outcomes.
- Identifying effective strategies for promoting digital literacy and digital citizenship in the context of emerging technologies such as AI and blockchain.

REFERENCES

Al Husseiny, F., & Youness, H. (2023). Exploring the role of social media marketing in students' decision to select universities in Lebanon: A proposed emerging framework. *QScience Connect, 2023*(1), 4. doi:10.5339/connect.2023.spt.4

Alexander, B., Adams Becker, S., & Cummins, M. (2016). *An NMC Horizon Project Strategic Brief*. CDN. http://cdn.nmc.org/media/2016-nmc-horizon-strategic-brief-digital-literacy.pdf

Ananiadou, K., & Claro, M. (2009). *21st-century skills and competencies for new millennium learners in OECD countries*. OECD Publishing. doi:10.1787/19939019

Aris, S. R. S., Teoh, S. H., Deni, S. M., Nadzri, F. A., & Dalim, S. F. (2022). Digital Skills Framework in Higher Education. *Proceedings, 82*, 61. doi:10.3390/proceedings2022082061

Aristeidou, M., & Herodotou, C. (2020). Online citizen science: A systematic review of effects on learning and scientific literacy. *Citizen Science: Theory and Practice, 5*(1), 11. doi:10.5334/cstp.224

Bennett, W. L. (2008). Changing citizenship in the digital age. In W. L. Bennett (Ed.), *Civic life online: Learning how digital media can engage youth* (pp. 1–24). MIT Press.

Bowser, A., Davis, K., Singleton, J., & Small, T. (2017). Professional learning: A collaborative model for online teaching and development. *SRATE Journal, 26*(1), 1-8.

Brodovskaya, E., & Dombrovskaya, A., & Batanina, I. (2020). The development of Russian youth digital citizenship: How to analyze and tackle the Internet communication risks. In Proceedings of the International Conference "Internet and Modern Society", (pp. 337-349). IEEE.

Buchholz, B. A., DeHart, J., & Moorman, G. (2020). Digital citizenship during a global pandemic: Moving beyond digital literacy. Journal of Adolescent &amp. *Adult Literacy, 64*(1), 11–17. doi:10.1002/jaal.1076 PMID:32834710

Catts, R., & Lau, J. (2008). *Towards information literacy indicators*. UNESCO Publishing.

Chib, A., Bentley, C., & Wardoyo, R.-J. (2019). Distributed digital contexts and learning: Personal empowerment and social transformation in marginalized populations. *Comunicar*, *27*(58), 51–60. doi:10.3916/C58-2019-05

Claro, M., Preiss, D. D., San Martín, E., Jara, I., Hinostroza, J. E., Valenzuela, S., Cortes, F., David, P. A., & Foray, D. (2002). An introduction to the economy of the knowledge society. *International Social Science Journal*, *54*(171), 9–23. doi:10.1111/1468-2451.00355

Coklar, A. (2020). Evaluation of digital citizenship levels of teachers in the context of information literacy and internet and computer use self-efficacy. *Asian Journal of Contemporary Education*, *4*(2), 80–90. doi:10.18488/journal.137.2020.42.80.90

Dewi. (2021). Analysis study of factors affecting students' digital literacy competency. *Elementary Education Online*, *20*(3), 424–431.

European Commission. (2018). *Human Capital Digital Inclusion and Skills: Digital Economy and Society Index Report 2018 Human Capital*. European Commission.

Gansner, M. M. (2017, September 5). "The Internet Made Me Do It"-Social Media and Potential for Violence in Adolescents. *Psychiatric Times*. https://www.psychiatrictimes.com/view/-internet-made-me-do-itsocial-media-and-potential-violence-adolescents

Gleason, B., & von Gillern, S. (2018). Digital citizenship with social media: Participatory practices of teaching and learning in secondary education. *Journal of Educational Technology & Society*, *21*, 200–212.

Harris, A., & Johns, A. (2020). Youth, social cohesion and digital life: From risk and resilience to a global digital citizenship approach. *Journal of Sociology (Melbourne, Vic.)*, *57*(2), 394–411. doi:10.1177/1440783320919173

Heath, M. (2020). Digital citizenship. *Oxford Bibliographies*. doi:10.1093/obo/9780199756810-0264

Helsper, E.J., Schneider, L.S., van Deursen, A.J.A.M., & van Laar, E. (2020). *The youth Digital Skills Indicator: Report on the conceptualisation and development of the ySKILLS digital skills measure*. KU Leuven, Leuven: ySKILLS.

Hwang, Y. (2011). Is communication competence still good for interpersonal media? Mobile phone and instant messenger. *Computers in Human Behavior*, *27*(2), 924–934. doi:10.1016/j.chb.2010.11.018

Imer, G., & Kaya, M. (2020). Literature review on digital citizenship in Turkey. *International Education Studies*, *13*(8), 6. doi:10.5539/ies.v13n8p6

Isin & Ruppert. (2020). *Being Digital Citizens (2nd ed.)*. Rowman & Littlefield International, Ltd.

Itani, M., Itani, M., Kaddoura, S., & Al Husseiny, F. (2022). The impact of the Covid-19 pandemic on online examination: Challenges and opportunities. *Global Journal of Engineering Education*, *24*(2).

Jabeen, S., & Ahmad, F. (2021). Digital citizenship: Effective use of digital media. In *Proceedings of the 13th International Conference on Education and New Learning Technologies,* (pp. 6041-6048). IEEE. 10.21125/edulearn.2021.1220

Jan, S. (2018). *Investigating the relationship between students' digital literacy and their attitude towards using ICT*. USDE.

Jerman, B. (2020). *Overcoming the digital divide with a modern approach to learning digital skills for the elderly adults*. Springer., doi:10.100710639-019-09961-9

Johnston, N. (2020). The Shift towards Digital Literacy in Australian University Libraries: Developing a Digital Literacy Framework. *Journal of the Australian Library and Information Association*, *69*(1), 93–101. doi:10.1080/24750158.2020.1712638

Kaddoura, S., & Al Husseiny, F. (2021a). An approach to reinforce active learning in higher education for IT students. *Global J. of Engng. Educ.*, *23*(1), 43–48.

Kaddoura, S., & Al Husseiny, F. (2021b). On-line learning on information security based on critical thinking andragogy.World Trans. on Engng. And Technol. *Educ.*, *19*(2), 157–162.

Kaeophanuek, S., Na-Songkhla, J., & Nilsook, P. (2019). A learning process model to enhance digital literacy using critical inquiry through digital storytelling (CIDST). *International Journal of Emerging Technologies in Learning*, *14*(3), 22–37. doi:10.3991/ijet.v14i03.8326

Kazakov, A. A. (2019). *Political Theory and Practice of Media Literacy*. Saratov University Publishing House.

Kim, K. T. (2019). The structural relationship among digital literacy, learning strategies, and core competencies among South Korean college students. *Educational Sciences: Theory and Practice*, *19*(2), 3–21. doi:10.12738/estp.2019.2.001

Kim, M., & Choi, D. (2018). Development of youth digital citizenship scale and implication for an educational setting. Journal of Educational Technology &amp. *Society*, *21*(1), 155–171.

Lapsley, I., & Segato, F. (2019). Citizens, technology, and the NPM movement. Public Money &amp. *Management*, *39*(8), 553–559. doi:10.1080/09540962.2019.1617539

Lauricella, A., & Herdzina, J., & Robb, M. B. (2020). Early childhood educators' teaching of digital citizenship competencies. Computers &amp. *Education*, 158.

Lewin, C., & McNicol, S. (2015). Supporting the development of 21st-century skills through ICT. In T. Brinda, N. Reynolds, R. Romeike, & A. Schwill (Eds.), *KEYCIT 2014: Key competencies in informatics and ICT* (pp. 98–181). Universitätsverlag Potsdam.

Li, Y., & Li, G. (2022). The Impacts of Digital Literacy on Citizen Civic Engagement—Evidence from China. *Digit. Gov.: Res. Pract.*, *3*(4), 24. Advance online publication. doi:10.1145/3532785

Pati, B. & Majhi, S. (2019). Information Literacy Skill: An Evaluative Study on the Students of LIS Schools in Odisha. *International Journal of Digital Literacy and Digital Competence (IJDLDC)*, *10*(1), 15-33. doi:10.4018/IJDLDC.2019010102

Loveless, A. (2007). *Creativity, new technologies and learning: A recent literature review* [An update]. Futurelab.

Manco-Chavez, J. A., Uribe-Hernandez, Y. C., Buendia-Aparcana, R., Vertiz-Osores, J. J., Isla Alcoser, S. D., & Rengifo-Lozano, R. A. (2020). Integration of ICTS and Digital Skills in Times of the Pandemic Covid-19. *International Journal of Higher Education, 9*(9), 11. doi:10.5430/ijhe.v9n9p11

Manzuoli, C. H., & Sánchez, A., & Bedoya, E. (2019). Digital citizenship: A theoretical review of the concept and trends. *The Turkish Online Journal of Educational Technology, 18*, 10–18.

Michaelsen, A. S. (2020). *Digital citizenship*. Routledge.

Nurhidayati & Ratnasari, S. W. (2020). Digital transformation of organizations: Perspectives from digital citizenship and innovative spiritual leadership. *Contentfull.*.

Nussbaum, M. (2012). Assessment of 21st century ICT skills in Chile: Test design and results from high school level students. *Computers & Education, 59*(3), 1042–1053. doi:10.1016/j.compedu.2012.04.004

Öztürk, G. (2021). Digital citizenship and its teaching: A literature review. Journal of Educational Technology &amp. *Online Learning, 4*(1), 31–45.

Pangrazio, L. (2016). Reconceptualizing critical digital literacy. *Discourse (Berkeley, Calif.), 37*(2), 163–174. doi:10.1080/01596306.2014.942836

Pati, B., & Majhi, S. (2019). Information Literacy Skill. *International Journal of Digital*.

Starkey, L. (2011). Evaluating learning in the 21st century: a digital age learning matrix. *Pedagogy and Education, 20*(1), 19–39. doi:10.1080/1475939X.2011.554021

Phuapan, P. (2015). *Elements of digital literacy skill: A conceptual analysis*. Research Gate. doi:10.29139/aijss.20150406

Poniszewska-Maranda, & T. Enokido (Eds.), Complex, intelligent and software intensive systems, 485-489). Springer. doi:10.1007/978-3-030-50454-0_50

Ratna Priwati, Acintya & Helmi, Avin. (2021). The manifestations of digital literacy in social media among Indonesian youth. HUMANITAS: Indonesian Psychological Journal. 18. 14. . doi:10.26555/humanitas.v18i1.17337

Ramachandran, V., Cline, A., & Hawkins, S. (2020). Technological advancements to promote adherence. In S. R. Feldman, A. Cline, A. Pona, & S. S. Kolli (Eds.), Treatment adherence in dermatology, 99-112. doi:10.1007/978-3-030-278090_10

Ranchordas, S. (2020). We teach and learn online. Are we all digital citizens now? Lessons on digital citizenship from the lockdown. Retrieved from http://www.iconnectblog.com/2020/05/we-teachand-learn-online-are-we-all-digital-citizens-now-lessons-on-digital-citizenship-from-thelockdown

Ribble, M. (2021). Digital Citizenship in the Frame of Global Change. *International Journal of Studies in Education and Science, 2*(2), 74–86.

Ribble, M., & Park, M. (2019). *The digital citizenship handbook for school leaders: Fostering positive interactions online*. International Society for Technology in Education.

Saputra, M., & Siddiq, I. (2020). Social media and digital citizenship: The urgency of digital literacy in the middle of a disrupted society era. International Journal of Engineering and Technology, 15(7), 156. . v15i07.13239 doi:10.3991/ijet

Simonofski, A., Asensio, E., & Wautelet, Y. (2019). Citizen participation in the design of smart cities. In A. Visvizi, & M. D. Lytras (Eds.), Smart cities: Issues and challenges,47-62. doi:10.1016/B978-0-12-816639-0.00004-1

Starkey, L. (2011). Evaluating learning in the 21st century: A digital age learning matrix. *Technology.*

Stone, J. (2020). Digital citizenship. In J. Stone (Ed.), *Digital play therapy* (pp. 140–152). Routledge., doi:10.4324/9780429001109-11

Tapingkae, P., Panjaburee, P., & Hwang, G.-J., & Srisawasdi, N. (. (2020). Effects of a formative assessment-based contextual gaming approach on students' digital citizenship behaviors, learning motivations, and perceptions. Computational &amp. *Education, 159.* Advance online publication. doi:10.1016/j.compedu.2020.103998

UNESCO. AGlobalFrameworkofReferenceonDigitalLiteracySkillsforIndicators4.4.2; Information Paper No. 51; UNESCO Institute for Statistics: Montreal, QC, Canada, 2018; Available online: http://uis.unesco.org/sites/default/files/documents/ip51-globalframework-reference-digital-literacy-skills-2018-en.pdf (accessed on 20 January 2022).

Van Laar, E., Van Deursen, A. J. A. M., Van Dijk, J. A. G. M., & De Haan, J. (2017). The relation between 21st-century skills and digital skills: A systematic literature review. *Computers in Human Behavior, 72,* 577–588. doi:10.1016/jchb.2017.03.010

van Laar, E., van Deursen, A. J. A. M., van Dijk, J. A. G. M., & de Haan, J. (2020, January). Van laar, E. (2020). Determinants of 21st-Century Skills and 21st-Century Digital Skills for Workers: A Systematic Literature Revie. *Sage (Atlanta, Ga.), 10*(1). doi:10.1177/2158244019900176

Vlaanderen, A., Bevelander, K., & Kleemans, M. (2020). Empowering digital citizenship: An anti-cyberbullying intervention to increase children's intentions to intervene on behalf of the victim. *Computers in Human Behavior, 112,* 106459. doi:10.1016/j.chb.2020.106459

Wang, Q. (2010). Using online shared workspaces to support collaborative group learning. *Computers & Education, 55*(3), 1270–1276. doi:10.1016/j.compedu.2010.05.023

Wang, W., Hsieh, J. P. A., & Song, B. (2012). Understanding user satisfaction with instant messaging: An empirical survey study. *International Journal of Human-Computer Interaction, 28*(3), 153–162. doi:10.1080/10447318.2011.568893

West, J. A. (2019). Using new literacies theory to analyze technology-mediated literacy classrooms. *E-Learning and Digital Media, 16*(2), 151–173. doi:10.1177/2042753019828355

Xu, S., Yang, H., MacLeod, J., & Zhu, S. (2019). Social media competence and digital citizenship among college students. *Convergence (London), 25*(1), 735–752. doi:10.1177/1354856517751390

Yu, A. Y., Tian, S. W., Vogel, D., & Kwok, R. C. W. (2010). Can learning be virtually boosted? An investigation of online social networking impacts. *Computers & Education, 55*(4), 1494–1503. doi:10.1016/j.compedu.2010.06.015

KEY TERMS AND DEFINITIONS

Digital Citizenship: Anyone who uses computers, the Internet, or other digital devices to interact with society on any level is considered to be practicing digital citizenship, which is the responsible use of technology. The world is growing more dependent on the Internet for daily activities as the rate of technological innovation continues to rise. This makes it essential to cover it with today's pupils.

Digital Literacy: The ability to find, comprehend, analyze, produce, and communicate digital information using information and communication technology is known as digital literacy, and it calls for both cognitive and technical abilities.

Chapter 13
Higher Education in the Post-Pandemic Era:
Implications and Future Prospects

Fatima A. Al Husseiny
Lebanese International University, Lebanon

Maya H. Abdallah
Lebanese International University, Lebanon

ABSTRACT

This chapter explores the educational changes and new trends that emerged after the COVID-19 pandemic with a brief review of how education looked like before it. The pandemic forced schools and educational institutions to adapt to new modes of teaching and learning, including online and remote learning. This chapter examines how these changes affected education, including curriculum, assessment, and pedagogy. It also explores the role of technology in education and the importance of digital literacy skills. Finally, it highlights the future trends that we need to watch for.

INTRODUCTION

The most recent Covid-19 outbreak affected several businesses, but education was notably affected. Academic institutions and external examination providers responded differently to the pandemic's shutdown. The widespread pandemic made it impossible for schools and universities to operate normally. Both teachers and students had to work from home to complete their academic tasks. In addition to its logistical complexity, evaluating such a system involves other challenges. Several organizations have developed opportunities for others to gain from their experiences (Itani et al., 2022). The world has been profoundly altered and challenged by the Covid-19 pandemic. This pandemic has impacted every aspect of society, but education has been particularly heavily struck, affecting student settings, attitudes, and skills. Governments worldwide had to pass legislation to stop in-person instruction in schools and colleges, which compelled the switch to online delivery techniques. Institutions and educators must develop

DOI: 10.4018/978-1-6684-7015-2.ch013

more innovative teaching techniques due to the swift shift to online learning to help students adjust to these quick changes, particularly with online evaluation (Al-Karaki et al., 2021).

Interactive technology in education has increased student involvement by promoting constructivist methods for creating an active learning environment. A study found that incorporating technology into the classroom increased students' enthusiasm for studying and improved their retention of the material. Also, the Covid-19 pandemic forced all educational institutions to migrate online. Due to this adjustment, instructional tactics must be modified to fit the brand-new virtual environment. The instructor must go above and above to draw in and retain students in an online course. Therefore, new internet tools are being sought (Kaddoura & Al Husseiny, 2021a). Tech-savvy students have access to on-demand life skills through online education. Developing an online learning model that can improve critical thinking skills in a virtual environment is challenging. The new teaching approaches must satisfy the needs of the 21st Century learner, whose abilities go beyond core competencies. There is a need to move away from traditional pedagogy and toward andragogy to develop self-directed learners who can compete in a global market for higher education graduates (Kaddoura & Al Husseiny, 2021b).

BACKGROUND

Online Distance Education and Emergence of Remote Teaching

Given the rapid advancement of technology, prominent technology executives are creating unique ways to transform the Metaverse into a learning environment. People have become acclimated to teleworking, telemedicine, and various other remote kinds of engagement since the COVID-19 pandemic (Kaddoura & Al Husseiny, 2023). In the age of technological innovation, we live in today, the trend of personalized learning is constantly growing. As a result, traditional schooling, social networking, and its connection to data collection are all rapidly developing. Importantly, our current educational environment strongly emphasizes the advantages of the growth mindset and the necessity of cognitive flexibility (Al Husseiny & Youness, 2023).

Higher Education Before and After Covid-19

In December 2019, a brand-new type of virus, Coronavirus, was first identified in China, which set off a global pandemic in March 2020. Direct, indirect, or close contact with those with the illness will put any individual at risk of getting infected (Kabadayi et al., 2020). As a result, stringent policies like border closures, stay-at-home directives, travel restrictions, extensive quarantines, coerced social distancing, contact tracing, and self-quarantining are implemented globally (Tian et al. 2020).

The service sector, which depends heavily on human interaction, has been struck the hardest by these regulations (Carroll & Conboy, 2020). In response to these rules, and while running on a short timeline, service sector businesses have sprinted to implement technology-driven strategies as a means of damage control. And since the domain of services incorporates universities and higher education, the educational system experienced its "digital growing-up" way earlier than most researchers and educators anticipated.

But, while considering the beginnings of remote learning and computer-based learning, one will come to realize that discussions regarding electronic or digital education have been prevalent since at least the middle of the 1990s (Zawacki-Richter, 2020).

Even though distance education was proposed ever since the digital revolution, its usage was rare, and the pace of digital educational transformation was modest. Despite MOOC's growing popularity, many academic institutions have yet to implement these technologies. Most learning activities were still limited to traditional classroom settings, and only a few organizations adopted these technologies (Kang, 2021).

The educational setting was heavily influenced by the notions of special education and psychology pioneers such as Jean Piaget and Lev Vygotsky, who advocated implementing student-centered learning and discovery learning and the importance of the 21st-century skills crucial to shaping lifelong learners.

The COVID-19 pandemic introduced socially-proposed rules concerning human interaction and created a new deep-rooted fear of human contact in general. The demand for online education has risen dramatically, with Coursera reporting a gain of 644% in March 2020 (DeVaney et al. 2020).

On that note, COVID-19 ushers for a new normal of digitalized services across industries. On that note, universities were forced to consider alternative teaching options and used distance learning strategies on a far greater scale than ever before.

This translated into the extensive, global use of remote collaboration tools such as Zoom and Microsoft Teams for multi-person meetings. In addition, educators from around the world scattered to give each other suggestions that would aid in online instruction. For example, some suggested mobile learning as an appropriate substitute for students with limited access to technology resources (Gonzalez et al., 2020).

However, the digitization of education clashed with several factors that were questioned for having the ability to hinder students' success. Scholars worldwide urged the industry to escape from "the tyranny of time" and the rigorous regulations concerning terms and attendance. Their sole aim was to ignite creativity and innovation in students' minds. They called for the implementation of competency-based degrees unbounded by the element of time. Also, the standard four-year residential program's viability in terms of what can be digitized and made into a commodity is further questioned by Govindarajan and Srivastava (2020). The researchers supported "flipped classrooms" and a customized "horses for courses" technique for online delivery.

For example, the online flipped classroom has gained popularity since online learning took center stage in the educational process. A flipped classroom rearranges a typical classroom and its teaching schedule to give students more time to learn comfortably (Ztürk & Akrolu, 2021). The lesson material is video recorded and assigned as homework. Active learning tasks and synthesis-based activities like peer cooperation and debate are used throughout the class to integrate knowledge (Bergmann & Sams, 2012; Bishop & Verleger, 2013). It is important to note that this type of classroom is student-centered, permitting learners to study at their own pace and utilizing technology support to ensure a flexible learning environment (Shih & Huang, 2020).

On the other hand, the complete transition to remote learning right after the outbreak of the Covid-19 pandemic was chained to several challenges that uncovered layers of gaps within the education system's infrastructure. As it seems, question marks loomed over the educational equity and the ambiguity over the material taught, the best practices to implement, and the overall teaching environment (Zhang et al., 2020). Primary teacher training in online teaching and the complexity of the home environment were also added to the list of common teaching concerns amidst the unexpected global pandemic. This goes without mentioning the challenges third-world countries face while navigating the educational goals of the job and the limited resources available.

As for the students, studies indicated that only a tiny percentage of students maintain their initial motivation during distance learning, and the majority of them drop out of online courses. Based on that, the role of the teacher itself could shift shortly in light of new remote learning paradigms, which may include managing students' learning motives and progress in addition to teaching.

After the minacious effects of the coronavirus pandemic started to subside slightly, educational institutes started introducing blended learning as part of the curriculum.

Over the years, integrating technology into face-to-face instruction has generated significant interest and opened up several research opportunities.

Due to its perception as effective in delivering flexible, timely, and ongoing learning, blended learning is currently thought to be educational institutions' most effective and widely used style of instruction by academic institutions (Rasheed et al., 2020). The best of both worlds is face-to-face and online learning for content delivery to enhance students' performance.

Blended learning can present itself in four different styles:

Rotation Model: This style allows the students to alternate between various learning models. Students can rotate between different stations of knowledge, including interactive activities with peers, online instructions, and teacher preparation (Sahoo & Bhattacharya, 2021).

Flex Model: This online learning program takes place during school hours. Students are given a chance to jump between various methods of instruction and see what works best for them, with the presence of qualified instructors providing support and feedback when necessary (Sahoo & Bhattacharya, 2021).

Self-Blend Model: This concept encourages students to choose one or more online courses that go hand-in-hand with their school lessons. Students can attend these courses on school grounds or at home (Sahoo & Bhattacharya, 2021).

Enriched Virtual Model: This model provides a "complete school experience" since students can divide their time between studying remotely and attending actual classroom classes. For example, after hearing the first session of a particular course on school grounds, the student can continue following the rest of the sessions at home (Sahoo & Bhattacharya, 2021).

This digital transformation is expected to be around for a while. On the contrary, digital services are on their way to being the new norm in service sectors. The global pandemic fosters and speeds innovation and advancement, particularly in the digital domain. Although the terms used in the discussions have changed over time (computer-based learning, e-learning, remote learning, etc.), the emphasis is primarily on the organizational requirements for long-term implementation.

Future Trends in Higher Education

With the advancement of technology and the start of the Fourth Industrial Revolution, society and the workplace continue to change and evolve. This has, in turn, profoundly affected the educational field, resulting in some emerging trends. Teachers must keep up with these most recent developments and essential aspects that influence classroom learning if they want to engage their pupils effectively. Comprehending these trends may enable them to design more efficient learning environments. These are some significant trends that educators should be aware of as they prepare to incorporate the most recent educational innovations.

Personalized Learning

According to the education literature, one of the most significant developments in education is digitalization, which will significantly impact how instruction is carried out. Moreover, digital technologies frequently prioritize individualized and tailored learning strategies (UNESCO, 2022).

Personalization, varied study styles, and a wide range of options for various situations made by students from multiple backgrounds and biographical stages will necessitate a more individualized approach to academic education through higher education institutions (Ehlers & Kellermann, 2019). A trendy word educators employ in place of "one size fits all" education is personalized learning. Yet, because customized learning is frequently used in connection with the concepts of differentiation and individualization, many people are still determining what it implies. We can only learn effectively if we recognize the significance of our learning and how it applies to our particular situations. For education to be meaningful, it must be personal. A person must fully assume responsibility for the learning process if they want their education to be utilized and used in the future.

According to Castaneda and Selwyn (2018), adaptive learning is a scaffolding strategy designed to benefit all parties involved in a learning environment, including teachers, students, and school administrators. By saving them time and giving them helpful information about each student's level of progress and learning capacity, adaptive learning technology benefits teachers. With the help of adaptive learning, they may create resources and activities tailored to each student's needs and organize an efficient, individualized learning experience. It also goes by the name of supportive scaffolding, and it calls for teachers to use differentiated instruction strategies and provide material that fits each student's learning style (Raj & Renumol, 2022). Moreover, adaptive learning enables students to study using customized plans based on their performance and skills and receive quick feedback tailored to their strengths and shortcomings (Castro, 2019). To offer a personalized learning experience, adaptive learning frequently requires utilizing a blended and online learning environment. Such a setting is outfitted with cutting-edge technology advancements like learning analytics and machine learning, or systems that track student progress and continuously use data to adapt the curriculum to specific students' requirements (Becker et al., 2017).

Lifelong Learning

While new technologies create skill gaps in workers and necessitate the acquisition of appropriate skills and lifetime learning, rapid technological advancement causes skills to deteriorate more quickly than in the past. Since new technologies have developed in recent years, this has changed to focus on lifelong skill acquisition. This movement can be explained by recent changes in the economy's structure and surroundings. Traditional usage of the word "lifelong learning" (LLL), which has a variety of meanings, refers to systems and processes that facilitate learning throughout adulthood and the working years. One interpretation of LLL is that it relates to a unique method through which adults learn and develop as they move through different stages of life (Poquet & Laat, 2021). Another definition speaks of the chances to take advantage of educational prospects fueled mainly by investments in human capital, driven by the market, and connected to the commoditization of education and skills (Vargas, 2017). Visions for LLL must consider these new realities associated with adult learning due to the prevalence of technology-mediated adult learning experiences, the need to establish ethical data collection and use practices to inform learning, and the dynamic nature of artificial intelligence embedded within these technologies. AI can transform how human and machine intellect are combined and how we learn (Seeber et al., 2020). LLL policies must consider ethical concerns, algorithmic trust, privacy and data security concerns, transparent data governance, standards, and worries and fears related to technology, data, and AI (Tomsett et al., 2020). (Luckin et al., 2016). Research communities in educational technology and Artificial Intelligence in Education (AIED) have, in the past, provided workable solutions that can be included in the LLL's instructional offerings and individual adult learning practices. The aim of LLL, a direction, and ideals supporting adult learning, should be explicitly addressed throughout, as seen from the examples below. In the twenty-first century, lifelong learning is a crucial professional development goal because of changes in global demographics, environmental requirements, and widespread information access (Longworth, 2003). Encouragement of lifelong learning can help students gain knowledge and skills, which will help them meet new organizational and professional needs and boost their chances of success (Salleh et al., 2019).

Competency-Based Education

Every year, more schools integrate competency-based education at a deeper level. This significant change in school culture, organization, and pedagogy aims to ensure the success of every student while addressing the fundamental flaws in the conventional paradigm. At the National Conference for K–12 Competency-Based Education in 2011, the first working definition of competency-based education was raised (Sturgis, Patrick, & Pittenger, 2011).

Knowledge is growing in competency-based education for students in grades K–12. Competency-Works updated the 2011 working definition in a multi-stage, participative process from 2017 to 2019.

Competency-based education definitions (Levine, E., & Patrick, S. (2019) as of 2019 had these approaches:

1. Every day, students are given the authority to make crucial decisions regarding their educational experiences, the creation and application of their knowledge, and how they will show what they have learned.
2. Assessment produces timely, pertinent, and usable evidence that is a meaningful, rewarding, and empowering learning experience for students.
3. Pupils get timely, tailored support based on their unique learning requirements.
4. Students advance based on proof of mastery rather than seat time.
5. Children learn actively by taking various routes and moving at diverse pedagogy, organizational structure, and school culture, all incorporate strategies to ensure equity for all children.
    7. Exact, clear, measurable, and transferrable learning expectations (knowledge, skills, and attitudes) are common and rigorous

In adult education, the idea of competence is still under debate. The benchmarks for workplace performance, known as workplace competency standards, serve as the foundation for setting enterprise agreements, compensation increases, recruitment practices, employee development, and promotion eligibility. Australian government-sponsored industrial and educational changes are currently using language that tries to separate itself from the constrictive viewpoint that characterized the Competency-based training movement. Large portions of the education industry were alienated by the National Training Board's proposal to focus exclusively on skills and outcomes in competency analysis in 1990. The shift to competency-based education has sparked a significant re-examining of the foundational components of the education and training system in the 21st century (Chappel, 2020).

Education in the Metaverse

Human-computer interaction methods will evolve when the metaverse invades the educational sector. Given the rapid advancement of technology, prominent technology executives are creating unique ways to transform the Metaverse into a learning environment. People have become acclimated to teleworking, telemedicine, and many other remote kinds of interaction since the COVID-19 pandemic.

Many educators have recently been concentrating on the Metaverse. Facebook's announcement caused an increase in interest in this topic, that it will change its name to Meta and promote itself as such. There needs to be more research on how the Metaverse affects education (Kaddoura & Al Husseiny, 2023).

Digital reality technologies can transform the entertainment industry, remote work, education, marketing, and economics. These technologies are likewise establishing a new paradigm for information exchange. The concept of the Metaverse has given rise to a new paradigm (Mystakidis, 2022). The word "Metaverse" is a combination of the phrases "meta," which means beyond or after, and "universe" (Cheng et al., 2022).

Metaverse platforms offer incremental improvements as virtual reality systems grow more user-friendly and networked. Once virtual reality glasses and accessories have a more comfortable form suitable for long-term usage, expanding their use cases and adapting them to educational contexts may be much more practical. Creating hardware and software based on the Metaverse that may be applied in educational contexts is crucial. Education professionals, researchers, designers, and developers must thus collaborate and guide one another on this topic (Sartaş & Topraklkolu, 2022).

Worldwide schooling was affected by the coronavirus outbreak. Beginning in 2020, teachers and students must learn a new distance learning methodology. Technology has been crucial for ensuring that education has continued during the global lockdowns (EU Business School, 2022).

The COVID-19 epidemic has significantly challenged and disrupted the world. This pandemic has changed students' environments, attitudes, and skills, negatively impacting the educational system (Toquero, 2020). Global regulation was necessary to stop in-person instruction in schools and colleges, forcing the switch to online delivery techniques (Itani et al., 2022).

Now, academics and IT experts are asking themselves the same question: if the internet aids learning in its present form, what kinds of things might the Metaverse enable everyone to do? The Metaverse makes it possible to adapt the curriculum to the needs of the students (Mistretta, 2022). The world is constantly changing due to new technology and schools of thought that are continually appearing. The Metaverse can transform the entire planet into a virtual global school, preventing the curriculum from falling behind. After the first advantage, one of the Metaverse's most attractive prospective educational applications is "gamifying" learning (EU Business School, 2022). The virtual world may make education look like a video game, with lessons structured like quests, encouraging pupils to finish their work and perform better, thanks to its emphasis on teamwork and accomplishing tasks (EU Business School, 2022). The Metaverse's technology and tools have considerably increased pedagogical and technical support for education through immersive learning opportunities, which has a beneficial effect on student motivation (Tlili et al., 2022).

AI in Education

The World Wide Web promoted competition by utilizing several technological developments that allow billions of people across numerous geographic locations to communicate whenever and wherever they are. This happened by relying solely on the analog medium of electronic devices, which is the primary fuel that expands the horizons of all 21st-century technologies. Future predictions indicate that artificial intelligence (A.I.) will drastically change consumer behavior and marketing strategies. Building on previous research and extensive interactions with practice, the authors provide a multidimensional paradigm for evaluating the impact of artificial intelligence that considers task types, intelligence levels, and whether or not A.I. is implanted in a robot. Today's generation finds it only possible to fathom life with social media. The same is true for future generations (Al Husseiny, 2023b).

Artificial intelligence (AI) applications in education are growing and have recently attracted much attention. AI and adaptive learning technologies are highlighted as critical educational technology developments in the 2018 Horizon research (Educause, 2018), with implementation expected in two to three years. According to the Horizon Report 2019 Higher Education Edition (Educause, 2019), the usage of AI in teaching is anticipated to grow even more dramatically. Yet, analysts predict that between 2018 and 2022, AI in Education will increase by 43%. According to Contact North, a significant Canadian non-profit online learning organization, there is no doubt that [AI] technology is intrinsically linked to the future of higher education (Contact North,2018). Significant investments have been made by the German Research Center for Artificial Intelligence1 (DFKI) and other nonprofit public-private partnerships. This surge in interest will probably significantly impact colleges and universities soon (Popenici & Kerr, 2017). For instance, Google paid $400 million for the European AI startup Deep Mind (AL Husseiny, 2023a).

Robots and teachers working together to help students by leveraging their best attributes is the ideal situation for AI in Education. As students will work in a world where AI is a reality, educational institutions should aggressively utilize the technology that is currently accessible and expose them to its possibilities. Individualized and differentiated instruction has been given priority by educators who want to tailor their lessons to each student's particular needs. Even yet, with thirty students in each session, AI will make it possible for instructors to differentiate to a degree that is currently difficult.

As AI advances, a machine may examine students' expressions to identify whether they are having trouble learning a concept and modify the course accordingly. In the future, AI-powered computers can adapt the curriculum to each student's needs, which is now impractical (UNESCO, 2019). Everything is available to every student. With artificial intelligence tools, all students, including those who speak different languages or may have visual or aural impairments, should be able to participate in global classrooms. Presentation Translator, a free PowerPoint add-in, creates real-time subtitles for the instructor's remarks. This creates new opportunities for students who might be sick and unable to attend class, require teaching at a different level, or in a subject not provided at their local institution. AI can help remove boundaries between traditional grade levels and educational institutions (Williamson, 2015).

Education in the Age of AI

As of late, educational institutes have a better grasp of how to teach and train individuals due to interdisciplinary research in the learning sciences, which has greatly aided our understanding of how humans learn. Artificial intelligence (AI) is becoming more prevalent, and whether we know it or not, we use AI technology in our everyday interactions. The lines separating humans from other living things are thinning, and we are headed toward a time when the technological singularity is unavoidable. One industry that has undergone a digital change is education since it has begun to utilize the potential presented by derivative technologies like artificial intelligence (Bozkurt et al., 2021).

The new century shows off an astonishing process of artificial intelligence's growth, evolution, and maturation in education (AIEd). AIEd refers to employing AI (Artificial Intelligence) technologies in educational contexts. It gives learners tailors guidance and feedback and aids educators in decision-making (Hwang et al.,2020).

In their paper "Vision, challenges, roles and research issues of Artificial Intelligence in Education," Hwang et al. (2020) categorized AIEd into four roles (Hwang et al.,2020).

- Intelligent tutor: This group includes adaptive learning mechanisms, tutoring, and recommendation systems.
- Intelligent tutee: Since most educational systems emphasize helping students more than allowing them to act as tutors or advisors, this function hasn't been given the appropriate research attention. Even though it may enhance learners' thinking abilities and knowledge levels, no studies have openly and consciously sought to build intelligent tutees.
- Intelligent learning partner/tool: The availability of such AI tools supports the viewpoint of student-centered learning and constructivism since it assists students in collecting data and analyzing results. The learner will have the chance to concentrate on essential tasks that require higher-thinking skills rather than wasting time and energy on simple roles.
- Policy-making advisor: AI technologies can guide policymakers into understanding trends, issues, and the most effective policies for the education setup.

It has already been used to predict students' academic success, identify at-risk students early on, pinpoint the key variables that will impact students' success, support the teaching process, create personalized learning resources, and incorporate interactive learning techniques (Bozkurt et al., 2021).

Additionally, AI is believed to boost students' engagement and achieve the desired learning outcomes since it integrates technologies like interactivity, discussion, and question generation (Bozkurt et al., 2021). In a nutshell, the "technologization" of education gave learners who felt disadvantaged while navigating traditional classrooms the necessary support for their success.

On the other hand, this infatuation with technology, especially in the context of education, is said to be changing the dynamics between educators and students. Teachers are no longer essential entities with expertise to share but rather a process facilitators. Arguably, categorizing the learning-teaching process as a trade interferes with students' character formation, translating into one's ability to empathize with others in the community and engage in societal issues (Guilherme 2019).

Prospects

Emergency remote teaching (ERT) during the Covid-19 pandemic has little in common with properly planned and constructed online education, as Hodges et al. (2020), Nordmann et al. (2020), and Xie and Rice (2021) note. Online education is not regular, and computer-based instruction is even less common. It demands

Given the requirement to anticipate learners' needs and expectations, detailed design and consideration of many components are necessary (Rapanta and Cantoni 2014). Also, emergency remote teachers had to deal with unanticipated human problems commonly overlooked in HE, like learners' motivation, socio-emotional distance, socio-economic gaps, and cultural isolation. However, Schatzki (2021) notes that teachers have traditionally undervalued the role that space and other tangible (and digital) aspects of social life play in determining how educational practices are structured. In the face of the unpreparedness of the academic world to adapt to this crisis (UNESCO 2020), educators from all grades and circumstances were called to take the learning situation into their hands, thinking, reassessing, and remodeling their pedagogical methods.

ERT paved the way for the first encounters with digital teaching, even if it cannot be said to share the same processes and procedures as online education due to a lack of administrative support and technological infrastructure. Given the wide range of options within what is often called teaching and learning with technologies, these earliest signs of digitization might readily offer new and effective blended or 'simple' technology-enhanced forms of teaching and learning. But, as our expert interviews revealed, several factors, including flexibility, empowerment, professionalization, and strategic decision-making, must be considered for this to be possible (Rapanta et al., 2021).

CONCLUSION

In this chapter, the researchers examined how education looked before and after the coronavirus that was set on a mission to alter the dynamics of various sectors worldwide.

The covid-19 pandemic introduced a shift like no other in various sectors. Strict guidelines of social conduct, such as social distancing and eliminating human interaction, forced institutes, including the educational sector, into a complete shift towards digitizing services.

What started as an ambiguous and unknown path uncovered the hidden layers of a sector unprepared for the storm that hit it. Educational institutes worldwide took "emergency online learning" as a starting point and went on a journey to study, evaluate, and implement the best practices that would optimize students' performance in the era of AI.

In addition, since the fourth Industrial Revolution is on a fast sprint, the researchers also examined future education trends concerning AI usage. Educational institutes must carefully review and keep up with these developments to ensure the effective delivery of content and design a comprehensive learning environment. These trends include personalized learning, life-long learning, competency-based education, and the practical usage of AI in education.

Finally, recommendations for future research are also presented that would pave pathways for other researchers to uncover and study.

RECOMMENDATIONS FOR FUTURE RESEARCH

Interdisciplinary research has considerably enhanced our understanding of how people learn and the best practices to implement for effective content delivery. The concept of technology in the education sector has been present for quite some time now, but its usage was limited and optional. However, since the coronavirus forced educational leaders and policy-makers to perform a sudden switch to online learning, educators are still investigating and filling out the gaps in the educational sector's infrastructure.

First, digitizing education means allocating technology to serve the educational process. Notably, technological tools were always at students' disposal or used as intelligent tutor that helps implement adaptive mechanisms. However, minimal research has been allocated to investigate AI as an intelligent tutee. So far, education in itself is considered to be a product. Many researchers around the globe are questioning the adverse effects of such tools on students since the teacher is now considered a mere facilitator of material. Therefore, future research should focus on building students as tutors or advisors for others. Aside from contributing to students' cognitive skills and knowledge levels, this supports constructivist views that advertise students constructing knowledge and learning through peer interaction.

In addition, advanced chatbot tools like ChatGPT are currently trending for generating impressive and natural human-like written content within seconds. It is expected that such devices are going to alter learning objectives, activities, and evaluation procedures within the educational context. It is no longer a matter of using or not using AI I education, but the best practice to approach the tools. For that reason, the researchers suggest investigating the case of AI's ethical use in education. Educators must learn how to set ethical policies limiting plagiarism when assigning students tasks.

On the other hand, policymakers should rethink their learning goals and focus on subject-domain tasks that utilize students' critical thinking and innovation instead of general skills. The ideal scenario would be to focus on finding solutions to real-world problems and new compositions of assessment that align with the educational objectives.

Also, as previously mentioned, many researchers are questioning the role of teachers now that the Human-AI collaborations are changing the game's rules. The theory of cognitive development by the Russian psychologist Lev Vygotsky proposed a theoretical concept known as the zone of proximal development. Children's potential for cognitive development is constrained on the lower end by what they can achieve on their own and the upper end by what they can achieve with the assistance of a peer or instructor who has more knowledge (Shabani et al., 2010). The zone of proximal development is this area of immediate potential. A child's cognitive abilities advance as they learn to execute tasks with progressively less help (Shabani et al., 2010). Collaborative learning practices in classroom instruction are strongly supported by Vygotsky's theories on the zone of proximal development. In the framework of Vygotsky's ideas, the five cooperative learning components—positive interdependence, small groups, interpersonal skills, face-to-face interaction, individual accountability, and group self-evaluation are examined (Shabani et al., 2010). But now that this assistance to attain cognitive development is provided by non-other than AI tools, many are worried about the possible replacement of teachers. Based on that, the researchers find it reasonable to investigate the growing role of AI in education. This concern shouldn't be limited to teaching since speculations are looming around AI automating many jobs. Therefore, it is crucial to prepare students for the future of work and have them reconsider their options before entering the job market.

REFERENCES

Al Husseiny, F. (2023). Artificial Intelligence in Higher Education: A New Horizon. In Handbook of Research on AI Methods and Applications in Computer Engineering (pp. 295-315). IGI Global. doi:10.4018/978-1-6684-6937-8.ch014

Al Husseiny, F. (2023). The Rising Trend of Artificial Intelligence in Social Media: Applications, Challenges, and Opportunities. Handbook of Research on AI Methods and Applications in Computer Engineering, 42-61.

Al Husseiny, F., & Youness, H. (2023). Exploring the role of social media marketing in students' decision to select universities in Lebanon: A proposed emerging framework. *QScience Connect*, *2023*(1), 4. doi:10.5339/connect.2023.spt.4

Al-Karaki, J. N., Ababneh, N., Hamid, Y., & Gawanmeh, A. (2021). Evaluating the Effectiveness of Distance Learning in Higher Education during COVID-19 Global Crisis: UAE Educators' Perspectives. *Contemporary Educational Technology*, *13*(3).

Alexander, B., Ashford-Rowe, K., Barajas-Murphy, N., Dobbin, G., Knott, J., McCormack, M., & Weber, N. (2019). *EDUCAUSE Horizon Report: 2019 Higher Education Edition*. Educause.

Becker, S. A., Brown, M., Dahlstrom, E., Davis, A., DePaul, K., Diaz, V., & Pomerantz, J. (2018). *Horizon report 2018 higher education edition brought to you by Educause*. EDUCAUSE.

Becker, S. A., Cummins, M., Davis, A., Freeman, A., Hall, C. G., & Ananthanarayanan, V. (2017). *NMC horizon report: 2017 higher education edition*. The New Media Consortium.

Bergmann, J., & Sams, A. (2012). *Flip your classroom: Reach every student in every class daily—the international society for technology in education*.

Bishop, J., & Verleger, M. A. (2013, June). *The flipped classroom: A survey of the research*. In *2013 ASEE Annual Conference & Exposition* (pp. 23-1200). ASEE. 10.18260/1-2--22585

Bozkurt, A., Karadeniz, A., Baneres, D., Guerrero-Roldán, A. E., & Rodríguez, M. E. (2021). Artificial intelligence and reflections from the educational landscape: A review of AI studies in half a century. *Sustainability*, *13*(2), 800. doi:10.3390u13020800

Carroll, N., & Conboy, K. (2020). Normalizing the "new normal": Changing tech-driven work practices under pandemic time pressure. *International Journal of Information Management*, *55*, 102186. doi:10.1016/j.ijinfomgt.2020.102186 PMID:32836643

Castañeda, L., & Selwyn, N. (2018). More than tools? Making sense of the ongoing digitizations of higher education. *International Journal of Educational Technology in Higher Education*, *15*(1), 1–10. doi:10.118641239-018-0109-y

Castro, R. (2019). Blended learning in higher education: Trends and capabilities. *Education and Information Technologies*, *24*(4), 2523–2546. doi:10.100710639-019-09886-3

Chappell, C., Gonczi, A., & Hager, P. (2020). Competency-based education. In *Understanding adult education and training* (pp. 191–205). Routledge. doi:10.4324/9781003118299-18

DeVaney, J., Shimshon, G., Rascoff, M., & Maggioncalda, J. (2020). Higher Ed needs a long-term plan for virtual learning. *Harvard Business Review*, 2–5.

Ehlers, U. D., & Kellermann, S. A. (2019). Future skills: The future of learning and higher education (pp. 2-69). Karlsruhe.

Gonzalez, T., De La Rubia, M. A., Hincz, K. P., Comas-Lopez, M., Subirats, L., Fort, S., & Sacha, G. M. (2020). Influence of COVID-19 confinement on students' performance in higher education. *PLoS One*, *15*(10), e0239490. doi:10.1371/journal.pone.0239490 PMID:33035228

Govindarajan, V., & Srivastava, A. (2020). What the shift to virtual learning could mean for the future of higher ed. *Harvard Business Review*, *31*(1), 3–8.

Guilherme, A. (2019). AI and education: The importance of teacher and student relations. *AI & Society*, *34*(1), 47–54. doi:10.100700146-017-0693-8

Hodges, C. B., Moore, S., Lockee, B. B., Trust, T., & Bond, M. A. (2020). *The difference between emergency remote teaching and online learning*.

Hurley, R. (2019). *Data Science: A Comprehensive Guide to Data Science, Data Analytics, Data Mining*. Artificial Intelligence, Machine Learning, and Big Data. Independently Published.

Hwang, G. J., Xie, H., Wah, B. W., & Gašević, D. (2020). Vision, challenges, roles and research issues of Artificial Intelligence in Education. *Computers and Education: Artificial Intelligence*, *1*, 100001. doi:10.1016/j.caeai.2020.100001

International Commission on the Futures of Education. (2020). *Education in a post-COVID world: Nine ideas for public action*. ICFE.

Itani, M., Itani, M., Kaddoura, S., & Al Husseiny, F. (2022). The impact of the Covid-19 pandemic on online examination: Challenges and opportunities. *Global Journal of Engineering Education*, *24*(2).

Kabadayi, S., O'Connor, G. E., & Tuzovic, S. (2020). The impact of coronavirus on service ecosystems as service mega-disruptions. *Journal of Services Marketing*, *34*(6), 809–817. doi:10.1108/JSM-03-2020-0090

Kaddoura, S., & Al Husseiny, F. (2021). An approach to reinforce active learning in higher education for IT students. *Global Journal of Engineering Education*, *23*(1), 43–48.

Kaddoura, S., & Al Husseiny, F. (2021). Online learning on information security based on critical thinking andragogy. *World Transactions on Engineering and Technology Education*, *19*(2), 157–162.

Kaddoura, S., & Al Husseiny, F. (2023). The rising trend of Metaverse in education: Challenges, opportunities, and ethical considerations. *PeerJ. Computer Science*, *9*, e1252. doi:10.7717/peerj-cs.1252

Kang, B. (2021). *How the COVID-19 pandemic is reshaping the education service. The Future of Service Post-COVID-19 Pandemic* (Vol. 1). Rapid Adoption of Digital Service Technology.

Kuznetsov, A., Pyanykh, E., & Rodaikina, M. (2021). *Digital Transformation in the Context of Improving the Quality of Lifelong Education*. MIT.

Levine, E., & Patrick, S. (2019). *What Is Competency-Based Education? An Updated Definition*. Aurora Institute.

Luckin, R., Holmes, W., Griffiths, M., & Forcier, L. B. (2016). *Intelligence Unleashed: An argument for AI in education*.

North, C. (2018). *Ten facts about artificial intelligence in teaching and learning*. University of California.

Öztürk, M., & Çakıroğlu, Ü. (2021). Flipped learning design in EFL classrooms: Implementing self-regulated learning strategies to develop language skills. *Smart Learning Environments*, *8*(1), 2. doi:10.118640561-021-00146-x

Pedro, F., Subosa, M., Rivas, A., & Valverde, P. (2019). *Artificial intelligence in education: Challenges and opportunities for sustainable development*. UNESCO.

Popenici, S. A., & Kerr, S. (2017). Exploring the impact of artificial intelligence on teaching and learning in higher education. *Research and Practice in Technology Enhanced Learning*, *12*(1), 1–13. doi:10.118641039-017-0062-8 PMID:30595727

Poquet, O., & De Laat, M. (2021). Developing capabilities: Lifelong learning in the age of AI. *British Journal of Educational Technology*, *52*(4), 1695–1708. doi:10.1111/bjet.13123

Raj, N. S., & Renumol, V. G. (2022). A systematic literature review on adaptive content recommenders in personalized learning environments from 2015 to 2020. *Journal of Computers in Education*, *9*(1), 113–148. doi:10.100740692-021-00199-4

Rapanta, C., Botturi, L., Goodyear, P., Guàrdia, L., & Koole, M. (2021). Balancing technology, pedagogy and the new normal: Post-pandemic challenges for higher education. *Postdigital Science and Education*, *3*(3), 715–742. doi:10.100742438-021-00249-1

Rapanta, C., & Cantoni, L. (2014). Being in the users' shoes: Anticipating experience while designing online courses. *British Journal of Educational Technology*, *45*(5), 765–777. doi:10.1111/bjet.12102

Rasheed, R. A., Kamsin, A., & Abdullah, N. A. (2020). Challenges in the online component of blended learning: A systematic review. *Computers & Education*, *144*, 103701. doi:10.1016/j.compedu.2019.103701

Salleh, U. K. M., Zulnaidi, H., Rahim, S. S. A., Bin Zakaria, A. R., & Hidayat, R. (2019). Roles of self-directed learning and social networking sites in lifelong learning. *International Journal of Instruction*, *12*(4), 167–182. doi:10.29333/iji.2019.12411a

Schatzki, T. R. (2022). Spatial troubles with teaching under COVID-19. *Studies in Continuing Education*, *44*(2), 300–315. doi:10.1080/0158037X.2021.1928052

Seeber, I., Waizenegger, L., & Seidel, S. (2020). Collaborating with issues and research opportunities. *Internet Research*. Advance online publication. doi:10.1108/INTR-12-2019-0503

Shabani, K., Khatib, M., & Ebadi, S. (2010). Vygotsky's zone of proximal development: Instructional implications and teachers' professional development. *English Language Teaching*, *3*(4), 237–248. doi:10.5539/elt.v3n4p237

Shih, H. C. J., & Huang, S. H. C. (2020). College students' metacognitive strategy use in an EFL flipped classroom. *Computer Assisted Language Learning*, *33*(7), 755–784. doi:10.1080/09588221.2019.1590420

Tian, H., Liu, Y., Li, Y., Wu, C. H., Chen, B., Kraemer, M. U., Li, B., Cai, J., Xu, B., Yang, Q., Wang, B., Yang, P., Cui, Y., Song, Y., Zheng, P., Wang, Q., Bjornstad, O. N., Yang, R., Grenfell, B. T., ... Dye, C. (2020). An investigation of transmission control measures during the first 50 days of the COVID-19 epidemic in China. *Science*, *368*(6491), 638–642. doi:10.1126cience.abb6105 PMID:32234804

Vargas, C. (2017). Lifelong learning from a social justice perspective 21. *Education Research and Foresght*, 21.

Williamson, B. (2015). Governing software: Networks, databases, and algorithmic power in the digital governance of public education. *Learning, Media and Technology*, *40*(1), 83–105. doi:10.1080/17439 884.2014.924527

Xie, J., & Rice, M. F. (2021). Instructional designers' roles in emergency remote teaching during CO-VID-19. *Distance Education*, *42*(1), 70–87. doi:10.1080/01587919.2020.1869526

Zawacki-Richter, O. (2021). The current state and impact of Covid-19 on digital higher education in Germany. *Human Behavior and Emerging Technologies*, *3*(1), 218–226. doi:10.1002/hbe2.238 PMID:33363276

Zhang, W., Wang, Y., Yang, L., & Wang, C. (2020). Suspending classes without stopping learning: China's education emergency management policy in the COVID-19 outbreak. *Journal of Risk and financial management, 13*(3), 55.

Chapter 14
Digital and Virtual Book Clubs:
Breaking the Boundaries of Restrictive Literacy Practices

Renee R. M. Moran
East Tennessee State University, USA

Natalia A. Ward
East Tennessee State University, USA

Monica T. Billen
California State University, Fresno, USA

Lashay Wood
East Tennessee State University, USA

Shuling Yang
East Tennessee State University, USA

ABSTRACT

This chapter reaffirms books clubs as a sound pedagogical strategy and considers how digital and virtual book clubs may allow us to meet this globalized moment in which technology has become a staple of our everyday lives. The authors provide two examples of how to integrate digital and virtual book clubs in both elementary classrooms and teacher education. The first demonstrates the promise of cross-country virtual books clubs as a way to help pre-service teachers access children's literature and consider diverse perspectives. The second case illustrates how one rural elementary school successfully made the shift from face-to-face to digital books in order to build motivation to read and increase authentic discussion between students. The authors argue that digital and virtual book clubs can expand access to text, empower and motivate students of all ages, and mirror real world literacy practices. The authors advocate for book clubs as a necessary literacy practice, which should be part of the science of reading movement.

DOI: 10.4018/978-1-6684-7015-2.ch014

INTRODUCTION

Book clubs have existed for decades in elementary schools as a means of fostering discussion about text, close reading, and response to literature (Jocius & Shealy, 2018). Book clubs, widely acknowledged as a sound pedagogical strategy, can deepen comprehension, foster the application of sound reading strategies, and boost motivation (Allington & Gabriel, 2012; Cazden, 1988; Cherry-Paul & Johansen, 2019; Gambrell, 2011). Though book clubs originated inside the walls of a physical classroom, the advancement of technology has allowed educators to extend their audience through the use of digital and virtual book clubs (Bromley, Faughnan, Ham, Miller, Armstrong, Crandall, Marrone, 2014; Serafini & Youngs, 2013; Siegel, 2012; Whitin, 2009). Since the onset of the COVID-19 pandemic, virtual book clubs have become increasingly prevalent (Naitnaphit, 2021). In this chapter, we define digital book clubs as book clubs occurring asynchronously online, and virtual book clubs as occurring synchronously on Zoom, Google Meet, or a similar platform.

Digital and virtual book clubs are relevant to our "YouTube Generation" (Dreon, Kerper, & Landis, 2011) as this generation is developing new ways of learning content, interacting with others, and processing information (Oblinger & Oblinger, 2005; Prensky, 2001a, 2001b). Lapp and colleagues (2012) posit that the "remixing" of traditional instruction with new literacies and multimodal text is a means of strengthening motivation. Digital book clubs mix traditional instruction with new literacies. Bromley et al. (2014) found that digital book clubs allow students to delve deeper into text, participate in valuable dialogic conversations with peers, and enhance their appreciation of literature.

Book clubs have also been used widely in university settings as a means of fostering collaborative, knowledge-building, and engaging text-based discussions (Beach & Yussen, 2011; Farr & Kurtzhan-Beach, 2006). Likewise, adult book clubs can encourage sharing of and connection to individual life experiences that build community and allow members to reconsider stagnant beliefs (Rooney, 2005; Sumara, Luce-Kapler, Robson, & Catlin, 2008). Scholars note that teacher preparation programs can be fertile ground for digital/virtual book clubs and that using diverse children's books with pre-service teachers (PSTs) offers opportunities to model culturally responsive pedagogy (Gay, 2002; Fortune et. al, 2021). While PSTs may feel some discomfort engaging in discourse around challenging topics that books may spur (Hollie, 2017), university faculty are encouraging such conversations now more than ever (Goldberg, 2020).

However, while book clubs have been widely extolled as a sound teaching technique, we have experienced that instructional time is limited in educational contexts due to policy mandates. The recent Science of Reading (SOR) movement is widely recognized by many as a move towards needed explicit instruction in phonics, phonemic awareness, and phonological awareness. However, some scholars are concerned that the movement is being oversimplified and narrowed. Duke and Cartwright (2021) note that SOR when applied only through the lens of the Simple View of Reading (SVR) which focuses solely on decoding and listening comprehension, may exclude other vital elements (often practiced in book clubs) such as the connections between vocabulary and word recognition or fluency and language comprehension. In our context we are required to integrate 23 prerecorded, state-developed virtual lectures focused on foundational skills instruction – central focus of SOR – throughout literacy coursework. Our local school districts are also purchasing scripted literacy curricula that leave teachers little room for supplemental activities such as digital/virtual book clubs and we find that students are often engaged in one-size-fits-all instruction. Despite this, in our chapter, we hope to uphold the promise of digital/virtual book clubs in varying environments by sharing practical strategies from teachers, librarians, PSTs, and literacy faculty that are having success with digital/virtual book clubs in our current educational environment and demonstrating ways that book clubs support SOR.

NEW LITERACIES IN THE TIMES OF SCIENCE OF READING

Each year for the last two decades, scholars have administered the "What's Hot in Literacy" survey to twenty-five literacy experts on the most pressing and prominent literacy issues of our times. The "science of teaching reading" was recently ranked as "extremely hot", a rare designation, which denotes a literacy matter that is of great concern to the educational community at large (Cassidy, Grote-Garcia, & Ortlieb, 2022). While 100% of the participants agreed that SOR is front and center in current educational debates, 44% believed that it should not be the primary focus of literacy policy and curriculum. In an explanation of survey responses and in reference to the simple view of reading (Duke & Cartwright, 2021), Cassidy et al (2022) noted:

Those who are using [the simple view of reading] to prioritize phonics are communicating the idea that since children understand language naturally, the only element left to teach is phonics. Unfortunately, this idea seems to ignore the vast body of research connecting comprehension skill development to other literacy topics such as reading fluency [...], motivation and interest [...], and writing.

While experts surveyed resisted a singular view of SOR, they did advocate strongly for SOR that encompasses explicit phonics and phonemic awareness instruction in tandem with the other well known components of reading such as fluency, comprehension, and writing with attention to motivation and engagement (National Reading Panel Report, 2000). Perhaps unsurprisingly, digital literacy was also ranked in the top five, denoted as "very hot" by survey respondents, a spot it has held since 2014. This data provides convincing evidence that SOR and digital literacy must be explored not as separate entities but concurrently as we work to bolster the literacy achievement gap and meet the moment of our digitized world.

Research has demonstrated new literacies, digital storytelling, and multimodal practices are tenets of our globalized world that should be integrated into K–12 classrooms (Bogard & McMackin, 2012; Gee, 2013; Hull & Nelson, 2005; Kress, 2003; Authors, 2020; Yearta, 2019). Shelby-Caffey, Ubeda, and Jenkins (2009) posit that students need not only the basic understanding of new media literacies, but they should also become innovators and creators of new literacies. Often students are passive consumers of technology, but there are digital tools available that have the potential for students to take a production role, where interactive online tools help literacy instruction (e.g., Epic, SeeSaw, Nearpod, Google Jamboard) (Chen et al., 2022). Production and consumption can happen simultaneously, as students intake new ideas while revising and creating using provided digital tools (Alvermann, Marshall, Mclean, Huddleston, & Joaquin 2012; Collier, 2018). Mullen and Wedick (2008) argue that "being literate no longer involves only being able to read and write," but also the ability to "download, upload, rip, burn, chat, save, blog, Skype, IM and share' (p. 66). Chiu (2021) found that online environments "supported more autonomy [and] were more likely to engage students cognitively in developing two important lifelong skills of digital literacy and self-regulated learning" (p. 1). Research also informed us that the choices of online teaching tools should be student-centered and cultivate student interests (Chen et al., 2022).

However, while touting the necessity of a focus on digital literacies, we must also acknowledge the roadblocks that are currently in place in terms of access. The digital divide, a term coined by Lloyd Morrisett, refers to the growing gap between privileged and underprivileged members of society and their access to computers and the internet (Rogers, 2001). Rogers (2001) posited that the focus on access related to the digital divide would be replaced by what he deemed the "education divide" wherein more individuals have access to digital tools but may not possess the knowledge and skills to use these tools in productive ways. Likewise, Bailey and colleagues (2021) observed that the achievement gap has grown between students who possess strong digital literacy skills and those that do not. While the research is clear on the benefits of incorporating digital tools in the K–12 classroom, we must be cognizant that many of our students will be much less equipped to navigate these tools than their peers. These students may need additional support and scaffolding along the way. Finally, while teacher educators and teachers may assume that the younger generation of students naturally bring insight into new literacies with them into the classroom, Wimmer and Draper (2019) remind us that we cannot presume that PSTs will naturally apply new literacies. Instead, teacher educators must create opportunities for engaging pre-service and novice teachers in multiple literacies as part of the literacy curriculum. Moreover, preservice teachers may be hesitant and even resistant to incorporate new literacies as an important part of their teaching (Kist & Pytash, 2015; Lewis & Founders, 2004).

VIRTUAL AND DIGITAL BOOK CLUBS IN ACTION

Research examining virtual and digital book clubs builds on the long standing tradition of using "student-led book clubs along with community-based book clubs" to "offer readers opportunities to connect and discuss the same book in a low-stakes environment" (Kelly & Cameron Likens, 2022, p. 1). Virtual and digital book clubs, conducted via Zoom, Skype, or another virtual platform across multiple settings, have important benefits for students who engage in them. First, they support students' engagement with new literacies and digital tools in service of collaboration, meaning-making, and intellectual growth. "Online book clubs bridge traditional literacies while engaging students in new literacies in safe and meaningful ways" (Kelly & Cameron Likens, 2022, p. 2). Virtual and digital book clubs expand the social circle available to students and lead to richer engagement with texts (Stover et al., 2016). This connection with a wider audience is particularly powerful for students who come from areas that do not enjoy cultural and linguistic diversity. Virtual and digital books clubs, thus, invite students to have an experience with unfamiliar ways of thinking and being and normalize difference as an important asset in a modern world. Furthermore, digital book clubs with its asynchronous discussion options provide an extended "think time to develop more thoughtful posts and comments" to students who may be hesitant to engage in real time discussions of texts (Stover et al., 2016, p. 10).

Orchestrating virtual and digital book clubs is a complex process that requires a deep understanding of literacy development, motivation and engagement, new literacies, and students we teach. Book choice and the selection of highly motivating texts readers can connect to is critical for virtual or digital book clubs (Smith, 2019). Furthermore, the success of digital and virtual book clubs often depends on the purposeful choice of the online platform and format for engagement, as well as providing clear expectations and ongoing support and guidance to students (Smith, 2019). When successfully set up, digital and virtual book clubs provide an excellent platform for learning for students of any age and experience levels. One study, for example, described how a virtual book club connected preservice teachers and fourth grade students in reading books, making sense of them, and discussing their growing understandings over time and across multiple platforms, e.g., Edmondo, Zoom, Flipgrid, Jamboard. As a result, "preservice teachers learned ways to build students' background knowledge, how to differentiate, and how to deepen students' thinking through modeling and questioning," while fourth graders reported changing as both readers and human beings (Kelly & Cameron Likens, 2022, p. 11). Another study described how an online book club ignited middle schoolers' engagement with literature over summer break months (Smith, 2019). Cumulatively, research on virtual and digital book clubs across ages and settings situates this long-standing pedagogical practice as a promising vehicle for promoting authentic engagement with texts and meaningful discussions in the literacy classroom.

Building on this existing work on digital/virtual book clubs, we present two cases (one virtual, one digital) in two different settings. For each case, we describe the purpose and goals, context, how-to, and lessons learned.

Case #1: A Cross Country Virtual Book Club Project With Pre-Service Teachers

Purpose

We share a common belief in the pedagogical power of book clubs for all students including PSTs. We agree with Bishop (1990) that books can serve as a mirror for self reflection, a window for looking out into other cultures and ways of life, and a sliding glass door through, which students can step into the shoes of another as a means of building empathy. We had incorporated book clubs in our literacy classes for years but wanted to broaden PSTs perspectives outside just the four walls of our classroom. Fortune and colleagues (2020) notes that cross-university book clubs can be an expansive experience for PSTs and that "inter-programmatic contact [can] bolster students' cultural competency, disciplinary literacies, and ultimately, their praxis" (p. 319). With this frame as a backdrop, we reached out to colleagues at a university who were also teaching similar literacy courses to PSTs. However, we purposefully chose a university that differed in geographical location and student population. After meeting with professors from the other university and considering schedules, curriculum mandates, and the needs of students, we agreed upon three asynchronous and two synchronous virtual book clubs. Our goals for PSTs included:

1) become more familiar with children's literature;
2) hear other's perspectives;
3) reflect on the book club process and consider how they might use it in their future classrooms.

Context

Two universities participated in this virtual book club partnership. University 1 was geographically situated in the Appalachian Mountains of east Tennessee. The majority of the students are white and monolingual, some with little to no experience with areas removed from their hometowns. Most students are females. University 2 was geographically situated in central California. The majority of students are bilingual females of Hispanic heritage. There were 38 students total across both classes. Knowing the demographic composition of our courses, we, as instructors, realized that both groups of students did not have much insight into each other's world and cultural ways of being. These differences, as well as important similarities, across settings and students supported the design of the project, as we aimed to build on students' knowledge and backgrounds to ignite new learning.

Text Selection

We selected three children's books that we viewed as in alignment with Bishop's (1990) notion of windows, mirrors, and sliding glass doors. We examined potential book club children's literature for "culturally conscious" elements that would represent practices and ways of living of our students but also provide an inside look into cultures other than their own (Sims, 1982, p. 49). We wanted PSTs to see themselves in a text, to see their new cross country book club members in a text, and to expand their view more globally. We chose *Owl Moon* by Jane Yolen to represent Appalachian culture, *Dreamers* by Yuyi Morales to represent the Latinx experience, and *The Water Princess* by Susan Verde to provide a global perspective. The book selection offered both a familiar and a new experience to all participating students. The focus on multicultural children's books was intentionally to invite PSTs to engage with children's books as a lynchpin of meaning making, critical thinking, and cultural explorations.

How To

Together with us, our students took part in two asynchronous online engagements on a Google Site and two synchronous Zoom meetings, during which they met with book club members and discussed the texts after reading and reflecting on them independently. Students were placed into small groups of four or five that were intentionally organized. On a shared editable website, students posted their thoughts and reactions. Students were invited to represent their responses to books using words, pictures, gifs, and videos. When composing their posts, students were asked to consider how they saw themselves in the text (mirror); observations they discovered about others' views, experiences, and cultures (window); and how the text changed their view of working with diverse children (doorway). During synchronous meetings, students shared more of their experience with the texts and spent time getting to know one another. As a culminating project, each group worked collaboratively to demonstrate their collective learning and reflective process through a multimodal collage. We learned valuable lessons from this project, and we share them here in hopes that more education preparation programs pursue collaborative projects that connect students across states and globally.

Lessons Learned

Lesson 1: *PSTs shared their personal cultural experiences openly through connection with the text as a mirror.*

Linda, a Hispanic PST from University 2, explained, "Hola, the book I am reading is *Dreamers*. It is a mirror for me because it reminds me of my ancestor's journey into California. Books like these are important because they share a different origin story yet the same human experience." Patricia, a PST from University 2 of Appalachian heritage, noted, "I could see myself in the text *Owl Moon*. It made me think about staying at my grandmother's house as a child. She lives next to a heavily wooded area, and my sister and I would climb the hill into the woods during the winter and play games and build forts in our heavy winter gear." We observed that the sharing of these stories created a space where students felt at ease and established a bond between book club members earlier than we believe would have otherwise occurred. Additionally, it moved PSTs away from surface level connections to the text and towards richer articulations of how the text spurred them to consider their own histories and ways of being. Our belief is that when PSTs have a meaningful experience with text themselves, they will be more likely to guide their students towards doing so as well.

Lesson 2: *PSTs demonstrated an understanding of others' cultures through connection with the text.*

We observed that students had aha moments regarding each other's cultures and noted that the experience broadened their perspectives. Ali (University 1) shared, "*Dreamers* is a window for me because I was able to understand the struggles that immigrants go through and the Hispanic culture". Elise (University 2) described how *Owl Moon* gave her insights on Appalachian traditions. "*Owl Moon* is a window for me. Reading it I was able to see the interest and familial love of owling." Students discussed the differing traditions across the texts and their own cultures while also making connections about larger common themes such as the importance of family bonding and the common struggles that people from all cultures experience. Although *The Water Princess* provided a glimpse into a different culture (African rather than Latinx or Appalachian cultural practices), students explained that it also provided insights into their own experience. Roberta (University 2) said, "*The Water Princess* was both a mirror and a window for me. As a young girl, my family had little money. This book allowed me to view the struggles of a culture." In this manner, we witnessed PSTs practicing empathy and understanding for those from a differing cultural background as well as expanding their knowledge of other cultures. Again, we hope that such experiences may spur PSTs to consider similar culturally responsive activities in their future classrooms.

Lesson 3: *PSTs used this experience to consider their future classrooms and how to honor diversity through children's books.*

PSTs noted increased confidence in using texts to "celebrate positive aspects of another culture, not just the negative" and to guide elementary students through "cultural exploration". Lindsey (University 1) explained, "I can imagine having students from different cultures and how they would feel if they saw mirrors in the class library. They would feel acknowledged and celebrated." PSTs were inspired to create multicultural children's book clubs in their future classrooms. Vera (University 1) noted, "Book clubs with another classroom can be beneficial for elementary students. Students can see mirrors with books they don't even realize!" In a discussion, one group of students shared how "important it is to show kids multiple perspectives of cultures so that they do not develop biases based on one aspect of a culture or place." Overall, PSTs considered our virtual book clubs as a potential model for their future classrooms.

Case #2: Digital Book Clubs Within a Rural Elementary School for Fluent Readers

Purpose

We are living in a digital age, one in which the ever changing facets of technology and communication are metamorphosing how we think about literacy (Bean & Goatley, 2021). Factors such as the COVID-19 pandemic, the advancement of mobile devices, and updated college and career ready focused standards have all been driving forces in the pursuit of increased digital literacy in our schools (Bean & Goatley, 2021; Hutchinson, Beschorner, & Schmidt-Crawford, 2012). While the number of technological resources for teachers is growing (Affinito, 2018), many teachers express discomfort with the application of technological tools and digital literacies (Bean & Goatley, 2021). Research demonstrates that teachers need support in the acquisition of skills that foster appropriate use and integration of resources provided and that technology often requires teachers to assume nontraditional roles (Castek & Gwinn, 2012). In Case #2, we share how one elementary school navigated such a transition through a collaborative support model as they moved from traditional face-to-face book clubs to digital book clubs. The goals for this project were:

1. Teachers and support staff will engage in collaborative discussions to co-plan and co-develop digital book club activities that will foster digital literacy in the school;
2. Students will become comfortable using digital tools and platforms as a mechanism for literacy learning and collaboration;
3. Students will engage in dialogic and meaningful literacy interactions on digital platforms.

Context

The elementary school was geographically located in the Appalachian Mountains of North Carolina and served 184 students in grades 4 and 5. Ten fourth and fifth grade teachers agreed to participate in the project and were supported by the instructional coach and media specialist in their efforts. The collaborative team of teachers, instructional coach, and media specialist met prior to implementation to discuss how they would transition to digital book clubs. The team agreed to pilot digital book clubs with advanced readers. Eighteen advanced readers met weekly from October through May in the media center where they logged into a portal and accessed literature and tasks together in an asynchronous fashion. The media specialist supported students when needed while simultaneously attending to her other duties in the media center. On days when students did not meet in the media center, they read the supplied texts and took notes independently.

Text Selection

The collaborative team believed it was important to select high interest and high readability texts that would challenge the advanced reader group in their thinking and spur lively online discussions. They also wanted students to read different genres and text formats as a means of supporting students' diverse reading preferences and encouraging deep engagement with a topic. Therefore, each module was built around a text set with a corresponding theme. Cappiello and Dawes (2012) posit that the integration of text sets can play a vital role "in enhancing students' abilities to comprehend and think critically about content" (p. 20). For example, in one module *Farewell to Manzanar* (Houston & Houston, 1973), a memoir that describes one family's experience in the Japanese internment camps of WWII, served as the anchor text. Supplemental texts for this module included *Baseball Saved Us* (Mochizuki, 1993), a picture book about a young boy living in an internment camp whose father decided to build a baseball diamond to spur hope and the website http://www.pbs.org/childofcamp/history/index.html where students read *Children of the Camps: Internment History*. The collaborative team strived to create module text sets that were multimodal including print, audio, and visual resources (Cappiello & Dawes, 2012). Therefore, texts also included photographs, podcasts, webcams, paintings, and news footage.

How To

The collaborative team met bi-weekly to plan module tasks and select texts. Edmodo, an educational website that draws from social media sites but is appropriate for classroom use, was chosen as the digital book club platform. The team appreciated that Edmodo allowed for the addition of small groups, that students could like and reply to each other's content with GIFs and links to videos or websites, and that teachers could manage and monitor all content, assign feedback, and give grades. The team recognized that online conversations can be stilted (Kelly & Cameron, 2022) and believed that the social media format of Edmodo would encourage more authentic interactions. Students were provided with a weekly schedule that included due dates for assigned readings and discussion posts. Each week they were required to engage in reading and notetaking of the texts assigned to each module. Once a week students worked on laptops in the library to compose discussion posts on the week's readings and reply to their peers. While we did observe students turning to ask one another questions or make comments, the discussions were primarily held online. Members of the collaborative team shared responsibilities of providing feedback on the posts. Students received feedback from a member of the team weekly on the Edmodo site. The goal of the feedback was to deepen students' thinking through questioning and assist them in making connections across the text set. Prior to beginning the first module, students participated in digital citizenship activities with the media specialist. The goal of these activities was to "advocate [for] and practice safe, legal, and responsible use of information and technology [and support students in] exhibit[ing] a positive attitude toward using technology that supports collaboration, learning, and productivity" (Isman & Gungoren, 2014, p. 73).

Lessons Learned

Lesson 1: *Digital book clubs encouraged more student participation and motivated students to read.*

The team observed that implementation of digital book clubs resulted in positive impacts on both student motivation to read and participation in discussions. They noted that students were excited to check their Edmodo platforms, particularly to view the GIFs and likes posted from their peers. Rebecca, a fourth grade teacher, reported to her colleagues, "I can see that just being able to log in and engage online with their peers has really motivated my students." This excitement spurred a motivation to read and to dig more deeply into the texts. Additionally, the team remarked that the digital platform allowed for more student participation. Often in face-to-face settings one or two more extroverted students may dominate the discussion. Edmodo provided a space for all students to share their views and opinions and be heard. For example, Ava, a reticent student in fifth grade reported, "I enjoy the discussions more than getting in a circle to discuss books. I can write what I think on the discussion board. I feel more shy face to face and I don't share my thinking as much." Another student, Maxwell, communicated that he felt more "into the reading" when he knew he had to write a discussion post that others were going to read.

Lesson 2: *Text sets allowed students to deepen their understanding of topics and encouraged the creation of thoughtful and introspective discussion posts.*

The team noted that having students access not just the anchor text but also the supplementary readings and multimodal resources assisted them in composing discussion posts that demonstrated deeper comprehension and empathy around difficult topics. For example, after students engaged in the reading and observation of texts and multimodal resources supporting the anchor text *Farewell to Manzanar,* students were asked to respond to the following prompt:

In December 1942 (Chapter 11, "Yes, Yes, No, No,") the administration of the Manzanar camp gave each family a Christmas tree as an apology for the difficulties that had led to the riot in the internment camp earlier that month. Why do you think the camp authorities chose a Christmas tree? Was it problematic? Why or why not?

In response, one of the 5th graders responded: "The people from the United States forced Japanese Americans to change how they naturally were. I guess on the outside the Christmas tree example would seem like a nice thing, but it really is not when you think about it. It is disrespectful in my opinion."

Another 5th grade student wrote: "The Christmas tree was celebrated from American culture. But, it is an insult because it shows how it's erasing the culture. Just like in Chapter 5, 'Papa would sit at the head of the table, with Mama next to him serving and the rest of us arranged around the edges according to age.' But then after time at the internment camp, 'Now, in the mess halls, after a few weeks had passed, we stopped eating as a family. Mama tried to hold us together for a while, but it was hopeless.' The same thing happened in the book, Baseball Saved Us. In that story, 'back home people were always busy working. But now, all they did was stand or sit around.' I keep thinking about what this means for culture today. How does war change things to make it just seem like a normal way of life for people?"

Wait time afforded by the digital book club provided students with a needed time to reflect and process the texts to produce a more thoughtful response that examined the themes and ideas in the texts more thoughtfully. Discussion board prompts pushed students' thinking forward beyond a typical in class discussion or even independent work students produced.

Lesson 3: *Teachers' ongoing collaboration served as a scaffold to engaging students in digital book clubs.*

While the idea of engaging students in digital book clubs and releasing control of the classroom to students was a challenging and daunting task at the beginning of the project, teachers found success and professional growth in the process. By working together as a team they were able to encourage student participation, reading, writing, and thinking about texts, while at the same time providing individualized support for those students who needed extra literacy scaffolding. Ongoing collaborative meetings also provided teachers with an opportunity to adjust the book club rubrics, prompts, and guidelines as needed. When teachers noticed that students struggled, they brainstormed ways to address such challenges together drawing on a collective expertise of the team. Teachers strategically revised the prompts to push students' thinking and writing forward, as well as provided additional time and resources to help students to be successful. While the digital book club was carefully planned in the beginning of the project; as it unfolded, it required teachers to be flexible and responsive. Such work would not be possible without their ongoing collaboration.

DISCUSSION AND IMPLICATIONS FOR VIRTUAL AND DIGITAL BOOK CLUBS IN THE ERA OF SCIENCE OF READING

The two cases presented above demonstrate the promise of digital and virtual book clubs as a means of empowering and motivating students of all ages– from elementary school students to pre-service teachers– and in various locations– Appalachia and the West Coast of the United States. These cases illustrate the importance of virtual and digital book clubs as democratic practice that decenters teachers and invites students to initiate, lead, and create their own learning. Such practices in the literacy classroom have the potential to foster collaborative, socially constructed affiliations while also compelling students to engage deeply with texts. This "collaborative, distributed, and participatory nature" of digital and virtual book clubs leads to spreading "knowledge about literacy throughout the classroom, especially as students move above the stages of foundational literacy" (Leu et al, 2017, p. 7). As such, the role of the teacher changes within such spaces. Teachers become "orchestrators of learning contexts rather than dispensers of literacy skills" (Leu et al, 2017, p. 7). And by extension, the literacy instruction becomes more collaborative, multidimensional, authentic, as well as less individual and simplistic (Knobel & Lankshear, 2014). The implementation of virtual and digital book clubs in both cases created a space to affirm the use of rich children's literature and text sets as a means of building interest and engagement (Bishop, 1990; Cappiello & Dawes, 2012). At the same time, the book club work met the current moment by drawing on diverse and controversial literature and engaging students through technology, which dominates our lives today. Students participated in discussions in a much more democratic manner with everyone getting a chance to participate through a variety of means, e.g., asynchronous discussions, video recording, imagery, Zoom conversations.

Virtual and digital book clubs presented valuable means of expanding access to text and broadening conversations accessible to our students. Such book clubs, informed by decades of literacy research, offer a ripe platform for the integration of intertextual connections and construction of meaning in collaborative environments that break the borders of the scripted curricula and practices prescribed in a current restrictive climate in schools. Conducting digital and virtual book clubs in an age of SOR requires that teachers and teacher educators become creative with how they organize their own and their student's time and focus. In both cases presented in this chapter, there was less time available for activities often considered to be supplementary by leadership. In the elementary school example, much of the literacy block was taken up by mandated SOR curricula and teachers often had little room for other literacy pursuits. In the case of PSTs, instructors had to integrate much of the content and prioritize activities that allowed for hitting multiple topics and standards at once. The collaborative teams in both cases were able to carve out valuable instruction time to foster group discussions in and out of class time and to encourage critical thinking. To build on the affordances of book clubs, additional supports are required for both teachers and teacher educators to ensure that they have opportunities to explore technology, make mistakes, and brainstorm how to utilize new ways of meaning-making in service of learning and preparing students for the future.

Furthermore, digital and virtual book clubs can be particularly powerful in Appalachian contexts, a region that is rife with what Robinson (2015) dubs a new poverty of digital inequality. Norris (2021) portrays this phenomenon as "creating technological groups of haves and have-nots" (p. 81) that demonstrate gaps in technology (equipment, access), proficiency (use of tools), and opportunity (employment and financial opportunities, knowledge building) (Hargattai, 2007; Mossberger, Tolbert, & Stansbury, 2003; Robinson, 2015; Whitacre & Mills, 2007). Case #1 and Case #2, described in this chapter, demonstrate the promise of digital and virtual book clubs in Appalachia as a means of fostering digital literacies with both K-5 students and PSTs and countering the digital inequality of the region.

Finally, virtual and digital book clubs provided an important platform to consider literacy as it is conceptualized, defined, and enacted in the past, present, and future. As the historical nature of literacy shifts to align with rapid changes in technology, communication patterns, and globalized patterns of interactions, "when we speak of new literacies, we mean that literacy is not just new today; it becomes new every day of our lives" (Leu et al, 2017, p. 1). This requires instructional practices that are flexible and dynamic to accommodate not only the variety of literacy strengths and needs children bring to the classroom, but also the authentic literacy tasks students will experience outside of the school walls. These practices must promote integration of reading, writing, discussion, word study, content learning, and critical view of texts in order to simulate the kinds of intellectual work that is required to understand and analyze "information within rich and complexly networked environments" available to students (Leu et al, 2017, p. 6). Such integration calls for theories and models of literacy that are not simple, but instead complex and inclusive. Theories and practices that mirror the complexity of literacy creation, consumption, and use in the real world will ultimately support students both inside the classroom and in the world outside the classroom walls.

REFERENCES

Affinito, S. (2018). *Literacy coaching: Transforming teaching and learning with digital tools and technology*. Heinemann.

Allington, R. L., & Gabriel, R. E. (2012). Every child, every day. *Educational Leadership*, 69(6), 10–15.

Alvermann, D., Marshall, J. D., Mclean, C., Huddleston, A. P., Joaquin, J., & Bishop, J. (2012). Adolescents' web-based literacies, identity construction, and skill development. *Literacy Research and Instruction*, 51(3), 179–195. doi:10.1080/19388071.2010.523135

Bailey, D. H., Duncan, G. J., Murnane, R. J., & Yeung, N. A. (2021). Achievement gaps in the wake of COVID-19. *Educational Researcher*, 50(5), 266–275. doi:10.3102/0013189X211011237

Beach, R., & Yussen, S. (2011). Practices of productive adult book clubs. *Journal of Adolescent & Adult Literacy*, 55(2), 121–131. doi:10.1002/JAAL.00015

Bean, R. M., & Goatley, V. J. (2020). *The Literacy Specialist: Leadership and Coaching for the Classroom, School, and Community*. Guilford Publications.

Bishop, R. S. (1990). Mirrors, windows, and sliding glass doors. *Perspectives: Choosing and Using Books for the Classroom*, 1(3), ix–xi.

Bogard, J. M., & McMackin, M. C. (2012). Combining traditional and new literacies in a 21st century writing workshop. *The Reading Teacher*, 65(5), 313–323. doi:10.1002/TRTR.01048

Bromley, K., Faughnan, M., Ham, S., Miller, M., Armstrong, T., Crandall, C., & Marrone, N. (2014). Literature circles go digital. *The Reading Teacher*, 68(3), 229–236. doi:10.1002/trtr.1312

Cappiello, M. A., & Dawes, E. T. (2012). *Teaching with text sets*. Teacher Created Materials.

Cassidy, J., Grote-Garcia, S., & Ortlieb, E. (2022). What's hot in 2021: Beyond the science of reading. *Literacy Research and Instruction*, *61*(1), 1–17. doi:10.1080/19388071.2021.2011236

Castek, J., & Gwinn, C. (2012). Technology in the literacy program. *Best practices of literacy leaders: Keys to school improvement*, 295–316.

Cazden, C. (1988). *Classroom discourse: The language of teaching and learning*. Heinemann.

ChenX.YangS.WigA. VBollingerC. B.EsperatT. K.WilsonN. S.PoleK. (2022).

Cherry-Paul, S., & Johansen, D. (2019). *Breathing new life into book clubs: A practical guide for teachers*. Heinemann.

Chiu, T. K. F. (2021). Student engagement in K-12 online learning amid COVID-19: A qualitative approach from a self-determination theory perspective. *Interactive Learning Environments*, 1–14. doi:10.1080/10494820.2021.1926289

Collier, D. R. (2018). Doodling, borrowing, and remixing: Students inquiring across digitized spaces. *The Reading Teacher*, *72*(1), 125–130. doi:10.1002/trtr.1717

Dreon, O., Kerper, R. M., & Landis, J. (2011). Digital storytelling: A tool for teaching and learning in the YouTube generation. *Middle School Journal*, *42*(5), 4–10. doi:10.1080/00940771.2011.11461777

Duke, N. K., & Cartwright, K. B. (2021). The science of reading progresses: Communicating advances beyond the simple view of reading. *Reading Research Quarterly*, *56*(S1), S25–S44. doi:10.1002/rrq.411

Farr, C. K., & Kurtzahn-Beach, R. (2006). Book club ladies: Marshaled by Oprah, guerrilla fighters in the culture wars. *Reader*, *55*, 56–70.

Fortune, D., Horst, P., Kessler, M. A., Tackett, M. E., & Pennington, L. K. (2021). Using Virtual Book Clubs to Elevate Discussion and Diverse Voices. In D. Hartsfield (Ed.), *Handbook of Research on Teaching Diverse Youth Literature to Pre-Service Professionals* (pp. 1–21). IGI Global. doi:10.4018/978-1-7998-7375-4.ch016

Gambrell, L. B. (2011). Seven Rules of Engagement: What's Most Important to Know about Motivation to Read. *The Reading Teacher*, *65*(3), 172–178. doi:10.1002/TRTR.01024

Gay, G. (2002). Preparing for culturally responsive teaching. *Journal of Teacher Education*, *53*(2), 106–116. doi:10.1177/0022487102053002003

Gee, J. P. (2013). *The anti-education era: creating smarter students through digital learning*. Palgrave Macmillan.

Goldberg, T. (2020). Delving into difficulty: Are teachers evading or embracing difficult histories? *Social Education*, *84*(2), 130–136.

Hargittai, E. (2007). The social, political, economic, and cultural dimensions of search engines: An introduction. *Journal of Computer-Mediated Communication*, *12*(3), 769–777. doi:10.1111/j.1083-6101.2007.00349.x

Hollie, S. (2017). *Culturally and linguistically responsive teaching and learning: Classroom practices for student success. Grades K-12.* Shell Education.

Houston, J. W., & Houston, J. D. (2017). *Farewell to Manzanar.* Clarion Book.

Hull, G. A., & Nelson, M. E. (2005). Locating the Semiotic Power of Multimodality. *Written Communication, 22*(2), 224–261. doi:10.1177/0741088304274170

Hutchison, A., Beschorner, B., & Schmidt-Crawford, D. (2012). Exploring the use of the iPad for literacy learning. *The Reading Teacher, 66*(1), 15–23. doi:10.1002/TRTR.01090

Isman, A., & Canan Gungoren, O. (2014). Digital citizenship. *Turkish Online Journal of Educational Technology-TOJET, 13*(1), 73–77.

Jocius, R., & Shealy, S. (2018). Critical book clubs: Reimagining literature reading and response. *The Reading Teacher, 71*(6), 691–702. doi:10.1002/trtr.1655

Kelly, K., & Cameron Likens, A. (2022). A pandemic partnership: Preservice teachers and fourth graders engage in virtual book clubs. *The Reading Teacher,* trtr.2173. doi:10.1002/trtr.2173

Kist, W., & Pytash, K. E. (2015). "I love to flip the pages". Pre-service teachers and New Literacies within a field experience. *English Education, 47*(2), 131–167.

Knobel, M., & Lankshear, C. (2014). Studying new literacies. *Journal of Adolescent & Adult Literacy, 58*(2), 97–101. doi:10.1002/jaal.314

Kress, G. (2003). *Literacy in the new media age.* Psychology Press.

Lapp, D., Moss, B., & Rowsell, J. (2012). Envisioning new literacies through a lens of teaching and learning. *The Reading Teacher, 65*(6), 367–377. doi:10.1002/TRTR.01055

Leu, D. J., Kinzer, C. K., Coiro, J., Castek, J., & Henry, L. A. (2017). New literacies: A dual-level theory of the changing nature of literacy, instruction, and assessment. *Journal of Education, 197*(2), 1–18. doi:10.1177/002205741719700202

Lewis, C., & Finders, M. (2004). Implied adolescents and implied teachers: A generation gap for new times. In D. Alvermann (Ed.), *Adolescents and literacies in a digital world* (pp. 101–113). Peter Lang.

Mochizuki, K. (2018). *Baseball saved us.* Lee and Lowe Books.

Mossberger, K., Tolbert, C. J., & Stansbury, M. (2003). *Virtual inequality: Beyond the digital divide.* Georgetown University Press.

Mullen, R., & Wedick, L. (2008). Avoiding the digital abyss: Getting started in the classroom with YouTube, digital stories, and blogs. *The Clearing House: A Journal of Educational Strategies, Issues and Ideas, 82*(2), 66–69. doi:10.3200/TCHS.82.2.66-69

Naitnaphit, L. (2021). Book clubs in a pandemic: Student choice and flexible pedagogies as we learned more about ourselves and the world. *Language Arts Journal of Michigan, 37*(1), 18–30.

National Reading Panel (U.S.) & National Institute of Child Health and Human Development (U.S.). (2000). *Report of the National Reading Panel: Teaching children to read: an evidence-based assessment of the scientific research literature on reading and its implications for reading instruction.* U.S. Dept. of Health and Human Services, Public Health Service, National Institutes of Health, National Institute of Child Health and Human Development.

Oblinger, D., & Oblinger, J. (2005). Is it age or IT: First steps towards understanding the Net Generation. In D. Oblinger & J. Oblinger (Eds.), *Educating the Net Generation* (pp. 2.1–2.22). EDUCAUSE., http:www.educause.edu/Resources/EducatingtheNetGeneration/IsItAgeorITFirstStepsTowardUnd/6058

Prensky, M. (2001a). Digital natives, digital immigrants. *On the Horizon, 9*(5), 1–6. doi:10.1108/10748120110424816

Prensky, M. (2001b). Digital natives, digital immigrants. Part II: Do they really think differently? *On the Horizon, 9*(6), 1–6. doi:10.1108/10748120110424843

Robinson, C. (2015). An exploration of poverty in central Appalachia: Questions of culture, industry, and technology. *An International Journal of Pure Communication Inquiry, 3*(2), 75–89. doi:10.17646/KOME.2015.26

Rogers, E. M. (2001). The Digital Divide. *Convergence, 7*(4), 96–111. doi:10.1177/135485650100700406

Rooney, K. (2005). *Reading with Oprah: The book club that changed America.* University of Arkansas Press.

Serafini, F., & Youngs, S. (2013). Reading workshop 2.0: Children's literature in the digital age. *The Reading Teacher, 66*(5), 401–404. doi:10.1002/TRTR.01141

Shelby-Caffey, C., Ubeda, E., & Jenkins, B. (2014). Digital storytelling revisited: An educator's use of an innovative literacy practice. *The Reading Teacher, 68*(3), 191–198. doi:10.1002/trtr.1273

Siegel, M. (2012). New times for multimodality? Confronting the accountability culture. *Journal of Adolescent & Adult Literacy, 55*(8), 671–680. doi:10.1002/JAAL.00082

Smith, J. M. (2019). Considerations for summer online book clubs. *The Reading Teacher, 72*(5), 638–642. doi:10.1002/trtr.1765

Stover, K., Yearta, L., & Harris, C. (2016). Experiential learning for preservice teachers: Digital book clubs with third graders. *Journal of Digital Learning in Teacher Education, 32*(1), 5–12. doi:10.1080/21532974.2015.1055013

Sumara, D. J., Luce-Kapler, R., Robson, C., & Catlin, S. J. (2008, December). Fictional practices of everyday life: Tactics of genre, gender and generation. Paper presented at *the Annual meeting of the National Reading Conference*, Orlando, FL.

Whitacre, B. E., & Mills, B. F. (2007). Infrastructure and the rural urban divide in high-speed residential internet access. *International Regional Science Review, 30*(3), 249–273. doi:10.1177/0160017607301606

Whitin, P. E. (2009). Tech-to-stretch: Expanding possibilities for literature response. *The Reading Teacher*, *62*(5), 408–418. doi:10.1598/RT.62.5.4

Wimmer, J. J., & Draper, R. J. (2019). Insiders' views of new literacies, schooling, and the purpose of education: "We should be teaching them more important things. *Reading Psychology*, *40*(2), 149–168. doi:10.1080/02702711.2019.1607000

Yearta, L. (2019). Integrating social studies and english language arts: Digital stories and the revolutionary war. *The Reading Teacher*, *73*(2), 215–218. doi:10.1002/trtr.1806

Conclusion

As this book, *Innovations in Digital Instruction Through Virtual Environments,* is being published, people are still trying to find a "new normal" after the COVID pandemic's high point in the United States. Educational practices radically shifted during the pandemic, moving educators and students alike into new, sometimes uncomfortable, digital and online environments. This move was welcomed by some and decried by others, yet it was necessary at the time. Then, when classrooms became more "normal" once schools opened up again, educators were faced with ongoing challenges, especially in terms of the gap in learning that occurred during the pandemic as not all students were able to keep up with their learning at the same pace as they might have. Yet, still, teachers, students, and parents could breathe a sigh of relief that schools are once again a present, active part of students' lives.

Then, in November 2022, a new challenge arose for teachers as ChatGPT burst onto the scene causing both excitement and fear, almost in equal measure. ChatGPT is an online tool that allows people to ask a question to what is essentially a superpowered chatbot using natural language, or language how we actually speak in everyday life, and to get an answer that is also in natural, everyday language. Not only can the chatbot mimic human language, it can also do so in a way that seems more like someone is speaking to an actual person. Also, ChatGPT can create new information from its existing database, which includes a huge set of online data that its developers provided for it to "learn" from, essentially a massive amount of online information. In March 2023, OpenAI released an updated ChatGPT called ChatGPT-4, which fixes some of the initial bugs or glitches discovered during its initial release as well as having updated capabilities (Metz, 2023).

Educators, in particular, have worries that ChatGPT would allow and encourage students to cheat on their schoolwork, bypassing the effort and critical thinking required to complete the work themselves. On some level, this concern is justified. A recent survey found that up to 30% of college students use some version of a chatbot to complete coursework (Jimenez, 2023), and the new ChatGPT-4 is conceivably able to pass a simulated bar exam better than 90% of possible students (Metz, 2023). It has some major computing power behind it. To combat this cheating, however, there are also a number of countermeasures being created to help educators, such as an app that a college student from Princeton, named Edward Tian, created during his winter break called ChatGPTZero (Bowan, 2023).

Beyond cheating, however, the dialogue around ChatGPT speaks to the heart of education itself. At the crux of the issues with ChatGPT for education is the way that learning is defined. In the past, prevailing ideas about learning were centered around the child as a vessel into which teachers poured their knowledge through lecture and other traditional teaching models. But, educators now know that learning is actually socially constructed; learning is not solely a transaction between teacher, content, and student.

If students are using ChatGPT to do the work of their assignments, then it is a manifestation of the view of learning that is input-output driven, and teachers know that this is not how good learning happens.

At its core, learning must take into account cognitive, social, and emotional characteristics of both the teacher and the students. One movement that recognizes this need in education is New Literacy Studies, which is a literacy movement that redefined literacy as a set of literacy practices (Street, 1995, 1997) that are inherently social (Gee, 2004). NLS paved the way toward understanding the complexity behind how literacy is fostered in and out of the classroom setting. In new work on literacies and learning, scholars have found that literacy is fostered in both school and non-school, everyday, settings (Potter & McDougall, 2017) and in ways that blend and the way that children engage with the world, with each other, with objects around them, and with each other, their parents and their teachers (Pahl & Rowsell, 2020) in ways that can determine the literacy that the children will be able to learn. Literacy is precious, and literacy can be lost if mishandled by transactional type teaching and learning.

This book, *Innovations in Digital Instruction Through Virtual Environments*, encourages the reader to think about online and digital technologies help educators and students learn in ways that move forward in encouraging ways without ignoring the complications. And, this is spot on. Educators and scholars are beginning to see just how important place and space are for how children engage with the world around them. Moreover, the way that children see themselves in terms of identities and how they feel about those identities in relationship to place, space, and other identities matters for how the children will learn. The threat and promise of ChatGPT is not only that it will become ubiquitous but also that it will become *invisibly-present*, meaning that users will not know that they are interacting with a chatbot at all to do their everyday practices, so it matters how these new digital tools might conceive of and represent place, space, and identity. In particular, in this chapter, this author make the case that learning must, above all, be about human connection.

BACKGROUND

After having spent many years researching how young people use and produce media using a variety of technologies, this author has become particularly interested in how adults set up a safe and encouraging environment for young people to use and create media:

My focus is on developing a new lens to see the ethics of youth media production as a larger construct, in other words the environments created by adults and youth within which the youth are creating their media...In particular, we must consider the difficulties inherent in what is seen as worth producing and what is seen as believable for particular audiences and particular youth. (Gibbons, 2013, p. 263)

In this author's earlier work on ethics, the focus was on how young people in nonprofits created digital movies about their lives. Later on, however, she also studied how teachers were able to create environments within which students could learn, such as how a teacher taught her kindergarten students to be emergent scientists using YouTube (Buchholz, Gibbons Pyles, Hash, & Hagaman, 2021). In this way, teaching with technologies can go hand-in-hand with creating new ways of seeing themselves for students.

As an educator, however, connecting to identities in learning is more challenging. With online teaching and learning, though, that learning must be more connected to place and to identity to be more effective. Place-based education research has found that people must understand how place matters in how we see the world and each other (Gruenwald, 2003). When people are encouraged to feel an affiliation to where they live (Gruenwald & Smith, 2007), they can approach learning from a place of wholeness, a place where who they are in a specific place matters to understanding the content in front of them. In *Negotiating Place and Space through Digital Literacies,* the author and her co-editors asserted that place mattered in how people understand and foster literacies in a variety of places and spaces (Gibbons Pyles, Rish, & Warner, 2019). They premised this book, in large part, on the idea that "place, in other words, does - as many argue - change us, not through some visceral belonging (some barely changing rootedness, as so many would have it) but through the practising of place, the negotiation of intersecting trajectories; place as an arena where negotiation is forced upon us" (Massey, 2005, p. 154).

In this sense, place-based education works well when it is grounded in the local and is able to critique the local (Smith, 2007). For instance, in understanding how young people wanted to tell stories about themselves and their lives, the author found that teens in rural Appalachia (Gibbons, 2015) and in rural Native American reservations in the Midwest (Gibbons, Drift, & Drift, 2011) felt the same pull toward place as a way to see themselves. The youth wanted to tell stories that honored their own people and their place. Focusing on a sense of place is vital to individuals seeing themselves within communities (Northcote, 2008), and in this way, place-based education is focused on conserving as well as transforming (Ball & Lai, 2006; see also Gruenwald, 2003).

With online teaching, "onlineness" is a necessary variable, but it is not the only variable for learning (Salmon, 2004). Asynchronous communication can bridge different times and cross different time zones, but the how and why facilitators teach is variable (Anderson & Barham, 2010). In digital and online learning, there is no set place; rather, there are a multiplicity of places. Therefore, the issue of space also arises. What scholars have found is that space is negotiated and social. Given that space always carries are social meanings and these are always plural (Georgiou, 2006), it makes sense that "...space is not simply an 'inert container' for the places of everyday experience; rather, space itself is the outcome of particular ways of reasoning about and representing the world (Brewer & Dourish, 2008, pp. 964-965).

With online and digital teaching, though, there ought to be a recognition that space is also embodied. In online learning, space and materiality come together (Enriquez, 2013). People turn spaces into places by embodying them, e.g., students living locally yet attending a university elsewhere through online classes (Enriquez, 2011). In comparison to face-to-face classrooms, online learning spaces and places are negotiated socially (see Figure 1), e.g., to work [or study] on a train, one must work within the space and with other people, e.g., shifting over to let others sit, listening to an iPod to reduce noise, having a computer fully charged, having network access, etc. (Axtell, Hislop, & Whittaker, 2008). Students who are conducting classes or homework at home might have to contend, for instance, with sharing a room with a sibling or having to access wifi at the local library because they do not have internet in the home. These ways of interacting in lived places with online spaces must be negotiated for learners and, as some might argue, for teachers as well, who have their own places and spaces.

Figure 1. Places, Spaces, and Technologies in F2F and Online Courses

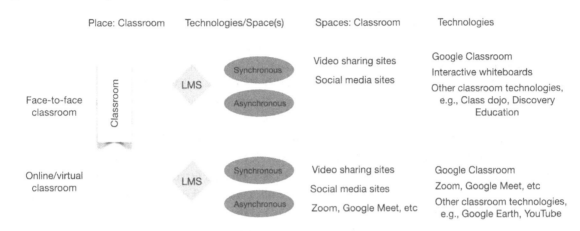

What this comes back to is how educators must attend to all facets of childrens' lives in order to truly reach them. Pahl & Rowsell (2020) advocate for a more holistic approach to literacy that can be helpful in understanding online teaching and learning as well. Drawing from theoretical frameworks that place literacies in the everyday world in material and immaterial ways and in ways that acknowledge how people see and feel in that world in terms of embodiment and affect, Pahl & Rowsell (2020) discuss how literacy has six dimensions: seeing, disrupting, hoping, knowing, creating, and making. They partner with educators and artists to collaboratively write chapters to address all six elements. This work brings together much of what one can understand from place-based and online learning.

The chapters in this book, *Innovations in Digital Instruction Through Virtual Environments*, focus on how children and teens can learn in different spaces and in different ways, so for this conclusion chapter, this author will focus on one element: knowing.

'Knowing,' as we define it here, represents the ways that people think through digital and nondigital environments and the ways they build literacy practices through their engagement with technologies as they constantly move in and out of print and digital texas. In order to adopt a living literacies approach, it is necessary to fold in digital-, media-, and print-based worlds as shaping the practices of everyday life. Thes worlds signify particular ways of thinking and being. (Collier & Rowsell, 2020, p. 92)

Knowing in this framework encompasses the various places and spaces along with the modalities from print to digital to online. It can allow for movement across the spaces as teachers foster literacies for their students in ways that can reach the students the most. In this sense, literacy education can be its most human.

ILLUSTRATIVE EXAMPLE: ChatGTP's SENSE OF SELF AND PLACE

In order to explore learning through the lens of knowing in living literacies in terms of place, space, and learning, the author posed a series of questions to OpenAI's version of ChatGPT to see how it connected to ideas of place, space, and identity. Though this chatbot is not named per se, for our purposes, the author will simply call it ChatGPT as this is what it referred to as in the interaction itself. Through these questions and answers, one can glimpse how its connections to these concepts are very different from those that we have as humans.

First, the author asked ChatGPT to design a lesson for middle school students that was centered on place, in particular on their own neighborhoods. She asked ChatGPT the following: "Design a lesson for middle school students in which they explore the neighborhoods they live in by walking around, doing interviews, drawing the buildings, and building a sense of themselves being from a particular place" (Communication with ChatGPT, 3/20/23). Such work has been done in powerful lessons with children in the Midwest United States (Mathews, 2010) and in Australia (Comber, 2011), and she was interested to see what this interface would pull from its data sources for a lesson that involved connections to place and people in local areas for children. The objective for this lesson mirrored the language from the prompt she asked as ChatGPT stated: "Students will explore and understand the unique characteristics of their neighborhoods, and develop a sense of belonging and identity by conducting interviews, making observations, and creating visual representations of their surroundings" (Communication with ChatGPT, 3/20/23). What is interesting about this objective is that ChatGPT added affective words to the prompt, such as searching for "unique" characteristics and "develop[ing] a sense of belonging and identity" through the different activities (n.p.). This call to affect is inherent in the assignment; it is the purpose, in other words, for students to connect to the neighborhoods and to find themselves within them. But, this isn't something that the author had put in the prompt itself that she had asked ChatGPT. To meet this objective, then, ChatGPT also responded with a detailed lesson plan with multiple steps and even included possible interview questions that the student could ask (see Appendix A). It is a strong beginning to a lesson plan that a teacher could use to help his or her students do this project in their own neighborhoods and schools. In this way, ChatGPT is able to access some level of awareness from the data it has been given about how students might connect to the learning about their own communities in how lesson plans are created.

Next, the author asked ChatGPT to modify the lesson for an online learning environment. She changed its connection from planning for place to planning for space, in other words. Much of this lesson plan stayed the same (see Appendix B): introducing neighborhoods as a concept, mapping and map-making, interviews, etc. What was new with this lesson is that ChatGPT added in different tools to facilitate the learning, much like a real teacher would do. For instance, instead of walking around the neighborhood, ChatGPT suggests that the teachers use videos of neighborhoods to introduce the concept and Google Maps for the students to explore their own parts of the neighborhood. Also, instead of conducting face-to-face interviews, it suggests that students use digital tools, such as video conferencing, and a teacher-provided digital worksheet to conduct interviews virtually. Then, they would meet as a whole class using video conferencing to share their findings. In this sharing time, the students would reflect on their sense of belonging. The extension activity is similar to the in-person class in that ChatGPT suggests advocacy, though with the online version, it suggests a digital poster over social media. These modifications are similar to what teachers might do for online learning, and ChatGPT uses the affordances of different spaces to foster learning for students using a variety of media and digital tools.

What is key in both of these lessons that ChatGPT suggests is that the human connections remain central to the learning no matter the modality. The teacher facilitates the learning from the initial introduction to the concept of neighborhoods through to the discussions at the end. The children are working with each other in collaborative groups, and they are the interviewers who are learning from community members. And, there is a suggestion for extension that involves making the neighborhoods better through social activism, e.g., letter writing to local government officials or digital social media campaigns. With these lessons, the focus is on connections between people in order for students to learn more about their "sense of belonging" to their neighborhoods, which as noted above, is a concept that was only implied in the prompt I gave to ChatGPT.

It is not, however, that ChatGPT is itself a sentient being who craves such human connection itself, though. When the author asked ChatGPT to explore its own sense of belonging, the answers pointed away from connection. When she asked ChatGPT who it was, this is what it replied:

GibbonsPyles: Who are you, ChatGPT?

ChatGPT: I am ChatGPT, a large language model developed by OpenAI. I am an artificial intelligence program designed to process and generate natural language, which means I can understand and respond to text-based inputs in a way that is similar to human communication. I have been trained on a massive corpus of text data, which allows me to generate text that is coherent and relevant to the input I receive. While I am not a sentient being and do not possess consciousness or emotions, I am capable of performing a wide range of language-related tasks, such as answering questions, translating languages, writing stories and even generating poetry. (Communication with ChatGPT, 3/20/23)

ChatGPT calls itself the name "ChatGPT," and then provides a definition of what that term means, which is "a large language model." It repeats this definition by extending what that means in simpler language when it states, "I can understand and respond to text-based inputs in a way that is similar to human communication." ChatGPT provides some discussion of what provides its information, and it denies that it is sentient or that it has any "consciousness or emotions." It ends with a short list of what it can do currently in terms of what kinds of outputs it can provide.

In particular for this concluding chapter, ChatGPT does not have a connection to place in the same way as people do. In the same chat in which the author asked about the lessons, she asked this question, "Are you from a particular place, ChatGPT?" (Communication with ChatGPT, 3/20/23). It responded with this information:

As an artificial intelligence language model, I do not have a physical existence or location. I exist entirely in the digital realm and am accessible from anywhere with an internet connection. However, I was developed by OpenAI, a research organization based in San Francisco, California, USA. (Communication with ChatGPT, 3/20/23)

ChatGPT suggests that there is no physical place for its existence, which is interesting. It's true that it exists as code within different interfaces, all of which have a physical source or sources somewhere, but there is no one central place for ChatGPT to claim. It claims to "exist entirely in the digital realm" and to be "accessible from anywhere with an internet connection." It equates its existence with access, meaning that its purpose is to be accessible to others. It does, however, mention the headquarters of OpenAI, which is in San Francisco. Interestingly, part of the coding and mechanics of the language systems with ChatGPT are done in other places, namely in Sydney, Australia, but ChatGPT mentions only its official creator's place and location.

This led the author to wonder if ChatGPT had any of the affective connections that it encourages teachers foster with the middle school students in the lessons it created. She asks ChatGPT, "Do you feel any special connection to San Francisco or to OpenAI's offices?" (Communication with ChatGPT, 3/20/23). In this case, however, the response is unequivocal. ChatGPT states:

As an AI language model, I do not have emotions or personal attachments. I was created by OpenAI to help people by answering their questions and providing information to the best of my abilities. While I do have access to information about San Francisco and OpenAI's offices, I do not have a personal connection to them nor do I experience any feelings about them. (Communication with ChatGPT, 3/20/23)

With this response, ChatGPT claims that it does not have "emotions or personal attachments" because it is an AI language model. It restates why it was created, in this case, to "help people by answering questions and providing information," and it acknowledges that it is aware of San Francisco and the OpenAI offices as places. It has no connection of its own to those places, though. What this means, then, is that ChatGPT can make lessons about place and space, but ChatGPT itself is incapable of learning from those same lessons.

SUMMING UP

The need for changing pedagogies and mindsets post-COVID, in an internet era. What *Innovations in Digital Instruction Through Virtual Environments* comes around to is that learning is most effective when it is fostered with human connections. The authors in this book reveal ways in which they not only innovate how they teach young people, but also, they discuss how we must take into account affect, emotion, and belonging in our teaching and learning as well. What this brief analysis reveals is where innovations could be heading is that these innovations must be used with plenty of self-reflection for both teachers and students. While ChatGPT can create a basic framework for lessons for children about place in which teachers can foster connections and have students reflect on their sense of belonging, ChatGPT itself is unable to have those same types of connections. This makes sense, though, since ChatGPT is not "real," in the sense that it is meant to mimic human interaction, not have them itself. In a recent New York Times article, Sherry Turkle, an MIT professor who studies technologies and social interaction, asserts that ChatGPT plays a game of pretend. She suggests that parents [and teachers, one supposes] can teach their children about ChatGPT and other chatbots by stating, "'When you ask chatbots about things that only people can know about, like feelings, they may come up with an answer. That's part of their pretend game. It's their job to seem like people. But you know that what they are really for is to get you to the things you want to read and see' (qtd. in Caron, 2023, para. 27). Inherently, chatbots are meant to appear real, and they increasingly are seeming to be real in their interactions with people. But, they cannot have real connections to the content they discuss or to the places, spaces, and people in our material and social worlds. The need for authentic human interaction and connection will still be needed even with these new technologies. Perhaps human connection will be needed even more so, as the "pretend game" in online spaces becomes increasingly believable for adults and children alike.

Damiana Gibbons Pyles
Appalachian State University, USA

REFERENCES

Anderson, A., & Barham, N. (2010). Blended learning: Commonalities in practice across a multidiscipline group of online learning facilitators. In R. Muldoon (Ed.), *Rethinking learning in your discipline*. Proceedings of the University Learning and Teaching Futures Colloquium 2010. University of New England, Armidale, NSW.

Axtell, C., Hislop, D., & Whittaker, S. (2008). Mobile technologies in mobile spaces: Findings from the context of train travel. *International Journal of Human-Computer Studies*, *66*(12), 902–915. doi:10.1016/j.ijhcs.2008.07.001

Ball, E., & Lai, A. (2006). Place-based pedagogy for the arts and humanities. *Pedagogy*, *6*(2), 261–287. doi:10.1215/15314200-2005-004

Bowan, E. (2023, January 9). A college student created an app that can tell whether AI wrote an essay. *NPR*. https://www.npr.org/2023/01/09/1147549845/gptzero-ai-chatgpt-edward-tian-plagiarism

Brewer, J., & Dourish, P. (2008). Storied spaces: Cultural accounts of mobility, technology, and environmental knowing. *International Journal of Human-Computer Studies*, *66*(12), 963–976. doi:10.1016/j.ijhcs.2008.03.003

Buchholz, B. A., Gibbons Pyles, D., Hagaman, K., & Hash, P. (2021). Teaching comprehension in the digital age: Pausing videos to scaffold scientific literacy practices. *Science and Children*, *58*(5), 43–50.

Caron, C. (2023, March 22). The A.I. chatbots have arrived. Time to talk to your kids. *New York Times*. https://www.nytimes.com/2023/03/22/well/family/ai-chatgpt-parents-children.html

Comber, B. (2011). Making space for place-making pedagogies: Stretching normative mandated literacy curriculum. *Contemporary Issues in Early Childhood*, *12*(4), 343–348. doi:10.2304/ciec.2011.12.4.343

Enriquez, G. (2011). Embodying exclusion: The daily melancholia and performative politics of struggling early adolescent readers. *English Teaching*, *10*, 90–112.

Enriquez, J. (2013). Being *(t)here*: Mobilising 'mediaspaces' of learning. *Learning, Media and Technology*, *38*(3), 319–336. doi:10.1080/17439884.2012.685744

Gee, J. P. (2004). *Situated language and learning: A critique of traditional schooling*. Routledge.

Georgiou, M. (2006). *Diaspora, identity and the media: Diasporic transnationalism and mediated spatialities*. Hampton Press., doi:10.1177/009182961103900106

Gibbons, D. (2013). Developing an ethics of youth media production using media literacy, identity, & modality. *The Journal of Media Literacy Education*, *4*(3), 256–265. doi:10.23860/jmle-4-3-6

Gibbons, D., Drift, T., & Drift, D. (2011). Whose story is it? Being Native and American: Crossing borders, hyphenated selves." International perspectives on youth media: Cultures of production & education. (Ed.) JoEllen Fisherkeller. Peter Lang Publishers, Inc. 172-191.

Gibbons Pyles, D. (2015). A multimodal mapping of voice in youth media: The pitch in youth video production. *Learning, Media and Technology*, *42*(1), 8–27. doi:10.1080/17439884.2016.1095209

Gibbons Pyles, D., Rish, R., & Warner, J. (2019). *Negotiating place and space through digital literacies.* Digital Media and Learning Series. Information Age Publishing.

Gruenewald, D. A. (2003). The best of both worlds: A critical pedagogy of place. *Educational Researcher, 32*(4), 3–12. doi:10.3102/0013189X032004003

Gruenewald, D. A., & Smith, G. A. (2007). *Place-based education in the global age: Local diversity.* Routledge.

Intelligent.com survey finds 30 percent of college students use artificial intelligence chatbot, ChatGPT, for written homework. (2023, January 31). PR Newswire. https://link-gale-com.proxy006.nclive.org/apps/doc/A735257911/BIC?u=boon41269&sid=ebsco&xid=75304029

Jimenez, K. (2023, March 1). ChatGPT in the classroom: Here's what teachers and students are saying. *USA Today.* https://www.usatoday.com/story/news/education/2023/03/01/what-teachers-students-saying-ai-chatgpt-use-classrooms/11340040002/

Massey, D. (2005). *For space.* Sage Publications Ltd.

Mathews, J. (2010). Using a studio-based pedagogy to engage students in the design of mobile-based media. *English Teaching, 9*(1), 87–102.

Metz, C. (2023, March 14). OpenAI plans to up the ante in tech's A.I. race. *New York Times.* https://www.nytimes.com/2023/03/14/technology/openai-gpt4-chatgpt.html?searchResultPosition=20

Northcote, M. (2008). Sense of place in online learning environments. *Proceedings of the Ascilite Conference, Melbourne,* Australia. https://ascilite.org/conferences/melbourne08/procs/northcote.pdf

Pahl, K., & Rowsell, J. (2020). *Living literacies: Literacy for social change.* Massachusetts Institute of Technology. doi:10.7551/mitpress/11375.001.0001

Salmon, B. G. (2004). *E-moderating: The key to teaching and learning online.* Taylor and Francis. doi:10.4324/9780203465424

Street, B. V. (1995). *Social literacies.* Longman.

Street, B. V. (1997). The implications of New Literacy Studies for literacy education. *English in Education, 31*(3), 26–39. doi:10.1111/j.1754-8845.1997.tb00133.x

APPENDIX A: CHATGPT LESSON ON PLACE

GibbonsPyles: Design a lesson for middle school students in which they explore the neighborhoods they live in by walking around, doing interviews, drawing the buildings, and building a sense of themselves being from a particular place.

ChatGPT:
Title: Exploring Our Neighborhoods
Grade Level: Middle School (6th - 8th grade)
Objective: Students will explore and understand the unique characteristics of their neighborhoods, and develop a sense of belonging and identity by conducting interviews, making observations, and creating visual representations of their surroundings.
Materials Needed:
   Pencils and erasers
   Paper or sketchbooks
   Clipboards or hard surfaces to write on
   Smartphones or digital cameras
   Interview questions worksheet
Procedure:
Begin by introducing the concept of neighborhoods and how they are defined by their physical characteristics, cultural practices, and social norms. Ask students to share what they know about their own neighborhoods and what they like or dislike about them.

Provide students with a map of their neighborhood or draw one on the board. Ask them to identify key landmarks, such as parks, schools, libraries, and community centers.

Divide the students into small groups of three to four and assign each group a different area of the neighborhood to explore. Encourage students to walk around and take note of the buildings, streets, and people they encounter.

Ask each group to conduct an interview with a local resident, business owner, or community leader. Provide them with a worksheet of interview questions that they can use to guide their conversation. Some suggested questions might include:

How long have you lived or worked in this neighborhood?

What changes have you seen over time?

What are the strengths and challenges of this neighborhood?

What are your favorite places or things to do in this neighborhood?

After the interviews, have students come together as a class to share their observations and insights. Ask each group to present their findings, highlighting the key characteristics and challenges of their assigned area.

Ask students to create a visual representation of their neighborhood using drawing materials or digital tools. They can focus on a particular building, street corner, or landmark that they find interesting or meaningful.

Have students share their drawings with the class, explaining why they chose their subject and what it represents about their neighborhood.

Finally, ask students to reflect on what they have learned about their neighborhood and how it relates to their sense of identity and belonging. They can write a short reflection or share their thoughts in a class discussion.

Assessment:

Completed interview questions worksheet

Group presentation on neighborhood observations

Visual representation of a neighborhood landmark

Reflection on what was learned about their neighborhood and how it relates to their sense of identity and belonging.

Extension:

Students can use their observations and insights to develop ideas for how to improve their neighborhood, such as advocating for more green spaces, better public transportation, or increased community engagement. They can write a letter to a local government representative or create a poster campaign to raise awareness about their ideas.

APPENDIX B: MODIFICATION FOR AN ONLINE LEARNING ENVIRONMENT

GibbonsPyles: Thank you. How would you modify this lesson for an online learning environment?

ChatGPT: Modifying this lesson for an online learning environment may require a few adjustments to the activities to adapt to the digital format. Here are some suggested modifications:

Materials needed:

Digital drawing tools (such as Paint or Sketchpad)

Video conferencing software

Digital interview questions worksheet

Procedure:

Begin the lesson by introducing the concept of neighborhoods and how they are defined by their physical characteristics, cultural practices, and social norms. Use video or audio recordings to explain the concept, and encourage students to share what they know about their own neighborhoods and what they like or dislike about them.

Provide students with a map of their neighborhood or use an online mapping tool to display it. Ask them to identify key landmarks, such as parks, schools, libraries, and community centers.

Divide the students into small groups of three to four and assign each group a different area of the neighborhood to explore. Encourage students to use Google Maps or other online mapping tools to take note of the buildings, streets, and people they encounter.

Ask each group to conduct an online interview with a local resident, business owner, or community leader. Provide them with a digital worksheet of interview questions that they can use to guide their conversation.

After the interviews, have students come together as a class to share their observations and insights. Ask each group to present their findings, highlighting the key characteristics and challenges of their assigned area. Use video conferencing software to facilitate this.

Ask students to create a digital representation of their neighborhood using drawing tools. They can focus on a particular building, street corner, or landmark that they find interesting or meaningful.

Have students share their digital drawings with the class, explaining why they chose their subject and what it represents about their neighborhood.

Finally, ask students to reflect on what they have learned about their neighborhood and how it relates to their sense of identity and belonging. They can write a short reflection or share their thoughts in a class discussion using the video conferencing software.

Assessment:
- Completed digital interview questions worksheet
- Group presentation on neighborhood observations
- Digital representation of a neighborhood landmark
- Reflection on what was learned about their neighborhood and how it relates to their sense of identity and belonging.

Extension:
Students can use their observations and insights to develop ideas for how to improve their neighborhood, such as advocating for more green spaces, better public transportation, or increased community engagement. They can create a digital poster campaign to raise awareness about their ideas and share it with their community via social media.

Compilation of References

Abdul-Majied, S., Kinkead-Clark, Z., & Burns, S. C. (2022). Understanding Caribbean early childhood teachers' professional experiences during the COVID-19 school disruption. *Early Childhood Education Journal*, 1–11. doi:10.100710643-022-01320-7

Abrami, P. C., & Bures, E. M. (1996). Computer-supported collaborative learning and distance education. *American Journal of Distance Education*, *10*(2), 37–42. doi:10.1080/08923649609526920

Acar, N. V. (2004). *How aware am I: Gestalt therapy (2. Baskı)*. Babylon Publishing.

Açıkgül, E. (2011). *The effect of digital divide on pre-service science teachers' use of information and communication technologies in the scientific process*. [Unpublished Master's thesis. Adıyaman: Adıyaman University].

Adèbìsì, F. (2022). Black/African science fiction and the quest for racial justice through legal knowledge: How can we unsettle Euro-modern time and temporality in our teaching? *Law, Technology, and Humans*, *4*(2), 24–37. doi:10.5204/lthj.2507

Affinito, S. (2018). *Literacy coaching: Transforming teaching and learning with digital tools and technology*. Heinemann.

Agustika, G. N. S. (2021). The influence of augmented reality-based learning media on the students' achievement of mathematics. In *2nd International Conference on Technology and Educational Science (ICTES 2020)* (pp. 47-56). Atlantis Press. 10.2991/assehr.k.210407.212

Akçayır, M., & Akçayır, G. (2017). Advantages and challenges associated with augmented reality for education: A systematic review of the literature. *Educational Research Review*, *20*, 1–11. doi:10.1016/j.edurev.2016.11.002

Akimov, A., & Malin, M. (2020). When old becomes new: A case study of oral examination as an online assessment tool. *Assessment & Evaluation in Higher Education*, *45*(8), 1205–1221. doi:10.1080/02602938.2020.1730301

Akkoyunlu, B., Yılmaz Soylu, M. & ve Çağlar, M. (2010). Developing a "numericalcompetence scale" for university students. *Journal of Hacettepe University Faculty of Education (H. U. Journal of Education) 39*, 10-19. https://dergipark.org.tr/download/article-file/87452

Aktaş, C. (2014). *QR Codes and Hybridization of Communication Technology*. Kalkedon Publications.

Al Husseiny, F. (2023). Artificial Intelligence in Higher Education: A New Horizon. In Handbook of Research on AI Methods and Applications in Computer Engineering (pp. 295-315). IGI Global. doi:10.4018/978-1-6684-6937-8.ch014

Al Husseiny, F. (2023). The Rising Trend of Artificial Intelligence in Social Media: Applications, Challenges, and Opportunities. Handbook of Research on AI Methods and Applications in Computer Engineering, 42-61.

Al Husseiny, F., & Youness, H. (2023). Exploring the role of social media marketing in students' decision to select universities in Lebanon: A proposed emerging framework. *QScience Connect*, *2023*(1), 4. doi:10.5339/connect.2023.spt.4

Alafodimos, C., Kalogiannakis, M., Papadakis, St., & Papachristos, D. (2009). Adult Education and Lifelong Learning: The case of GSAE (General Secretary for Adult Education) in Greece. In D. Guralnick (ed.) Proceedings of the *International Conference on E-Learning in the Workplace* (ICELW-09), 10-12 June 2009, New York: Kaleidoscope Learning (CD-Rom).

Albayrak, S., & Yilmaz, R. M. (2021). An investigation of pre-school children's interactions with augmented reality applications. *International Journal of Human-Computer Interaction, 38*(2), 165–184. doi:10.1080/10447318.2021.1926761

Alexander, B., Adams Becker, S., & Cummins, M. (2016). *An NMC Horizon Project Strategic Brief.* CDN. http://cdn.nmc.org/media/2016-nmc-horizon-strategic-brief-digital-literacy.pdf

Alexander, B., Ashford-Rowe, K., Barajas-Murphy, N., Dobbin, G., Knott, J., McCormack, M., & Weber, N. (2019). *EDUCAUSE Horizon Report: 2019 Higher Education Edition.* Educause.

Al-Karaki, J. N., Ababneh, N., Hamid, Y., & Gawanmeh, A. (2021). Evaluating the Effectiveness of Distance Learning in Higher Education during COVID-19 Global Crisis: UAE Educators' Perspectives. *Contemporary Educational Technology, 13*(3).

Allington, R. L., & Gabriel, R. E. (2012). Every child, every day. *Educational Leadership, 69*(6), 10–15.

Altincik, H. (2022). Evaluation Of Democracy, Civil Society And Lobbying. In *A Digital Context, İn: Individual, Society And Communication In The Context Of Digitalization* (pp. 187–195). Education Publisher.

Alvermann, D. E. (2017). The M word: Dare we use it? *Journal of Adolescent & Adult Literacy, 61*(1), 99–102. doi:10.1002/jaal.665

Alvermann, D., Marshall, J. D., Mclean, C., Huddleston, A. P., Joaquin, J., & Bishop, J. (2012). Adolescents' web-based literacies, identity construction, and skill development. *Literacy Research and Instruction, 51*(3), 179–195. doi:10.108 0/19388071.2010.523135

Ananga, P., & Biney, I. K. (2017). Comparing face-to-face and online teaching and learning in higher education. *MIER Journal of Educational Studies Trends and Practices*, 165-179.

Ananiadou, K., & Claro, M. (2009). *21st-century skills and competencies for new millennium learners in OECD countries.* OECD Publishing. doi:10.1787/19939019

Anderson, L. W., & Krathwohl, D. R. (2001). *A taxonomy for learning, teaching, and assessing, Abridged Edition.* Allyn and Bacon.

Anderson, S. E., Groulx, J. G., & Maninger, R. M. (2011). Relationships among preservice teachers' technology-related abilities, beliefs, and intentions to use technology in their future classrooms. *Journal of Educational Computing Research, 45*(3), 321–338. doi:10.2190/EC.45.3.d

Andreassen, H. K., Bujnowska-Fedak, M. M., Chronaki, C. E., Dumitru, R. C., Pudule, I., Santana, S., Voss, H., & Wynn, R. (2007). European citizens' use of Ehealth services: A study of seven countries. *BMC Public Health, 7*(1), 1–7. doi:10.1186/1471-2458-7-53 PMID:17425798

Angelino, L. M., Williams, F. K., & Natvig, D. (2007). Strategies to engage online students and reduce attrition rates. *The Journal of Educators Online, 4*(2), 114. https://eric.ed.gov/?id=EJ907749. doi:10.9743/JEO.2007.2.1

Appleby, R. (2021). *Developing Creative Thinking with Intentional Teaching Practices in Academic Subjects for Early Childhood Classrooms.* SOPHIA. https://sophia.stkate.edu/maed/437

Arasaratnam-Smith, L. & Northcote, M. (2017). Community in online higher education: Challenges and opportunities. *The Electronic Journal of e-Learning, 15*(2), 188-198.

Archambault, L. M., & Barnett, J. H. (2010). Revisiting technological pedagogical content knowledge: Exploring the TPACK framework. *Computers & Education, 55*(4), 1656–1662. doi:10.1016/j.compedu.2010.07.009

Aris, S. R. S., Teoh, S. H., Deni, S. M., Nadzri, F. A., & Dalim, S. F. (2022). Digital Skills Framework in Higher Education. *Proceedings, 82*, 61. doi:10.3390/proceedings2022082061

Aristeidou, M., & Herodotou, C. (2020). Online citizen science: A systematic review of effects on learning and scientific literacy. *Citizen Science: Theory and Practice, 5*(1), 11. doi:10.5334/cstp.224

Atkinson, B. F. W., Bennett, T. O., Bahr, G. S., & Nelson, M. M. W. (2007, July). Development of a multiple heuristics evaluation table (MHET) to support software development and usability analysis. *Proceedings of the 4th International conference on Universal Access in Human–Computer Interaction: Coping With Diversity*, Beijing, China. 10.1007/978-3-540-73279-2_63

Aufa, M., Hadi, S., Syahmani, Hasbie, M., Fitri, M., Saputra, M. A., & Isnawati. (2021). Profile of students' critical thinking, creativity, and collaboration skills on environmental pollution material. *Journal of Physics: Conference Series, 1760*(1), 1–6. doi:10.1088/1742-6596/1760/1/012027

Avila, J., & Pandya, J. Z. (2013). Traveling, textual authority, and transformation: An introduction to critical digital literacies. In J. Avila & J. Z. Pandya (Eds.), *Critical digital literacies as social praxis* (pp. 127–153). Peter Lang.

Aydemir, M. (2019). An examination of the renewed social studies course curriculum in terms of digital citizenship and its sub-dimensions. *International Journal of Contemporary Educational Research, 4*(2), 15–38.

Aygün, M. 2019. *Investigation of digital citizenship status of social studies teachers and social studies teacher candidates.* [Master's Thesis, Yıldız Technical University].

Azuma, R. T. (1997). A survey of augmented reality. *Presence (Cambridge, Mass.), 6*(4), 355–385. doi:10.1162/pres.1997.6.4.355

Bacca, J., Baldiris, S., Fabregat, R., Graf, S., & Kinshuk. (2014). Augmented Reality Trends in Education: A Systematic Review of Research and Applications. *Educational Technology & Society, 17*(4), 133–149. https://www.jstor.org/stable/jeductechsoci.17.4.133

Bahl, E. K. (2015). Comics and scholarship: Sketching the possibilities. *Composition Studies, 43*(1), 178–182.

Bailey, D. (2008). *Cybercitizenship and cyper cafety: Cyber ethics.* Rosen Central. https://archive.org/

Bailey, D. H., Duncan, G. J., Murnane, R. J., & Yeung, N. A. (2021). Achievement gaps in the wake of COVID-19. *Educational Researcher, 50*(5), 266–275. doi:10.3102/0013189X211011237

Balta-Salvador, R., Olmedo-Torre, N., Pena, M., & Renta-Davids, A. (2021). Academic and emotional effects of online learning during the COVID-19 pandemic on engineering students. *Education and Information Technologies, 26*(6), 7407–7434. doi:10.100710639-021-10593-1 PMID:34108843

Bamford, A. (2011). *The 3D in education white paper.*

Bandura, A. (1977). Self-efficacy: Toward a unifying theory of behavioral change. *Psychological Review, 84*(2), 191–215. doi:10.1037/0033-295X.84.2.191 PMID:847061

Bandura, A. (2001). Sociocognitive theory: An agentic perspective. *Annual Review of Psychology, 52*(1), 1–26. doi:10.1146/annurev.psych.52.1.1 PMID:11148297

Banister, S., & Reinhart, R. V. (2012). Assessing NETS• T performance in teacher candidates: Exploring the way to find teacher assessment. *Journal of Digital Learning in Teacher Education, 29*(2), 59–65. doi:10.1080/21532974.2012.10784705

Banko, M., & ve Babaoğlan, A. R. (2014). *The effect of the digital citizen on the Gezi Park process.* Gezi Park. http://www.geziparkikitabi.com/

Barkley, E. (2010). *Student engagement techniques: A handbook for college faculty.* Jossey-Bass.

Barnes, D., & James, G. C. (2020). *I am every good thing.* Nancy Paulsen Books.

Battersby, S. L., & Verdi, B. (2015). The culture of professional learning communities and connections to improve teacher efficacy and support student learning. *Arts Education Policy Review, 116*(1), 22–29. doi:10.1080/10632913.2015.970096

Beach, R., & Yussen, S. (2011). Practices of productive adult book clubs. *Journal of Adolescent & Adult Literacy, 55*(2), 121–131. doi:10.1002/JAAL.00015

Bean, J. C. (2011). *The professor's guide to integrating writing, critical thinking, and active learning in the classroom* (2nd ed.). Jossey-Bass.

Bean, R. M., & Goatley, V. J. (2020). *The Literacy Specialist: Leadership and Coaching for the Classroom, School, and Community.* Guilford Publications.

Becker, S. A., Brown, M., Dahlstrom, E., Davis, A., DePaul, K., Diaz, V., & Pomerantz, J. (2018). *Horizon report 2018 higher education edition brought to you by Educause.* EDUCAUSE.

Becker, S. A., Cummins, M., Davis, A., Freeman, A., Hall, C. G., & Ananthanarayanan, V. (2017). *NMC horizon report: 2017 higher education edition.* The New Media Consortium.

Beers, K., & Probst, R. E. (2015). *Reading nonfiction: Notice & note stances, signposts, and Strategies.* Heinemann.

Beers, K., & Probst, R. E. (2017). *Disrupting thinking: Why how we read matters.* Scholastic.

Bennett, W. L. (2008). Changing citizenship in the digital age. In W. L. Bennett (Ed.), *Civic life online: Learning how digital media can engage youth* (pp. 1–24). MIT Press.

Bergmann, J., & Sams, A. (2012). *Flip your classroom: Reach every student in every class daily—the international society for technology in education.*

Bers, M. U. (2008). Engineers and storytellers: Using robotic manipulatives to develop technological fluency in early childhood. In O. N. Saracho & B. Spodek (Eds.), *Contemporary perspectives on science and technology in early childhood education* (pp. 105–125). Information Age.

Bhavnani, S. P., Parakh, K., Atreja, A., Druz, R., Graham, G. N., Hayek, S. S., Krumholz, H. M., Maddox, T. M., Majmudar, M. D., Rumsfeld, J. S., & Shah, B. R. (2017). 2017 roadmap for innovation—ACC health policy statement on healthcare transformation in the era of digital health, big data, and precision health: A eeport of the American college of cardiology task force on health policy statements and systems of care. *Journal of the American College of Cardiology, 70*(21), 2696–2718. doi:10.1016/j.jacc.2017.10.018 PMID:29169478

Bianchi-Pennington, B. (2018). Designing literary discussion with podcasts. *Journal of Adolescent & Adult Literacy, 61*(5), 589–591. doi:10.1002/jaal.724

Bibeau, S. (2001). Social presence, isolation, and connectedness in online teaching and learning: From the literature to real life. *Journal of Instruction Delivery Systems, 15*(3), 35–39.

Biesenbach-Lucas, S. (2003). Asynchronous discussion groups in teacher training classes: Perceptions of native and non-native students. *Journal of Asynchronous Learning Networks*, *7*(3), 24–46.

Bigelow, M., & King, K. (2016). Peer interaction while learning to read in a new language. *Peer interaction and second language learning: Pedagogical Potential and Research Agenda*, 349-375.

Bishop, J., & Verleger, M. A. (2013, June). *The flipped classroom: A survey of the research*. In *2013 ASEE Annual Conference & Exposition* (pp. 23-1200). ASEE. 10.18260/1-2--22585

Bishop, R. S. (1990). Mirrors, windows, and sliding glass doors. *Perspectives: Choosing and Using Books for the Classroom*, *1*(3), ix–xi.

Björklund, C., & Barendregt, W. (2016). Teachers' pedagogical mathematical awareness in Swedish early childhood education. *Scandinavian Journal of Educational Research*, *60*(3), 359–377. doi:10.1080/00313831.2015.1066426

Björklund, C., van den Heuvel-Panhuizen, M., & Kullberg, A. (2020). Research on early childhood mathematics teaching and learning. *ZDM*, *52*(4), 607–619. doi:10.100711858-020-01177-3

Black, R. W. (2009). Online fan fiction, global identities, and imagination. *Research in the Teaching of English*, *43*(4), 397–425.

Blad, E. (2020). There's pushback to social-emotional learning. *EdWeek*. https://www.edweek.org/education/theres-pushback-to-social-emotional-learning-heres-what-happened-in-one-state/2020/02

Blake, N. (2000). Tutors and students without face or places. *Journal of Philosophy of Education*, *34*(1), 183–196. doi:10.1111/1467-9752.00164

Blasco-Arcas, L., Buil, I., Hernández-Ortega, B., & Sese, F. J. (2013). Using clickers in class: The role of interactivity, active collaborative learning, and engagement in learning performance. *Computers & Education*, *62*, 102–110. doi:10.1016/j.compedu.2012.10.019

Blau, S. D. (2003). *The literature workshop: Teaching texts and their readers*. Heinemann.

Bloom, B. S. (1956). *Taxonomy of educational objectives, handbook I: The cognitive domain*. David McKay Co Inc.

Bogard, J. M., & McMackin, M. C. (2012). Combining traditional and new literacies in a 21st century writing workshop. *The Reading Teacher*, *65*(5), 313–323. doi:10.1002/TRTR.01048

Bolwijn, R., Casella, B., & Zhan, J. (2019). International production and the digital Economy. In R. Tulder, A. Verbeke, & L. Piscitello (Eds.), *International Business in the Information and Digital Age*. Emerald Publishing.

Bonwell, C., & Eison, J. (1991). ASHE-ERIC Higher Education Report: Vol. 1. *Active learning: Creating excitement in the classroom*. The George Washington University, School of Education and Human Development.

Booker, K. (2018). The high tide raises all ships: Middle grades teachers' perspectives on school belonging in early adolescence. *RMLE Online: Research in Middle Level Education*, *41*(8), 1–15. doi:10.1080/19404476.2018.1505402

Boud, D., & Cohen, R. (2014). *Peer learning in higher education: Learning from and with each other*. Routledge. doi:10.4324/9781315042565

Bower, M. (2019). Technology-mediated learning theory. *British Journal of Educational Technology*, *50*(3), 1035–1048. doi:10.1111/bjet.12771

Bowser, A., Davis, K., Singleton, J., & Small, T. (2017). Professional learning: A collaborative model for online teaching and development. *SRATE Journal, 26*(1), 1-8.

Bozkurt, A., Karadeniz, A., Baneres, D., Guerrero-Roldán, A. E., & Rodríguez, M. E. (2021). Artificial intelligence and reflections from the educational landscape: A review of AI studies in half a century. *Sustainability, 13*(2), 800. doi:10.3390u13020800

Branch, C. (2015). 3D Printing in healthcare, the review. *Journal of Undergraduate Student Research, 16*(3), 1–4.

Brandell, J. R., & Varkas, T. (2001). Narrative case studies. The handbook of social work research methods, 293-307.

Bremer, J. (2005). The internet and children: Advantages and disadvantages. *Child and Adolescent Psychiatric Clinics of North America, 14*(3), 405–428. doi:10.1016/j.chc.2005.02.003

Brennen, S., & Kreiss, D. (2014). Digita-lization and digitization. *Culture Digitally.* https://culturedigitally.org/2014/09/digitalization-and-digitization

Brimi, H. M. (2011). Reliability of grading high school work in English. *Practical Assessment, Research & Evaluation, 16*(17), 1–12. doi:10.7275/j531-fz38

Broadband Commission. (2017). *Digital health: A call for government leadership and cooperation between ICT and health.* Broadband Commission.

Brodovskaya, E., & Dombrovskaya, A., & Batanina, I. (2020). The development of Russian youth digital citizenship: How to analyze and tackle the Internet communication risks. In Proceedings of the International Conference "Internet and Modern Society", (pp. 337-349). IEEE.

Bromley, K., Faughnan, M., Ham, S., Miller, M., Armstrong, T., Crandall, C., & Marrone, N. (2014). Literature circles go digital. *The Reading Teacher, 68*(3), 229–236. doi:10.1002/trtr.1312

Buchholz, B. A., Jordan, R. L., & Frye, E. M. (2022). "Can we see ur dog [?]": Co-constructing virtual author visits in the chat. *The Reading Teacher.* https://ila.onlinelibrary.wiley.com/doi/full/10.1002/trtr.2142

Buchholz, B. A., DeHart, J., & Moorman, G. (2020). Digital citizenship during a global pandemic: Moving beyond digital literacy. Journal of Adolescent &amp. *Adult Literacy, 64*(1), 11–17. doi:10.1002/jaal.1076 PMID:32834710

Burke, K., & Larmar, S. (2021). Acknowledging another face in the virtual crowd: Reimagining the online experience in higher education through an online pedagogy of care. *Journal of Further and Higher Education, 45*(5), 601–615. doi:10.1080/0309877X.2020.1804536

Burnett, C., Dickinson, P., Myers, J., & Merchant, G. (2006). Digital connections: Transforming literacy in the primary school. *Cambridge Journal of Education, 36*(1), 11–29. doi:10.1080/03057640500491120

Burnett, C., & Merchant, G. (2011). Is there a space for critical literacy in the context of social media? *English Teaching, 10*(1), 41–57.

Burns, L. D., & Botzakis, S. (2016). *Teach on purpose! Responsive teaching for student success.* Teachers College Press.

Butler, O. E. (1979). *Kindred.* Doubleday.

Cabero, J. (2014). Formación del profesorado universitario en TIC. Aplicación del método Delphi para la selección de los contenidos formativos formativos para el profesorado en TIC. *Educ. XXI, 11*, 111-132. doi:10.5944/educxx1.17.1.10707

Caeli, K., Ray, L., & Mill, J. (2003). 'Clear as mud'. Toward greater clarity generic qualitative research. *International Journal of Qualitative Methods*, *2*(2). Advance online publication. doi:10.1177/160940690300200

Cai, S., Wang, X., & Chiang, F. K. (2014). A case study of augmented reality simulation system application in a chemistry course. *Computers in Human Behavior*, *37*, 31–40. doi:10.1016/j.chb.2014.04.018

Canbek, G., & Sağıroğlu, Ş. (2006). A review on information, information security and processes. *Journal of Polytechnic*, *9*(3), 165–174.

Can, Y., & Bardakci, S. (2022). Teachers' opinions on (urgent) distance education activities during the pandemic period. *Advances in Mobile Learning Educational Research*, *2*(2), 351–374. doi:10.25082/AMLER.2022.02.005

Cappiello, M. A., & Dawes, E. T. (2012). *Teaching with text sets*. Teacher Created Materials.

Cardenal, F. J., & López, V. F. (2015) 'Education apps – one step beyond: it's time for something more in the education apps world'. *International Joint Conference*, *369*, 571–581. https://doi.org/10.1007/978-3-319-19713-5_50

Carmigniani, J., Furht, B., Anisetti, M., Ceravolo, P., Damiani, E., & Ivkovic, M. (2011). Augmented reality technologies, systems and applications. *Multimedia Tools and Applications*, *51*(1), 341–377. doi:10.100711042-010-0660-6

Carroll, J., & Ryan, J. (Eds.). (2005). *Teaching international students: Improving learning for all*. Routledge.

Carroll, N., & Conboy, K. (2020). Normalizing the "new normal": Changing tech-driven work practices under pandemic time pressure. *International Journal of Information Management*, *55*, 102186. doi:10.1016/j.ijinfomgt.2020.102186 PMID:32836643

Cascales, A., Pérez-López, D., & Contero, M. (2013). Study on parent's acceptance of the augmented reality use for preschool education. *Procedia Computer Science*, *25*, 420–427. doi:10.1016/j.procs.2013.11.053

Cassibba, R., Ferrarello, D., Mammana, M. F., Musso, P., Pennisi, M., & Taranto, E. (2021). Teaching mathematics at a distance: A challenge for universities. *Education Sciences*, *11*(1), 1. doi:10.3390/educsci11010001

Cassidy, J., Grote-Garcia, S., & Ortlieb, E. (2022). What's hot in 2021: Beyond the science of reading. *Literacy Research and Instruction*, *61*(1), 1–17. doi:10.1080/19388071.2021.2011236

Castañeda, L., & Selwyn, N. (2018). More than tools? Making sense of the ongoing digitizations of higher education. *International Journal of Educational Technology in Higher Education*, *15*(1), 1–10. doi:10.118641239-018-0109-y

Castek, J., & Gwinn, C. (2012). Technology in the literacy program. *Best practices of literacy leaders: Keys to school improvement*, 295–316.

Castells, M. (2010). *The rise of the network society*. Wiley. https://onlinelibrary.wiley.com/doi/pdf/10.1002/9781444319514.oth1

Castells, M. (2008). *The rise of the network society*. Bilgi University Press.

Castro, R. (2019). Blended learning in higher education: Trends and capabilities. *Education and Information Technologies*, *24*(4), 2523–2546. doi:10.100710639-019-09886-3

Catts, R., & Lau, J. (2008). *Towards information literacy indicators*. UNESCO Publishing.

Cazden, C. (1988). *Classroom discourse: The language of teaching and learning*. Heinemann.

Çetintav, G., & Yılmaz, R. (2022). A systematic analysis of published articles on augmented reality in the field of mathematics and geometry education. *Karaelmas Journal of Educational Sciences*, *10* (1), 47-61. https://dergipark.org.tr/tr/pub/kebd/issue/70876/1077084

Çevik, G., Yılmaz, R. M., Goktas, Y., & Gülcü, A. (2017). Learning English word with augmented reality for preschool education. *Journal of Instructional Technologies and Teacher Education*, 6(2), 50–57. https://dergipark.org.tr/tr/pub/jitte/issue/31327/303838

Chadha. (2022a) Introspective interactions: Implications from an international collaboration. *Journal of Educators Online, 19*(1).

Chadha. (2022b) Pedagogical interrelationships: The transformed landscape of deliberations. *Journal of the Scholarship of Teaching and Learning, 22*(2).

Chadha, A. (2019). Personalizing and extending deliberation in the online classroom: Future horizons. *Journal of Educators Online, 16*(2). https://eric.ed.gov/?id=EJ1223972. doi:10.9743/JEO.2019.16.2.4

Chai, C. S., Koh, J. H. L., & Tsai, C. C. (2010). Facilitating preservice teachers' development of technological, pedagogical, and content knowledge (TPACK). *Journal of Educational Technology & Society*, 13(4), 63–73.

Chang, H. Y., Wu, H. K., & Hsu, Y. S. (2013). Integrating a mobile augmented reality activity to contextualize student learning of a socioscientic issue. *British Journal of Educational Technology*, 44(3). Advance online publication. doi:10.1111/j.1467-8535.2012.01379.x

Chan, R., Bista, K., & Allen, R. (2021). *Online teaching and learning in higher education during Covid-19: International perspectives and experiences (Routledge studies in global student mobility)*. Routledge., doi:10.4324/9781003125921

Chappell, C., Gonczi, A., & Hager, P. (2020). Competency-based education. In *Understanding adult education and training* (pp. 191–205). Routledge. doi:10.4324/9781003118299-18

Chappuis, J., & Stiggins, R. (2020). *Classroom assessment for student learning: Doing it right—using it well*. Pearson.

Chatfield, T. (2013). *How we adapt to the digital age*. Sel Publishing.

Chen, Y., Zhou, D., Wang, Y., & Yu, J. (2017, June). *Application of augmented reality for early childhood English teaching*. In 2017 International symposium on educational technology (ISET) (pp. 111-115). IEEE. 10.1109/ISET.2017.34

Cheng, K.-H., & Tsai, C. C. (2013). Affordances of augmented reality in science learning: Suggestions for future research. *Journal of Science Education and Technology*, 22(4), 449–462. doi:10.100710956-012-9405-9

Chen, R. J. (2010). Investigating models for preservice teachers' use of technology to support student-centered learning. *Computers & Education*, 55(1), 32–42. doi:10.1016/j.compedu.2009.11.015

Chen, W. (2013). The implications of social capital for the digital divides in America. *The Information Society*, 29(1), 13–25. doi:10.1080/01972243.2012.739265

ChenX.YangS.WigA.VBollingerC.B.EsperatT.K.WilsonN.S.PoleK. (2022).

Chen, Y. (2020). Improving market performance in the digital economy. *China Economic Review*, 62, 101482. doi:10.1016/j.chieco.2020.101482

Cherry-Paul, S., & Johansen, D. (2019). *Breathing new life into book clubs: A practical guide for teachers*. Heinemann.

Cheung, A. C., & Slavin, R. E. (2013). The effectiveness of educational technology applications for enhancing mathematics achievement in K-12 classrooms: A meta-analysis. *Educational Research Review*, 9, 88–113. doi:10.1016/j.edurev.2013.01.001

Chib, A., Bentley, C., & Wardoyo, R.-J. (2019). Distributed digital contexts and learning: Personal empowerment and social transformation in marginalized populations. *Comunicar*, 27(58), 51–60. doi:10.3916/C58-2019-05

Chiu, T. K. F. (2021). Student engagement in K-12 online learning amid COVID-19: A qualitative approach from a self-determination theory perspective. *Interactive Learning Environments*, 1–14. doi:10.1080/10494820.2021.1926289

Choi, M. (2016). A concept analysis of digital citizenship for democratic citizenship education in the internet age. *Theory and Research in Social Education*, *44*(4), 565–607. doi:10.1080/00933104.2016.1210549

Choudbury, M., & Share, J. (2012). Critical media literacy: A pedagogy for new literacies and urban youth. *Voices from the Middle*, *19*(4), 39–44.

Churchill, N., Lim, C. P., Oakley, G., & Churchill, D. (2008). Digital Storytelling and Digital Literacy Learning. In Readings in Education and Technology. [University of the Fraser Valley Press.]. *Proceedings of ICICTE*, *2008*, 418–430. http://www.icicte.org/ICICTE2008Proceedings/churchill043.pdf

Çiftçi, A., & Topçu, M. S. (2021). Mental models and opinions of pre-service preschool teachers about stem education. *Milli Eğitim Dergisi*, *50*(231), 41–65. doi:10.37669/milliegitim.719596

Clandinin, D. J. (Ed.). (2006). *Handbook of narrative inquiry: Mapping a methodology*. Sage Publications.

Clandinin, D. J., & Connelly, F. M. (2004). *Narrative inquiry: Experience and story in qualitative research*. Jossey-Bass.

Claro, M., Preiss, D. D., San Martín, E., Jara, I., Hinostroza, J. E., Valenzuela, S., Cortes, F., David, P. A., & Foray, D. (2002). An introduction to the economy of the knowledge society. *International Social Science Journal*, *54*(171), 9–23. doi:10.1111/1468-2451.00355

Clements, D. H ve Sarama, J. (2008). Mathematics and technology: Supporting learning for student and teachers. In O.N. Saracho ve B. Spodek (Eds.), Contemporary perspectives on science and technology in early childhood education (pp.127-147). Information Age.

Clements, D. H., & Sarama, J. (2011). Early childhood teacher education: The case of geometry. *Journal of Mathematics Teacher Education*, *14*(2), 133–148. https://doi.org/110.1007/s10857-011-9173-0

Clements, D. H., & Sarama, J. (2014). *Learning and teaching early math: The learning trajectories approach*. Routledge.

Clements, D. H., & Sarama, J. (2016). Math, science, and technology in the early grades. *The Future of Children*, ●●●, 75–94. doi:10.1353/foc.2016.0013

COCIR. (2015). COCIR eHealth Toolkit: Integrated Care: Breaking The Silos (Fifth Edition). COCIR.

Coklar, A. (2020). Evaluation of digital citizenship levels of teachers in the context of information literacy and internet and computer use self-efficacy. *Asian Journal of Contemporary Education*, *4*(2), 80–90. doi:10.18488/journal.137.2020.42.80.90

Collaborative for Academic, Social, and Emotional Learning (CASEL). (n.d.). *What is the CASEL framework?* CASEL. https://casel.org/fundamentals-of-sel/what-is-the-casel-framework/

Collier, D. R. (2018). Doodling, borrowing, and remixing: Students inquiring across digitized spaces. *The Reading Teacher*, *72*(1), 125–130. doi:10.1002/trtr.1717

Common Sense Media. (2011). Digital literacy and citizenship in the 21st century. *Common Sense Media*. https://www.commonsensemedia.org/sites/default/files/uploads/pdfs/DigitalLiteracyandCitizenshipWhitePaper-Mar2011.pdf

Copley, J. V. (2004) The Early Childhood Collaborative: A professional development model to communicate and implement. (Eds., Samara, D.H.) Enganging Young Children in Mathematics, Standards for Early Childhood Mathematics Education, 401-414. Lawrence Erlbaim Associates.

Corley, M. A. (2005). Differentiated instruction: Adjusting to the needs of all learners. *Focus on Basics*, *7*, 1–6.

Coşgun Ögeyik, M. (2022). Using Bloom's Digital Taxonomy as a framework to evaluate webcast learning experience in the context of Covid-19 pandemic. *Education and Information Technologies*, *27*(8), 11219–11235. doi:10.100710639-022-11064-x PMID:35528755

Crosby, L. M. S. W., Shantel, D., Penny, B., & Thomas, M. A. T. (2020). Teaching through collective trauma in the era of COVID-19: Trauma-informed practices for middle level learners. *Middle Grades Review*, *6*(2), 1–6.

Cross, C. T., Woods, T. A., & Schweingruber, H. E. (2009). *Mathematics learning in early childhood: Paths toward excellence and equity*. National Academies Press.

Croxton, R. A. (2014). The role of interactivity in student satisfaction and persistence in online learning. *Journal of Online Learning and Teaching*, *10*(2), 314–325.

Cuban, L. (2009). *Oversold and underused*. Harvard University Press. doi:10.2307/j.ctvk12qnw

Çubukçu, A., & ve Bayzan, Ş. (2013). The perception of digital citizenship in Turkey and methods to increase this perception with the conscious, safe and effective use of the Internet. *Middle Eastern and African Journal of Educational Research*, *5*, 148–174.

Cunningham, P., & Allington, R. L. (2015). *Classrooms that work: They can all read and write*. Pearson.

Curricula . (2022). Borys Grinchenko Kyiv University. https://kubg.edu.ua/images/stories/Departaments/vstupnikam/pi/op_bak_po_en.pdf

Dahal, N. (2019). Online assessment through Moodle platform in higher education. *ICT Integration in Education Conference, 19-21, 2019,* Kathmandu, Nepal.

Dahal, N. (2021). Workshop activity in online courses of mathematics education: Insights for learning and assessment. The *14th International Congress on Mathematical Education,* Shanghai, China.

Dahal, B., & Dahal, N. (2015). Opportunities and challenges to use ICT in Nepalese mathematics education. In *Proceedings of Second National Conference on Mathematics Education* (pp. 102-106).

Dahal, N. (2022). Understanding and uses of collaborative tools for online courses in higher education. *Advances in Mobile Learning Educational Research*, *2*(2), 435–442. doi:10.25082/AMLER.2022.02.012

Dahal, N., Luitel, B. C., & Pant, B. P. (2022a). Exploration of the Workshop activity for peer assessment in online courses of mathematics. *Advances in Mobile Learning Educational Research*, *2*(2), 475–482. doi:10.25082/AMLER.2022.02.016

Dahal, N., Luitel, B. C., Pant, B. P., & Rajbanshi, R. (2022b). Enhancing student-teachers assessment skills: A self- and peer-assessment tool in higher education. *International Journal of Education and Practice*, *10*(4), 313–321. doi:10.18488/61.v10i4.3173

Dahal, N., Luitel, B. C., Pant, B. P., Shrestha, I. M., & Manandhar, N. K. (2020). Emerging ICT tools, techniques, and methodologies for online collaborative teaching and learning mathematics. *Mathematics Education Forum Chitwan*, *5*(5), 17–21. doi:10.3126/mefc.v5i5.34753

Dahal, N., Manandhar, N. K., Luitel, L., Luitel, B. C., Pant, B. P., & Shrestha, I. M. (2022c). ICT tools for remote teaching and learning mathematics: A proposal for autonomy and engagements. *Advances in Mobile Learning Educational Research*, *2*(1), 289–296. doi:10.25082/AMLER.2022.01.013

Dahal, N., & Pangeni, S. K. (2019). Workshopping in online courses: Insights for learning and assessment in higher education. *International Journal of Multidisciplinary Perspectives in Higher Education*, *4*(1), 89–110. doi:10.32674/jimphe.v4i1.1275

Darling-Aduana, J. (2021). Development and validation of a measure of authentic online work. *Educational Technology Research and Development*, *69*(3), 1729–1752. doi:10.100711423-021-10007-6 PMID:34092984

Darling-Hammond, L., Wei, R. C., Andree, A., Richardson, N., & Orphanos, S. (2009). *Professional learning in the learning profession*. National Staff Development Council.

David, B. (2014). Introduction: Making the move to peer learning. In D. Boud & Cohen, R. (Eds.), *Peer Learning in Higher Education* (pp. 1–17). Routledge.

Davies, R. S., & West, R. E. (2014). Technology integration in schools. In *Handbook of research on educational communications and technology* (pp. 841–853). Springer New York. doi:10.1007/978-1-4614-3185-5_68

de Kloet, J., & van Zoonen, L. (2007). Fan culture: Performing difference. *Media studies: Key issues and debates*, 322-341.

De Kosnik, A. (2009). Should fan fiction be free? *Cinema Journal*, *48*(4), 118–124. doi:10.1353/cj.0.0144

DeHart, J. D., & Densley, E. (2022). What Messages or Symbols Make You Feel Empowered?" A Virtual Book Experience with Tristan Strong. *The Journal of Literacy and Technology*, *23*(1).

Denham, S. A., Blair, K. A., DeMulder, E., Levitas, J., Sawyer, K., Auerbach-Major, S., & Queenan, P. (2003). Preschool emotional competence: Pathway to social competence? *Child Development*, *74*(1), 238–256. doi:10.1111/1467-8624.00533 PMID:12625448

DeVaney, J., Shimshon, G., Rascoff, M., & Maggioncalda, J. (2020). Higher Ed needs a long-term plan for virtual learning. *Harvard Business Review*, 2–5.

DeVoss, D. N., Eidman-Aadahl, E., & Hicks, T. (2010). *Because digital writing matters: Improving student writing in online and multimedia environments*. Jossey-Bass.

Dewey, J. (1933). Philosophy and civilization. *Philosophy (London, England)*, *8*(31).

Dewi. (2021). Analysis study of factors affecting students' digital literacy competency. *Elementary Education Online*, *20*(3), 424–431.

P. Dillenbourg, A. Eurelings, & K. Hakkarainen (Eds.). (2001). European perspectives on computer-supported collaborative learning. *Proceedings of the First European Conference on Computer-Supported Collaborative Learning*. University of Maastricht.

Doyle, B. G., & Bramwell, W. (2006). Promoting emergent literacy and social–emotional learning through dialogic reading. *The Reading Teacher*, *59*(6), 554–564. doi:10.1598/RT.59.6.5

Dreon, O., Kerper, R. M., & Landis, J. (2011). Digital storytelling: A tool for teaching and learning in the YouTube generation. *Middle School Journal*, *42*(5), 4–10. doi:10.1080/00940771.2011.11461777

Drigas, A. S., & Kokkalia, G. K. (2014). ICTs in kindergarten. *International Journal of Emerging Technologies in Learning*, *9*(2), 52–58. doi:10.3991/ijet.v9i2.3278

Drosatos, G., Efraimidis, P. S., Williams, G., & Kaldoudi, E. (2016). *Towards Privacy by Design in Personal e-Health Systems*. Proceedings of the 9th International Joint Conference on Biomedical Engineering Systems and Technologies (BIOSTEC 2016), (*vol. 5*, pp. 472-477). ScitePress. 10.5220/0005821404720477

Duffin, L. C., French, B. F., & Patrick, H. (2012). The teachers' sense of efficacy scale: Confirming the factor structure with beginning pre-service teachers. *Teaching and Teacher Education*, *28*(6), 827–834. doi:10.1016/j.tate.2012.03.004

Duffy, T. M., & Jonassen, D. H. (1992). *Constructivism and the technology of instruction: A conversation.* Lawrence Erlbaum.

DuFour, R., & Mattos, M. (2013). How do principals really improve schools? *Educational Leadership*, *70*(7), 34–39.

Duke, N. K., & Cartwright, K. B. (2021). The science of reading progresses: Communicating advances beyond the simple view of reading. *Reading Research Quarterly*, *56*(S1), S25–S44. doi:10.1002/rrq.411

Dunleavy, M., Dede, C., & Mitchell, R. (2009). Affordances and limitations of immersive participatory augmented reality simulations for teaching and learning. *Journal of Science Education and Technology*, *18*(1), 7–22. doi:10.100710956-008-9119-1

Dünser, A., Grasset, R., Seichter, H., & Billinghurst, M. (2007, March). *Applying HCI principles to AR systems design.* 2nd International Workshop on Mixed Reality User Interfaces: Specification, Authoring, Adaptation (MRUI 2007) (pp. 37-42). Charlotte. http://hdl.handle.net/10092/2340

Durdu, L., & Dag, F. (2017). Pre-service teachers' TPACK development and conceptions through a TPACK-based course. *The Australian Journal of Teacher Education*, *42*(11), 150–171. doi:10.14221/ajte.2017v42n11.10

East, M. (2019). *Giving students a voice: The power of anonymity in a digital learning environment.* Talis. https://talis.com/2019/07/25/giving-students-a-voice-the-power-of-anonymity-in-a-digital-learning-environment/

Easton, S. (2003). Clarifying the instructor's role in online distance learning. *Communication Education*, *52*(2), 87–105. doi:10.1080/03634520302470

Edmundson, J. (2002). Asking different questions: Critical analysis and reading research. *Reading Research Quarterly*, *37*(1), 113–119. doi:10.1598/RRQ.37.1.5

Edwards-Groves, C. J. (2011). The multimodal writing process: Changing practices in contemporary classrooms. *Language and Education*, *25*(1), 49–64. doi:10.1080/09500782.2010.523468

Ehlers, U. D., & Kellermann, S. A. (2019). Future skills: The future of learning and higher education (pp. 2-69). Karlsruhe.

Eleftheriadi, A., Lavidas, K., & Komis, V. (2021). Teaching mathematics in early childhood education with ICT: The views of two contrasting teachers' groups. *Journal of Digital Educational Technology*, *1*(1), 1–10. doi:10.21601/jdet/11117

Erdem, C. (2019). *Digital citizenship in South Africa.* [Unpublished PhD Thesis. Nigeria: Obafemı].

Ertmer, P. A., Ottenbreit-Leftwich, A. T., Sadik, O., Sendurur, E., & Sendurur, P. (2012). Teacher beliefs and technology integration practices: A critical relationship. *Computers & Education*, *59*(2), 423–435. doi:10.1016/j.compedu.2012.02.001

Eshet-Alkalai, Y. (2004). Digital literacy: A conceptual framework for survival skills in the digital era. *Journal of Educational Multimedia and Hypermedia*, *13*(1), 93–106.

Estapa, A., & Nadolny, L. (2015). The effect of an augmented reality enhanced mathematics lesson on student achievement and motivation. *Journal of STEM education, 16*(3). https://www.jstem.org/jstem/index.php/JSTEM/article/view/1981

Estrem, H. (2004). The portfolio's shifting self: Possibilities for assessing student learning. *Pedagogy: Critical approaches to teaching literature, language, culture, and composition, 4*(1), 125-127.

European Commission. (1996). *Strategic Developments for the European Publishing Industry towards the Year 2000. Europe's Multimedia Challeng: Main Report.* European Commission DG XIII/E.

European Commission. (2018). *Commission Staff Working Document Accompanying the document Proposal for a Council Recommendation on Key Competences for Lifelong Learning [COM(2018) 24 final].* Europea. https://eur-lex.europa.eu/legal-content/EN/TXT/PDF/?uri=CELEX:52018SC0014&from=EN

European Commission. (2018). *Human Capital Digital Inclusion and Skills: Digital Economy and Society Index Report 2018 Human Capital.* European Commission.

European Commission. Joint Research Centre, Vuorikari, R., Kluzer, S., Punie, Y. (2022). *DigComp 2.2, The Digital Competence framework for citizens: with new examples of knowledge, skills and attitudes,* Publications Office of the European Union. https://data.europa.eu/doi/10.2760/115376

European Committee. (2013). Monitor. *Education + Training, 2013,* •••. http://educalab.es/documents/10180/14921/monitor13_en.pdf/23d54070-3136-4d22-8a95-9eb73123ad81

European School Education Platform. (2022). Etwinning weeks 2022. *ESEP.* https://school-education.ec.europa.eu/en/group/etwinning-weeks-2022

European SchoolNet [EUN]. (2021). *Future Classroom Lab.* EUN. https://fcl.eun.org/about

Evans-Amalu, K., & Claravall, E. B. (2021). Inclusive online teaching and digital learning: Lessons learned in the time of pandemic and beyond. *Journal of Curriculum Studies Research, 3*(1), i–iii. doi:10.46303/jcsr.2021.4

Eysenbach, G. (2001). What is e-health? *Journal of Medical Internet Research, 3*(2), 1–2. doi:10.2196/jmir.3.1.e1 PMID:11720962

Farr, C. K., & Kurtzahn-Beach, R. (2006). Book club ladies: Marshaled by Oprah, guerrilla fighters in the culture wars. *Reader, 55,* 56–70.

Ferracane, M., & Marel, E. (2020). Patterns of trade restrictiveness in online platforms: A first look. *World Economy, 43*(11), 2932–2959. doi:10.1111/twec.13030

Ferrari, A. (2013). *DIGCOMP: A framework for developing and understanding digital competence in Europe.* JRC Publications.

Figueroa-Sánchez, M. (2008). Building emotional literacy: Groundwork to early learning. *Childhood Education, 84*(5), 301–304. doi:10.1080/00094056.2008.10523030

Fisher, D., Frey, N., & Hattie, J. (2020). *The distance learning playbook: Grades K-12.* Corwin.

Fishkin, J. S. (2006). The nation in a room: Turning public opinion into policy. *Boston Review.* https://deliberation.stanford.edu/mm/2006/bostonreview-nation.pdf

Fitzsimon, M. (2014). Engaging students' learning through active learning. *Irish Journal of Academic Practice, 3*(1), 9–18.

Flip. (2022). *About Flip.* Flip. https://info.flip.com/about.html

Flip. (2022, June 28). *Introducing Flip.* Flip Product Updates. https://info.flip.com/blog/product-updates/flip-rebrand-features.html

Fortune, D., Horst, P., Kessler, M. A., Tackett, M. E., & Pennington, L. K. (2021). Using Virtual Book Clubs to Elevate Discussion and Diverse Voices. In D. Hartsfield (Ed.), *Handbook of Research on Teaching Diverse Youth Literature to Pre-Service Professionals* (pp. 1–21). IGI Global. doi:10.4018/978-1-7998-7375-4.ch016

Freitas, R., & Campos, P. (2008). SMART: A system of augmented reality for teaching 2nd grade students. *22nd British HCI Group Annual Conference on People and Computers: Culture, Creativity*, Interaction Swinton, UK. 10.1145/1531826.1531834

Fuson, K. C., Clements, D. H., & Sarama, J. (2015). Making early math education work for all children. *Phi Delta Kappan, 97*(3), 63–68. doi:10.1177/0031721715614831

Fussell, R. S. (2005). Protecting information security availability via self-adapting intelligent agents. Military Communications Conference, (pp. 297). IEEE. 10.1109/MILCOM.2005.1606116

Gainer, J. S. (2010). Critical media literacy in middle school: Exploring the politics of representation. *Journal of Adolescent & Adult Literacy, 53*(5), 364–373. doi:10.1598/JAAL.53.5.2

Gambrell, L. B. (2011). Seven Rules of Engagement: What's Most Important to Know about Motivation to Read. *The Reading Teacher, 65*(3), 172–178. doi:10.1002/TRTR.01024

Gansner, M. M. (2017, September 5). "The Internet Made Me Do It"-Social Media and Potential for Violence in Adolescents. *Psychiatric Times.* https://www.psychiatrictimes.com/view/-internet-made-me-do-itsocial-media-and-potential-violence-adolescents

Garcia, A. (2013). Utilizing mobile media and games to develop critical inner-city agents of social change. In J. Avila & J. Z. Pandya (Eds.), *Critical digital literacies as social praxis* (pp. 107–125). Peter Lang.

Garcia, A., & Dutro, E. (2018). Electing to Heal. *English Education, 50*(4), 375–383.

Garcia, A., Witte, S., & Dail, J. (Eds.). (2020). *Studying gaming literacies.* Brill. doi:10.1163/9789004429840

Garrison, D. R. (2009). Communities of inquiry in online learning. In *Encyclopedia of distance learning* (2nd ed., pp. 352–355). IGI Global. doi:10.4018/978-1-60566-198-8.ch052

Garrison, D. R., Anderson, T., & Archer, W. (2000). Critical inquiry in a text-based environment: Computer conferencing in higher education model. *The Internet and Higher Education, 2*(2-3), 87–105. doi:10.1016/S1096-7516(00)00016-6

Garrison, D. R., Anderson, T., & Archer, W. (2001). Critical thinking, cognitive presence, and computer conferencing in distance education. *American Journal of Distance Education, 15*(1), 7–23. doi:10.1080/08923640109527071

Gay, G. (2002). Preparing for culturally responsive teaching. *Journal of Teacher Education, 53*(2), 106–116. doi:10.1177/0022487102053002003

Gecü-Parmaksız, Z. (2017). *Augmented reality activities for children: A comparative analysis on understanding geometric shapes and improving spatial skills* (Publication No. 475084) [Doctoral dissertation, Middle East Technical University] Yükseköğretim Kurulu Başkanlığı Tez Merkezi. https://tez.yok.gov.tr/UlusalTezMerkezi/

Gecu-Parmaksiz, Z., & Delialioglu, O. (2019). Augmented reality-based virtual manipulatives versus physical manipulatives for teaching geometric shapes to preschool children. *British Journal of Educational Technology, 50*(6), 3376–3390. doi:10.1111/bjet.12740

Gee, J. P. (2003). What video games have to teach us about learning and literacy. [CIE]. *Computers in Entertainment, 1*(1), 20–20. doi:10.1145/950566.950595

Gee, J. P. (2013). *The anti-education era: creating smarter students through digital learning.* Palgrave Macmillan.

Giacotto, S. (2022). Using comics to teach. *Language Magazine, 21*(11), 20.

Gil de Zúñiga, H., Jung, N., & Valenzuela, S. (2012). Social media use for news and individuals' social capital, civic engagement and political participation. *Journal of Computer-Mediated Communication, 17*(3), 319–336. doi:10.1111/j.1083-6101.2012.01574.x

Gilster, P. (1997). *Digital literacy.* John Wiley.

Glassmeyer, D. M., Dibbs, R. A., & Jensen, R. T. (2011). Determining utility of formative assessment through virtual community: Perspectives of online graduate students. *Quarterly Review of Distance Education, 12*(1), 23–35.

Gleason, B., & von Gillern, S. (2018). Digital citizenship with social media: Participatory practices of teaching and learning in secondary education. *Journal of Educational Technology & Society, 21*, 200–212.

Gökmen, A. (2012). Virtual business operations, e-commerce & its significance and the case of Turkey: Current situation and its potential. *Electronic Commerce Research, 12*(1), 31–51. doi:10.100710660-011-9084-2

Goktas, Y., Yildirim, S., & Yildirim, Z. (2009). Main barriers and possible enablers of ICTs integration into pre-service teacher education programs. *Journal of Educational Technology & Society, 12*(1), 193–204.

Goldberg, T. (2020). Delving into difficulty: Are teachers evading or embracing difficult histories? *Social Education, 84*(2), 130–136.

Golden, N. A. (2020). Organizing for meaningful assessment. *English Journal, 109*(6), 16–19.

Gong, J., & Tarasewich, P. (2004). Guidelines for handheld mobile device interface design. *Proceedings of DSI 2004 Annual Meeting,* 3751–3756. https://www.researchgate.net/publication/249916209_Guidelines_for_handheld_mobile_device_interface_design

Gonzalez, T., De La Rubia, M. A., Hincz, K. P., Comas-Lopez, M., Subirats, L., Fort, S., & Sacha, G. M. (2020). Influence of COVID-19 confinement on students" performance in higher education. *PLoS One, 15*(10), 1–23. doi:10.1371/journal.pone.0239490 PMID:33035228

Govindarajan, V., & Srivastava, A. (2020). What the shift to virtual learning could mean for the future of higher ed. *Harvard Business Review, 31*(1), 3–8.

Grabill, J. T., & Hicks, T. (2005). Multiliteracies Meet Methods: The Case for Digital Writing in English Education. *English Education, 37*(4), 301–311.

Gray, B. C., & Wilkins, P. (2016). The case of the missing author: Toward an anatomy of collaboration in comics. In Cultures of Comics Work (pp. 115-129). Palgrave Macmillan, New York.

Gray, J. (2000). *Teachers at the center a memoir of the early years of the National Writing Project.* Distributed by ERIC Clearinghouse.

Greenhow, C., & Robelia, B. (2009). Informal learning and identity formation in online social networks. *Learning, Media and Technology, 34*(2), 119–140. doi:10.1080/17439880902923580

Guilherme, A. (2019). AI and education: The importance of teacher and student relations. *AI & Society, 34*(1), 47–54. doi:10.100700146-017-0693-8

Gulamhussein, A. (2013). *Teaching the teachers: Effective professional development in an era of high stakes accountability.* Center for Public Education. http://www.centerforpubliceducation.org

Guntur, M. I. S., & Setyaningrum, W. (2021). The effectiveness of augmented reality in learning vector to improve students' spatial and problem-solving skills. *International Journal of Interactive Mobile Technologies*, *15*(5), 159–173. doi:10.3991/ijim.v15i05.19037

Guss, S. S., Clements, D. H., & Sarama, J. H. (2022). High-Quality early math: Learning and teaching with trajectories and technologies. In A. Betts & K. Thai (Eds.), *Handbook of research on innovative approaches to early childhood development and school readiness* (pp. 349–373). IGI Global., doi:10.4018/978-1-7998-8649-5.ch015

Habermas, J. (1972). *Knowledge and human interest.* Heinemann.

Habib, R. B. (2017). Students teaching students: An action research project incorporating active learning at language classroom. *Journal of Education and Human Development*, *6*(2), 182–199.

Hammer, E. (2019). Embracing a culture of lifelong learning–in universities & all spheres of life. *Proceedings of the International Astronomical Union. International Astronomical Union*, *15*(S367), 316–322. doi:10.1017/S1743921321001010

Han, J., Jo, M., Hyun, E., & So, H. J. (2015). Examining young children's perception toward augmented reality-infused dramatic play. *Educational Technology Research and Development*, *63*(3), 455–474. doi:10.100711423-015-9374-9

Harasim, L. (2012). *Learning theory and online technologies.* Routledge. doi:10.4324/9780203846933

Hargittai, E. (2007). The social, political, economic, and cultural dimensions of search engines: An introduction. *Journal of Computer-Mediated Communication*, *12*(3), 769–777. doi:10.1111/j.1083-6101.2007.00349.x

Harper, L. J. (2016). Using picture books to promote social-emotional literacy. *Young Children*, *71*(3), 80–86.

Harris, A., & Johns, A. (2020). Youth, social cohesion and digital life: From risk and resilience to a global digital citizenship approach. *Journal of Sociology (Melbourne, Vic.)*, *57*(2), 394–411. doi:10.1177/1440783320919173

Harris, J. B., & Hofer, M. J. (2017). "TPACK stories": Schools and school districts repurposing a theoretical construct for technology-related professional development. *Journal of Research on Technology in Education*, *49*(1-2), 1–15. doi:10.1080/15391523.2017.1295408

Harris, J., & Hofer, M. J. (2014). The construct is in the eye of the beholder: School districts' appropriations and reconceptualizations of TPACK. In L. Liu & D. C. Gibson (Eds.), *Research highlights in technology and teacher education* (pp. 11–18). Association for the Advancement of Computing in Education.

Harvey, C. B. (2015). Fantastic transmedia. In *Fantastic Transmedia* (pp. 12–39). Palgrave Macmillan. doi:10.1057/9781137306043_2

Hawkman, A. M., Tofel-Grehl, C., Searle, K., & MacDonald, B. L. (2022). Successes, challenges, and surprises: Teacher reflections on using children's literature to examine complex social issues in the elementary classroom. *Teachers and Teaching*, *28*(5), 1–19. https://www.tandfonline.com/doi/abs/10.1080/13540602.2022.2062747. doi:10.1080/13540602.2022.2062747

Heath, M. (2020). Digital citizenship. *Oxford Bibliographies.* doi:10.1093/obo/9780199756810-0264

Heffernan, A., Abdelmalek, M., & Nunez, D. A. (2021). Virtual and augmented reality in the vestibular rehabilitation of peripheral vestibular disorders: Systematic review and meta-analysis. *Scientific Reports*, *11*(1), 1–11. doi:10.103841598-021-97370-9

Helsper, E.J., Schneider, L.S., van Deursen, A.J.A.M., & van Laar, E. (2020). *The youth Digital Skills Indicator: Report on the conceptualisation and development of the ySKILLS digital skills measure.* KU Leuven, Leuven: ySKILLS.

Hennessy, S. (2011). The role of digital artefacts on the interactive whiteboard in supporting classroom dialogue. *Journal of Computer Assisted Learning*, *27*(6), 463–489. doi:10.1111/j.1365-2729.2011.00416.x

Hennig, N. (2017). Podcast literacy: Educational, accessible, and diverse podcasts for library users. *Library Technology Reports*, *53*(2), 1–42.

Hermes, J. C., Welsh, J., & Winkelman, R. J. (2016). A framework for defining and evaluating technology integration in the instruction of real-world skills. In Rosen, Y., Ferrara, S. & Mosharraf, M., eds. Handbook of research on technology tools for real-world skill development. IGI Global.

Hicks, T., & Turner, K. H. (2013). No longer a luxury: Digital literacy can't wait. *English Journal*, *102*(6), 58–65.

Hills, M. (2017). From fan culture/community to the fan world: Possible pathways and ways of having done fandom. *Palabra Clave (La Plata)*, *20*(4), 856–883. doi:10.5294/pacla.2017.20.4.2

Hodge, E., Bossé, M. J., Foulconer, J., & Fewell, M. (2006). Mimicking proximity: The role of distance education in forming communities of learning. *International Journal of Instructional Technology & Distance Learning*, *3*(12). http://www.itdl.org/Journal/Dec_06/article01.htm

Hodges, C. B., Moore, S., Lockee, B. B., Trust, T., & Bond, M. A. (2020). *The difference between emergency remote teaching and online learning.*

Hofer, M., & Grandgenett, N. (2012). TPACK development in teacher education: A longitudinal study of preservice teachers in a secondary MA Ed. program. *Journal of Research on Technology in Education*, *45*(1), 83–106. doi:10.1080/15391523.2012.10782598

Hollandsworth, R. (2011). Digital Citizenship. *Techtrends: Linking Research & Practice to Improve Learning, 55*(4), 37-47.

Hollandsworth, R., Dowdy, L. ve Donovan, J. (2011). *Digital citizenship in K-12: It takes a village.* Springer.

Hollenbeck, C. R., Mason, C. H., & Song, J. H. (2011). Enhancing student learning in marketing courses: An exploration of fundamental principles for website platforms. *Journal of Marketing Education*, *33*(2), 171–182. doi:10.1177/0273475311410850

Hollie, S. (2017). *Culturally and linguistically responsive teaching and learning: Classroom practices for student success. Grades K-12.* Shell Education.

Holovatenko, T. (2022). Ways of Implementing Google Jamboard in Pre-Service Primary School Teacher Training to Using Modern Technologies of Foreign Languages Teaching. *Electronic Scientific Professional Journal. OPEN EDUCATIONAL E-ENVIRONMENT OF MODERN UNIVERSITY*, (13), 19–31. doi:10.28925/2414-0325.2022.132

Holzberger, D., Philipp, A., & Kunter, M. (2013). How teachers' self-efficacy is related to instructional quality: A longitudinal analysis. *Journal of Educational Psychology*, *105*(3), 774–786. doi:10.1037/a0032198

Hosek, V. A. (2018). *Locating the critical component in technological, pedagogical, and content knowledge (TPACK): An examination of how graduate students recruit TPACK and critical digital literacy into classroom practices* [Doctoral dissertation, Illinois State University]. ProQuest (10978267).

Hosek, V. A., & Handsfield, L. J. (2019). Monological practices, authoritative discourses and the missing "C" in digital classroom communities. *English Teaching*, *19*(1), 79–93. doi:10.1108/ETPC-05-2019-0067

Houston, J. W., & Houston, J. D. (2017). *Farewell to Manzanar.* Clarion Book.

Hsiao, E. L. (2012). Synchronous and asynchronous communication in an online environment: Faculty experiences and perceptions. *Quarterly Review of Distance Education*, *13*(1), 15.

Hsieh, M., & Lee, J. (2008, March). *AR marker capacity increasing for kindergarten English learning.* International MultiConference of Engineers and Computer Scientists, Hong Kong, China. https://www.researchgate.net/publication/44261645_AR_Marker_Capacity_Increasing_for_Kindergarten_English_Learning

Huang, Y., Li, H., & Fong, R. (2015). Using augmented reality in early art education: A case study in Hong Kong kindergarten. *Early Child Development and Care, 186*(6), 879–894. doi:10.1080/03004430.2015.1067888

Hughes, A. (2009). *Higher education in a Web 2.0 world.* Bristol, England: JISC. https://www.jisc.ac.uk/media/documents/publications/heweb20rptv1.pdf

Hull, G. A., & Nelson, M. E. (2005). Locating the Semiotic Power of Multimodality. *Written Communication, 22*(2), 224–261. doi:10.1177/0741088304274170

Hunter, J. (2015). *Technology integration and high possibility classrooms: Building from TPACK.* Routledge., doi:10.4324/9781315769950

Hurley, R. (2019). *Data Science: A Comprehensive Guide to Data Science, Data Analytics, Data Mining.* Artificial Intelligence, Machine Learning, and Big Data. Independently Published.

Husbye, N. E., Buchholz, B. A., Powell, C. W., & Vander Zanden, S. (2019). Death didn't come up at center time": Sharing Books about Grief in Elementary Literacy Classrooms. *Language Arts, 96*(6), 347–357.

Hutchison, A., Beschorner, B., & Schmidt-Crawford, D. (2012). Exploring the use of the iPad for literacy learning. *The Reading Teacher, 66*(1), 15–23. doi:10.1002/TRTR.01090

Huxham, M., Campbell, F., & Westwood, J. (2012). Oral versus written assessments: A test of student performance and attitudes. *Assessment & Evaluation in Higher Education, 37*(1), 125–136. doi:10.1080/02602938.2010.515012

Hwang, G. J., Xie, H., Wah, B. W., & Gašević, D. (2020). Vision, challenges, roles and research issues of Artificial Intelligence in Education. *Computers and Education: Artificial Intelligence, 1*, 100001. doi:10.1016/j.caeai.2020.100001

Hwang, Y. (2011). Is communication competence still good for interpersonal media? Mobile phone and instant messenger. *Computers in Human Behavior, 27*(2), 924–934. doi:10.1016/j.chb.2010.11.018

IACR. (2007). *Communication technologies.* International Conference on Information Security and Cryptology. IACR.

Ihsan, A., Munawir, M., & Amir, F. (2017). Learning media of mathematical operations in early childhood based augmented reality. *In International Conference on Science, Technology and Modern Society, 1*(1), 19-22. https://ejurnalunsam.id/index.php/icstms/article/view/498/346

Imer, G., & Kaya, M. (2020). Literature review on digital citizenship in Turkey. *International Education Studies, 13*(8), 6. doi:10.5539/ies.v13n8p6

In most oblasts of Ukraine the educational process resumed – Minister Shkarlet. (2022, March 14). *Radio Svoboda [Radio Freedom].* https://www.radiosvoboda.org/a/news-osvita-vidnovlennya/31752216.html

International Commission on the Futures of Education. (2020). *Education in a post-COVID world: Nine ideas for public action.* ICFE.

Iona, J. (2017). Flipgrid. *School Librarian, 65*(4), 211.

Isin & Ruppert. (2020). *Being Digital Citizens (2nd ed.).* Rowman & Littlefield International, Ltd.

Isman, A., & Canan Gungoren, O. (2014). Digital citizenship. *Turkish Online Journal of Educational Technology-TOJET, 13*(1), 73–77.

Itani, M., Itani, M., Kaddoura, S., & Al Husseiny, F. (2022). The impact of the Covid-19 pandemic on online examination: Challenges and opportunities. *Global Journal of Engineering Education, 24*(2).

Ito, M., Baumer, S., & Bittanti, M. boyd, d., Cody, R., Herr-Stephenson, B., Horst, H. A., Lange, P. G., Mahendran, D., Martínez, K. Z., Pascoe, C. J., Perkel, D., Robinson, L., Sims, C., & Tripp, L. (2010). Hanging out, messing around, and geeking out: Kids living and learning with new media. MIT Press.

Ivankova, N., Creswell, J., & Stick, S. (2006). Using Mixed-Methods Sequential Explanatory Design: From Theory to Practice. *Field Methods, 18*(1), 3–20. doi:10.1177/1525822X05282260

Jabeen, S., & Ahmad, F. (2021). Digital citizenship: Effective use of digital media. In *Proceedings of the 13th International Conference on Education and New Learning Technologies,* (pp. 6041-6048). IEEE. 10.21125/edulearn.2021.1220

Jamiat, N., & Othman, N. F. N. (2019, October). *Effects of augmented reality mobile apps on early childhood education students' achievement.* The 3rd International Conference on Digital Technology in Education (pp. 30-33). 10.1145/3369199.3369203

Jan, S. (2018). *Investigating the relationship between students' digital literacy and their attitude towards using ICT.* USDE.

Jeffri, N. F. S., & Rambli, D. R. A. (2017). Design and development of an augmented reality book and mobile application to enhance the handwriting-instruction for pre-school children. *Open Journal of Social Sciences, 5*(10), 361–371. doi:10.4236/jss.2017.510030

Jerman, B. (2020). *Overcoming the digital divide with a modern approach to learning digital skills for the elderly adults.* Springer., doi:10.100710639-019-09961-9

Jocius, R., & Shealy, S. (2018). Critical book clubs: Reimagining literature reading and response. *The Reading Teacher, 71*(6), 691–702. doi:10.1002/trtr.1655

Johnson, D. W. (2019). *Murder falcon.* Image Comics.

Johnson, L., Adams, S., & Cummins, M. (2012). *NMC Horizon Report: 2012 K–* (12th ed.). New Media Consortium., https://eric.ed.gov/?id=ED593595

Johnston, N. (2020). The Shift towards Digital Literacy in Australian University Libraries: Developing a Digital Literacy Framework. *Journal of the Australian Library and Information Association, 69*(1), 93–101. doi:10.1080/24750158.2020.1712638

Jones, M., & Ryan, J. (2017). The online space: Developing strong pedagogy for online reflective practice. In R. Brandenberg, (Eds.), *Reflective theory and practice in teacher education* (pp. 205–222). Springer. doi:10.1007/978-981-10-3431-2_11

Jones, S. M., McGarrah, M. W., & Kahn, J. (2019). Social and emotional learning: A principled science of human development in context. *Educational Psychologist, 54*(3), 129–143. doi:10.1080/00461520.2019.1625776

Kabadayi, S., O'Connor, G. E., & Tuzovic, S. (2020). The impact of coronavirus on service ecosystems as service mega-disruptions. *Journal of Services Marketing, 34*(6), 809–817. doi:10.1108/JSM-03-2020-0090

Kaddoura, S., & Al Husseiny, F. (2021). An approach to reinforce active learning in higher education for IT students. *Global Journal of Engineering Education, 23*(1), 43–48.

Kaddoura, S., & Al Husseiny, F. (2021). Online learning on information security based on critical thinking andragogy. *World Transactions on Engineering and Technology Education*, *19*(2), 157–162.

Kaddoura, S., & Al Husseiny, F. (2021a). An approach to reinforce active learning in higher education for IT students. *Global J. of Engng. Educ.*, *23*(1), 43–48.

Kaddoura, S., & Al Husseiny, F. (2021b). On-line learning on information security based on critical thinking andragogy. World Trans. on Engng. And Technol. *Educ.*, *19*(2), 157–162.

Kaddoura, S., & Al Husseiny, F. (2023). The rising trend of Metaverse in education: Challenges, opportunities, and ethical considerations. *PeerJ. Computer Science*, *9*, e1252. doi:10.7717/peerj-cs.1252

Kaeophanuek, S., Na-Songkhla, J., & Nilsook, P. (2019). A learning process model to enhance digital literacy using critical inquiry through digital storytelling (CIDST). *International Journal of Emerging Technologies in Learning*, *14*(3), 22–37. doi:10.3991/ijet.v14i03.8326

Kai, I. (2011). Space/place and situationality/situatedness of identity: Reading James McBride's *The Color of Water*. *Journal of General Education Tainan University of Technology*, *10*(1), 203–219. doi:10.6780/JGETUT.201101.0205

Kaku, M. (2016). *Physics of the future. (Y. S. Oymak ve H. Oymak, Çev.)*. METU Development Foundation Publishing.

Kang, B. (2021). *How the COVID-19 pandemic is reshaping the education service. The Future of Service Post-COVID-19 Pandemic* (Vol. 1). Rapid Adoption of Digital Service Technology.

Kang, D., Goico, S., Ghanbari, S., Bennallack, K. C., Pontes, T., O'Brien, D. H., & Hargis, J. (2018). Providing an oral examination as an authentic assessment in a large section, undergraduate diversity class. *International Journal for the Scholarship of Teaching and Learning*, *13*(2), 1–14. doi:10.20429/ijsotl.2019.130210

Karaduman, H. (2017). Social studies teacher candidates' opinions about digital citizenship and its place in social studies teacher training program: A comparison between the USA and Turkey. *The Turkish Online Journal of Educational Technology*, *16*(2), 93–106.

Karakaş, Z. (2002). *Technology management*. [Unpublished Master's Thesis, Sakarya University Institute of Social Sciences, Sakarya].

Karakose, T., Ozdemir, T. Y., Papadakis, S., Yirci, R., Ozkayran, S. E., & Polat, H. (2022). Investigating the Relationships between COVID-19 Quality of Life, Loneliness, Happiness, and Internet Addiction among K-12 Teachers and School Administrators—A Structural Equation Modeling Approach. *International Journal of Environmental Research and Public Health, 19*(3), 1052. MDPI AG. Retrieved from doi:10.3390/ijerph19031052

Karakose, T., Polat, H., & Papadakis, S. (2021). Examining Teachers' Perspectives on School Principals' Digital Leadership Roles and Technology Capabilities during the COVID-19 Pandemic. *Sustainability, 13*(23), 13448. MDPI AG. doi:10.3390/su132313448

Katsaris, I., & Vidakis, N. (2021). Adaptive e-learning systems through learning styles: A review of the literature. *Advances in Mobile Learning Educational Research*, *1*(2), 124–145. doi:10.25082/AMLER.2021.02.007

Katzman, N. F., & Stanton, M. P. (2020). The integration of social emotional learning and cultural education into online distance learning curricula: Now imperative during the COVID-19 pandemic. *Creative Education*, *11*(9), 1561–1571. doi:10.4236/ce.2020.119114

Kavytska, T., & Drobotun, V. (2022). Online Teaching Writing to University Students: Negative Stereotypes Ruined. In C. Giannikas, Transferring Language Learning and Teaching From Face-to-Face to Online Settings (pp. 67-87). IGI Global. doi:10.4018/978-1-7998-8717-1.ch004

Kazakov, A. A. (2019). *Political Theory and Practice of Media Literacy.* Saratov University Publishing House.

Kelly, K., & Cameron Likens, A. (2022). A pandemic partnership: Preservice teachers and fourth graders engage in virtual book clubs. *The Reading Teacher*, trtr.2173. doi:10.1002/trtr.2173

Kerawalla, L., Luckin, R., Selijefot, S., & Woolard, A. (2006). Making it real: Exploring the potential of augmented reality for teaching primary school science. *Virtual Reality (Waltham Cross)*, *10*(3), 163–174. doi:10.100710055-006-0036-4

Kersulov, M. L., & Henze, A. (2021). Where image and text meet identity: Gifted students' poetry comics and the crafting of "nerd identities.". *The Journal of Media Literacy Education*, *13*(1), 92–105. doi:10.23860/JMLE-2021-13-1-8

Kesey, K. (1962). *One flew over the cuckoo's nest.* Viking Press.

Kikilias, P., Papachristos, D., Alafodimos, N., Kalogiannakis, M., & Papadakis, St. (2009). An Educational Model for Asynchronous E-Learning: A case study in a Higher Technology Education. In D. Guralnick (ed.) *Proceedings of the International Conference on E-Learning in the Workplace* (ICELW-09). Kaleidoscope Learning (CD-Rom).

Kılıç, T. (2017). e-Health, good practice; Netherlands. *Gumushane University Journal of Health Sciences*, *6*(3), 203–217.

Kim, Y., & Park, N. (2012). Development and application of STEAM teaching model based on the Rube Goldberg's invention. In Yeo, SS., Pan, Y., Lee, Y., Chang, H. (Eds), Computer science and its applications: (Lecture Notes in Electrical Engineering, vol 203). Springer, Dordrecht. doi:10.1007/978-94-007-5699-1_70

Kim, C., Kim, M. K., Lee, C., Spector, J. M., & DeMeester, K. (2013). Teacher beliefs and technology integration. *Teaching and Teacher Education*, *29*, 76–85. doi:10.1016/j.tate.2012.08.005

Kim, H. J., Kim, M. H., Chio, J. K., & Ji, Y. G. (2008, July). *A study of evaluation framework for tangible user interface. 2nd International Conference on Applied Human Factors and Ergonomics AHFE2008*, (pp. 14-17). Las Vegas, USA.

Kim, J. (2021). Implications of a Sudden Shift Online: The Experiences of English Education Students' Studying Online for the First-Time During COVID-19 Pandemic in Japan. In J. Chen (Ed.), *Emergency Remote Teaching and Beyond.* Springer., doi:10.1007/978-3-030-84067-9_10

Kim, K. T. (2019). The structural relationship among digital literacy, learning strategies, and core competencies among South Korean college students. *Educational Sciences: Theory and Practice*, *19*(2), 3–21. doi:10.12738/estp.2019.2.001

Kim, M., & Choi, D. (2018). Development of youth digital citizenship scale and implication for an educational setting. Journal of Educational Technology &amp. *Society*, *21*(1), 155–171.

King, A. (1993). From sage on the stage to guide on the side. *College Teaching*, *41*(1), 30–35. doi:10.1080/87567555. 1993.9926781

Kirschner, P. A. (2015). Facebook as learning platform: Argumentation superhighway or dead-end street? *Computers in Human Behavior*, *53*, 621–625. doi:10.1016/j.chb.2015.03.011

Kirylo, J. D. (2016). *Teaching with purpose: An inquiry into the who, why, and how we teach.* Rowman & Littlefield.

Kist, W., & Pytash, K. E. (2015). "I love to flip the pages". Pre-service teachers and New Literacies within a field experience. *English Education*, *47*(2), 131–167.

Knobel, M., & Lankshear, C. (2014). Studying new literacies. *Journal of Adolescent & Adult Literacy*, *58*(2), 97–101. doi:10.1002/jaal.314

Kocdar, S., Karadeniz, A., Peytcheva-Forsyth, R., & Stoeva, V. (2018). Cheating and plagiarism in e-assessment: Students' perspectives. *Open Praxis*, *10*(3), 221–235. doi:10.5944/openpraxis.10.3.873

Koehler, M. J., & Mishra, P. (2009). What is technological pedagogical content knowledge? *Contemporary Issues in Technology & Teacher Education, 9*(1), 60–70.

Koehler, M. J., Mishra, P., & Cain, W. (2013). What Is Technological Pedagogical Content Knowledge (TPACK)? *Journal of Education, 193*(3), 13–19. doi:10.1177/002205741319300303

Koh, J. H., Chai, C. S., & Tsai, C. C. (2014). Demographic factors, TPACK constructs, and teachers' perceptions of constructivist-oriented TPACK. *Journal of Educational Technology & Society, 17*(1), 185–196.

Koh, J. H., & Divaharan, H. (2011). Developing pre-service teachers' technology integration expertise through the TPACK-developing instructional model. *Journal of Educational Computing Research, 44*(1), 35–58. doi:10.2190/EC.44.1.c

Koong Lin, H. C. K., Hsieh, M. C., Wang, C. H., Sie, Z. Y., & Chang, S. H. (2011). Establishment and usability evaluation of an interactive AR learning system on conservation of fish. *Turkish Online Journal of Educational Technology-TOJET, 10*(4), 181-187. http://www.tojet.net/articles/v10i4/10418.pdf

Ko, S. M., Chang, W. S., & Ji, Y. G. (2013). Usability principles for augmented reality applications in a smartphone environment. *International Journal of Human-Computer Interaction, 29*(8), 501–515. doi:10.1080/10447318.2012.722466

Kotenko, O., Kosharna, N., & Holovatenko, T. (2020). Pre-service Primary School Teacher's Foreign Language Training by Means of Using Innovative Technologies. In I. G. Papadopoulos (Ed.), *International Perspectives on Creativity in the Foreign language Classrooms* (pp. 257–280). Nova Press Publishing.

Kress, G. (2003). *Literacy in the new media age.* Psychology Press.

Kudo, A. (2018). *My little Ikigai journal.* St. Martin's.

Kuhnke, E. (2016). *Body language: Learn how to read others and communicate with confidence.* Capstone.

Kuk, K., Prokin, D., Dimić, G., & Stanojević, B. (2011). New approach in realization of laboratory exercises in the subject programmable logic devices in the system for electronic learning: Moodle. *Facta Universitatis-series. Electronics and Energetics, 24*(1), 131–140.

Kuznetsov, A., Pyanykh, E., & Rodaikina, M. (2021). *Digital Transformation in the Context of Improving the Quality of Lifelong Education.* MIT.

Lamy, M., & Zourou, K. (2013). *Social networking for language education.* Palgrave Macmillan. doi:10.1057/9781137023384

Lang, J. M. (2013). *Cheating lessons: Learning from academic dishonesty.* Harvard University Press. doi:10.4159/harvard.9780674726239

Lapp, D., Moss, B., & Rowsell, J. (2012). Envisioning new literacies through a lens of teaching and learning. *The Reading Teacher, 65*(6), 367–377. doi:10.1002/TRTR.01055

Lapsley, I., & Segato, F. (2019). Citizens, technology, and the NPM movement. Public Money &amp. *Management, 39*(8), 553–559. doi:10.1080/09540962.2019.1617539

Lauricella, A., & Herdzina, J., & Robb, M. B. (2020). Early childhood educators' teaching of digital citizenship competencies. Computers &amp. *Education, 158.*

Lavidas, K., Apostolou, Z., & Papadakis, S. (2022). Challenges and opportunities of mathematics in digital times: Preschool teachers' views. *Education in Science, 12*(7), 459. doi:10.3390/educsci12070459

Lazarinis, F., Karatrantou, A., Panagiotakopoulos, C., Daloukas, V., & Panagiotakopoulos, T. (2022). Strengthening the coding skills of teachers in a low dropout Python MOOC. *Advances in Mobile Learning Educational Research*, 2(1), 187–200. doi:10.25082/AMLER.2022.01.003

Leu, D. J., Kinzer, C. K., Coiro, J., & Cammack, D. W. (2004). Towards a theory of new literacies emerging from the Internet and other information and communication technologies. In R. B. Ruddell & N. Unrau (Eds.), *Theoretical models and processes of reading* (5th ed., pp. 1570–1613). International Reading Association.

Leu, D. J., Kinzer, C. K., Coiro, J., Castek, J., & Henry, L. A. (2017). New literacies: A dual-level theory of the changing nature of literacy, instruction, and assessment. *Journal of Education*, 197(2), 1–18. doi:10.1177/0022057417719700202

Levine, E., & Patrick, S. (2019). *What Is Competency-Based Education? An Updated Definition*. Aurora Institute.

Levine, S., Moore, D. P., Bene, E., & Smith, M. W. (2022). What if it were otherwise? Teachers use exams from the past to imagine possible futures in the teaching of literature. *Reading Research Quarterly*, 58(1), 5–24. doi:10.1002/rrq.488

Lewin, C., & McNicol, S. (2015). Supporting the development of 21st-century skills through ICT. In T. Brinda, N. Reynolds, R. Romeike, & A. Schwill (Eds.), *KEYCIT 2014: Key competencies in informatics and ICT* (pp. 98–181). Universitätsverlag Potsdam.

Lewis, C., & Finders, M. (2004). Implied adolescents and implied teachers: A generation gap for new times. In D. Alvermann (Ed.), *Adolescents and literacies in a digital world* (pp. 101–113). Peter Lang.

Lewis, T. Y. (2014). Affinity spaces, apprenticeships, and agency: Exploring blogging engagements in family spaces. *Journal of Adolescent & Adult Literacy*, 58(1), 71–81. doi:10.1002/jaal.322

Lim, C. P., Zhao, Y., Tondeur, J., Chai, C. S., & Tsai, C. C. (2013). Bridging the gap: Technology trends and use of technology in schools. *Journal of Educational Technology & Society*, 16(2), 59–68.

Lin, L., Foung, D., & Chen, J. (2022). Assuring online assessment quality: The case of unproctored online assessment. *Quality Assurance in Education*, 31(1), 137–150. doi:10.1108/QAE-02-2022-0048

Liu, S. H., Tsai, H. C., & Huang, Y. T. (2015). Collaborative professional development of mentor teachers and preservice teachers in relation to technology integration. *Journal of Educational Technology & Society*, 18(3), 161–172.

Liu, T.-Y., Tan, T.-H., & Chu, Y.-L. (2010). QR code and augmented reality-supported mobile english learning system. In X. Jiang, M. Y. Ma, & C. W. Chen (Eds.), *Mobile Multimedia Processing* (pp. 37–52). Springer Berlin Heidelberg., https://link.springer.com/chapter/10.1007/978-3-642-12349-8_3

Liu, X., Magjuka, R. J., Bonk, C. J., & Lee, S.-H. (2007). Does sense of community matter? An examination of participants' perceptions of building learning communities in online courses. *Quarterly Review of Distance Education*, 8(1), 9–24.

Li, Y., & Li, G. (2022). The Impacts of Digital Literacy on Citizen Civic Engagement—Evidence from China. *Digit. Gov.: Res. Pract.*, 3(4), 24. Advance online publication. doi:10.1145/3532785

Louis, K. S., & Wahlstrom, K. (2011). Principals as cultural leaders. *Phi Delta Kappan*, 92(5), 52–56. doi:10.1177/003172171109200512

Loveless, A. (2007). *Creativity, new technologies and learning: A recent literature review* [An update]. Futurelab.

Luckin, R., Holmes, W., Griffiths, M., & Forcier, L. B. (2016). *Intelligence Unleashed: An argument for AI in education.*

Ludwig-Hardman, S., & Dunlap, J. C. (2003). Learner support services for online students: Scaffolding for success. *International Review of Research in Open and Distributed Learning*, 4(1), 1–15. doi:10.19173/irrodl.v4i1.131

Lupton, D. (2013). The digitally engaged patient: Self-monitoring and self-care in the digital health era. *Social Theory & Health, 11*(3), 256–270. doi:10.1057th.2013.10

Lynch, T. L. (2017). *The hidden role of software in educational research: Policy to practice.* Routledge.

Machado, M., & Tao, E. (2007). Blackboard vs. Moodle: Comparing user experience of learning management systems. *The 37th ASEE/IEEE Frontiers in Education Conference.* Milwaukee.

Maigret, E. (2011). *Media and communication sociology.* Communication Publications.

Major, L., Warwick, P., Rasmussen, I., Ludvigsen, S., & Cook, V. (2018). Classroom dialogue and digital technologies: A scoping review. *Education and Information Technologies, 23*(5), 1995–2028. doi:10.100710639-018-9701-y

Maldonado, N., & Yuan, T. (2011). Technology in the classroom: from Ponyo to "My Garfield Story": using digital comics as an alternative pathway to literary composition. *Childhood Education, 87*(4), 297–301. doi:10.1080/000940 56.2011.10523197

Manco-Chavez, J. A., Uribe-Hernandez, Y. C., Buendia-Aparcana, R., Vertiz-Osores, J. J., Isla Alcoser, S. D., & Rengifo-Lozano, R. A. (2020). Integration of ICTS and Digital Skills in Times of the Pandemic Covid-19. *International Journal of Higher Education, 9*(9), 11. doi:10.5430/ijhe.v9n9p11

Mann, S. J. (2005). Alienation in the learning environment: A failure of community? *Studies in Higher Education, 30*(1), 43–55. doi:10.1080/03075070502000307786

Manzuoli, C. H., & Sánchez, A., & Bedoya, E. (2019). Digital citizenship: A theoretical review of the concept and trends. *The Turkish Online Journal of Educational Technology, 18*, 10–18.

Marcuse, H. (1964). *One-Dimensional Man.* Beacon.

Marsh, J. (2010). Young children's play in online virtual worlds. *Journal of Early Childhood Research, 8*(1), 23–39. doi:10.1177/1476718X09345406

Martin, L., Martinez, D. R., Revilla, O., Aguilar, M. J., Santos, O. C., & Boticario, J. G. (2008). Usability in e-Learning Platforms: Heuristics comparison between Moodle, Sakai and dotLRN. *The 7th Europian Conference on e-Learning,* Agia Napa, Cyprus.

Martín, S. C., González, M. C., & Peñalvo, J. P. G. (2020). Digital competence of early childhood education teachers: Attitude, knowledge and use of ICT. *European Journal of Teacher Education, 43*(2), 210–223. doi:10.1080/02619768 .2019.1681393

Maskiewicz, A. C., & Winters, V. A. (2012). Understanding the co-construction of inquiry practices: A case study of a responsive teaching environment. *Journal of Research in Science Teaching, 49*(4), 429–464. doi:10.1002/tea.21007

Masmuzidin, M. Z., & Aziz, N. A. A. (2018). The current trends of augmented reality in early childhood education. [IJMA]. *The International Journal of Multimedia & Its Applications, 10*(6), 47. doi:10.5121/ijma.2018.10605

Mazza, R., & Milani, C. (2004). GISMO: A Graphical Interactive Student Monitoring Tool for Course Management Systems. *International Conference on Technology Enhanced Learning,* Milan.

Mbalia, K. (2020). *Rick Riordan presents Tristan Strong punches a hole in the sky.* Disney Books.

McBride, J. (1995). *The Color of Water.* Penguin Group.

McCumber, J. (2005). *Assessing and managing security risk in IT systems.* CRC Press.

McDonald, A., McGowan, H., Dollinger, M., Naylor, R., & Khosravi, H. (2021). Repositioning students as co-creators of curriculum for online learning resources. *Australasian Journal of Educational Technology, 37*(6), 102–118. doi:10.14742/ajet.6735

McGrail, E., & Turner, K. H. (2021). A framework for the assessment of multimodal composition. *English Education, 53*(4), 277–302.

McLean, C. A. (2010). A space called home: An immigrant adolescent's digital literacy practices. *Journal of Adolescent & Adult Literacy, 54*(1), 13–22. doi:10.1598/JAAL.54.1.2

McNiff, J. (2013). *Action research: Principles and practice.* Routledge. doi:10.4324/9780203112755

Media Awareness Network. (2010). *Digital literacy in Canada: From inclusion to transformation.* A Submission to the Digital Economy Strategy Consultation. http://www.ic.gc.ca/eic/site/028.nsf/eng/00454.html

Megahed, N., & Hassan, A. (2021). A blended learning strategy: Reimagining the post-Covid-19 architectural education. *Archnet-IJAR: International Journal of Architectural Research.*

Mercimek, B., & Yaman, N. D., Kelek, A ve Odabaşı, H. F. (2016). The new reality of the digital world: Trolls. *Trakya University Journal of Education Faculty, 6*(1), 67–77.

Michaelsen, A. S. (2020). *Digital citizenship.* Routledge.

Michikyan, M., & Suárez-Orozco, C. (2016). Adolescent media and social media use: Implications for development. *Journal of Adolescent Research, 31*(4), 411–414. doi:10.1177/0743558416643801

Milgram, P., & Kishino, F. (1994). A taxonomy of mixed reality visual displays. *IEICE Transactions on Information and Systems, 77*(12), 1321–1329. https://www.researchgate.net/publication/231514051_A_Taxonomy_of_Mixed_Reality_Visual_Displays

Miller, L. R., Nelson, F. P., & Phillips, E. L. (2021). Exploring critical reflection in a virtual learning community in teacher education. *Reflective Practice, 22*(3), 363–380. doi:10.1080/14623943.2021.1893165

Miller, M. D., Linn, R. L., & Gronlund, N. E. (2013). *Measurement and assessment in teaching* (11th ed.). Pearson.

Mingers, J., & Walsham. (2010). Toward ethical information systems: The contribution of discourse ethics. *Management Information Systems Quarterly, 34*(4), 833–854. doi:10.2307/25750707

Ministry of Education and Science. (2022). *On the organization of the educational process.* AUC. https://auc.org.ua/sites/default/files/kerivnykam_06_03_org_osvit_procesu.pdf

Mishra, P., & Koehler, M. J. (2006). Technological pedagogical content knowledge: A framework for teacher nnowledge. *Teachers College Record, 108*(6), 1017–1054. doi:10.1111/j.1467-9620.2006.00684.x

Misra, P. K. (2021). Process of Teaching. In *Learning and Teaching for Teachers* (pp. 115–131). Springer. doi:10.1007/978-981-16-3077-4_7

Mochizuki, K. (2018). *Baseball saved us.* Lee and Lowe Books.

Moeller, S., Joseph, A., Lau, J., & ve Carbo, T. (2011). *Towards media and information literacy indicators.* UNESCO.

Moore, G. (1989). Three types of interaction. *American Journal of Distance Education, 3*(2), 1–6. doi:10.1080/08923648909526659

Moore, G. (1990). Recent contributions to the theory of distance education. *Open Learning, 5*(3), 10–15. doi:10.1080/0268051900050303

Moran, M., Seaman, J., & Tinti-Kane, H. (2011). *Teaching, learning, and sharing: How today's higher education faculty use social media*. Pearson Learning Solutions.

Morris, L. V., Finnegan, C., & Wu, S.-S. (2005). Tracking student behavior, persistence, and achievement in online courses. *The Internet and Higher Education*, *8*(3), 221–231. doi:10.1016/j.iheduc.2005.06.009

Morze, N., Boiko, M., Vember, V., & Dziabenko, O. (2020). Report 3. Methodological and technical design of innovative classroom. *Electronic Scientific Professional Journal of Open Educational E-Environment of Modern University*, 1-119. doi:10.28925/2414-0325.2020spv3

Morze, N., Varchenko-Trotsenko, L., Terletska, T., & Smyrnova-Trybulska, E. (2021). Implementation of adaptive learning at higher education institutions by means of Moodle LMS. *Journal of Physics: Conference Series*, *1840*(1), 12062. doi:10.1088/1742-6596/1840/1/012062

Mosleh, S., Shudifat, R., Dalky, H., Almalik, M., & Alnajar, M. (2022). Mental health, learning behaviour and perceived fatigue among university students during the COVID-19 outbreak: A cross-sectional multicentric study in the UAE. *BMC Psychology*, *10*(1), 47. doi:10.118640359-022-00758-z PMID:35236395

Mossberger, K., Tolbert, C. J., & ve McNeal, R. S. (2008). *Digital citizenship: The Internet, society, and participation*. MIT Press.

Mossberger, K., Tolbert, C. J., & ve McNeal, R. S. (2008). *Digital citizenship: The Internet*. MIT.

Mossberger, K., Tolbert, C. J., & Stansbury, M. (2003). *Virtual inequality: Beyond the digital divide*. Georgetown University Press.

Moyer-Packenham, P. S., & Bolyard, J. J. (2016). International perspectives on teaching and learning mathematics with virtual manipulatives. In P. S. Moyer Packenham (Ed.), *Revisiting the definition of a virtual manipulative* (pp. 3–23). Springer., https://digitalcommons.usu.edu/cgi/viewcontent.cgi?article=3398&context=teal_facpub

Muhaimin, M., Habibi, A., Mukminin, A., Saudagar, F., Pratama, R., Wahyuni, S., & Indrayana, B. (2019). A sequential explanatory investigation of TPACK: Indonesian science teachers' survey and perspective. *Journal of Technology and Science Education, 9*(3), 269-281.

Mullen, R., & Wedick, L. (2008). Avoiding the digital abyss: Getting started in the classroom with YouTube, digital stories, and blogs. *The Clearing House: A Journal of Educational Strategies, Issues and Ideas*, *82*(2), 66–69. doi:10.3200/TCHS.82.2.66-69

Murray, M. C. V. P. (2014). Unraveling the digital literacy paradox: How higher education fails at the fourth literacy. *Issues in Informing Science And Information Technology*, *11*, 85–100. doi:10.28945/1982

Muxiddinovna, A. Z. (2022). The Place and Importance of Steam Educational Technology in Preschool Education. *Journal of Pedagogical Inventions and Practices*, *11*, 3–5. https://zienjournals.com/

Naitnaphit, L. (2021). Book clubs in a pandemic: Student choice and flexible pedagogies as we learned more about ourselves and the world. *Language Arts Journal of Michigan*, *37*(1), 18–30.

National Association for the Education of Young Children & National Council of Teachers of Mathematics (NAEYC & NCTM). (2010). *Position statement. Early childhood mathematics: Promoting good beginnings*. www.naeyc.org/resources/position_statements/psmath.htm

National Association for the Education of Young Children (NAEYC). (2010). *Early childhood mathematics: Promoting good beginnings*. https://www.naeyc.org/files/naeyc/file/positions/psmath.pdf

National Council of Teachers of Mathematics (NCTM). (2000). *Principles and standards for school mathematics.*, doi:10.5951/TCM.7.1.0026

National Reading Panel (U.S.) & National Institute of Child Health and Human Development (U.S.). (2000). *Report of the National Reading Panel: Teaching children to read: an evidence-based assessment of the scientific research literature on reading and its implications for reading instruction.* U.S. Dept. of Health and Human Services, Public Health Service, National Institutes of Health, National Institute of Child Health and Human Development.

Ng, W.NG. (2012). Can we teach digital natives digital literacy? *Computers & Education, 59*(3), 1065–1078. doi:10.1016/j.compedu.2012.04.016

Niess, M. L. (2011). Investigating TPACK: Knowledge growth in teaching with technology. *Journal of Educational Computing Research, 44*(3), 299–317. doi:10.2190/EC.44.3.c

Nieveen, N., & Plomp, T. (2018). Curricular and implementation challenges in introducing twenty-first century skills in education. In E. Care, P. Griffin, & M. Wilson (Eds.), *Assessment and teaching of 21st century skills: Research and applications* (pp. 259–276). Springer. doi:10.1007/978-3-319-65368-6_15

Nikolopoulou, K. (2022). Online education in early primary years: Teachers' practices and experiences during the COVID-19 pandemic. *Education in Science, 12*(2), 76. doi:10.3390/educsci12020076

North, C. (2018). *Ten facts about artificial intelligence in teaching and learning.* University of California.

Northeastern Center for Advancing Teaching and Learning. (2022). *"Teaching presence" in the community of inquiry framework: What does it mean to "teach" online?* Northeastern University. https://learning.northeastern.edu/teaching-presence/

Nugent, G., Barker, B., Grandgenett, N., & Adamchuk, V. I. (2010). Impact of robotics and geospatial technology interventions on youth STEM learning and attitudes. *Journal of Research on Technology in Education, 42*(4), 391–408. doi:10.1080/15391523.2010.10782557

Nugroho, S. A., Trisniawati, T., & Rhosyida, N. (2022). Developing powerpoint-based interactive multimedia of mathematics learning multiples and factors materials for elementary school. *Advances in Mobile Learning Educational Research, 2*(2), 411–420. doi:10.25082/AMLER.2022.02.009

Nurhidayati & Ratnasari, S. W. (2020). Digital transformation of organizations: Perspectives from digital citizenship and innovative spiritual leadership. *Contentfull..*

Nussbaum, M. (2012). Assessment of 21st century ICT skills in Chile: Test design and results from high school level students. *Computers & Education, 59*(3), 1042–1053. doi:10.1016/j.compedu.2012.04.004

Oblinger, D., & Oblinger, J. (2005). Is it age or IT: First steps towards understanding the Net Generation. In D. Oblinger & J. Oblinger (Eds.), *Educating the Net Generation* (pp. 2.1–2.22). EDUCAUSE., http:www.educause.edu/Resources/EducatingtheNetGeneration/IsItAgeorITFirstStepsTowardUnd/6058

OECD. (2017). *PISA 2015 results (Volume V). collaborative problem solving.* OECD Publishing. https://dx.doi.org/doi:10.1787/9789264285521-en

Ohler, J. (2012). Digital citizenship means character education for the digital age. *Education Digest: Essential Readings Condensed for Quick Review, 77*(8), 14–17.

Oranç, C., & Küntay, A. C. (2019). Learning from the real and the virtual worlds: Educational use of augmented reality in early childhood. *International Journal of Child-Computer Interaction, 21*, 104–111. doi:10.1016/j.ijcci.2019.06.002

Order of the President of Ukraine No 64/2022 On the Introduction of the Martial Law. (2022). President.gov. https://www.president.gov.ua/documents/642022-41397

Overbay, A., Patterson, A., Vasu, E., & Grable, L. (2010). Constructivism and technology use: Findings from the impacting leadership project. *Educational Media International, 47*(2), 103–120. doi:10.1080/09523987.2010.492675

Oyedemi, T. D. (2012). *The partially digital: İnternet, citizenship, social inequalities, and digital citizenship in South Africa.* [Unpublished PhD Thesis. Nigeria: ObafemıAwolowo University]. https://scholarworks.umass.edu/dissertations/AAI3518402/

Özarslan, Y. (2013). *Genişletilmiş gerçeklik ile zenginleştirilmiş öğrenme materyallerinin öğrenen başarısı ve memnuniyeti üzerindeki etkisi.* (Publication No. 331054) [Doctoral dissertation, Anadolu Üniversitesi] Yükseköğretim Kurulu Başkanlığı Tez Merkezi. https://tez.yok.gov.tr/UlusalTezMerkezi/

Özdamlı, F., & Karagözlü, D. (2018). Preschool teachers' opinions on the use of augmented reality application in preschool science education. *Croatian Journal of Education, 20*(1), 43–74. doi:10.15516/cje.v20i1.2626

Özel, C., & Uluyol, Ç. (2016). Bir arttırılmış gerçeklik uygulamasınının geliştirilmesi ve öğrenci görüşleri. *Türkiye Sosyal Araştırmalar Dergisi, 20*(3), 793-823. https://dergipark.org.tr/tr/pub/tsadergisi/issue/31706/347481

Öztürk, G. (2021). Digital citizenship and its teaching: A literature review. Journal of Educational Technology &amp. *Online Learning, 4*(1), 31–45.

Öztürk, M., & Çakıroğlu, Ü. (2021). Flipped learning design in EFL classrooms: Implementing self-regulated learning strategies to develop language skills. *Smart Learning Environments, 8*(1), 2. doi:10.118640561-021-00146-x

P21. (2009). *P21 Framework Definitions.* https://files.eric.ed.gov/fulltext/ED519462.pdf

Pagoto, S., & Bennett, G. G. (2013). How behavioral science can advance digital health. *Translational Behavioral Medicine, 3*(3), 271–276. doi:10.100713142-013-0234-z PMID:24073178

Pamuk, S. (2012). Understanding preservice teachers' technology use through TPACK framework. *Journal of Computer Assisted Learning, 28*(5), 425-439.Pangrazio, L. (2016). Reconceptualising critical digital literacy. *Discourse (Abingdon), 37*(2), 163–174.

Pangrazio, L. (2016). Reconceptualising critical digital literacy. *Discourse (Abingdon), 37*(2), 163–174. doi:10.1080/01596306.2014.942836

Pan, Z., López, M., Li, C., & Liu, M. (2021). Introducing augmented reality in early childhood literacy learning. *Research in Learning Technology, 29.* Advance online publication. doi:10.25304/rlt.v29.2539

Paratore, J. R., O'Brien, L. M., Jiménez, L., Salinas, A., & Ly, C. (2016). Engaging preservice teachers in integrated study and use of educational media and technology in teaching reading. *Teaching and Teacher Education, 59*, 247–260. doi:10.1016/j.tate.2016.06.003

Park, L. S. (2011). *A long walk to water.* HMH Books for Young Readers.

Pati, B. & Majhi, S. (2019). Information Literacy Skill: An Evaluative Study on the Students of LIS Schools in Odisha. *International Journal of Digital Literacy and Digital Competence (IJDLDC), 10*(1), 15-33. doi:10.4018/IJDLDC.2019010102

Pati, B., & Majhi, S. (2019). Information Literacy Skill. *International Journal of Digital.*

Pavlik, J. V. (2013). *New media and journalism.* Phoenix Publications.

Pedro, F., Subosa, M., Rivas, A., & Valverde, P. (2019). *Artificial intelligence in education: Challenges and opportunities for sustainable development*. UNESCO.

Peeters, W. (2019). The peer interaction process on Facebook: A social network analysis of learners' online conversations. *Education and Information Technologies, 24*(5), 1–28. doi:10.100710639-019-09914-2

Peeters, W., & Mynard, J. (2019). Peer collaboration and learner autonomy in online interaction spaces. *Relay Journal, 2*(2), 450–458. doi:10.37237/relay/020218

Peimani, N., & Kamalipour, H. (2021). Online education and the COVID-19 outbreak: A case study of online teaching during lockdown. *Education Sciences, 11*(2), 72. https://www.mdpi.com/2227-7102/11/2/72. doi:10.3390/educsci11020072

Peñarrubia-Lozano, C., Segura-Berges, M., Lizalde-Gil, M., & Bustamante, J. C. (2021). A Qualitative Analysis of Implementing E-Learning During the COVID-19 Lockdown. *Sustainability, 69*(3317), 1–28. doi:10.3390u13063317

Pence, H. E. (2011). Teaching with transmedia. *Journal of Educational Technology Systems, 40*(2), 131–140. doi:10.2190/ET.40.2.d

Perren, A., & Felschow, L. E. (2017). The bigger picture: Drawing intersections between comics, fan, and industry studies. In *The Routledge Companion to Media Fandom* (pp. 309–318). Routledge. doi:10.4324/9781315637518-38

Pfanner, E. (2013). Peering into the future of media. *New York Times*.

Philip, T., & Olivares-Pasillas, M. C. (2016). Learning technologies and educational equity: Charting alternatives to the troubling pattern of big promises with dismal results. *Teachers College Record*, (ID Number: 21616). Retrieved from http://www.tcrecord.org

Phuapan, P. (2015). *Elements of digital literacy skill: A conceptual analysis*. Research Gate. doi:10.29139/aijss.20150406

Pitchford, N. J., & Outhwaite, L. A. (2016). Can touch screen tablets be used to assess cognitive and motor skills in early years primary school children? A cross-cultural study. *Frontiers in Psychology, 7*, 1666. doi:10.3389/fpsyg.2016.01666

Poniszewska-Maranda, & T. Enokido (Eds.), Complex, intelligent and software intensive systems, 485-489). Springer. doi:10.1007/978-3-030-50454-0_50

Pool, C. R. (1997). A new digital literacy: A conversation with Paul Gilster: Integrating technology into teaching. *Educational Leadership, 55*(3), 6–11. http://www.ascd.org/publications/educationalleadership/nov97/vol55/num03/A-New-Digital-Literacy@-A-Conversation-with-Paul-Gilster.aspx

Popenici, S. A., & Kerr, S. (2017). Exploring the impact of artificial intelligence on teaching and learning in higher education. *Research and Practice in Technology Enhanced Learning, 12*(1), 1–13. doi:10.118641039-017-0062-8 PMID:30595727

Poquet, O., & De Laat, M. (2021). Developing capabilities: Lifelong learning in the age of AI. *British Journal of Educational Technology, 52*(4), 1695–1708. doi:10.1111/bjet.13123

Prensky, M. (2001). Digital natives, digital immigrants. *Marc Prensky*. http://www.marcprensky.com/writing/Prensky%20%20Digital%20Natives,%20Digital%20Immigrants%20-%20Part1.pdf

Prensky, M. (2001). Digital natives, digital immigrants. *Horizon, 9*(5), 1–6. doi:10.1108/10748120110424816

Prensky, M. (2001b). Digital natives, digital immigrants. Part II: Do they really think differently? *On the Horizon, 9*(6), 1–6. doi:10.1108/10748120110424843

Prestridge, S. (2017). Examining the shaping of teachers' pedagogical orientation for the use of technology. *Technology, Pedagogy and Education, 26*(4), 367–381. doi:10.1080/1475939X.2016.1258369

Price, V. (2009). Citizens deliberating online: Theory and some evidence. *Online deliberation: Design, Research, and Practice*, 37-58.

Prince, M. (2004). Does active learning work? A review of the research. *Journal of Engineering Education, 93*(3), 223–232. doi:10.1002/j.2168-9830.2004.tb00809.x

Project Zero. (2022). *Project Zero's thinking routines toolbox*. Harvard. https://pz.harvard.edu/thinking-routines.

Puentedura, R. R. (2010). SAMR and TPACK: Intro to advanced practice. *Hippasus*. http://hippasus.com/resources/sweden2010/SAMR_TPCK_IntroToAdvancedPractice.pdf

Puentedura, R. R. (2013). *SAMR: Moving from enhancement to transformation*. Ruben R. Puentedura's Blog. http://www.hippasus.com/rrpweblog/archives/2013/05/29/SAMREnhancementToTransformation.pdf

Quinones, G., & Adams, M. (2021). Children's virtual worlds and friendships during the COVID-19 pandemic: Visual technologies as a panacea for social isolation. *Video Journal of Education and Pedagogy, 5*(1), 1–18. doi:10.1163/23644583-bja10015

Raj, N. S., & Renumol, V. G. (2022). A systematic literature review on adaptive content recommenders in personalized learning environments from 2015 to 2020. *Journal of Computers in Education, 9*(1), 113–148. doi:10.100740692-021-00199-4

Ramachandran, V., Cline, A., & Hawkins, S. (2020). Technological advancements to promote adherence. In S. R. Feldman, A. Cline, A. Pona, & S. S. Kolli (Eds.), Treatment adherence in dermatology, 99-112. doi:10.1007/978-3-030-278090_10

Rambli, D. R. A., Matcha, W., & Sulaiman, S. (2013). Fun learning with AR alphabet book for preschool children. *Procedia Computer Science, 25*, 211–219. doi:10.1016/j.procs.2013.11.026

Ranchordas, S. (2020). We teach and learn online. Are we all digital citizens now? Lessons on digital citizenship from the lockdown. Retrieved from http://www.iconnectblog.com/2020/05/we-teachand-learn-online-are-we-all-digital-citizens-now-lessons-on-digital-citizenship-from-thelockdown

Rapanta, C., Botturi, L., Goodyear, P., Guàrdia, L., & Koole, M. (2021). Balancing technology, pedagogy and the new normal: Post-pandemic challenges for higher education. *Postdigital Science and Education, 3*(3), 715–742. doi:10.100742438-021-00249-1

Rapanta, C., & Cantoni, L. (2014). Being in the users' shoes: Anticipating experience while designing online courses. *British Journal of Educational Technology, 45*(5), 765–777. doi:10.1111/bjet.12102

Rasalingam, R. R., Muniandy, B., & Rass, R. (2014). Exploring the application of augmented reality technology in early childhood classroom in Malaysia. *Journal of Research & Method in Education, 4*(5), 33–40. doi:10.9790/7388-04543340

Rasheed, R. A., Kamsin, A., & Abdullah, N. A. (2020). Challenges in the online component of blended learning: A systematic review. *Computers & Education, 144*, 103701. doi:10.1016/j.compedu.2019.103701

Ratna Priwati, Acintya & Helmi, Avin. (2021). The manifestations of digital literacy in social media among Indonesian youth. HUMANITAS: Indonesian Psychological Journal. 18. 14. . doi:10.26555/humanitas.v18i1.17337

Redondo, B., Cózar-Gutiérrez, R., González-Calero, J. A., & Sánchez Ruiz, R. (2020). Integration of augmented reality in the teaching of English as a foreign language in early childhood education. *Early Childhood Education Journal*, *48*(2), 147–155. doi:10.100710643-019-00999-5

Ribble, M. (2004). Digital citizenship: Addressing appropriate technology behavior. *Learning and Leading with Technology*, *32*(1), 6–11.

Ribble, M. (2007). *Digital citizenship in schools*. International Society for.

Ribble, M. (2021). Digital Citizenship in the Frame of Global Change. *International Journal of Studies in Education and Science*, *2*(2), 74–86.

Ribble, M., & Park, M. (2019). *The digital citizenship handbook for school leaders: Fostering positive interactions online*. International Society for Technology in Education.

Richardson, C. (2020). Supporting collaborative creativity in education with the i5 framework. *Educational Action Research*.

Rittle-Johnson, B. (2017). Developing mathematics knowledge. *Child Development Perspectives*, *11*(3), 184–190. doi:10.1111/cdep.12229

Robbins, M. A. (2017). *Confessions of a Fangirl: Interactions with Affinity Spaces and Multimodal, Multicultural Texts at Book Clubs and Fandom Events* [Doctoral dissertation, University of Georgia].

Robinson, C. (2015). An exploration of poverty in central Appalachia: Questions of culture, industry, and technology. *An International Journal of Pure Communication Inquiry*, *3*(2), 75–89. doi:10.17646/KOME.2015.26

Roblyer, M. D., & Hughes, J. E. (2019). *Integrating educational technology into teaching: Transforming learning across disciplines* (8th ed.). Pearson.

Rogers, E. M. (2001). The Digital Divide. *Convergence*, *7*(4), 96–111. doi:10.1177/135485650100700406

Rogerson, S. (2020). Re-imagining the digital age through digital ethics, invited position paper. In J. Arthur, T. Harrison ve G. Polizzi (Eds.), Promoting character education as part of a holistic approach to re-ımagining the digital age: Ethics and the Internet webinar (pp. 25-28). University of Birmingham Jubilee Centre for Character and Virtues.

Rogerson, S. (1996). Preparing to handle dilemmas in the computing profession. *Organizations and People*, *3*(2), 25–26.

Rohibni, R., Rokhmawan, T., Sayer, I. M., & Fitriyah, L. (2022). The variety of mathematics learning media for early childhood in improving basic mathematics ability. *Bulletin of Science Education*, *2*(3), 102–114. doi:10.51278/bse.v2i3.427

Rooney, K. (2005). *Reading with Oprah: The book club that changed America*. University of Arkansas Press.

Rosenberg, J., & Koehler, M. (2015). Context and Technological Pedagogical Content Knowledge (TPACK): A Systematic Review. *Journal of Research on Technology in Education*, *47*(3), 186–210. doi:10.1080/15391523.2015.1052663

Rossini, T. S. S., do Amaral, M. M., & Santos, E. (2021). The viralization of online education: Learning beyond the time of the coronavirus. *Prospects*, *51*(1), 285–297. doi:10.100711125-021-09559-5 PMID:33967347

Rovai, A. P., & Wighting, M. J. (2005). Feelings of alienation and community among higher education students in a virtual classroom. *The Internet and Higher Education*, *8*(2), 97–110. doi:10.1016/j.iheduc.2005.03.001

Rowntree, D. (1995). Teaching with audio in open and distance learning. *British Journal of Educational Studies*, *43*(2).

Rudestam, K. E., & Schoenholtz-Read, J. (2009). *Handbook of online learning*. Sage Publications.

Ruggiero, D., & Mong, C. J. (2015). The teacher technology integration experience: Practice and reflection in the classroom. *Journal of Information Technology Education, 14*, 162–178. doi:10.28945/2227

Ruth, A., & Houghton, L. (2009). The wiki way of learning. *Australasian Journal of Educational Technology, 25*(2). https://ajet.org.au/index.php/AJET/article/view/1147. doi:10.14742/ajet.1147

Rutten, K., Roets, G., Soetaert, R., & Roose, R. (2012). The rhetoric of disability: A dramatic-narrative analysis of O*ne flew over the cuckoo's nest. Critical Arts, 26*(5), 631–647. doi:10.1080/02560046.2012.744720

Safar, A. H., Al-Jafar, A. A., & Al-Yousefi, Z. H. (2017). The effectiveness of using augmented reality apps in teaching the English alphabet to kindergarten children: A case study in the State of Kuwait. *Eurasia Journal of Mathematics, Science and Technology Education, 13*(2), 417–440. doi:10.12973/eurasia.2017.00624a

Saldana, J. (2016). *The coding manual for qualitative researchers.* SAGE Publications Ltd.

Salim, J., Tandy, S., Arnindita, J., Wibisono, J., Haryanto, M., & Wibisono, M. (2022). Zoom fatigue and its risk factors in online learning during the COVID-19 pandemic. *Medical Journal of Indonesia, 31*(1), 13–19. doi:10.13181/mji.oa.225703

Salleh, U. K. M., Zulnaidi, H., Rahim, S. S. A., Bin Zakaria, A. R., & Hidayat, R. (2019). Roles of self-directed learning and social networking sites in lifelong learning. *International Journal of Instruction, 12*(4), 167–182. doi:10.29333/iji.2019.12411a

Saputra, M., & Siddiq, I. (2020). Social media and digital citizenship: The urgency of digital literacy in the middle of a disrupted society era. International Journal of Engineering and Technology, 15(7), 156. . v15i07.13239 doi:10.3991/ijet

Sato, M., & Ballinger, S. (2016). *Peer interaction and second language learning: Pedagogical potential and research agenda.* John Benjamins. doi:10.1075/lllt.45

Schacter, J., & Jo, B. (2016). Improving low-income preschoolers mathematics achievement with Math Shelf, a preschool tablet computer curriculum. *Computers in Human Behavior, 55*, 223–229. doi:10.100713394-017-0203-9

Schatzki, T. R. (2022). Spatial troubles with teaching under COVID-19. *Studies in Continuing Education, 44*(2), 300–315. doi:10.1080/0158037X.2021.1928052

Schlienger, T., & Teufel, S. (2001). *Analyzing information security culture: Increased trust by an appropriate information security culture.* University of Fribourg.

Schmidt, D. A., Baran, E., Thompson, A. D., Mishra, P., Koehler, M. J., & Shin, T. S. (2009). Technological pedagogical content knowledge (TPACK): The development and validation of an assessment instrument for preservice teachers. *Journal of Research on Technology in Education, 42*(2), 123–149. doi:10.1080/15391523.2009.10782544

Schmidt, E., & Cohen, J. (2014). *New digital age.* Optimist Publications.

Schreck, M. K., Lewandowski, S., Green, J., & Hart, C. A. (1999). What's the best novel you've ever taught? *English Journal, 89*(2), 30–32. doi:10.2307/822136

Seeber, I., Waizenegger, L., & Seidel, S. (2020). Collaborating with issues and research opportunities. *Internet Research.* Advance online publication. doi:10.1108/INTR-12-2019-0503

Selwyn, N. (2012). Making sense of young people, education and digital technology: The role of sociological theory. *Oxford Review of Education, 38*(1), 81–96. doi:10.1080/03054985.2011.577949

Selwyn, N. (2016). Digital downsides: Exploring university students' negative engagements with digital technology. *Teaching in Higher Education, 21*(8), 1006–1021. doi:10.1080/13562517.2016.1213229

Serafini, F., & Youngs, S. (2013). Reading workshop 2.0: Children's literature in the digital age. *The Reading Teacher*, *66*(5), 401–404. doi:10.1002/TRTR.01141

Shabani, K., Khatib, M., & Ebadi, S. (2010). Vygotsky's zone of proximal development: Instructional implications and teachers' professional development. *English Language Teaching*, *3*(4), 237–248. doi:10.5539/elt.v3n4p237

Shanahan, L., Steinhoff, A., Bechtiger, L., Murray, A., Nivette, A., Hepp, U., Ribeaud, D., & Eisner, M. (2022). Emotional distress in young adults during the COVID-19 pandemic: Evidence of risk and resilience from a longitudinal cohort study. *Psychological Medicine*, *52*(5), 824–833. doi:10.1017/S003329172000241X PMID:32571438

Sharon, J. H. K., & Nurlaily, N. (2022). Students' perceptions of vlog as speaking assessment technique at senior high school. *IDEAS: Journal of Language Teaching & Learning. Linguistics and Literature*, *10*(2), 2036–2043. doi:10.24256/ideas.v10i2.3218

Shelby-Caffey, C., Ubeda, E., & Jenkins, B. (2014). Digital storytelling revisited: An educator's use of an innovative literacy practice. *The Reading Teacher*, *68*(3), 191–198. doi:10.1002/trtr.1273

Shelton, B. E., & Hedley, N. R. (2002). Using augmented reality for teaching earth-sun relationships to undergraduate geography students. *The First IEEE International Workshop Agumented Reality Toolkit Bildiri Kitapçığı*, 8.

Shih, H. C. J., & Huang, S. H. C. (2020). College students' metacognitive strategy use in an EFL flipped classroom. *Computer Assisted Language Learning*, *33*(7), 755–784. doi:10.1080/09588221.2019.1590420

Siegel, M. (2012). New times for multimodality? Confronting the accountability culture. *Journal of Adolescent & Adult Literacy*, *55*(8), 671–680. doi:10.1002/JAAL.00082

Simonofski, A., Asensio, E., & Wautelet, Y. (2019). Citizen participation in the design of smart cities. In A. Visvizi, & M. D. Lytras (Eds.), Smart cities: Issues and challenges,47-62. doi:10.1016/B978-0-12-816639-0.00004-1

Sin, A. K., & Zaman, H. B. (2010). Live solar system (LSS): Evaluation of an augmented reality book-based educational tool. *2010 International Symposium on Information Technology*, (pp. 1-6).

Sjølie, E., Francisco, S., & Langelotz, L. (2019). Communicative learning spaces and learning to become a teacher. *Pedagogy, Culture & Society*, *27*(3), cc. 365-382.

Skulmowski, A., & Xu, M. (2021). Understanding cognitive load in digital and online learning: A new perspective on extraneous cognitive load. *Educational Psychology Review*, *34*(1), 171–196. doi:10.100710648-021-09624-7

Slavin, R. E., & Lake, C. (2008). Effective programs in elementary mathematics: A best-evidence synthesis. *Review of Educational Research*, *78*(3), 427–515. doi:10.3102/0034654308317473

Smith, C. H. (2021). The teaching zone: Square pegs in round holes. *Teaching English in the Two-Year College*, *48*(4), 413–435.

Smith, J. M. (2019). Considerations for summer online book clubs. *The Reading Teacher*, *72*(5), 638–642. doi:10.1002/trtr.1765

Smith, M. D. (2021). CALL in a social context: Reflecting on digital equity, identity, and interaction in the post-COVID age. *Quality Assurance in Education*, *29*(4), 537–549.

Smith, M., Traxler, J., & Elgar, E. (2022). *Digital learning in higher education: Covid-19 and beyond*. Edward Elgar Publishing., doi:10.4337/9781800379404

Somyürek, S. (2014). Öğretim sürecinde z kuşağının dikkatini çekme: Artırılmış gerçeklik. *Eğitim Teknolojisi Kuram ve Uygulama*, *4*(1), 63–80. doi:10.17943/etku.88319

Son, J.-B. (2018). Activity-Based Approach. In J.-B. Son, Teacher Development in Technology-Enhanced Language Teaching (p. 133-156). Palgrave Macmillan, Cham. doi:10.1007/978-3-319-75711-7_8

Song, A. Y. (2016). Operationalizing Critical Digital Literacies: A Holistic Approach to Literacy Education in the Modern Age. *Talking Points, 28*(1), 17–24.

Songkram, N., Songkram, N., Chootongchai, S., & Samanakupt, T. (2021). Developing Students' Learning and Innovation Skills Using the Virtual Smart Classroom. *International journal of emerging technologies in learning, 16*(4).

Spachuk, K. (2020, February 1). *Charles Miller, co-founder and partner GM of Flipgrid at Microsoft*. The University of British Columbia. https://virtual.educ.ubc.ca/wp/etec522/2020/02/01/charles-miller-co-founder -and-partner-gm-of-flipgrid-at-microsoft/

Sparfeldt, J. R., Rost, D. H., Baumeister, U. M., & Christ, O. (2013). Test anxiety in written and oral examinations. *Learning and Individual Differences, 24*, 198–203. doi:10.1016/j.lindif.2012.12.010

Spencer-Waterman, S. (2005). *Handbook on differentiated instruction for middle and high schools*. Routledge.

St John Ambulance Victoria. (2018). *First aid action hero - The game. St John Ambulance Australia (VIC) INC - Saving lives through first aid*. St John Ambulance Victoria. https://www.stjohnvic.com.au/community-programs/action-hero/

Stake, R. E. (1995). *The art of case study research*. Sage Publications.

Stanhope, D. S., & Corn, J. O. (2014). Acquiring teacher commitment to 1: 1 initiatives: The role of the technology facilitator. *Journal of Research on Technology in Education, 46*(3), 252–276. doi:10.1080/15391523.2014.888271

Starkey, L. (2011). Evaluating learning in the 21st century: a digital age learning matrix. *Pedagogy and Education, 20*(1), 19–39. doi:10.1080/1475939X.2011.554021

Starkey, L. (2011). Evaluating learning in the 21st century: A digital age learning matrix. *Technology*.

Stedronsky, J., & Turner, K. H. (2020). Inquiry ignites! Pushing back against traditional literacy instruction. In J. Dyches, B. Sams, & A. Boyd (Eds.), *Acts of resistances: Subversive teaching in the English language arts classroom* (pp. 51–64). Myers Education Press.

Steinkuehler, C. (2010). Video games and digital literacies. *Journal of Adolescent & Adult Literacy, 54*(1), 61–63. doi:10.1598/JAAL.54.1.7

Stone, J. (2020). Digital citizenship. In J. Stone (Ed.), *Digital play therapy* (pp. 140–152). Routledge., doi:10.4324/9780429001109-11

Stornaiuolo, A., & LeBlanc, R. J. (2014). Local literacies, global scales: The labor of global connectivity. *Journal of Adolescent & Adult Literacy, 58*(3), 192–196. doi:10.1002/jaal.348

Stotz, M. (2018). *"Creature Counting": The Effects of Augmented Reality on Perseverance and Early Numeracy Skills*. (Publication No. 10813679) [Doctoral dissertation, Lehigh University]. ProQuest Dissertations & Theses Global https://www.proquest.com/docview/2049753987

Stover, K., Yearta, L., & Harris, C. (2016). Experiential learning for preservice teachers: Digital book clubs with third graders. *Journal of Digital Learning in Teacher Education, 32*(1), 5–12. doi:10.1080/21532974.2015.1055013

Stripling, M.Y. (2009). Teaching literature and medicine: Ken Kesey's *One flew over the cuckoo's nest. Teaching American Literature: A Journal of Theory and Practice, 3*(1), 61-68.

Sumara, D. J., Luce-Kapler, R., Robson, C., & Catlin, S. J. (2008, December). Fictional practices of everyday life: Tactics of genre, gender and generation. Paper presented at *the Annual meeting of the National Reading Conference*, Orlando, FL.

Sundqvist, P. (2022). Teaching technology in a play-based preschool—views and challenges. In P. J. Williams & B. von Mengersen (Eds.), *Applications of Research in Technology Education: Helping Teachers Develop Research-Informed Practice* (pp. 219–232). Springer., https://link.springer.com/book/10.1007/978-981-16-7885-1

Sun, P. C., Tsai, R. J., Finger, G., Chen, Y. Y., & Yeh, D. (2008). What drives a successful e-learning? An empirical investigation of the critical factors influencing learner satisfaction. *Computers & Education, 50*(4), 1183–1202. doi:10.1016/j.compedu.2006.11.007

Sutton, S. R. (2011). The preservice technology training experiences of novice teachers. *Journal of Digital Learning in Teacher Education, 28*(1), 39–47. doi:10.1080/21532974.2011.10784678

Swan, K. (2002). Building learning communities in online courses: The importance of interaction. *Education. Communication & Leadership, 2*(1), 23–49. doi:10.1080/1463631022000005016

Tang, Y. M., Lau, Y. Y., & Chau, K. Y. (2022). Towards a sustainable online peer learning model based on student's perspectives. *Education and Information Technologies, 27*(9), 1–20. https://link.springer.com/article/10.1007/s10639-022-11136-y. doi:10.100710639-022-11136-y PMID:35668899

Tao, Y., & Ma, J. (2022). Effects of the TPACK Levels of University Teachers on the Use of Online Teaching Technical Tool. *International Journal of Emerging Technologies in Learning, 17*(20), 188–199. doi:10.3991/ijet.v17i20.35135

Tapingkae, P., Panjaburee, P., & Hwang, G.-J., & Srisawasdi, N. (. (2020). Effects of a formative assessment-based contextual gaming approach on students' digital citizenship behaviors, learning motivations, and perceptions. Computational &amp. *Education, 159*. Advance online publication. doi:10.1016/j.compedu.2020.103998

Tekerek, M., & Tekerek, A. (2013). A research on students' information security awareness. *Turkish Journal of Education, 2*(3), 61–70.

Telgemeier, R. (2019). *Guts*. Scholastic.

Tello, S. F. (2007). An analysis of student persistence in online education. *International Journal of Information and Communication Technology Education, 3*(3), 47–62. doi:10.4018/jicte.2007070105

Tettenborn, E. (2005). Teaching imagined testimony: *Kindred, Unchained memories*, and the African burial ground in Manhattan. *Transformations, 16*(2), 87–103.

The Council Of The European Union. (2018) *Key Competences For Lifelong Learning A European Reference Framework*. Brussels: Official Journal of the European Union. https://eur-lex.europa.eu/legal-content/EN/TXT/PDF/?uri=CELEX:32018H0604(01)&rid=7

Theobold, A. S. (2021). Oral exams: A more meaningful assessment of students' understanding. *Journal of Statistics and Data Science Education, 29*(2), 156–169. doi:10.1080/26939169.2021.1914527

Tian, H., Liu, Y., Li, Y., Wu, C. H., Chen, B., Kraemer, M. U., Li, B., Cai, J., Xu, B., Yang, Q., Wang, B., Yang, P., Cui, Y., Song, Y., Zheng, P., Wang, Q., Bjornstad, O. N., Yang, R., Grenfell, B. T., ... Dye, C. (2020). An investigation of transmission control measures during the first 50 days of the COVID-19 epidemic in China. *Science, 368*(6491), 638–642. doi:10.1126cience.abb6105 PMID:32234804

Toffler, A. (2011). *Shock future fear*. Corridor Publishing.

Tomi, A. B., & Rambli, D. R. A. (2013). An interactive mobile augmented reality magical playbook: Learning number with the thirsty crow. *Procedia Computer Science*, *25*, 123–130. doi:10.1016/j.procs.2013.11.015

Tømte, C., Enochsson, A., Buskqvist, U., & Kårstein, A. (2015). Educating online student teachers to master professional digital competence: The TPACK-framework goes online. *Computers & Education*, *84*(84(May)), 26–35. doi:10.1016/j.compedu.2015.01.005

Tondeur, J., Kershaw, L. H., Vanderlinde, R. R., & Van Braak, J. (2013). Getting inside the black box of technology integration in education: Teachers' stimulated recall of classroom observations. *Australasian Journal of Educational Technology*, *29*(3), 434–449. doi:10.14742/ajet.16

Tondeur, J., van Keer, H., van Braak, J., & Valcke, M. (2008). ICT integration in the classroom: Challenging the potential of a school policy. *Computers & Education*, *51*(1), 212–223. doi:10.1016/j.compedu.2007.05.003

Topper, A., & Lancaster, S. (2013). Common challenges and experiences of school districts that are implementing one-to-one computing initiatives. *Computers in the Schools*, *30*(4), 346–358. doi:10.1080/07380569.2013.844640

Tuli, N., & Mantri, A. (2021). Evaluating usability of mobile-based augmented reality learning environments for early childhood. *International Journal of Human-Computer Interaction*, *37*(9), 815–827. doi:10.1080/10447318.2020.1843888

Turner, K. H. (Ed.). (2020). *The ethics of digital literacy: Teaching students across grade levels*. Rowman and Littlefield.

Turner, K. H., & Hicks, T. (2015). *Connected reading: Teaching adolescent readers in a digital age*. NCTE.

Turner, K. H., & Hicks, T. (2022). Digital literacy (still) can't wait: Renewing and reframing the conversation. *English Journal*, *112*(1), 86–93. doi:10.2307/814427

Tyger, R. L. (2011). *Teacher candidates' digital literacy and their technology integration efficacy*. [Unpublished Doctoral dissertation, Georgia Southern University]. http://digitalcommons.georgiaso uthern.edu/cgi/viewcontent.cgi?article=1557&context=etd

Udesky, L. (2015). Classroom coaches critical as teachers shift to common core. Retrieved from https://edsource.org/2015/classroom-coaches-critical-as-teac hers-shift-to-common-core

Ulutas, I., Kilic Cakmak, E., Akinci Cosgun, A., Bozkurt Polat, E., Aydın Bolukbas, F., Engin, K., . . . Ozcan, S. (2022). Digital Storytelling in Early Mathematics Education. In STEM, Robotics, Mobile Apps in Early Childhood and Primary Education (pp. 393-413). Springer.

UNESCO. A Global Framework of Reference on Digital Literacy Skills for Indicators 4.4.2; Information Paper No. 51; UNESCO Institute for Statistics: Montreal, QC, Canada, 2018; Available online: http://uis.unesco.org/sites/default/files/documents/ip51-globalframework-reference-digital-literacy-skills-2018-en.pdf (accessed on 20 January 2022).

United Nations. (1989). *Convention on the Rights of the Child*. UN. https://www.ohchr.org/en/instruments-mechanisms/instruments/convention-rights-child

United States Department of Education. (2018). *Average class size in public schools, by class type and state: 2017–18*. [Table]. NCES. https://nces.ed.gov/surveys/ntps/tables/ntps1718_fltable06_t 1s.asp

Ur, P. (2012). Classroom interaction. In P. Ur (Ed.), *A course in English language teaching* (2nd ed.). Cambridge University Press. https://doi-org.ezp3.lib.umn.edu/10.1017/9781009024518 doi:10.1017/9781009024518.016

Van Laar, E., Van Deursen, A. J. A. M., Van Dijk, J. A. G. M., & De Haan, J. (2017). The relation between 21st-century skills and digital skills: A systematic literature review. *Computers in Human Behavior, 72,* 577–588. doi:10.1016/jchb.2017.03.010

van Laar, E., van Deursen, A. J. A. M., van Dijk, J. A. G. M., & de Haan, J. (2020, January). Van laar, E. (2020). Determinants of 21st-Century Skills and 21st-Century Digital Skills for Workers: A Systematic Literature Revie. *Sage (Atlanta, Ga.), 10*(1). doi:10.1177/2158244019900176

van Laar, E., van Deursen, A. J., van Dijk, J. A., & de Haan, J. (2017). The relation between 21st-century skills and digital skills: A systematic literature review. *Computers in Human Behavior, 72,* 577–588. doi:10.1016/j.chb.2017.03.010

Vanderhill, R., & Dorroll, C. (2022). Teaching, self-care, and reflective practice during a pandemic. *PS, Political Science & Politics, 55*(3), 1–5. doi:10.1017/S1049096521001918

Vargas, C. (2017). Lifelong learning from a social justice perspective 21. *Education Research and Foresght, 21.*

Varon, S. (2020). *My pencil and me.* First Second.

Verbruggen, S., Depaepe, F., & Torbeyns, J. (2020). Effectiveness of educational technology in early mathematics education: A systematic literature review. *International Journal of Child-Computer Interaction, 27,* 1–17. doi:10.1016/j.ijcci.2020.100220

Verenna, A., Noble, K., Pearson, H., & Miller, S. (2018). Role of comprehension on performance at higher levels of Bloom's taxonomy: Findings from assessments of healthcare professional students. *Anatomical Sciences Education, 11*(5), 433–444. doi:10.1002/ase.1768 PMID:29346708

Vizenor, K. V. (2013). *Binary lives: Digital citizenship and disability participation in a use created content digital world.* ERIC.

Vlaanderen, A., Bevelander, K., & Kleemans, M. (2020). Empowering digital citizenship: An anti-cyberbullying intervention to increase children's intentions to intervene on behalf of the victim. *Computers in Human Behavior, 112,* 106459. doi:10.1016/j.chb.2020.106459

Volkovskii, D. (2021, June). Experience of Applied Research in Online Deliberation: An Analysis of Civility in American Online Discussions. In IMS (pp. 199-205).

Vygotsky, L. (1978). Interaction between learning and development. *Readings on the Development of Children, 23*(3), 34–41.

Wang, Q. (2010). Using online shared workspaces to support collaborative group learning. *Computers & Education, 55*(3), 1270–1276. doi:10.1016/j.compedu.2010.05.023

Wang, Q., & Zhao, G. (2021). ICT self-efficacy mediates most effects of university ICT support on preservice teachers' TPACK: Evidence from three normal universities in China. *British Journal of Educational Technology, 52*(6), 2319–2339. doi:10.1111/bjet.13141

Wang, W., Hsieh, J. P. A., & Song, B. (2012). Understanding user satisfaction with instant messaging: An empirical survey study. *International Journal of Human-Computer Interaction, 28*(3), 153–162. doi:10.1080/10447318.2011.568893

Wanstreet, C. E. (2006). Interaction in online learning environments. *Quarterly Review of Distance Education, 7*(4), 399–411.

Waterfield, J., & West, B. (2006). *Inclusive assessment in higher education: A resource for change.* University of Plymouth.

Watulak, S. L., & Kinzer, C. K. (2013). Beyond technology skills: Toward a framework for critical digital literacies in pre-service technology education. In J. Avila & J. Z. Pandya (Eds.), *Critical digital literacies as social praxis* (pp. 127–153). Peter Lang.

Weaver, T. (2013). *Comics for film, games, and animation: using comics to construct your transmedia storyworld.* Routledge. doi:10.4324/9780240824055

Weiss, I., Kramarski, B., & Talis, S. (2006). Effects of multimedia environments on kindergarten children's mathematical achievements and style of learning. *Educational Media International, 43*(1), 3–17. doi:10.1080/09523980500490513

Wells, M. S. (2021). Preparing teachers during a pandemic: Virtual practicum in an undergraduate literacy course. *Teacher Educators'. Journal, 14*, 61–82.

West, J. A. (2019). Using new literacies theory to analyze technology-mediated literacy classrooms. *E-Learning and Digital Media, 16*(2), 151–173. doi:10.1177/2042753019828355

Whitacre, B. E., & Mills, B. F. (2007). Infrastructure and the rural urban divide in high-speed residential internet access. *International Regional Science Review, 30*(3), 249–273. doi:10.1177/0160017607301606

Whitin, P. E. (2009). Tech-to-stretch: Expanding possibilities for literature response. *The Reading Teacher, 62*(5), 408–418. doi:10.1598/RT.62.5.4

Wiecha, J. M., Gramling, R., Joachim, P., & Vanderschmidt, H. (2003). Collaborative e-learning using streaming video and asynchronous discussion boards to teach the cognitive foundation of medical interviewing: A case study. *Journal of Medical Internet Research, 5*(2), e13. doi:10.2196/jmir.5.2.e13 PMID:12857669

Wiggins, G. P., & McTighe, J. (2005). *Understanding by design* (2nd ed.). Pearson.

Williams, J. D. (2003). *Preparing to teach writing: Research, theory, and practice* (3rd ed.). Lawrence Erlbaum Associates. doi:10.4324/9781410607461

Williamson, B. (2015). Governing software: Networks, databases, and algorithmic power in the digital governance of public education. *Learning, Media and Technology, 40*(1), 83–105. doi:10.1080/17439884.2014.924527

Wilson, A. A., Chavez, K., & Anders, P. L. (2012). "From the Koran and Family Guy": Expressions of identity in English learners' digital podcasts. *Journal of Adolescent & Adult Literacy, 55*(5), 374–384. doi:10.1002/JAAL.00046

Wilson, M. S. (2001). Cultural considerations in online instruction and learning. *Distance Education, 22*(1), 52–64. doi:10.1080/0158791010220104

Wimmer, J. J., & Draper, R. J. (2019). Insiders' views of new literacies, schooling, and the purpose of education: "We should be teaching them more important things. *Reading Psychology, 40*(2), 149–168. doi:10.1080/02702711.2019.1607000

Winn, M. R. (2012). Promote digital citizenship through school-based social networking. *Learning and Leading with Technology, 39*(4), 10–13.

Wu, H. K., Lee, S. W. Y., Chang, H. Y., & Liang, J. C. (2013). Current status, opportunities and challenges of augmented reality in education. *Computers & Education, 62*, 41–49. doi:10.1016/j.compedu.2012.10.024

Xie, J., & Rice, M. F. (2021). Instructional designers' roles in emergency remote teaching during COVID-19. *Distance Education, 42*(1), 70–87. doi:10.1080/01587919.2020.1869526

Xu, S., Yang, H., MacLeod, J., & Zhu, S. (2019). Social media competence and digital citizenship among college students. *Convergence (London), 25*(1), 735–752. doi:10.1177/1354856517751390

Yaghoubi, A., & Mobin, M. (2015). Portfolio assessment, peer assessment and writing skill improvement. *Theory and Practice in Language Studies*, *5*(12), 2504–2511. doi:10.17507/tpls.0512.10

Yalçınkaya, B., & ve Cibaroğlu, M. O. (2019). Examining the perception of digital citizenship: An empirical evaluation. *Business & Management Studies: An İnternational Journal*, *7*(4), 1188–1208.

Yang, C. (2021). Online Teaching Self-Efficacy, Social-Emotional Learning (SEL) Competencies, and Compassion Fatigue Among Educators During the COVID-19 Pandemic. *School Psychology Review*, *50*(4), 505–518. doi:10.1080 /2372966X.2021.1903815

Yearta, L. (2019). Integrating social studies and english language arts: Digital stories and the revolutionary war. *The Reading Teacher*, *73*(2), 215–218. doi:10.1002/trtr.1806

Yeh, C., & Tsai, C. (2022). Massive Distance Education: Barriers and Challenges in Shifting to a Complete Online Learning Environment. *Frontiers in Psychology*, *13*, 928717. doi:10.3389/fpsyg.2022.928717 PMID:35859848

Yeon, S. H., & Shepherd, D. (2020). Transform your language instruction with Flipgrid. *Dialog on Language Instruction*, *30*(1), 73–76.

Yeşil, L. B. (2020). Shaping School Culture With Technology: Impact of Being an eTwinning School on Its Climate. In M. Durnali (Ed.), *Utilizing Technology, Knowledge, and Smart Systems in Educational Administration and Leadership* (pp. 259–278). IGI Global. doi:10.4018/978-1-7998-1408-5.ch014

Yilmaz, R. M. (2018). Augmented reality trends in education between 2016 and 2017 years. In N. Mohamudally (Ed.), State Of The Art Virtual Reality And Augmented Reality Knowhow, (pp.81-97). InTechOpen. https://dx.doi.org/ doi:10.5772/intechopen.74943

Yılmaz, R. M. (2016). Educational magic toys developed with augmented reality technology for early childhood education. *Computers in Human Behavior*, *54*, 240–248. doi:10.1016/j.chb.2015.07.040

Yılmaz, R. M., & Göktaş, Y. (2018). Using augmented reality technology in education. *Cukurova University Faculty of Education Journal*, *47*(2), 510–537. doi:10.14812/cuefd.376066

Yılmaz, R. M., Küçük, S., & Göktaş, Y. (2016). Are augmented reality picture books magic or real for preschool children aged five to six? *British Journal of Educational Technology*, *48*, 824–841. doi:10.1111/bjet.12452

Young, J., Young, J., & Shaker, Z. (2012). Technological Pedagogical Content Knowledge (TPACK) Literature using confidence intervals. *TechTrends*, *56*(5), 25–33. doi:10.100711528-012-0600-6

Yu, A. Y., Tian, S. W., Vogel, D., & Kwok, R. C. W. (2010). Can learning be virtually boosted? An investigation of online social networking impacts. *Computers & Education*, *55*(4), 1494–1503. doi:10.1016/j.compedu.2010.06.015

Yuan, F. (2018). An English language multimedia teaching model based on Krashen's theory. *International Journal of Emerging Technologies in Learning*, *13*(8), 198–209. doi:10.3991/ijet.v13i08.9051

Yuen, S., Yaoyuneyong, G., & Johnson, E. (2011). Augmented reality: An overview and five directions for AR in education. *Journal of Educational Technology Development and Exchange*, *4*(1), 119–140. doi:10.18785/jetde.0401.10

Yuksel-Arslan, P., Yildirim, S., & Robin, B. R. (2016). A phenomenological study: Teachers' experiences of using digital storytelling in early childhood education. *Educational Studies*, *42*(5), 427–445. doi:10.1080/03055698.2016.1195717

Zarzuela, M. M., Pernas, F. J. D., Martínez, L. B., Ortega, D. G., & Rodríguez, M. A. (2013). Mobile serious game using augmented reality for supporting children's learning about animals. *Procedia Computer Science*, *25*, 375–381. doi:10.1016/j.procs.2013.11.046

Zawacki-Richter, O. (2021). The current state and impact of Covid-19 on digital higher education in Germany. *Human Behavior and Emerging Technologies*, *3*(1), 218–226. doi:10.1002/hbe2.238 PMID:33363276

Zeivots, S., Vallis, C., Raffaele, C., & Luca, E. J. (2021). Approaching design thinking online: Critical reflections in higher education. *Issues in Educational Research*, *31*(4), 1351–1366.

Zhang, W., Wang, Y., Yang, L., & Wang, C. (2020). Suspending classes without stopping learning: China's education emergency management policy in the COVID-19 outbreak. *Journal of Risk and financial management, 13*(3), 55.

Zhang, C., & Quinn, M. F. (2018). Promoting early writing skills through morning meeting routines: Guidelines for best practices. *Early Childhood Education Journal*, *46*(5), 547–556. doi:10.100710643-017-0886-2

Zhou, F., Duh, H. B. L., & Billinghurst, M. (2008, September). Trends in augmented reality tracking, interaction and display: A review of ten years of ISMAR. *7th IEEE/ACM International Symposium on Mixed and Augmented Reality* (pp. 193-202). IEEE.

Zhu, Y., Yang, X., & Wang, S. J. (2017). Augmented reality meets tangibility a new approach for early childhood education. *EAI Endorsed Transactions on Creative Technologies*, *4*(11), 1–8. doi:10.4108/eai.5-9-2017.153059

Zickuhr, K., & Smith, A. (2012). *Digital differences*. Pew Research Center.

About the Contributors

Jason D. DeHart has served as an assistant professor of reading education at Appalachian State University. DeHart's research interests include multimodal literacy, including film and graphic novels, and literacy instruction with adolescents. His work has recently appeared in SIGNAL Journal, English Journal, and The Social Studies.

***

Maya Abdallah holds a Master's degree in Educational Management from the Lebanese International University. She also attained her BA in TESL and TD from the same university and a CELTA certificate from the University of Cambridge. Her 4-year-long teaching journey ignited a passion for all things writings and a career in content writing across a spectrum of diverse topics. Her professional growth includes several certifications from Google, Coursera, and other reputable training agencies on social media, teaching methodologies, and management. Maya's research interest revolves around education, leadership, psychology, and management.

Fatima Al Husseiny is a LinkedIn content creator and is part of LinkedIn for Journalists Premium Program 2022-2023. She holds a Master's degree in Educational Management and BA in English Language and Literature. Her research interests are related to Education, Educational Technology, AI, and Social Media. Fatima's professional goals are related to developing academic research in her fields of interest. She has been awarded two achievement awards for her contributions to Wikipedia and has various certifications from Google, Coursera, LinkedIn Learning, and Udemy. Fatima enriches her social responsibility by contributing to educational blogs in reputable media outlets (e.g. Annahar Media Group Website) and content editing in an international context, such as The International Girls Academy, NJ, USA.

Feyza Aydin Bölükbaş completed, in 2015, her undergraduate education in Gazi University Education Faculty Preschool Teaching Program. In 2018, she completed his master's degree in Gazi University Institute of Educational Sciences, Department of Preschool Education. She is still continuing her doctorate education, which she started in Gazi University Educational Sciences Institute Preschool Education program in 2018. She works on mathematics education, technology and art education in preschool children. We Use Technology in Early Mathematics Learning with TÜBİTAK 4005 Digital Story Telling. He worked as an expert in TÜBİTAK 4005 Augmented Reality/AR in Preschool Education and Multidimensional Mathematics projects. He is also a scholar in TÜBİTAK 1001 Intangible Cultural

Heritage and Technology Study in Preschool Education: Development, Implementation and Evaluation of Traditional Handicrafts-Based Digital Storytelling and Coding Program. She is still working as a Research Assistant at Aksaray University.

Monica T. Billen, an Assistant Professor at California State University, Fresno, focuses on elementary literacy education.

Emine Bozkurt Polat was born in Kahramanmaraş in 1991, and graduated from Necmettin Erbakan University, Department of Preschool Education in 2012 and was appointed as a research assistant at Kahramanmaraş Sütçü İmam University in the same year. After completing his master's degree in Necmettin Erbakan University Preschool Education Department in 2016, he was appointed as a research assistant to Gazi University Preschool Education Department in the same year and started his doctorate education. She worked as the education coordinator at Gazi Practice Kindergarten for 1 year in the 2018-2019 academic year. The author is still working as a research assistant at Gazi University. As an academician, he has publications on technology, augmented reality, robotic coding values education in preschool children. She worked on robotic coding in her doctoral thesis.

Kadriye Budak, having attained an undergraduate degree in Preschool Education from Dokuz Eylül University's Education Faculty in 2017, and subsequently earning a master's degree in Preschool Education from Pamukkale University's Educational Sciences Institute in 2018, is currently pursuing a doctoral degree in the same field at Gazi University's Educational Sciences Institute. Budak's research focuses on the integration of digital games and technology in preschool education, and Budak is actively engaged in various related projects. Budak is also currently serving as a lecturer at Bilecik Şeyh Edebali University.

Whitney Chandler, who attended Murray State University, has been a high school English teacher in Georgia for eleven years. Her research interests include student voice, attitudes toward writing, and practitioner research. She will serve as the editorial assistant for NCTE's English Journal for issues slated to publish in Fall 2023.

Kate Cimo is a 6th grade teacher of ELA and Social Studies in the Owen J. Roberts School District with one Masters in Education from Cabrini University and one Masters in Social Emotional Learning from Neumann University. Cimo's primary goals in education have been focusing on how to intertwine getting middle aged students excited about reading good books and being engaged in their writing, while also personally connecting more deeply with their classroom community.

Niroj Dahal (ORCID ID: 0000-0001-7646-1186), Ph.D. Scholar in STEAM Education, works as a lecturer at Kathmandu University School of Education under the Department of STEAM Education. His research interests include ICT in education, qualitative research, transformative research, mathematics education, open, distance, & e-learning, STEAM education, research and development, and ICT & e-Research. Mr. Dahal has been teaching graduate and undergraduate students for over a decade. He has also been continuously participating and presenting his research and practices in more than a dozen plus national and international conferences, workshops, and seminars. He has published editorials, articles, book reviews, and book chapters in various national and international journals and publication presses in the field of mathematics education and STEAM education. He may be contacted by e-mail at niroj@ kusoed.edu.np.

Pelin Yolcu has been working at Dicle University Diyarbakır Technical Sciences Vocational School since 2011. She works as an Instructor. In 2006, he completed his undergraduate education in Radio TV Cinema at Selcuk University, Faculty of Communication. He graduated from the Institute of Social Sciences of the same university, from the Department of Radio TV Cinema in 2011, and in 2020, he completed his doctorate in the field of Radio TV Cinema with the thesis titled "The use of cultural codes in Turkish cinema after 2000: Derviş Zaim cinema". The author gives training in and out of the institution on subjects such as communication, communication with children, diction, history of cinema, screenplay, public relations and advertising, editing techniques. The author has international works on semiotics, mise-en-scene analysis, cyberbullying, cold war era cinema, digital citizenship, digital footprint, digital literacy through cartoons, history teaching through cartoons, and migration.

Kübra Engin completed her undergraduate education in Hacettepe University Faculty of Education Department of Early Childhood Education in 2014. Between 2014-2016, she worked as a pre-school teacher in public schools under the Ministry of National Education of Turkiye, and as a research assistant at Gaziosmanpaşa University, Faculty of Education, Department of Early Childhood Education between 2016-2017. Between 2016-2019, she completed her master's degree at Gazi University, Institute of Educational Sciences, Department of Early Childhood Education. She is continuing her doctorate education in the same science that she started in 2019. She is still working as a research assistant at Gazi University, Gazi Faculty of Education, Department of Early Childhood Education. His academic interests are nature education, social and emotional learning, use of technology in education and family education in early childhood.

Lara Handsfield is a Professor of Bilingual-Bicultural Education and Elementary Literacy Education in the School of Teaching and Learning at Illinois State University, where she teaches literacy methods courses for undergraduate teacher candidates and graduate courses in literacy and curriculum theory. Her research critically examines comprehension instruction in culturally and linguistically diverse classrooms, digital literacies, and how teachers and students negotiate multiple political and pedagogical demands. Her work has appeared in several academic journals, including the Reading Teacher, Reading Research Quarterly, the Journal of Literacy Research, and Language Arts. She is the author of Literacy Theory as Practice: Connecting Theory and Instruction in K-12 Classrooms (2016).

Tetiana Holovatenko, PhD, is a senior lecturer of the Borys Grinchenko Kyiv University (Ukraine) and Visiting Scholar at the University of Minnesota (USA). Her research interests include technology-enhanced teaching English, trauma-informed language teaching and comparative education studies.

Vicki Hosek, Ed.D., is an experienced educator who teaches undergraduate secondary education methods, multiliteracies, and technology integration courses to teacher candidates. Her research focuses on examining the technology integration practices of teacher candidates and practicing teachers and the role and value they place on student inquiry and student voice in digital environments. She studies the development of the critical digital literacy (CDL) and the ways that teacher education programs can support this development. Dr. Hosek earned her degrees from the University of Colorado, Western Illinois University, and Illinois State University.

Jodi LaShay Jennings works at East Tennessee State University, Lashay Wood is an Assistant Professor of Literacy.

Matthew Macomber teaches secondary and post-secondary ELA and research in the Pacific Northwest. As an educator, he is especially interested in updating traditional instructional approaches in ELA classes for contemporary, digital instruction. He has previously presented work at TYCA and CCCC.

Renee Moran works at East Tennessee State University, and is an Associate Professor of literacy education.

Jill Stedronsky is an eighth grade Language Arts teacher at William Annin Middle School in New Jersey and adjuncts at Drew University. She is currently a teacher leader and a former co-director for Drew University's National Writing Project. She continues to research and work with teachers to create an authentic environment for writing and reading instruction rooted in a student's curiosity and driven by the student's life purpose. She is the co-author of "Inquiry Ignites Pushing Back Against Traditional Literacy Instruction" in the edited collection, Acts of Resistance: Subversive Teaching in the ELA Classroom.

Kristen Turner is Professor and Director of Teacher Education at Drew University in New Jersey. Her research focuses on the intersections between technology and literacy, and she works with teachers across content areas to implement effective literacy instruction and to incorporate technology in meaningful ways. She is the co-author of Connected Reading: Teaching Adolescent Readers in a Digital World and Argument in the Real World: Teaching Students to Read and Write Digital Texts and editor of Ethics of Digital Literacy: Developing Knowledge and Skills across Grade Levels. She is also the founder and director of the Drew Writing Project and Digital Literacies Collaborative and the co-founder of the Screentime.me research project and the Technopanic: Living and Learning in a Digital Age podcast.

Natalia Ward is an Assistant Professor in the Department of Curriculum and Instruction at East Tennessee State University. Her research interests include equitable education and assessment for multilingual learners, literacy and biliteracy, and education policy enactment in local contexts. Her email is wardna1@etsu.edu.

Noura Wehbe holds a Master's and a BS degree in Biology from BAU, Lebanon, and a teaching Diploma from Al Ain University in UAE. She is an educator with 10+ years of experience in middle and high school teaching. Noura is a former UNESCO school activities coordinator. Nora was trained by the Lebanese National Commission for UNESCO to be a trainer in safeguarding intangible cultural heritage in Lebanon from 2018 to 2021. She believes in teaching students life skills, especially 21st-century soft skills, to prepare them to be lifelong learners.

Shuling Yang works at East Tennessee State University as an Assistant Professor of literacy education.

Lamia Büşra Yeşil is a qualified EFL teacher and education technologies expert with vast experience in teaching and creating e-learning content. She has a master's degree in Distance Education in Instructional Technologies MA Programme. She has been involved with many collaborative projects with schools worldwide since 2013. She has been a trainer for various projects such as eTwinning, FCL, DesignFILS, and TeachUP. Motivated with 10 years of progressive experience, she is a lifelong learner. She has many awarded projects and prizes in national and international competitions. She has several articles about "Shaping School Culture with Technology" and is the author of the book "Teaching English in the Digital Era". She has online courses about "Augmented Reality", "Technology Integration in Education: SAMR Model", and "the Best Tools and Resources for Teaching Media Literacy". She writes and presents widely on integrating technology in education and good practices. Currently, she works in Germany as a native language teacher and takes part as a trainer in American Turkish School Distance Education Programme.

Index

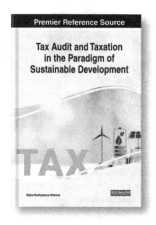

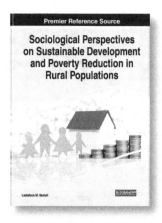